WANNA COOK?

THE COMPLETE, UNOFFICIAL
COMPANION TO
BREAKING BAD

e w
c

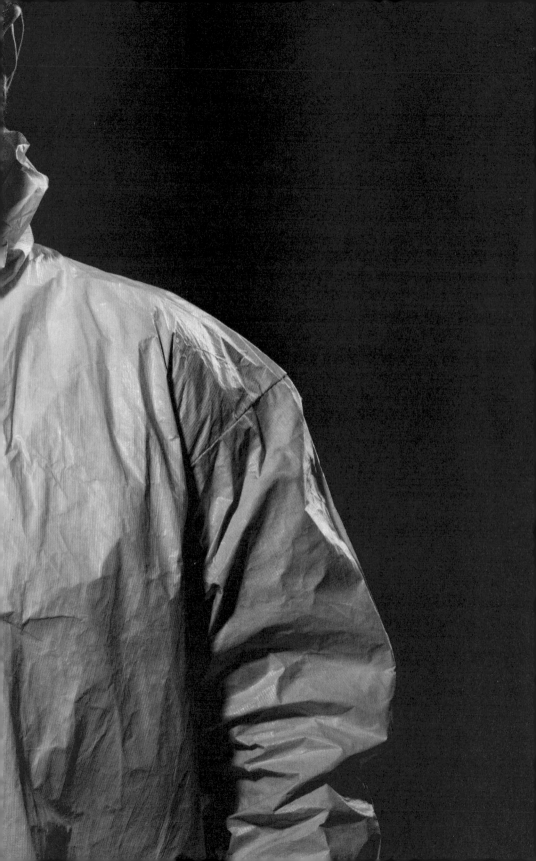

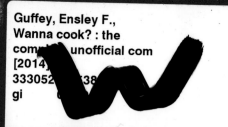
...AL COMPANION TO

BREAKING BAD

183.84   +6

W anna

74
2-8-18-32-12-2

58.93   +2
                +3

Co ok?

27
2-8-15-2

+

**K. DALE
KOONTZ**

w press

Published by ECW Press
2120 Queen Street East, Suite 200
Toronto, Ontario, Canada M4E 1E2
416-694-3348 / info@ecwpress.com

MIX
Paper from
responsible sources
FSC® C016245

Library and Archives Canada Cataloguing in Publication

Guffey, Ensley F., author
Wanna cook? : the complete unofficial companion
to Breaking bad / Ensley F. Guffey, K. Dale Koontz.

ISBN 978-1-77041-117-3 (pbk.)
Also issued as: 978-1-77090-497-2 (pdf);
978-1-77090-498-9 (epub)

1. Breaking bad (Television program : 2008).
I. Koontz, K. Dale, 1968–, author II. Title.

PN1992.77.B74G84 2014   791.45'72
C2013-908028-7   C2013-908029-5

Editor for the press: Jennifer Hale
Cover design: Natalie Olsen, Kisscut Design
Cover image: © Chris Wilson/Alamy
Inside cover images: retro periodic table © Dvougao/
istockphoto.com; background © lostandtaken.com
Type: Troy Cunningham
wisps © iAmManab/brusheezy.com
Printing: Friesens 5 4 3 2 1
PRINTED AND BOUND IN CANADA

ENSLEY F. GUFFEY

For my mother, Pat Guffey,
who always believed.
And for Dale,
sine qua non.

K. DALE KOONTZ

For Ensley, who always
made his deadlines, made
sure I made mine, and
loved me every step of
the way.

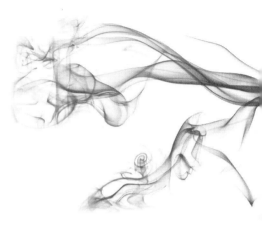

SPOILER WARNING

While we have tried to keep the individual episode recaps as free from spoilers as Walt's meth is free of impurities, the same cannot be said for the six brief *What's Cooking* essays throughout the book. These sections, which open and close the guide with others placed at the end of each season, are written assuming that you've watched the entire run of *Breaking Bad*. So if you *haven't* yet seen the whole series, you might want to skip over these sections until you have. If there is anything crucial to the episode analysis in those essays, we'll include the basic information again in the episode guides.

ACKNOWLEDGMENTS

Books do not write themselves and they are never the result of the sole efforts of those whose names are on the cover. We could not — flat-out *could not* — have written this book without the generous assistance of a great number of people. First and foremost, we'd like to thank Vince Gilligan and his amazingly talented cast and crew for bringing *Breaking Bad* to television in the first place. Thanks for the journey — even for the darkest parts of it. We'd also like to extend special thanks to Michael Slovis for being so generous with his time and insight into the production of *Breaking Bad*.

Thanks to Emily Schultz, Erin Creasey, Troy Cunningham, Crissy Calhoun, Laura Pastore, David Caron, and the rest of the incredible team at ECW Press for their help in shepherding this manuscript into the slick final printed copy you hold in your hands. John Hale, *Breaking Bad* fan and father of our skilled editor, generously allowed us to use photographs from his trip to Albuquerque, where he eschewed tours and tracked down filming locations all by himself. All of these folks helped bring *Wanna Cook?* into the world, and made it beautiful.

Neva Howell was a lifesaver with her transcription help, and Cleveland Community College provided welcome support in the early days of this project. The faculties of the Departments of History at the University of North Carolina at Greensboro and East Tennessee State University also provided encouragement and support as Ensley moved deeper and deeper into "nontraditional research." Special thanks are also due to David Lavery, who insisted we watch the show in the first place.

And a final word for our editor, Jen Hale. Ah, Jen, whose red pen ruthlessly separated the wheat from the chaff. You prodded us, encouraged us, laughed with us, and held our hands when we didn't think we could pull this off. You are the best and most generous of editors. Can we do this again soon?

What's Cooking

CHANGE WE CAN BELIEVE IN

There is a term used in critical analysis of television called "emotional realism." First used by Ien Ang to describe the lure of the original *Dallas*, emotional realism basically means that while we know that the show is a work of fiction, we can be carried away by it because it "feels" real. We identify with characters' experiences because we or someone we know has experienced something similar, or because the world of the TV show shares points of similarity with the real world we inhabit every day. In the case of *Breaking Bad*, hopefully very few (if any!) viewers have experienced the specific situations in which the characters in the show find themselves embroiled, but the world they live in is our world, complete with crystal meth, drug cartels, medical bills, missed opportunities, and family ties. We know Walt's world intimately, so it feels real.

But . . . how many of us have responded to devastating news like a diagnosis of lung cancer by deciding we'll go into the illegal drug trade, with all of its inherent risks and deadly violence? It's not exactly the expected reaction, no matter what the family financial situation. So why do we believe the transformation from milquetoast, sad-sack Walter White to dangerously unstable, murderous Heisenberg? Or the wannabe-gangsta Jesse Pinkman of season 1 into a hard, calculating killer with a conscience? Or good-ol'-boy Hank Schrader, DEA badass, to a guy who's looking forward to being out of the cop business to furiously bitter disabled mineral-hound to truly brilliant detective? We accept these radical changes in behaviors and personalities in fictional characters because creator Vince Gilligan, the *Breaking Bad* writers, the crew, and the magnificent ensemble cast manage to show these changes happening in a very realistic, recognizable way.

This brings us to Dr. Lonnie Athens, the sociologist and criminologist who, in 1995, published his theory of "dramatic self-change," which describes the process by which all of us undergo significant and fundamental alterations in the way we view and interact with the world and society based upon personal experience and social reactions to those experiences. According to Athens, this process is extremely difficult and can take a long time, so it usually only occurs in response to sudden and/or significant changes in our lives or living situations. The unexpected death of a loved one, say, or maybe a diagnosis of terminal lung cancer, or seeing a bunch of people get blown to hell by a booby-trapped severed head on the back of a tortoise. These situations happen to everyone (well, maybe not the tortoise thing), and usually more than once in a lifetime, so they are things with which we are all thoroughly familiar. Athens theorizes that dramatic self-change occurs in five stages: fragmentation, provisional unity, praxis, consolidation, and social segregation. Since this type of self-change is one of the central themes in *Breaking Bad*, we thought we'd look at the process at work in *Breaking Bad* and its characters, and hopefully shed some light on why it is that we are able to buy Walt's, Jesse's, Hank's, and others' journeys as being "real."

Each of us has an unconscious collection of what Athens calls "phantom companions," which in their simplest form can be thought of as the voices of our experience. This is the reservoir of experience and advice we accumulate throughout our lives and from various social interactions. This includes everything from Mom's advice for safely bundling up in cold weather to Dad's tips on preparing the perfect steak to what to wear to a funeral — all of the various information we possess that allows us to deal with life as it occurs, accrued through our own experiences, particularly social ones. The first step in dramatic self-change occurs when we experience something so completely outside of our normal frame of reference that no combination of this phantom community allows us to effectively deal with the current situation. When the self is faced with something it is unable to deal with in its present form, it fragments. Whether the experience in question is generally deemed positive, like winning a $250 million lottery, or negative, like losing a limb, the end result — fragmentation — is traumatic. For Walt, the traumatic event that destroyed his worldview is, of course, his cancer diagnosis. Nothing Walt has ever experienced, no voice from his past or present, has prepared him to deal with this, and he is, in the end, unequipped to handle the situation.

Jesse Pinkman's great traumatic moments occur with the death of Jane, and again when he murders Gale in "Full Measure." Hank Schrader experiences fragmentation several times during the series. First when he begins to suffer signs of PTSD after shooting Tuco Salamanca, a situation exacerbated by his experiences in Mexico, then again in the aftermath of his shoot-out with the Salamanca cousins, and finally as he begins again to dig into the mysterious Heisenberg. For Skyler, fragmentation occurs through two separate events. First when she discovers the web of Walt's lies and then with the revelation of what he's actually been up to. For Marie, the pivotal events are Skyler learning about her shoplifting, and Hank's shooting. All of these characters are presented with situations that they are simply unable to navigate successfully using their old selves — the usual collection of experiences and advice — and so they find themselves confused and adrift in strange and frightening circumstances.

In the face of such trauma, people begin to create a new "phantom community," a new set of advice and theoretical guidelines to deal with the new experience and any similar ones they might encounter in the future. For Walt, this means interpreting the shattering of his world as an opportunity to free himself from all of the constraints he has been operating under for his entire life. From his perspective, if, as his cancer diagnosis suggests, he will die very soon, then there is no reason to play by the rules anymore. The result is the construction of what Athens terms a provisional unity, a new construction of self that the person believes might enable him or her to deal with the new experience. After Jane's death Jesse decides that he is "the bad guy," and after shooting Gale it is not until Mike takes him under his wing that Jesse begins to construct his provisional unity as a loyal henchmen and real gangster. Hank eventually finds new hope in a life with Marie outside of the DEA, and reconstructs himself again after his shooting by returning to the core of police work: investigation. Skyler chooses to deal herself into Walt's criminal enterprises, trying to refashion herself as a criminal strategist. Marie responds to Hank's shooting by becoming the completely devoted, loving, and self-sacrificing wife. All of these are what might be called working hypotheses of how to deal with the changed world, and all of them are very provisional until they are tested in the world through Athens's next step, praxis.

After constructing a new, provisional self, a person has to try that self out in the real world by attempting to use the newly formed ideas and advice to deal with the same or similar situations that had caused the fragmentation to begin with. Walt starts cooking meth and becomes an increasingly violent actor in the drug world. Jesse attempts to become a stone-cold dealer who doesn't care about anyone, including himself. Hank dives into mineral collection and cataloging. Skyler embarks on detailed story making for her and Walt, and near-obsessive plans for laundering Walt's money. Marie puts on a smile and pretends Hank's anger and bitterness towards her doesn't hurt. In each case, the characters are trying out the new selves they have put together in order to deal with the changed world they find themselves in. This doesn't always work well, or at all. Walt discovers that it's not as simple as making quality meth and selling it for big money, but he's successful enough to muddle through. Jesse can't be the bad guy in the face of Andrea and Brock, and can't continue to not care when he feels needed and necessary. At the same time, however, parts of his bad guy persona work quite well, giving him a hardness and courage he was lacking. Minerals can't inspire Hank's real passion. Skyler is unprepared for the realities of large-scale money laundering and the realities of the drug world, and her elaborate plans come to naught in the face of the all-too-human element of Ted's greed. Poor Marie simply can't survive Hank's unending assaults on her supportive efforts. Walt and Jesse's provisional selves, while not 100 percent successful, prove functional enough to retain, if only in part. Hank's prove wholly inadequate to deal with his new experiences. Skyler's and Marie's also fail to provide the means to deal with their new worlds.

When provisional unities/selves fail in praxis, people are back at square one, confused and searching for a way to make the world comprehensible and navigable. For Marie this confusion manifests in increasingly risky shoplifting and the spinning of elaborate fantasy lives she shares with people at open houses until she is caught and her distress brings in one of Hank's friends to help. For Skyler, her elaborate schemes leave her back where she started: terrified, dependent on Walt, and searching for a way to understand what is happening around her. Hank must try again, finally finding that it is a return to pure investigative work freed from ambition or pressures that provides a functioning new self. For all of these characters the process has been extraordinarily difficult, and their struggles echo within us, mirroring those of our own lives.

Once a working self has been tested, it must be either accepted or rejected. Remember that a successful new self can be good or bad, famous or infamous, as long as it allows the person to deal with an experience similar to the one that caused the original fragmentation. Importantly, the process of acceptance or rejection — consolidation, as Athens terms it — is heavily reliant on other people, and the social response to the new self's actions. This step is vital in Walt's case. His new self is very, very dark, progressively arrogant, dangerous, and violent. However, it has also proven effective in allowing Walt to survive and even prosper in radically dangerous experiences. Further, his new self has brought recognition that his old one never received. He began as a good nobody, but becomes a bad somebody, famed for his meth, his violence, and his meteoric rise in the criminal world. For perhaps the first time since graduate school, Walt is respected, and feels a measure of pride and self-worth, even if the causes of such feelings are true crimes in every sense of the word. Walt chooses to keep his new self, his Heisenberg, because other people have responded to his actions with respect, even fear. And Walt likes being the object of both. Jesse too, in a more quiet way, has consolidated his new self, based upon the reactions of Gus, Mike, Andrea, Brock, and even Walt. Hank has found validation again in the eyes of the DEA, and Marie in Hank. Skyler, it seems, is still adrift.

The final phase in dramatic self-change is called social segregation. The new self naturally seeks the company of those who appreciate it, and who may share similar views of the world. Walt briefly finds this in his early relationship with Gus, but his new self takes him progressively further away from his family, and into the criminal underworld, until he is able to connect with Héctor Salamanca in a very fundamental way in order to eliminate Gus. Jesse, after seeking approval from Walt for so long, begins to draw closer to Andrea and Brock who, in their own way, have lived through the same traumas as Jesse. While Walt's social segregations take him away from family, Jesse's draw him towards it. Hank and Marie too are drawn to their family by their experiences, particularly to one another. Relationships change, and a new social group begins to emerge.

As we watch these characters go through the often torturous, repetitive process of dramatic self-change, we are increasingly drawn deeper into the world of *Breaking Bad*. With excruciating attention to detail and the realities of human experience, Vince Gilligan and Company give us such realistic portrayals of this process from the different perspectives of several distinct individuals that we are able to follow, to pull for a character making one choice, and to rail at them for making another. We become involved because we all have walked this painful path at some point, and most of us have so many times. It feels real, and so Walt, Jesse, Hank, Skyler, Marie, and the lives they live also feel real.

And *that*, friends and neighbors, is Quality TV.

EPISODE GUIDE
SEASON ONE

1

Starring:

BRyan Cranston (Walter White)

A**AR**on Paul (Jesse Pinkman)

An**Na** Gunn (Skyler White)

Dea**N** Norris (Hank Schrader)

Betsy Brandt (Marie Schrader)

RJ Mit**Te** (Walter White, Jr.)

ilot/Breaking Bad

Original air date: January 20, 2008
Written and directed by: Vince Gilligan

"I prefer to see [chemistry] as the study of change . . . that's all of life, right? It's the constant, it's the cycle. It's solution — dissolution, just over and over and over. It is growth, then decay, then — transformation! It is fascinating, really." — Walter White

We meet Walter White, Jesse Pinkman, and Walt's family. Walt is poleaxed by some tragic news. With nothing to lose, Walt decides to try to make one big score, and damn the consequences. For that, however, he needs the help of Jesse Pinkman, a former student turned loser meth cook and drug dealer.

From the moment you see those khakis float down out of a perfectly blue desert sky, you know that you're watching a show like nothing else on television. The hard beauty and stillness of the American Southwest is shattered by a wildly careening RV driven by a pasty white guy with a developing paunch wearing only a gas mask and tighty-whities.

What the hell?

Like all pilots, this one is primarily exposition, but unlike most, the exposition is beautifully handled as the simple background of Walter's life. The use of a long flashback as the body of the episode works well, in no small part due to Bryan Cranston's brilliant performance in the opening, which gives us a Walter White so obviously, desperately out of his element that we immediately wonder how this guy wound up pantsless in the desert and apparently determined to commit suicide-by-cop. After the opening credits, the audience is taken on an intimate tour of Walt's life. Again, Cranston sells it perfectly. The viewer is presented with a middle-aged man facing the back half of his life from the perspective of an early brilliance and promise that has somehow imploded into a barely-making-ends-meet existence as a high school chemistry teacher. He has to work a lousy second job to support his pregnant wife and disabled teenage son and still can't afford to buy a water heater.

Executive producer and series creator Vince Gilligan, along with the cast and crew (Gilligan & Co.), take the audience through this day in the life of Walt, and it's just one little humiliation after another. The only time Walt's eyes sparkle in the first half of the episode is when he is giving his introductory lecture to his chemistry class. Here Walt transcends his lower-middle-class life in an almost poetic outpouring of passion for this incredible science. Of course, even that brief joy is crushed by the arrogant insolence of the archetypal high school jackass who stays just far enough inside the line that Walt can't do a damn thing about him. So this is Walt and his life, as sad sack as you can get, with no real prospects of improvement, a brother-in-law who thinks he's a wuss, and a wife who doesn't even pay attention during birthday sex.

Until everything changes.

The sociologist and criminologist Lonnie Athens would likely classify Walt's cancer diagnosis as the beginning of a "dramatic self change," brought on by something so traumatic that a person's self — the very thoughts, ideas, and ways of understanding and interacting with the world — is shattered, or "fragmented," and in order to survive, the person must begin to replace that old self, those old ideas, with an entirely new worldview. (Athens and his theories are discussed much more fully in the previous *What's Cooking* essay, but since we warned you not to read that if you don't want to risk spoilage, the basic — and spoiler-free — parts are mentioned here.) *Breaking Bad* gives us this fragmentation beautifully. Note how from the viewer's perspective Walt is upside down as he is moved into the MRI machine, a motif smoothly repeated in the next scene with Walt's reflection in the top of the doctor's desk. Most discombobulating of all, however, is the consultation with the doctor. At first totally voiceless behind the tinnitus-like ambient soundtrack and faceless except for his chin and lips, the doctor and the news he is imparting are made unreal, out of place, and alien. As for Walt, in an exquisite touch of emotional realism, all he can focus on is the mustard stain on the doctor's lab coat. How many of us, confronted with such tragic news, have likewise found our attention focused, randomly, illogically, on some similar mundanity of life?

It is from this shattered self that Walt begins to operate and things that would have been completely out of the question for pre-cancer Walt are now actual possibilities — things like finding a big score before he dies by making and selling pure crystal meth. Remember that Walt is a truly brilliant chemist, and knows full well what crystal meth is and what it does to people who use it. He may not know exactly what he's getting into, but he knows what he is doing.

(ALBERT L. ORTEGA/PR PHOTOS)

Enter Jesse Pinkman (Aaron Paul, best known previously for his role on *Big Love*), a skinny white-boy gangster wannabe who, under the name "Cap'n Cook," makes a living cooking and selling meth. He's also an ex-student of Walt's, and after being recognized by his former teacher during a drug bust, Walt has all the leverage he needs to coerce Jesse into helping him. Why does he need him? Because, as Walt says, "you know the business, and I know the chemistry." Symbolizing just how far beyond his old life Walt is moving, he and Jesse park their battered RV/meth lab in the desert outside of Albuquerque, far from the city and any signs of human life. All that is there is a rough dirt road and a "cow house" in the distance. The desert is a place without memory, a place outside of things, where secrets can be kept, and meth can be cooked. This is where Walt lives now.

It is in this desert space that Walt becomes a killer, albeit in self-defense. Ironically, the one thing that Walt views as holding the keys to the secret of life — chemistry — becomes the means to end lives. Walt, a father, teacher, and an integral part of an extended family — in other words, an agent of life and growth — has now become a meth cook, using chemical weapons to kill his enemies. Walter White has become an agent of death.

The transformation is just beginning, but already Skyler (Anna Gunn, previously known for her roles on *The Practice* and *Deadwood*) is having some trouble recognizing her husband: "Walt? Is that you?"

LAB NOTES

HIGHLIGHT

JESSE TO WALT: "Man, some straight like you — giant stick up his ass all of a sudden at age what? Sixty? He's just going to break bad?"

DID YOU NOTICE

* This episode has the first (but not the last!) appearance of Walt's excuse that he's doing everything for his family.
* There's an award on the wall in Walt's house commemorating his contributions to work that was awarded the Nobel Prize back in 1985. The man's not a slouch when it comes to chemistry, so what's happened since then?
* At Walt's surprise birthday party, Walt is very awkward when he handles Hank's gun.
* Speaking of Hank (Dean Norris, whose other roles include the TV series *Medium*, and the movies *Total Recall* and *Little Miss Sunshine*), he waits until the school bus has left the neighborhood before ordering his team into the meth lab, showing what a good and careful cop he is.
* Maybe it's just us, but J. P. Wynne High School (where Walt teaches chemistry) seems to have the most well-equipped high school chemistry lab in the country.
* As Walt receives his diagnosis, the doctor's voice and all other sounds are drowned out by a kind of numbing ringing, signifying a kind of psychic overload that prevents Walt from being fully engaged with the external world. This effect will be used again several times throughout the series.
* Walt literally launders his money to dry it out, foreshadowing what's to come.

SHOOTING UP

- ◆ Thanks to John Toll, who served as cinematographer for the first season of *Breaking Bad*, the show has one of the most distinctive opening shots ever. Just watch those empty khaki pants flutter across a clear sky. *Breaking Bad* loves certain camera angles and this section is where we'll point out some of the shots that make the show stand out.

- ◆ Look at that taped non-confession Walt makes for his family when he thinks the cops are coming for him. We're used to watching recordings of characters — shows are filmed (or taped), but here, we're watching him recording himself on tape. Who's the real Walt?

TITLE Many pilot episodes share the name with the title of the show and *Breaking Bad*'s pilot is no exception. Vince Gilligan, who grew up in Farmville, Virginia, has stated that "breaking bad" is an American Southernism for going off the straight and narrow. When you bend a stick until it breaks, the stick usually breaks cleanly. But sometimes, sticks (and men) break bad. You can wind up in the hospital with a splinter in your eye, or you can wind up in Walter White's world. Either way, it's no kind of good.

INTERESTING FACTS Show creator Vince Gilligan's early educational experience was at J. P. Wynne Campus School in Farmville, Virginia. He recycled the name for the high school in *Breaking Bad*.

SPECIAL INGREDIENTS

WHAT IS CRYSTAL METH, ANYWAY?

While there is some evidence that methamphetamine can be found naturally in several species of acacia plants, commercial meth-making involves chemistry, not agriculture. The history of the drug dates back to 1893 when Japanese chemist Nagai Nagayoshi first synthesized the substance from ephedrine. The name "methamphetamine" was derived from elements of the chemical structure of this new compound: **meth**yl **a**lpha-**m**ethyl**ph**eny-**leth**yl**amine**. In the United States, meth is a Schedule II controlled substance, which the Drug Enforcement Administration defines as a substance that may have some accepted medical use, but also has a high likelihood of being abused and causing dependence. Other Schedule II substances include opium and cocaine.

Crystal meth is a very pure, extremely potent form of methamphetamine that is usually smoked like crack cocaine, but can also be crushed and snorted, injected, or even inserted into the anus or urethra where it dissolves into the bloodstream. Among other ailments, prolonged meth use can result in rapid decay and loss of teeth (known as "meth mouth"); drug-related psychosis that can persist for weeks, months, or even years after use is discontinued; and, oh yeah, death. Crystal meth is highly addictive and is such a horrifically vicious drug that in 2008 *The Economist* reported that in Pierce County, Washington, where 589 meth labs were found in 2001, some police and residents were relieved to see an uptick in crack use as an indicator that the meth trade was declining!

Make no mistake: what Walt and Jesse are doing is a Bad Thing.

Unfortunately, you don't need a trained chemist like Walter White to whip up a batch of meth. In fact, there are many recipes for home-cooking meth and one of the most popular uses a method that sounds downright patriotic: in the "Red, White, and Blue" method, the red is red phosphorus, white is the ephedrine or pseudoephedrine, and blue is iodine, used to make hydroiodic acid. The cook obtains these ingredients from items such as lye, anhydrous ("without water") ammonia, iodine, hydrochloric acid, matches (Emilio is scraping match heads when viewers first meet him), ephedrine (which is found in sinus medications such as Sudafed), drain cleaner, ether, lighter fluid, and brake fluid. *Ick.*

Another downside of meth manufacturing is the stew of toxic fumes that are created as by-products. As seen in the pilot episode, a careless cook can be exposed to highly toxic phosphine gas by overheating the red phosphorus used in the cooking process. Other toxins can include mercury and hydrogen gas — also known as the stuff that blew up the *Hindenburg*. Now you know why Walt made Emilio toss out his cigarette.

MUSTARD GAS VERSUS PHOSPHINE GAS

HANK: Meth labs are nasty on a good day. You mix that shit wrong and you've got, uh, mustard gas.
WALT: Phosphine gas.

Both of these gases are best avoided, to be sure, but there is a significant difference. According to the Centers for Disease Control, mustard gas (or, more accurately, "sulfur mustard") is a chemical warfare agent that was first used by the German Empire in September 1917 against the forces of Imperial Russia at Riga during World War I. Mustard gas is a "vesicant" or blistering agent, which means it causes blistering both externally and internally on the skin, eyes, throat, esophagus, and lungs, with the blisters sometimes forming several hours after exposure to the gas. Mustard gas was not always lethal, depending on the dose or whether or not any gas had been inhaled. Victims often suffered agonizing pain from burns, blindness, and bleeding, both external and internal, and many who survived were disabled for the rest of their lives. Unlike chlorine, phosgene, or even tear gas, gas masks did not protect the wearer from mustard gas, which could cause disabling chemical burns on any part of a soldier's exposed skin. Furthermore, mustard gas sank low and lingered for weeks, making occupation of trenches extremely dangerous for friend and foe alike. Mustard gas has no recognized medical use and its use in combat is now a violation of the United Nations' Chemical Weapons Convention.

Phosphine gas is far more deadly. According to the California Office of Environmental Health Hazard Assessment, phosphine gas is an unintended and potentially lethal (just ask Emilio!) by-product of meth manufacturing using the hydroiodic acid/red phosphorus method. Phosphine gas has no effect on the skin, and causes only mild to moderate irritation to the eyes, but produces rapid and horrific effects if inhaled. Low-level, short-term exposure can cause coughing and severe lung irritation. Neurological effects include dizziness, convulsions, and coma. The results of long-term or high-level exposure to phosphine gas (as in a poorly ventilated RV, for example) include pulmonary edema; convulsions; damage to the kidney, liver, and heart; and death. Phosphine gas was also used during World War I, but unlike mustard gas, quick and proper use of gas masks proved an effective countermeasure. In non-gaseous form, phosphine is used in the manufacture of semi-conductors and compound conductors. Pellets containing phosphine that react with atmospheric water or a rodent's stomach acids are used for pest control, and phosphine gas is also used as an aerosol insecticide because it leaves no residue on the products it is applied to.

Meth isn't the only thing that gets cooked on *Breaking Bad*. Meals are a big part of the show, indicating how things are going at any given time: is the White family sitting down to a home-cooked meal or is it a dinner of takeout? And, while it is a well-known fact that teenage boys can wolf down copious quantities of food, Junior (aka "Flynn") eats more breakfasts than should be allowed by law. In fact, *Breaking Bad* memes and drinking games have sprung up around Junior's breakfasts, so keep an eye out for how many times you see him at the breakfast table.

Walt's home life has an important marker associated with breakfast — the birthday bacon. For his 50th birthday at the start of season 1, breakfast is a celebration with Skyler spelling out "50" in veggie bacon on his plate. There will be two future instances of bacon spelling out something for Walter; watch how much his circumstances have changed each time.

The Cat's in the Bag

Original air date: January 27, 2008
Written by: Vince Gilligan **Directed by:** Adam Bernstein

"We got loose ends here!" — Jesse Pinkman

Walt begins lying to his family and friends, and is forced to decide just how far he is going to take things. Meanwhile, Jesse makes a terrible mess.

A lot of Walt's character is revealed in this episode. He attempts to blame Jesse for their situation, and tries desperately to convince himself that he can strike some kind of deal with Krazy-8 (Max Arciniega) that will let everyone go their separate ways. Walt is obviously in over his head. He has entered a world so fundamentally different from the lower-middle-class suburbia that he knows that he can't quite come to grips with it. He clings desperately to the idea that rational men can come to equitable agreements that benefit all sides, despite personal experience that the world of crystal meth is anything but reasonable. It is Walt who decides that they have to kill Krazy-8, even though Jesse has been immersed in the drug world far longer than Walt has. Further, it's Walt who comes up with the idea of dissolving the bodies in hydrofluoric acid. It's also interesting that the ostensibly "gangsta" Jesse is unwilling to commit murder, though he agrees it is probably necessary. This will not be the only time Walt's willing to go further than Jesse and it won't be the only time Jesse balks at using violence to eliminate a roadblock.

Jesse and Walt's developing relationship is also handled nicely, particularly as they bicker like an old married couple over exactly what type of plastic container Jesse needs to buy to dissolve the bodies in. The comic relief of Jesse "trying on" the bins in the aisle of the store is brilliant, as are Walt's fumbling attempts to roll a joint to make his work easier. Nor do Gilligan & Co. forget to show us how Walt's new double life and newly precarious sense of self affect his relationships with his family, particularly Skyler. When Walt is late for the sonogram appointment and Skyler presses him, he calmly, coldly, and quite unexpectedly tells her to leave him alone, and Anna Gunn's expression leaves the viewer in no doubt that this is a new attitude from Walt with which her character is completely unfamiliar. The "revelation" that Walt's been smoking pot is yet more evidence that Walt is no longer exactly the man he has been for most of their life together.

Indeed, Walt is moving further from the life he has always known towards a new world where, despite his formidable intelligence, his ignorance of the rules make him a danger to everyone he knows. Walt and Jesse are sloppy criminals, and — at best — Walt is not nearly as smart as he thinks he is. They leave one of the gas masks in the desert, Jesse doesn't listen to Walt about the right kind of plastic, and Walt doesn't bother to explain why they need a specific type. Walt can't bring himself to kill and even provides Krazy-8 with food, water, toilet paper, and even hand sanitizer, all of which lets Krazy-8 know Walt isn't prepared to kill him. It is no coincidence that, as Jesse hits his pipe to get up the guts to take care of Emilio's body, *The Three Stooges* is playing on his TV. It makes for a lovely metaphor for Walt and Jesse's fumbling attempts to deal with the consequences of their actions.

These dark problems of morality, murder, and body disposal are the result of a choice made by Walt and Jesse to try to escape any legal consequences for their actions in the desert. They would undoubtedly have to do some jail time, but going to the police would put an end to the entire mess once and for all, and in Walt's case, it's likely that a decent lawyer would be able to parlay the trauma of Walt's cancer diagnosis into mitigating circumstances. Even gassing Krazy-8 and Emilio (stuntman and actor John Koyama, who has guested on *24*, *Alias*, and *Grey's Anatomy*) is an act of self-defense. Once they decide to cover up the evidence of their crime, and especially once Walt decides to hope that Krazy-8 dies from his exposure to the gas rather than take him to a hospital, they have crossed a moral line. Of course, so has the viewer, because the audience roots for these two stooges, and thus is captured in the moral ambivalence of the show already. The viewer knows that Walt and Jesse are not really good guys, but wants to root for them anyway. It is a wonderfully original position to be in, and the viewer has become complicit through the desire to see if and how they will handle this new darkness.

LAB NOTES

HIGHLIGHT

> **JESSE:** "And why'd you go and tell her I was selling you weed?"
> **WALT:** "It seemed preferable to admitting that I cook crystal meth and killed a man."

(ALBERT L. ORTEGA/PR PHOTOS)

DID YOU NOTICE

- The kids who find the gas mask in the desert are cute, but also in old clothes, which are a little ragged. They are poor and apparently Native American. The little girl putting the mask on is a great touch, as Walt and Jesse's activities will ultimately affect people they don't even know about.
- The decor in Jesse's house is very old-lady-ish: patterns, floral prints, lace table runners, china cabinets filled with knickknacks, etc. Not really what we expect a meth cook/gangbanger's house to look like.
- Check out how Walt falls back on technical language to find euphemisms for what he wants to do: "chemical discorporation" instead of "dissolve the bodies in acid." Walt does this a *lot*; when a situation (especially one he created) becomes uncomfortable, he lapses into "tech talk" to give himself some distance. He often does this to convince himself that, while he's involved in the meth trade, he's not as bad as the *real* "bad guys." After all, he's "doing it for his family."

- Walt insists that he and Jesse are in this as equal partners when he's desperate, and when it is to his own advantage. This is a recurring motif in their relationship throughout the series.

MISCALCULATIONS Hydrofluoric acid does indeed eat through glass and most metals and plastics. Despite this, it is considered a "weak" acid because it doesn't completely dissociate (i.e. break down into its component ions) in water. Would it work to dissolve a body? Yes. However, it is a bit unusual for a high school chemistry lab to have such a large stock of the stuff, if any at all. Walt's choice of hydrofluoric acid is itself unusual, as he should know that lye (sodium hydroxide), a much more readily available, less widely corrosive base, when mixed with water would reduce a human body to liquid sludge and fragile bones. Given that lye could also easily and safely be used in and washed down the drain of a tub (indeed it is found in most drain clog removers), and is much more commonly available, it is puzzling that Walt wouldn't use it instead. However, as we will see throughout the series, Walt is a smart guy, but when he's under pressure he doesn't come up with an obvious solution. Instead, he'll choose the most complicated solution that he knows no one else would ever think of — probably because it's so darned complicated in the first place. Also, the fumes given off by either hydrofluoric acid or lye would have likely required Walt and Jesse to wear gas masks in the house constantly. Exposure to the fumes from the glop that falls through the ceiling would have been extraordinarily dangerous, as hydrofluoric acid is extremely toxic, affecting nerve function and causing systemic toxicity in humans, reacting with calcium in the blood and potentially causing cardiac arrest. Walt and Jesse, however, are unmasked at the time.

SHOOTING UP
- This episode introduces some of *Breaking Bad*'s trademark camera angles. The first is during the coin flip. The camera is positioned at a point that is above where the ceiling would be, and looks down on Walt and Jesse as the coin, spinning in slow motion, rises into focus in the foreground, hangs, and falls back towards Walt and Jesse's upturned faces. This type of shot will occur several times during the series, and seems to always serve to underscore the significance of a particular scene.

- Throughout the series, Gilligan & Co. employ what is called a point-of-view (POV) shot. Simply put, a camera is positioned so that the viewer sees what things would look like from the point of view of a given person or, importantly in *Breaking Bad*, a particular object. The type of POV shot that will become a trademark of *Breaking Bad*'s cinematography is first seen when Jesse is putting Emilio's body in the tub and dousing it with the acid. The camera is positioned "under" the tub, and looking up "through" it, as if the bottom of the tub was clear. This up-and-through POV shot will become one of the most recognizable bits of camera work in the series.
- Walt's position when he wakes up on the bathroom floor will also be repeated as the series progresses: left side of the face mashed against the floor, drooling. This positioning and the angling of the shot to make it appear that the person is vertical at first will be used several more times with different characters.

MUSIC Clyde McPhatter's "You're Movin' Me" makes for hilarious background music to Krazy-8's abortive escape.

INTERESTING FACTS Jesse lists DeVry University under "Education" on his (ahem) "MyShout" page, where he apparently studied data systems management. DeVry is a for-profit institution that has come under fire in the past, with students often complaining of deceptive loan practices and substandard instruction.

SPECIAL INGREDIENTS

CHIRALITY, THALIDOMIDE, AND METHAMPHETAMINE

When lecturing to his chemistry class about "chirality," Walt uses his hands as an example — your right and left hands are mirror images of each other, but they can't be completely superimposed on each other. In other words, your two hands won't totally line up. In organic chemistry, the same concept exists: some molecules exist as almost mirror images (called *enantiomers*), but with vastly different properties. Walt uses the drug thalidomide as an example. One enantiomer of the drug is a substance that prevents nausea and thalidomide was marketed as a drug to combat morning sickness in pregnant women. However, the other enantiomer of the drug is a powerful substance that causes severe developmental defects. Before the drug was banned for use in pregnant women, thousands of babies were born with severe birth defects, including missing limbs and flipper-like appendages. Walt doesn't mention it to his class, but meth is also chiral. One enantiomer is a decongestant, while the other is an addictive psychostimulant.

A nd the Bag's in the River

1.03

Original air date: February 10, 2008
Written by: Vince Gilligan **Directed by:** Adam Bernstein

"There's nothing but chemistry here." — Walter White

Walt and Jesse clean up their messes as Walt contemplates a weighty decision. Meanwhile, Marie goes shopping.

One of the best elements of this episode is the look viewers get at the "secondary" characters. More than any show in recent years, *Breaking Bad* takes the time to create fully realized characters at all levels. There really is no such thing as a bit part in *Breaking Bad*. As the show progresses, even tertiary characters get to be whole people rather than cardboard cutouts. Right from the get-go we are shown that Walt is close with family, including his in-laws Hank and Marie Schrader (Betsy Brandt who has had roles in the movies *Magic Mike*, *Shelf Life*, and *Jeremy Fink and the Meaning of Life* and on the TV series *The Michael J. Fox Show*). They do things together, hang out, have family nights, and while they occasionally annoy the hell out of each other (and the viewer!), they truly care. Marie seems to be the quintessential nosy sister who always needs to be in the middle of things, getting the attention. When she does not get the spotlight she craves, such as when a salesgirl at the shop rudely ignores her, she rebels by casually shoplifting a pair of shoes while carrying on a normal phone conversation with her husband. Marie and Hank both have good jobs and no kids, so clearly her need to shoplift arises from some non-financial motivation.

Then there's Hank, who could easily be read as the stereotypical good-ol'-boy cop. A jock, a jerk, and a shallow ass. Or is he? In his own way, Hank tries to be a positive influence on Walter Jr. (RJ Mitte), even to the point of acting as a surrogate father when he tries to scare him straight about drugs. Junior obviously idolizes his uncle Hank, and Hank is equally crazy about his nephew. One of the best little moments in this episode is when Hank saves Junior's pride in front of Wendy the Meth Whore (Julia Minesci) by telling her that Junior broke his leg playing football. There's a tremendous amount of compassion under Hank's testosterone-fueled dickishness.

This episode could have been an hour of utter grimness if not for the use of humor by Gilligan & Co. The bit where Walt and Jesse are outside hosing Emilio-goo off themselves while standing in brightly colored kiddy-pools is simply priceless, offering a contrast between happy innocence and their utter physical, mental, and moral exhaustion. This scene, displaying the blackest of black humor, feels like an homage to *Pulp Fiction*, which boasts a similar darkly funny scene in which Vincent (John Travolta) and Jules (Samuel L. Jackson) are hosed off in the backyard following an accidental shooting. Also nice is Hank's call to Marie, which in many shows would be just a husband checking in with his wife while he's at work — except in this instance, Hank's in the middle of a meth bust surrounded by agents in hazmat suits. The couple's ho-hum chat about family stuff is delightfully skewed for the viewer.

The core of the episode, however, is the choice faced by Walt. With Krazy-8 chained to a pole in Jesse's basement, Walt, having lost the coin toss in "The Cat's in the Bag," is supposed to kill him and thus tidy up what he thinks is the last loose end. Walt's moral debate is handled with more than a little surrealism, including a scene where he sits down with Krazy-8, who we learn is named Domingo ("Sunday" in English) and shares a couple of beers and brief life stories, like two guys from the same town having met in a bar, but oh so entirely different. Krazy-8 is the first person Walt has told about his cancer. The scene between the two men in the basement is really sublime, intimate in a very deep way. Domingo himself plays Walt from their very first scene together, calling Walt by name, and making sure Walt sees him as a real person with a name of his own, and a family, and even a degree in business administration from the University of New Mexico. In the end, of course, Walt kills him, but the discovery that Domingo had secreted a dagger-like shard of broken plate in his pocket allows Walt to rationalize his actions as self-defense. Nonetheless, we've seen Walt make his choice and take another step down an increasingly dark road.

LAB NOTES

HIGHLIGHT

KRAZY-8: "This line of work doesn't suit you."

DID YOU NOTICE

* While using the toilet to flush Emilio's remains at the beginning of the episode, we see Walt making a list with reasons not to kill Krazy-8 on one side and reasons to kill him on the other. On the "con" side are: "It's the moral thing to do; Judeo-Christian principles; You are not a murderer; Sanctity of life; He may listen to reason; Post-traumatic stress; Won't be able to live with yourself; Murder is wrong." On the "pro" side is only one item, but it's a doozy: "He'll kill your entire family if you let him go."
* Krazy-8 is chained to the pole with a U-lock, a type of lock used for bicycles and scooters that is supposedly extremely difficult to break or cut.
* Hank's partner Steven "Gomey" Gomez (Steven Michael Quezada) refers to the meth found in the trap car as "too damn white." Nice little play on Walter White's last name here.
* The meth motel, or "Crystal Palace," is actually named the Crossroads Motel, and at the end of the episode, Walt is on an overpass looking out over the highway beneath. He's at his own crossroads, as the events of the past few days have made clear.
* No one is enjoying sex in these first episodes. Sky isn't paying attention in the pilot, Jesse is so paranoid he's looking out of the window even as Wendy climbs on top of him, and Walt isn't exactly all there for the bout that closed the pilot and opened "The Cat's in the Bag."

SHOOTING UP

* One of the consistently great elements on *Breaking Bad* is the cold open. In TV terms, a "cold open" is the scene (or scenes) before the opening credits, and *Breaking Bad* will make some of the most creative

use of this space ever seen on television. The up-and-through shot of Walt and Jesse cleaning up liquefied Emilio puts the viewer down in the muck, both literally and figuratively. The background flashback of a young, graduate-student Walt listing the chemical composition of the human body with a raven-haired old flame is an incredibly powerful counterpoint to what Walt is dealing with in the present. Walt has moved from the fun theoretical exercise of figuring out what makes a man, to gathering together those very chemical compounds and literally flushing them down the toilet.

- The use of color in this episode is exquisite, particularly when Walt reconstructs the broken plate. The yellow plate shards are placed atop two shades of green tiles, with the darker green underlying the missing piece, drawing the eye to the missing portion and subtly emphasizing the dagger-like shape.

- Walt's flashbacks also use color to good effect, with an overall blue tint to the light to clearly differentiate them from the present day scenes.

- When Walt passes out from coughing, the next shot of him is with the left side of his face mashed to the floor, drooling, with the camera oriented at first to make it appear that Walt is vertical rather than horizontal, a composition used before in "The Cat's in the Bag."

TITLE The last episode ("The Cat's in the Bag") goes with this one (". . . And the Bag's in the River") to form a quote from the 1957 film *Sweet Smell of Success*, a movie Gilligan has listed as a favorite due to its rapid-fire dialogue. The phrase means that a problem has been handled and that there's nothing to worry about. While Walt's problem may have been handled by the end of this episode, there are still consequences to worry about.

INTERESTING FACT When going through Krazy-8's car in the desert, Hank and Gomez refer to it as a "trap car." Simply put, a trap car is a vehicle used by drug dealers/transporters that has been modified with hidden compartments, booby traps, concealed weapons, even rear halogen lights to blind pursing police. It's worth mentioning that Hank finds the hidden compartment after Gomez had already searched it, showing once again that Hank is *very good* at what he does.

SPECIAL INGREDIENTS

BAKING SODA

During the cleanup of Emilio's remains, Walt is liberally dusting the goo with baking soda. Baking soda is an amazing substance that can be used for many purposes, from treating jellyfish stings to keeping cut flowers fresh to a gardening-soil additive to grow sweeter tomatoes. It can also be used as an antacid both internally and externally, and, of course, it helps neutralize odors. Baking soda (sodium bicarbonate) is amphoteric, meaning that it reacts with both acids and bases, and thus is a handy neutralizing agent to have in any chemistry lab. In most cases baking soda does not react in such a way as to be harmful, so you don't even have to worry about using too much of it. In Walt and Jesse's situation, it is likely that the hydrofluoric acid had been sufficiently diluted by, well, Emilio (we Homo sapiens are about 60 percent water, after all). The soda would be effective even on such a corrosive substance, which is important if Walt and Jesse hope to stop it from eating through another floor. Using baking soda on the goo would also reduce the odor and the toxic fumes produced by the acid.

C ancer Man

1.04

Original air date: February 17, 2008
Written by: Vince Gilligan **Directed by:** Jim McKay

"What am I, some kind of criminal or something?"
— Jesse Pinkman

Walt and Jesse both try to get out of the meth trade. Meanwhile, Jesse tries to mend some fences with his family.

Where the previous episode revealed more about the individual secondary characters, this one brings them all together. We learn that Hank isn't just a random agent in the DEA, but in charge of a section of agents. The fact that Walt's meth is incredibly pure (99.1 percent) also means that Walter has probably shot to the top of Hank's "Most Wanted" list, though neither of them knows it. There are some lovely, funny moments in the cold opening and opening scenes, particularly the transition from Hank talking to his team about a new badass cook in town, to pale, paunchy Walt brushing his teeth. The up-and-through shot of the grilling barbecued chicken brings us into the heart of the episode: families.

Walt, Skyler, Junior, Hank, and Marie have all gathered for a family cookout at the Whites' house, and from their attitudes and comfort level, it appears that such family gatherings are regular events. This is a tight group, and their reaction to the news of Walt's cancer shows us exactly how close they are. Marie may be a nitpicky bitch, and Hank a masculinized jerk, but when the chips are down they are there for their family. Walt is really lucky to have this kind of built-in support system, but he just can't see it, because his pride is rearing up. When Hank assures Walt that no matter what happens he will take care of Sky and the kids, Walt can't stand the idea that another man might have to take care of his family. Whatever Walt might say, or however he might rationalize things, this is the real reason behind his decision to cook meth: his pride. He's not doing it for his family; he's doing it for himself and for some twisted sense of what it means to be a man. Thus he won't even consider borrowing money from Hank to pay for his treatment. In fact, he doesn't seem to even really want treatment.

(ANDREW EVANS/PR PHOTOS)

Why? Walt sees the cancer diagnosis as liberating. To Walt it seems that none of the old rules or constraints on his behavior apply anymore, because he has nothing to lose. Jail? He'll be dead in a matter of weeks or months. Death? It's coming for him sooner rather than later anyway. Laws? What are the cops going to do, kill him? Almost breaking the leg of the muscle-bound teenager who was making fun of Walter Jr. in "Pilot/Breaking Bad," and blowing the hell out of Ken the Bluetooth-Douche's car in this episode are acts so far outside of the pre-cancer parameters of Walt's usual life that no one (even Walt at first) would ever think he was capable of them. So too is his decision to cook meth. Walt isn't Walt anymore. The trauma of the cancer diagnosis has shattered his old worldview, his old self, and thus spurred the construction and emergence of a new, different, even dangerous self.

The problems that are just beginning to arise for Walt lie in how this new self perceives and affects the world around it. Those effects are already becoming apparent as Walt's criminal activities contaminate the family space. Walt has hidden his cash in the central-air intake vent in his unborn daughter's nursery, from whence it is sucked throughout the house when the system kicks on. This is a really well-executed metaphor for the ultimate impossibility of separating Walt's family life from his criminal one. Walt can try to keep his suburban, weekend-cookout life separate from his meth-cooking wizard life, even going so far as to take to the desert to do his cooking, but the two strands will cross. When they do, the chemicals he uses in his meth life will invariably poison his other one and the nice, normal life he's trying to preserve is going to be forever tainted.

This episode also gives us a look into Jesse's family, a quintessential upper-middle-class suburban household right down to the Latina maid. Jesse's parents obviously have worked hard to provide a good life and education for their children. Jesse's younger brother, Jake (Benjamin Petry, recognizable from *3:10 to Yuma*), seems to be every parent's dream: smart, talented, engaged, and well mannered. Not everything is as it seems in the Pinkman house, however, and Gilligan & Co. do an exquisite job of exploding the middle-class American myth. There is no reason to believe that Jesse himself did not receive the same benefits and chances as Jake, but somewhere he went off-track. The scene where we see Jesse going through his old trunk, revealing in his younger self the makings of a talented artist and a really good kid is one of the most quietly poignant moments in the series.

Beyond these relatively simple lines, we are being shown something darker and sadder: the realities of addiction. It's easy to view Jesse's parents as uncaring jerks, but this episode is giving the viewer more than just the obvious family history as his parents agonize over what to do about Jesse's sudden, drug-addled reappearance. They wonder what drugs he's on this time, if they need to set conditions, preparing themselves to lay down the law and keep to it this time. These are people who have obviously been through the wringer before, who love their oldest son, but have reached the point that the families of addicts must reach if they don't want the addict to drag them down with him or her: refusal to tolerate or enable the addict's behavior and addiction. They know they can't save Jesse, so they have done what was necessary to try to save themselves and Jake. Jesse has lied to them and betrayed their trust and love so many times before that they can't really believe anything he says. This is a realistic and convincingly brutal depiction of a family dealing with addiction, and that ain't pretty. We sympathize with Jesse, but in doing so we have to realize that his current relationship with his family is of his own making.

LAB NOTES

HIGHLIGHT

JAKE: "It's a piccolo, actually."

JESSE: "Dude! Play some Jethro Tull!"

DID YOU NOTICE

* The ringing as Walt's doctor explains the possible side effects of treatment is the same effect as when Walt got the original diagnosis, as is the unintelligible fading of the doctor's voice.
* The "Tampico Furniture" plate on Walt Jr.'s old crib in the nursery. This is the store Krazy-8's father owns.
* During his briefing to his DEA team, Hank mentions cartel-run "Superlabs" for meth manufacture in Mexico. Both Superlabs and the Mexican cartel's interest in them will recur in the series.

SHOOTING UP

* The up-and-through shot of the grilling chicken makes the cooking meat queasily reminiscent of the bloody goo Walt and Jesse were cleaning up the cold open of ". . . And the Bag's in the River."
* Check out the camera and audio effects when Jesse gets completely tweaked and flees his house in a paranoid panic — the Mormons as killer bikers, the flash-cuts, lighting changes, and aural hallucinations of helicopters circling, all topped off by the cheery ringing of the missionary's bicycle bell.

TITLE "Cancer Man" is a reference to William B. Davis's character on *The X-Files*, where Vince Gilligan was a writer, consultant, producer, and executive producer from 1995 to 2002.

MUSIC Jesse tells his little brother to play some Jethro Tull on his piccolo. Jethro Tull is a British rock band fronted by Ian Anderson, who often stands on one foot while playing the flute. The band has been around since 1967 and has sold well over 60 million albums.

SPECIAL INGREDIENTS

GLUING STAB WOUNDS

Domingo/Krazy-8 didn't go out gently, and Walt came away from Jesse's basement with some fairly serious wounds on his leg from the makeshift ceramic dagger. In this episode Walt uses "Acrylate Glue: Instant Bonding Agent" to glue his wounds together after cleaning and disinfecting them. The fictional brand name is based upon the chemical name for the adhesive agent in various super glues called cyanoacrylate. During the Vietnam War, the U.S. military used cyanoacrylate spray glues to stop wounds from bleeding in the field so that wounded soldiers had a higher chance of surviving to reach medical facilities out of the combat zone. Super Glue, Krazy Glue, etc. could indeed be used as an adhesive stitching to close wounds, but such household glues are not recommended for medical use because they may contain other chemicals that can irritate the skin (note how Walt winces when he applies the glue) or even cause burns as the glue works by reacting with the moisture in the air to polymerize into a resin, a process that produces heat. There are medical grade cyanoacrylate glues that are designed for use on wounds and that do not have such potentially painful side effects, but they are not readily available to folks like Walt who are trying to avoid the complications inherent in showing up at the ER with stab wounds.

AMERICAN HEALTH INSURANCE

Breaking Bad can be interpreted in part as an indictment of the American healthcare system. As Walt is being loaded into the ambulance following his collapse at the car wash in the pilot episode, he asks the EMTs if this is really necessary, as he doesn't have very good insurance. While Walt's lack of insurance isn't the only reason he makes the choices he makes, the dismal fact remains that the United States stands alone among developed countries in not providing universal healthcare coverage to its citizens. (Not just developed countries either. Per person, Thailand's gross domestic product is one-fifth that of the U.S.'s, yet only one percent of the Thai population lacks health insurance. Ironically, over the last decade, Mexico has dramatically expanded access to sophisticated treatment for its citizens, so maybe Walt should throw in with the Mexican cartels for the health coverage . . . although no cartel representative seems to mention that benefit.)

In 2010, the United States Census Bureau reported that 16.3 percent of people in the U.S. (a percentage that translates into 49.9 million individuals) lacked health insurance coverage. The Affordable Care Act (ACA) was signed into law in 2010 and has been upheld by the U.S. Supreme Court. However, a number of states are attacking portions of the ACA, which is intended to — among other things — end lifetime caps on insurance benefits and end the denial of coverage based on pre-existing health conditions. Before the ACA it was okay for a company to refuse to pay for, let's say, treatment for heart disease for you if you had been diagnosed with heart disease *before* you signed up for coverage. To borrow a title from season 3 of *Breaking Bad*, it is Kafkaesque. You can only get coverage if you don't need coverage.

Keep in mind, Walt has coverage — it's just not very good. In the U.S., many people with children have to make some nasty decisions. Walt's a high school teacher — in most school systems, his coverage would be cheap, but adding Skyler and Junior (especially Junior, who was born with cerebral palsy, a condition that often requires frequent and expensive therapies) can be astronomical. One way to deal with this is to opt for a higher out-of-pocket deductible and to pay a higher percentage of the costs. Walt's situation is better than many, but it's worth remembering that outstanding healthcare costs contributed to more than 60 percent of recent personal bankruptcies in the U.S.

No matter how you slice it, Walt can't afford his cancer.

Gray Matter

Original air date: February 24, 2008
Written by: Patty Lin **Directed by:** Tricia Brock

"Wanna cook?" — Walter White

Jesse and Walt discover that going straight isn't as easy as they thought. Meanwhile, Walt catches up with old friends and Skyler stages an intervention.

The thing about a real job is that, without education, experience, and marketable skills, you generally have to start at the bottom, and the bottom doesn't pay. After his first experience with meth making and dealing, Walt swears off cooking (though he certainly takes his share of the profits from the sales), and now he and Jesse have to figure out what they're going to do instead. Jesse's willing to look for jobs, but will only accept a certain standard of employment. Sure, dancing around in a foam costume and flipping a sign around isn't exactly on the top of anyone's Monster.com search criteria, but it's honest work, although the pay is probably lousy and Jesse does have bills. Instead, though, he refuses the offer, and we get the sense that it has as much to do with Jesse's sense of pride as with the job itself. Interestingly, his brief experience with Walt has infected Jesse with some of his old teacher's perfectionism when it comes to meth. He even shows off his newfound knowledge of chemistry nomenclature, and actually throws out an entire batch of meth for not being up to his new and exacting standards.

Jesse is hungry for a sense of worth and purpose. Dismissed as a loser by his parents, and also by Walt, Jesse is desperate to be good at something and to have a chance to prove himself. The only viable possibility seems to be cooking meth, and we begin to see that Jesse, for all of his failing grades in high school and seeming idiocy, is far from stupid. He's picked up a lot from a single cook with Walt and discovered ambitions that had long been sleeping. The role reversal where Jesse is now is the all-business cook and easily annoyed by his friend Badger's horseplay is a nice, funny touch. Unfortunately for Jesse, despite all he has learned thus far, his chemistry skills are nowhere near the level of Walt's, and he simply cannot make the quality product by himself that he can make with Walt. At least, not yet.

Walt's going through some self-worth issues too, and we get another glimpse into his past with the appearance of Elliott and Gretchen Schwartz (Adam Godley, whose credits include *Charlie and the Chocolate Factory*, *Around the World in 80 Days*, and *Elizabeth: The Golden Age*; and Jessica Hecht whose significant roles include *Bored to Death*, *Friends*, and *Sideways*). She was the fetching brunette we saw in Walt's flashbacks in ". . . And the Bag's in the River." They're old grad school friends and business partners who now have made it big and, despite his early involvement, have done it without Walt. The disparity in economic and social status between the Whites and the Schwartzes is well done. Walt and Skyler show up to Elliott's party dressed to the nines, but in clothes that are more than a little out of date, with Walt in a double-breasted navy suit coat with gold buttons that makes him look like something out of a satire on '70s-era yacht clubs. They stand out even more among the rest of the guests who are all dressed casually, beigely, and yet also expensively. This is obviously not Walt and Sky's world. However, when Walt's gift to Elliott is opened after a series of extravagant gifts (which include a Fender Stratocaster guitar played and signed by Eric Clapton), it proves to be the most thoughtful, meaningful present of them all.

It is this side of Walt that brings the viewer so willingly along on his journey into darkness and makes the audience root for him, because he can be such a sweet and thoughtful man. It is easy to see why his family loves him so much, why even old friends still have such a powerful affection for him. Walt is a good guy. He works two jobs to let Sky stay home and write. His love and support for Walter Jr. is obvious, and he has surrounded himself with a family that, while sometimes dysfunctional, is ultimately a source of tremendous love and strength. You can't help but like the guy.

Until his pride crops up and overshadows everything else.

Offered a chance at a job at Gray Matter, which comes with excellent insurance and presumably a much larger paycheck than teaching at a public high school, Walt becomes furious and refuses as soon as he finds out it's a sinecure arising out of Elliott's desire to help him. Remember, this is an entirely legal and aboveboard opportunity for Walt to provide for his family and cover his medical expenses. Indeed, it is even likely that Walt would soon become a true asset to the company if he would take the time to sharpen his skills and knowledge. From what we learn at the party, he may well be the most brilliant chemist there. But Walt's having none of it. He would rather cook meth, risk his family, and die than accept what he sees as a handout. Tragic flaw, anyone?

At the core of this episode are the themes pride and money. Taken together, Walt and Jesse paint a portrait of an American Dream that they have both found to be more myth than reality. Jesse's choices have left him fundamentally unequipped to prosper in the legitimate working world. Walt's decisions have left him in a position where, even though he has a job and insurance, neither is really good, and trying to live up to the role of the sole wage-earner and support his family has led to a really crappy second job with him still only barely making ends meet. Worse, neither is in a position to find a way out of their respective predicaments. Neither of them can afford a drop in income while they train / retrain for better opportunities. Indeed, it is Walt's almost pathological concern with money that leads to his refusal to undergo cancer treatment, which leads in turn to the most sublime scene in this season: Skyler's intervention, where Walt's family comes together to try to talk him into getting treatment for his cancer.

Breaking Bad has a number of truly memorable scenes and the "home intervention" is one of them. Beautifully and truthfully written, the intervention showcases the amazing talents of the ensemble cast comprising Walt's extended family. The actors in the scene convey heartbreak, humor, anger, and bewilderment by turns. Junior, who has to use crutches every single day just to get around, is pissed off that his dad is so willing to give up and he lets Walt hear about it. Skyler doesn't really care what opinion her sister Marie might have and Hank doesn't like Marie being attacked. The "talking pillow" is unable to keep these people calm and at one point, it looks like the whole thing will disintegrate into a yelling match. But the scene belongs to Walt, who explains with quiet dignity that he's thought through his decision to not seek treatment. This is his choice, by God, and he wants it to be respected: "Sometimes I feel that I never actually make any of my own choices. My entire life — it just seems I never had a real say about any of it." Of course, Walt is taking a different kind of extreme measure in the face of his disease, so it's best to take what he says with a grain of salt. In the end, Walt can't do what he thinks he must without Jesse, and Jesse can't do what he thinks he must without Walt. The RV will roll on.

LAB NOTES

HIGHLIGHT
SKYLER: "Not yet, please. I have the talking pillow."

DID YOU NOTICE
* The "talking pillow" is inscribed with the feel-good slogan "Find Joy in the Little Things." Solid advice that the White family fails to heed.
* When he gets in trouble trying to illegally buy beer, Junior calls Hank, rather than Walt. Hank calls him on that and asks Sky and Marie not to tell Walt that Junior called him instead. Again Hank is stepping in as Junior's surrogate father, and also shows sensitivity towards the emotional currents of the family, including Walt's pride.
* Notice the stack of books on the bedside table. Skyler is reading up on both pregnancy and dealing with cancer. One title, *While Waiting*, could deal with either subject.

SHOOTING UP Time-lapse photography is an integral part of *Breaking Bad*'s cinematography, particularly in desert cook scenes. Keep an eye out for it and you'll see it popping up over and over again. It's always beautifully done — both aesthetically and in terms of advancing the storyline.

TITLE "Gray Matter" refers to the name of Elliott and Gretchen's very successful company. Gray is a mix of black and white and, in this case, it represents a blending of Elliott's last name, "Schwartz" (German for "black"), and Walter's last name, "White." However, Walt is no longer a part of the company, and hasn't been for a long time.

SPECIAL INGREDIENTS

CEREBRAL PALSY

A friend of *Breaking Bad*'s creator Vince Gilligan was born with cerebral palsy and Gilligan conceived the role of Walt Jr. as a tribute to him. Junior has cerebral palsy, as does RJ Mitte, the young actor cast in the role. Mitte has used the role to increase the visibility of actors with disabilities and the challenges they face. He serves as a spokesman for an advocacy campaign known as "I AM PWD," which stands for "Inclusion in the Arts and Media of Performers with Disabilities." It's an important issue, given that about 20 percent of the population has some form of disability, but only about one percent of speaking parts in television portray disability — roles often played by non-disabled actors. In part, this is due to access issues — if you're in a wheelchair, simply getting to the audition poses problems that other actors don't have to deal with. Further, many "disabled roles" are cardboard cutouts instead of fully realized people. This stereotype is something Mitte is working to change and the role of Walt Jr. has given him quite a platform. Junior is a pretty typical teenager. He wants his driver's license and he loves his family while trying to carve out his own identity, often displaying a quick temper and sharp mouth. He just also happens to need crutches and an extra few seconds to get his thoughts out.

Mitte's own case of cerebral palsy is less pronounced than Walt Jr.'s — Mitte doesn't need crutches, for example. Cerebral palsy is actually a group of disorders caused by injuries to or abnormalities of the brain, often happening prior to birth or shortly thereafter. Cerebral palsy often manifests in impaired movement. In particular, muscles of the arms and legs are often tight and rigid, without the flexibility most of us enjoy. A person with cerebral palsy may also have other conditions relating to problems associated with abnormal brain development, but frequently the intellectual capacity is completely normal. While there is no cure, treatments and therapies can assist a person with cerebral palsy to lead a full and independent life.

CRYSTALLOGRAPHY

A former graduate school colleague at Elliott's party introduces Walt as a "master of crystallography." This is a branch of science that studies the arrangement of atoms in solids. Originally, crystals were studied based on their geometry to deduce angles and symmetry of the crystal in question, which involved lots of both patience and higher mathematics. Now, the crystal sample is targeted by a beam and the resulting diffraction patterns are analyzed. (X-ray diffraction, neutron diffraction, or electron diffraction are all common methods in this uncommon field.) It still involves near-endless patience and lots of high mathematics.

How could such a specialized field result in a multimillion dollar company such as Gray Matter? Outside of pure chemistry, crystallography is a useful tool for materials engineers who are looking for methods to develop nanotechnology use. Crystallography is also used by biologists studying proteins. For example, the double-helix structure of DNA familiar to most high-school chemistry students was first developed through crystallographic data.

Crazy Handful of Nothin'

Original air date: March 2, 2008
Written by: Bronwen Hughes **Directed by:** George Mastras

"A little tweak of chemistry." — Walter White

Walt and Jesse are cooking again, and Walt wants to move product wholesale, despite Jesse's warnings. Meanwhile, Hank demonstrates why he's so very good at his job.

The cold open to "Crazy Handful of Nothin'" gives us Walt and Jesse back in the RV with Walt laying down the law. Walt wants to be in the background so Jesse can deal with customers, and after their experiences with Emilio and Krazy-8, Walt insists that there be no more violence. During this lovely speech we see a flash-forward to the end of the episode where a shaven-headed, badass-looking Walt carries a bloody bag out of a blasted building. Looks like Walt's no violence rule won't last long.

The cold open sets up the disparity between what Walt imagines the drug business to be and what it actually is. More, it reveals a central fact about Walt himself: he thinks he can control things — and people too. Despite ostensibly having teamed up with Jesse because Jesse knows the business, Walt is completely unwilling to listen to him when Jesse tries to explain the realities of that business. Instead, Walt wants things to be a certain way and therefore he stubbornly insists that they *are* that way. When Jesse remains unwilling, Walt alternately bullies and cajoles Jesse into trying to work out an agreement with Krazy-8's replacement as distributor, despite Jesse's fear. Indeed, Walt is manipulating everyone in his life, and congratulating himself on being smarter than anyone else. He uses his cancer to manipulate Skyler, playing on her emotions with no thought for her whatsoever. He plays the feckless academic with Hank, and allows the soft-spoken, terribly kind custodian, Hugo (played by Pierre Barrera, who is primarily a set dresser rather than an actor), to be jailed and lose his job because of Walt's own carelessness.

All this happens because Walt is brilliant in the "book smart" way, but lacks both emotional smarts and street smarts. In fact, in those two areas, he's sometimes a complete idiot. After stealing all the equipment necessary to make quality meth from the high school chemistry lab, Walt doesn't even think about altering the inventory lists. Hank, who may not know chemistry but sure as hell knows meth making, easily identifies the missing equipment as just what you'd need to outfit a quality meth lab, and the unaltered inventory sheets directly connect the gas mask and all of the rest of the equipment to Walt's lab. The viewer can't help but notice the surprised look on Walt's face when he realizes just how familiar his brother-in-law is with the meth-making business. After years of knowing Walt as a hapless, harmless sort of man, Hank can't conceive of Walt being a meth-making maniac. That single fact prevents Walt from becoming the DEA's number one suspect in their search for the new mastermind meth cook. It also keeps Walt from being a suspect in the sudden disappearance of the DEA's meth snitch, who turns out to have been Krazy-8.

Walt's arrogance also leads him to start playing a dangerous game with Hank. Realizing that Hank doesn't think him capable of the crimes he's actually committed, Walt begins to take a little too much pleasure in dancing on the razor's edge with Hank, as seen during their not-quite-friendly card game, where Walt bluffs Hank into folding despite Walt having "a handful of nothing." Walt's expression reveals how much he is enjoying besting Hank and how a family poker game has, in his twisted mind, turned into further proof that Walt is capable of outsmarting any potential foe. Walt's arrogance, however, blinds him to the fact that while he resents Hank for underestimating *him*, he's making the dangerous mistake of underestimating just how intelligent his brother-in-law is.

This is not the best mental state for Walt to be in, for this episode also gives us the first of the series' real villains, the extraordinarily frightening Tuco Salamanca, played with tremendous gusto by Raymond Cruz (also known for roles on *Nip/Tuck*, *CSI: Miami*, and *The Closer*). Tuco is murder in a snakeskin-patterned silk shirt, and is the antithesis to Walt's fantasy of a rational drug world where the rules of legal business and commerce still apply. Instead Tuco is dangerously erratic, and murderously sociopathic, capable of shifting from laughing hail-fellow-well-met to brutal violence with no warning and for the most trivial of reasons. Tuco is the id run wild, and the very definition of what Lonnie Athens terms a "dangerous, violent criminal." Tuco is the true face of the drug business, but it is Jesse, not Walt, who pays the price for Walt's hubris and arrogance.

It takes Tuco, however, to reveal who this new Walt is. For five episodes now Walt has been moving further and further away from his old self as he creates a new way of viewing and interacting with the world in the wake of his cancer diagnosis. Skyler has seen it, Walter Jr. above all knows his dad's gone weird, Hank overlooks it because it is so radically different from pre-cancer Walt, and even Jesse has noted that this Mr. White is not the same person who taught him high school chemistry. The question is, just who or what is Walt becoming? Head shaved, in a black porkpie hat, going balls-out with high explosives into Tuco's den, Walt finally gives us the answer: "Heisenberg."

From here on out, nothing is certain.

LAB NOTES

HIGHLIGHT

> WALT: "Yes, that's what we need! We need a distributor. Do you know anyone like that?"
> JESSE: "Yeah. I mean I used to . . . until you killed him."

DID YOU NOTICE

+ The science fair projects lining the wall of Walt's classroom when Hank comes to visit include one for "nasty teeth," or "meth mouth."
+ Lots of poker playing in the White/Schrader households. In the last episode, Hank uses a poker metaphor to explain his thinking to Walt and here Walt turns that around on Hank with his bluff.
+ Jesse instantly recognizes Walt's chemo patch and is familiar with the stages of cancer.
+ When Walt gets sick from the chemo while cooking, he encourages Jesse to finish the cook, giving him a kind of pep talk and assuring him

that he can do it. Walt's opinion of Jesse's skills as a cook is a recurring topic in the series.

TITLE The title of this episode comes from a quote in the 1967 film *Cool Hand Luke* and it has two meanings. On one hand, it refers to Walt's bluffing during the family poker game, during which Marie comments that Walt won the hand even though he was holding "a handful of nothing." In fact, the poker scene between the two men seems to be a direct homage to the film. Walt won his bluff with Hank, but sometimes you have to show your cards first, as Walt does with the small amount of mercury fulminate he uses to convince Tuco of his point of view. Bluffing with a handful of nothing is a risky move, because it relies on your ability to convince others that you are one kind of person rather than another, an ability that Walt and Cool Hand Luke seem to share.

MUSIC The montage and music as Jesse sells the batch of meth is brilliantly done, with that hideous blue-green fluorescent lighting all around to give an added 3 a.m. too-bright feeling to things.

SPECIAL INGREDIENTS

STAGES OF LUNG CANCER

Walt has been diagnosed with Stage III lung cancer. Just what does that mean? First, it's important to understand that cancer is not just one disease. Instead, the term refers to out-of-control cell growth that results in tumors in the body. While benign tumors can be safely removed and tend to be localized, malignant tumors grow aggressively and spread, or metastasize, throughout the body. Lung cancer tends to metastasize early, making it both life-threatening and difficult to treat.

The "stage" of the disease refers to how much the cancer has spread. Accurate staging may require blood chemistry tests, X-rays, and more sophisticated scans such as MRI and CT scans. Determining the stage of the cancer helps determine the best course of treatment and also provides the prognosis of the patient. There are four stages to non-small-cell lung cancers, also known as NSCLC. NSCLC are the most common type of lung cancers, accounting for about 80 percent of all cases. Stages include:

* In Stage I, the cancer is confined to the lung.

- In Stages II and III, the cancer has grown beyond the lung, but is still confined to the chest, with larger, more invasive tumors gaining the "Stage III" classification.
- In Stage IV, the cancer has spread beyond the chest to other parts of the body.

The five-year survival rate for a person whose lung cancer is first diagnosed at Stage III is not good. Every individual is different — Walt's not a smoker, for instance, which helps — but the overall percentage of people who are alive five years after a Stage III diagnosis of lung cancer is under 25 percent. Knowing all this, Walt's despair and drastic behavior becomes easier to understand.

MERCURY FULMINATE

Walt uses mercury fulminate to explosively convince Tuco to see things his way and to pay for the meth he took from Jesse. Walt sets this up earlier in the episode with another chemistry lecture where he explains the nature of chemical reactions, and even gives the formula for the degradation of fulminated mercury into its constituent elements: $Hg(OCN)_2 = Hg + 2CO_2 + N_2$.

Mercury fulminate decomposes in a chemical reaction called detonation, meaning that the chemicals involved combust so rapidly that the resulting gas expands faster than the speed of sound, creating a violent shock wave that can be highly destructive, as Tuco and his crew can testify. However, Gilligan & Co. have taken some artistic liberties with the chemistry here. If the huge crystals Walt gives Tuco are all really mercury fulminate, then he is the greatest crystallographer who has ever lived. In fact, real-world experiments with crystallizing mercury fulminate resulted in crystals less than one millimeter long. Also, mercury fulminate is notoriously unstable, and with the rough handling Walt's bag of "meth" receives, it is likely that it would have exploded much sooner, and certainly the rest of the bag would have gone up when the piece Walt threw did.

HEISENBERG

Walt takes his street name from Werner Karl Heisenberg (1901–1976) who was a German theoretical physicist. Heisenberg is best known for the "uncertainty principle" in quantum physics that (in a *very* boiled-down-to-basics definition) asserts that there is an intrinsic limit on the accuracy with which pairs of properties can be simultaneously known. Heisenberg was referring to physical properties of a particle, such as velocity and position. The more precisely one is known (velocity, for example), the less precisely the other (position, in this example) can be known or determined. At any given instant, you can accurately know one or the other, but not both.

Brilliant. The more Walt becomes Heisenberg, the less certain we are of Walt. Sure, Walt could have just gone for "Chameleon Man" or given the Southwestern context, "Gila Monster," but you have to admit, "Heisenberg" has style and dash. (Heisenberg also died of cancer, a disease that is very much on Walt's mind these days.)

In a series of lectures given in the mid-'50s, Heisenberg also said, "What we observe is not nature itself, but nature exposed to our method of questioning." In other words, nothing is pure. The questions you choose to ask frame the answers you will receive. This is another problem for Walt — he doesn't understand the fullness of the vat of evil he's begun to swim in, so he can't see the trouble that will come from that failure to understand.

No-Rough-Stuff-Type Deal

1.07

Original air date: March 9, 2008
Written by: Peter Gould **Directed by:** Tim Hunter

"Hey, what are we doing way out here? What happened, did they close the mall?" — Tuco Salamanca

Walt and Jesse figure out how to cook on a large scale. Meanwhile, Walt finally begins to see just how dangerous Tuco can be.

What started with Walt getting off on bluffing Hank in a (mostly) friendly game of poker is beginning to escalate. Now Walt's looking for illicit thrills everywhere, as he and Sky demonstrate in the back seat of the Aztek in the school parking lot. Parked beside a police cruiser — the same cruiser an officer drove to the school to talk to the PTO about the dangers of crystal meth — Walt once again tests how far he can push the envelope before getting caught. And as for the Heisenberg half of his life, despite his experience with Tuco, Walt's made a deal. Unfortunately Walt fails to listen to Jesse, and again gets the two embroiled in a heap of trouble.

In this episode, *Breaking Bad* again takes the viewer to a place without memory, except instead of a desert, we're in a deserted junkyard surrounded by towers of slowly rusting, wrecked cars. The thing about such forgotten spaces is that their privacy also comes with a dark side: anything can happen in such places. Walt thought he was being smooth and smart in choosing an abandoned location to meet Tuco, but learns the hard way that he doesn't know what the hell he's doing. Public spaces are far safer for drug meets.

To this point Jesse's not been much more than a wannabe, but during this first meet in the junk-yard, he shows far more bravery than Walt. Unlike him, Jesse knows exactly what he's dealing with when it comes to Tuco, from personal experience: an "insane ass-clown, dead-eyed killer." Walt hasn't figured that out yet, but he will. In the meantime, for Jesse to meet with Tuco after being so viciously brutalized takes some real guts, and proves that he's not the loser we thought he was at the beginning of the season.

(IZUMI HASEGAWA/PR PHOTOS)

Walt's greed begins to ramp up now, and he's never satisfied, making promises he doesn't have the ability to keep, and always pushing for more. He desires the rush of living dangerously, without realizing the truth of that phrase. Walt's schemes require spending most of the money they've already made on re-equipping the RV, and of course Walt convinces Jesse — with a mixture of contempt and first-day-of-the-rest-of-your-life speeches — to do all the dangerous work of finding and buying the supplies. Walt wants more, but he doesn't want to take any risks himself. In truth, Walt would probably be able to acquire the equipment they need faster and more easily than Jesse, but this way he takes on none of the risk such a shopping trip would entail. Plus, if anything goes wrong, he can blame it on Jesse. For Walt, having someone to blame is always important, and that someone can never be himself. In the end, however, Walt has to join Jesse in taking a big risk, and despite once again using his knowledge of chem-istry to good effect, Walt reveals his shortcomings when he discovers that a bulk chemical supply warehouse doesn't store chemicals in single-gallon jugs. Confronted with the unexpected, Walt improvises — badly — bitching at Jesse all the while and forgetting that the best way to move a full barrel is by rolling it on its side.

Walt's not the only one operating under delusions of grandeur and enjoying living outside of the law, as we see with Marie's over-the-top baby shower gift, which she shoplifted from a high-end store. Confronted with her actions Marie denies, denies, and denies, even trying to turn things around by blaming Sky for returning it. Again, with Marie it's about attention; she wanted to have the best gift at the shower, thus making the day at least somewhat about her rather than Skyler and the baby. Watch Skyler's own acting ability, as she quickly and efficiently lies her way out of trouble at the store where she's tried to return Marie's "gift." In the end, Sky may well be a better liar and manipulator than even Walt.

At the baby shower, Walt and Hank have a very interesting conversation by the pool, where they have retreated from the hen party inside. As Hank smokes an illegal Cuban cigar, the men discuss just what should be legal and what should be prohibited. Walt's conversation here is another example of him enjoying dancing around his secrets with Hank.

Again the audience is treated to some wonderful humor, not just in Jesse and Walt's heist, but during the subsequent distillation process in Jesse's basement, while his realtor is holding an open house upstairs. Gilligan & Co. obviously understand the absolute necessity of comic relief in a show that would otherwise be too dark for viewers. Having to deal with Walt's march into moral depravity without any relief from the grim and gore would be unbearable, but the show's brilliant writing and the perfect timing of the cast's performances gives us the necessary release of laughter and light, and adds that extra sublime bit of humanity that makes *Breaking Bad* so addictive (if you'll pardon the term). In the end, however, the viewer is reminded of what is really going on as Walt and Jesse again find themselves in the forgotten spaces of the junkyard with a monster. A chance comment by one of his henchmen, Gonzo (Cesar Garcia who had a role in *Drive* and guest spots on episodes of *Criminal Minds* and *Weeds*), sends Tuco into a rage with such bloody and terrifying results that Jesse and Walt can do nothing but stand by and watch. We end the season on Walt's face, and it's clear by his expression that he finally, *finally* begins to realize what he's gone into business with.

LAB NOTES

HIGHLIGHT
JESSE: "Yeah, Mr. White! Yeah — science!"

DID YOU NOTICE
- The "Meth = Death" poster behind the cop at the PTO meeting.
- Hank's face when Sky opens Marie's gift is telling. He knows immediately that the tiara is stolen.
- Check out how weirdly normal Walt and Sky are on the couch as they recount their weekend to one another.

SHOOTING UP
- The lingering shot of the support pole in Jesse's basement where Krazy-8 was chained and died is another example of using relatively long shots of specific objects to imbue them with narrative meaning and importance.
- The film-within-a-film technique used for the baby shower is really nice, and gives the viewer another look at why everyone wants to like Walt. His message to his unborn daughter is truly touching and reveals the finest parts of Walt's character. It also recalls the use of the same technique in "Pilot/Breaking Bad" when Walt taped his non-confession.
- Junior's boob close-up is hilarious and a nice touch of the reality of what happens when you hand a 16-year-old a video camera.

TITLE The title references a quote from the 1996 Coen Brothers film *Fargo*. In that film, a man sets up the kidnapping of his wife in what is supposed to be "a no-rough-stuff-type deal" that goes horribly wrong. Like Walt, the character in *Fargo* doesn't know what he's gotten himself into until it's too late.

MUSIC As Walt and Jesse stare horrified after Tuco's nonchalant departure we hear Gnarls Barkley's "Who's Gonna Save My Soul," a perfect piece to end on.

SPECIAL INGREDIENTS

ETCH A SKETCH THERMITE

To break into the chemical company, Walt and Jesse (in their pom-pom ski masks) are going to need to blow open a substantial padlock, and Walt uses the powder inside an Etch A Sketch pad. Can you really do that with a child's toy? Well, chemistry is interesting.

If you pry open the toy and remove the aluminum powder that coats the screen, you have half the ingredients for thermite. All you need now is some form of metal oxide (even rust could do, since rust is chemically a form of iron oxide) and a heat source. The thermite mixture itself isn't explosive, but it can create very high temperatures around a small area; temperatures high enough to weld metal together without conventional welding equipment. Walt and Jesse use a gas torch as a heat source to get the reaction started and their Great Heist is underway.

METH USED TO BE LEGAL

So you've got a drug so bad for you that its use causes skin lesions, tooth loss, extreme insomnia, hallucinations, paranoia, and death. Yet as the menfolk discuss by the pool during the baby shower, meth was legal, albeit only through prescription, until the early 1980s. During World War Two, both Allied and Axis forces freely distributed meth to soldiers, no doubt causing many cases of addiction. (This didn't start with WWII — thousands of soldiers in the American Civil War came home addicted to powerful drugs such as morphine that was used to treat pain. Opium was often added to patent medicines during that time as well.) One side effect of meth use is acute alertness, so millions of tablets were distributed to tank crews, aircraft personnel, and foot soldiers.

Following WWII, meth was widely prescribed by physicians in America for the treatment of narcolepsy, Parkinson's disease, depression, and alcoholism. (Yep, trade in a boozy nose for meth mouth. *There's* a step in the right direction!) Gradually, the medical uses of meth were halted, although it is still prescribed in the U.S., primarily for the treatment of attention deficit disorder and obesity. In an attempt to shut down the clandestine manufacture of the drug, laws were passed in the United States in 1983 to prohibit the possession of equipment and ingredients to manufacture the drug. With the passage of the federal Combat Methamphetamine Epidemic Act of 2005, stark limits were placed on the purchase of the drug's main ingredients — ephedrine and pseudoephedrine, and drugs containing those ingredients were required to be placed behind pharmacy counters to cut down on theft. These laws have had an impact on domestic production of meth, but as *Breaking Bad* shows, the manufacture and distribution of the drug continues to be rampant.

SPEED KILLS

BODY COUNT
Walt: 2 (Emilio and Krazy-8)

BEATDOWNS
Jesse: 2 (by Krazy-8 and by Tuco)
Gonzo: 1 (by Tuco)

What's Cooking

WALTER WHITE
AND THE ANTIHERO

Fans and critics alike often refer to Walt as an "antihero." What does that term actually mean? Where does it come from? Is that what Walt — a central character viewers sympathize with, even though he's done repulsive, evil things — actually is? And if he is, why is a character who has done so many awful things so popular with viewers?

Before we can meaningfully discuss the antihero (a character who upends the usual narrative apple cart), we need to understand the basics. Traditionally, stories have been structured with a *protagonist* and an *antagonist*. The term *protagonist* comes from the Greek word "protagonistes," which means "chief actor." This is the central character of the story and is the character the audience is intended to identify with most strongly. The conflict of the story arises from the negative interaction between the protagonist and the antagonist (from the Greek *antagonists*, which means "opponent" or "rival"). The antagonist is usually a person who opposes the protagonist, but the antagonist can also be an inhuman force of nature that the protagonist must fight and overcome, such as the shark in *Jaws*. Traditionally, the protagonist possesses heroic qualities, such as being courageous and morally good, while the antagonist is more villainous, exhibiting qualities such as double-dealing and cruelty. In simple terms, think of good-tempered Bullwinkle J. Moose (protagonist) contending with the nefarious scheming of Pottsylvanian spy and professional no-goodnik Boris Badenov (antagonist).

An *antihero* is a protagonist who lacks these heroic qualities. The term has been further refined to include protagonists who exhibit qualities normally associated with villains, such as greed and violence, as well as possessing non-heroic qualities, such as selfishness and cowardice. Significantly for this discussion, antiheroes may circumvent or break the law in order to achieve goals that they see as noble. While the term *antihero* is first dated to 1714, characters fitting the definition of an antihero can be found well before that time. Shylock from Shakespeare's *The Merchant of Venice* (around 1596) is one example, as is Lucifer from Milton's *Paradise Lost* (1667). Also pitching their tents in the antihero camp are Raskolnikov from Dostoevsky's *Crime and Punishment* (1866) and Severus Snape from Rowling's Harry Potter series. And let's not leave out the antiheroines, who include Becky Sharp from Thackeray's *Vanity Fair* (1847) and Scarlett O'Hara from Mitchell's *Gone with the Wind* (1936).

On television, antiheroes have never been more popular than they are today. Many of these antiheroes have been involved in law enforcement, which has traditionally been portrayed as one of the more heroic occupations. Vic Mackey (*The Shield*) is a long way from Sheriff Andy Taylor (*The Andy Griffith Show*) and Lieutenant Theo Kojak (*Kojak*). Of course, television antiheroes can be found in professions other than law enforcement, such as advertising (Don Draper of *Mad Men*), "waste management" (Tony Soprano of *The Sopranos*), forensic blood-spatter analyst (Dexter Morgan of *Dexter*), and motorcycle club management (Jax Teller of *Sons of Anarchy*). So how does a mild-mannered high school chemistry teacher become one of the most popular antiheroes of all time? After all, *Breaking Bad*'s viewer ratings increased with every season and the finale episode shattered records. In addition, three of the show's lead actors (Cranston, Gunn, and Paul) have been honored with Emmy Awards and the show itself took home the "Outstanding Drama Series" Emmy at the 2013 awards — and will certainly be in the running for the 2014 award season, which will consider the final eight episodes. No doubt about it, Walter White is popular. But why are the adventures of a manipulative meth kingpin "must-see" television?

It can be argued that antiheroes have become more prevalent as our society has become more conflicted, and in post-9/11 America the television antihero has taken a firm hold of the viewing public. Using this argument, it's as if we don't fully trust the knight in shining armor anymore — like The

Who, we're determined that we won't get fooled again. We've had too many real-world betrayals by those in positions of authority in the government, clergy, Scouting, and sports for us to be comfortable with simple stories of White Hats and Black Hats. We live in a world of gray and we've grown more comfortable with conflicted moral messages. In a way, the hero-or-antihero debate is the age-old argument of Superman versus Batman. Superman is good, dependable, and true, and will go to great lengths to avoid killing, while Batman is psychologically damaged from childhood trauma and will likely as not use violence to solve the immediate problem. Yet many prefer the gritty Dark Knight to the noble Son of Krypton. However, in the case of both Batman and Superman, the characters are ultimately *heroes* — that is, they do the right thing and fight on the side of good, although their methods differ. Antiheroes are not so constrained, often acting out of purely selfish motives.

With *Breaking Bad*, we have something new — we actually *see* the transformation of normal guy into immoral antihero. That Walter White *is* an antihero is beyond doubt. He remains the protagonist of *Breaking Bad* throughout the show, but his qualities are decidedly non-heroic. Walt's choices may not be our choices, but the factors that drive him to cross one moral line after another are events we understand all too well: crappy job, mounting medical bills, credit card debt, and a midlife crisis sparked by asking himself the question "Just what have I accomplished with my life?" and not liking the answer. When the viewer joins them, Tony Soprano is already a mobster and Dexter Morgan is already a sociopath, but Walter White is simply an Everyman and turns into a monster before our very eyes.

As viewers know, Walt begins his journey as a pathetic figure: he's a brilliant chemist who is just scraping by working for low pay and little respect as a high school chemistry teacher. His paycheck is not enough to move the family out of the "starter home" he and his wife purchased 16 years ago and they have growing problems with debt. Walt sees himself as a failure as a provider, but he sees no other way to live — until he is diagnosed with lung cancer. Oddly freed from his humdrum life by this terrible news, Walt begins his journey from being a forgettable nobody to being "Heisenberg" — ruthless meth kingpin. He initially justifies his foray into the meth manufacturing business by claiming that he wants to leave his family financially secure after the cancer kills him, but that excuse quickly falls by the wayside. At first,

Walt needs Jesse to act as his guide. Walt has always lived a straight-arrow sort of life and he knows the chemistry, but is willing to admit that he doesn't know the business. Quickly, however, Walt feels he has outgrown his need for Jesse's guidance.

Walt's insistence that all of his illegal actions are being done for his family echoes the so-called "Heinz dilemma" posed by psychologist Lawrence Kohlberg. The Heinz dilemma explores ethics and morality by asking students to speculate on the following: Heinz has a very sick wife whom he loves very much. Only one druggist has the drug that will cure her and he charges an exorbitant price for the drug. Heinz cannot raise the funds to purchase the drug and the druggist refuses to lower his price. Desperate, Heinz breaks into the shop and steals the drug. The question is: Was Heinz correct in doing so? This is very much like Walt's justification for manufacturing meth — he wants to leave his family comfortable. However, Walt is not personifying the Heinz dilemma. In the Heinz dilemma, the husband is only concerned about his wife's health; he's not worried about the tidiness of his burglary. Walt doesn't want to just churn out massive amounts of street meth, although Jesse points out that they're making poison and their customers don't care about whether or not their high was created in a scientifically clean environment. Walt's constant emphasis on professional standards is evidence of Walt's pride at work. Pride is one of the chief antiheroic qualities and is certainly one of Walt's chief characteristics. Also, Heinz takes a single, desperate action. Walt takes one, then another, then another, then another until he's unrecognizable to all around him.

Herein lies the appeal of Walt. Vince Gilligan has created a character who does dreadful, horrible things — including poisoning a child, killing a man just for telling him the truth, and standing by while allowing a girl to die — yet we watch with concentrated fascination. Walt's antiheroic choices are not our choices, but we see his path and almost understand it; after all, everyone has a breaking point. How far can a man be pushed before breaking the law looks like a viable option? And, just as important, after reaching that point, how much further is that man willing to go? In Walt's case, he doesn't make one batch of meth. Instead, he takes increasingly dark actions, one after another after another, digging himself ever deeper and corroding nearly all those who brush against his penumbra of evil, including Combo, Tomás, Victor, and Andrea. While he may not actively intend any of the horrible things that happen as a result of his career-switch, that buys him no redemption — if you don't want the effect, don't be the cause. Walt's utter refusal to own the consequences of his actions is a deplorable weakness — compared to *Sons of Anarchy*, for example, where Jax Teller hurts and kills those who defy him or threaten his family, and he never enjoys doing so. But he acknowledges that yeah, he did those things and he'd do them again if necessary. Walt lacks even that degree of honesty.

EPISODE GUIDE

SEASON TWO

2

Seven Thirty-Seven

Original air date: March 8, 2009
Written by: J. Roberts **Directed by:** Bryan Cranston

"They got book learnin', but no street skills." — Hank Schrader

Things go from bad to worse in Walt and Jesse's relationship with Tuco. Meanwhile, Skyler is getting fed up with Walt's behavior.

Season 2 of *Breaking Bad* begins right where season 1 left off: in the forgotten spaces of the junkyard where Tuco has been revealed as a dangerously violent psychopath, capable of turning on his own people in an instant. Walt now begins to understand exactly who he has insisted on becoming business partners with, but reveals his continuing, almost willful ignorance by thinking that he can plan to retire from the meth business in just 11 weeks. Indeed, Walt's arrogance and disdain for others really begin to stand out in this episode. He believes that his scientific expertise makes him smarter and more capable than everyone else around him, yet in reality, he often makes things more complicated than they need to be. Think of the methylamine heist last season, where Walt came up with a complicated plan to steal barrels of a difficult-to-obtain substance and used thermite in an ingenious way . . . but didn't think about the presence of security cameras and lugged the heavy barrels out rather than rolling them.

Walt's plan to use ricin to kill Tuco is another example of his arrogance getting in the way of things. Neither he nor Jesse are familiar with handguns, but an elaborate scheme based on Walt's opinion of Tuco as a "degenerate," and one that will take 48 to 72 hours to work, is bound to blow up in their faces, especially given Tuco's penchant for direct and violent measures. Walt's judgment — that they have no choice but to kill Tuco — is extremely suspect. After all, Walt has plenty of other choices he could make. He could go to the police or the DEA, for instance, but that choice comes with consequences that Walt doesn't want to face. For Walt, murder has now become a viable, and more acceptable, solution to problems.

Then there is Walt's truly disturbing sexual assault on Skyler in their kitchen. Symptomatic of Walt's own descent into degeneracy, his need for physical comfort very swiftly turns violent, and though Skyler clearly tells him "no," Walt refuses to hear it. He wants what he wants and he wants it right now. The fact that Skyler is pregnant adds another layer of horror to Walt's attack. The White house is becoming less and less of a refuge as Walt brings more and more of the violence of his other life home with him, harming those he loves and slowly destroying their home life. What Walt is supposedly doing for the good of his family is in fact destroying it. As a result, Skyler finally breaks in this episode, no longer able to keep silent on Walt's cancer, his strange behavioral changes, her unexpected pregnancy, and Marie's apparent kleptomania. Interestingly, it is Hank in whom she unexpectedly and angrily confides, and who offers clumsy but sincere comfort to her. Again, Hank is present for Walt's family while Walt is absent.

Walt's newfound acceptance of violence is accompanied by an equally newfound terror dogging his every step and murdering his sleep. His precautions to protect his family are ludicrous, and his willingness to abandon Jesse to fend for himself is again telling, placing Jesse in the category of people that Walt views as utterly disposable. Walt doesn't care about Jesse, not really. In fact, one begins to wonder if Walt truly cares about anyone besides himself. He certainly says he does, but his choices give a different story. The darkness of the episode is fortunately broken by a wide vein of black humor provided largely by Hank, both during Sky's breakdown and at the crime scene at the junkyard where No-Doze (actor and stuntman Jesus Jr.) and Gonzo's bodies have been discovered after a freak accident. Hank's investigation also provides a more subtle humor as Walt, Jesse, and Tuco become the victims of a very dark farce of *I Love Lucy*–style misunderstandings and ill-drawn conclusions that lead all of them to assume the worst.

LAB NOTES

HIGHLIGHT

JESSE: "Ricin beans?"

DID YOU NOTICE

- Walt puts down the "Heisenberg hat" before going to talk with Skyler, perhaps trying to put his entire other life aside with it. In removing the hat to enter the house, Walt makes an attempt to separate his two selves. The problem is, Heisenberg isn't the hat; it's Walt.
- Walt Jr. comes in after Walt's assault on Skyler and sees the smudge of her face cream on the refrigerator door. This brief bit emphasizes Junior's position on the outside of things, dramatically affected by what's going on with his parents, yet denied knowledge of what's actually happening, and unable to change things, or even prepare for any changes that are coming. This position is emphasized again and again throughout the series.

- Marie and Hank's house is larger, more modern, and cleaner than Walt and Skyler's. Marie and Hank both work in relatively well-paying jobs and have no children. The subtle contrast to Walt and Skyler's home and financial situation is telling, and is part of the fuel for Walt's prideful refusal to ask Hank for help.
- A tick of Marie's character is revealed in her kitchen with her precise arrangement of Splenda packs that she lines up on the counter, tears in exactly the same way in sequence from right to left, and neatly folds together, all while chattering away, and with really bad Muzak jazz playing in the background. Watch for this routine to be repeated.
- The ringing in Walt's ears as he stands before the TV in shock recalls the similar ringing during the doctor's office visits in season 1.
- Despite Walt's opinion of him, Jesse is far more aware of the world they are now living in. When Walt tells him to run, Jesse is already prepared with his cash tucked away in a duffel bag. No scrambling around in air ducts for him.
- Hank's skill as a detective is again subtly emphasized as, despite being late to the scene, he is the one who figures out exactly what happened to Gonzo and No-Doze in the junkyard.
- Jesse's pimped-out car looks pretty, but runs poorly. The sheen is all exterior.

MISCALCULATIONS Walt tells Jesse that the KGB used ricin in the tip of an umbrella in the "late 1920s." This is wrong in several ways — see the story of Georgi Markov's assassination below — including the fact that the assassination happened in 1978, and the KGB did not exist as such until 1954. In the 1920s the USSR's intelligence/internal security agencies were the Cheka (1917–1922), the NKVD (1922–1946), GPU (1922–1923), and the OGPU (1923–1934).

SHOOTING UP
- The use of color in this episode is especially noteworthy, beginning with the shocking pink of the half-roasted teddy bear in the Whites' pool, a jarring bit of color among the grayscale of the cold opening that gives added significance to the battered stuffed toy. Attention to color continues with Skyler's avocado green face cream, beginning

with another lingering, significance-imparting shot of the jar reminiscent of the similar shot of Walt's present to Elliott in season 1's "Gray Matter." The color continues through the sexual assault, when Sky's mask is partly smeared against the refrigerator door to be seen by Walter Jr., and is picked up in the following scene, which opens with Jesse at the Dog House, eating guacamole dip that is the same color and texture as Skyler's face cream.

- When Walt sets the Heisenberg hat down in the car, the hat is shot in blurry forced perspective — when an object is placed extremely near the camera, making it appear larger than it actually is — while the house, Walt, and Skyler seem very small.
- The setup shot of Skyler applying lotion to her very pregnant belly adds an additional layer of brutality to Walt's subsequent assault on her.
- The guacamole dip POV of Jesse's head between the front and rear ends of the neon "Dog House" sign is lovely, and a nice reminder that Jesse is operating way outside of the comforts of his usual house, and doing something wrong to boot, a situation often summed up by saying that someone is "in the doghouse."

TITLE "Seven Thirty-Seven" is an obvious reference to the amount of money Walt calculates that he needs to make from meth to set his family up after his death: $737,000. It also begins a sequence of titles throughout season 2, heralded by black-and-white cold opens, which tell a one-sentence tale. It begins here: "Seven Thirty-Seven . . ."

INTERESTING FACTS Bryan Cranston makes his *Breaking Bad* directorial debut with this episode.

SPECIAL INGREDIENTS

CASTOR BEANS TO RICIN
Would Walt's plan to create ricin from castor beans and then use the poison to eliminate Tuco actually work? Just maybe, but ricin is such a nasty substance that Walt and Jesse need to be very careful to not poison themselves in the process. The castor plant is a lush ornamental plant that can grow up to 15 feet high with little care. It is also quite resistant to pests, which should make it an

ideal landscaping plant. However, by producing seedpods (they aren't actually "beans") that can be both attractive to children and very poisonous to them, maybe a nice cactus would make a better housewarming gift.

The oil derived from the castor plant is one of the world's most important and commonly used industrial vegetable oils. Castor oil is commonly used in paints and varnishes. It holds up well under high temperatures and is used as a lubricant in high-performance racing engines. It's also a basic ingredient in the production of nylon. Taken by mouth, castor oil acts as a laxative and can be used topically to relieve cramps and joint pain.

Ricin does not occur in the oil of the castor plant, so don't worry. Ricin is a by-product of the extraction process and is found in the leftover mash after the oil is extracted. It is a particularly nasty poison and is fatal to humans in *very* low doses. A single milligram is deadly if ingested and half that amount can kill a fully grown adult if the ricin is injected. (Topical contact — on the skin or in the eyes — is dangerous but typically not fatal.) Ricin acts by shutting down the ribosomes that carry out protein synthesis in cells. Interestingly, by attacking the cellular structures that are responsible for protein synthesis, ricin has been posited as a possible "magic bullet" for cancer treatment, if the key can be found that will allow the modified ricin to only target the malignant cancer cells. That's a very big "if" right now, and Walt isn't interested in that research. He only wants to refine the ricin from the seeds and use it as an agent of death.

And death by ricin, by the way, is horrible. The first symptoms (coughing, fever, and stomach pains) appear anywhere from three to 12 hours after exposure. Inhalation of ricin causes lung damage, including fluid in and swelling of the lung tissue. If the ricin is ingested, the victim experiences vomiting and bloody, persistent diarrhea along with dehydration. The victim will likely die within five days of exposure. There is no known antidote for ricin poisoning.

GEORGI MARKOV POISON-TIP UMBRELLA ASSASSINATION

As a lethal, slow-acting poison, it has been speculated that ricin is the perfect murder weapon, since the ricin could be given to the intended victim and still give the murderer plenty of time to get away before symptoms become obvious. Indeed, one of the most famous (and officially unsolved) incidents of the Cold War involved ricin and a plot straight out of a spy thriller.

Georgi Markov was a Bulgarian novelist and playwright. He fled

Bulgaria's Communist regime and defected to the West in 1969. He eventually settled in London where he worked as a broadcast journalist for a number of organizations, including BBC World Service, Radio Free Europe, and Germany's Deutsche Welle. He used these forums to harshly criticize the Bulgarian regime, especially Todor Zhivkov, who was the head of the Communist state.

On September 7, 1978 (which was also Zhivkov's birthday), Markov walked to a bus stop to catch the bus that would take him to his job at the BBC. He suddenly felt a slight sting, as if a bug had bitten him, on the back of his right thigh. He looked behind him and saw a man picking an umbrella off the ground. The man quickly crossed the street to a taxi, which drove away. This man has never been positively identified.

When Markov arrived at the BBC, he noticed a small red mark at the site of the sting. That evening he developed a fever and he was admitted to a London hospital where he died three days later. An autopsy showed that the cause of death was ricin poisoning. The ricin had been placed in a pellet that was then injected into Markov through the "umbrella." Carefully crafted to ensure that the poison got into Markov's body and wasn't just on his skin, the pellet had two tiny holes drilled into it sealed with a substance that would melt at the temperature of the human body. Once the pellet was injected, the coating melted away and the ricin spread throughout Markov's bloodstream. Even if the doctors treating Markov had known about the elaborate plot, they wouldn't have been able to do anything. Markov's fate was sealed when he felt the jab of the umbrella at the bus stop.

There is strong evidence that the Soviet KGB arranged the murder to silence the dissident. An Italian citizen by the name of Francesco Gullino has been named the prime suspect in the Markov murder, but no one has ever been formally charged.

G rilled

2.02

Original air date: March 15, 2009
Written by: George Mastras **Directed by:** Charles Haid

"I like doing business with a family man. There's always a lot of collateral." — Tuco Salamanca

Walt and Jesse try to survive Tuco's "hospitality." Meanwhile, Hank's search for Walt turns into a search for Jesse.

Walt's greed and refusal to listen to Jesse's warnings come very close to getting them both killed in this episode. Furthermore, Walt's already shaky web of schemes and lies begins to fray and to gravely affect his family. The montage of Skyler and Marie putting out flyers carries a sense of frantic urgency and frustration at being able to do so little, and the continuing tension between Sky and Marie isn't making things any easier, particularly as Marie still seems to think that if she denies stealing the tiara long enough, eventually everyone will believe her and the problem will just go away.

Meanwhile, back at the (deserted) ranch, Walt's stupidity and Tuco's insanity come close to creating a perfect storm. The oh-so-clever scheme to do Tuco in with ricin fails utterly, and it's blind luck that Walt and Jesse are able to get away with their lives. During these hijinks, "Grilled" introduces Héctor "Tio" Salamanca, played by the amazing Mark Margolis (a film veteran who has been in everything from *The Wrestler, Black Swan*, and *Requiem for a Dream* to *I Shot Andy Warhol, Ace Ventura: Pet Detective*, and *Scarface*).

Héctor doesn't say a word in the entire episode, yet Margolis's use of breathing and a sharply limited range of motion and facial expressions communicate clearly and eloquently. There are damn few actors who have ever lived who can convey hate with a look the way Margolis can. Of course, the audience, like Walt and Jesse, has no idea who Tio is beyond Tuco's uncle — and Gilligan & Co. use that to their full advantage. Tio is presented as the next best thing to a vegetable, but *Breaking Bad* appearances often deceive, and he may actually be the smartest guy in the house.

(BILLY BENNIGHT/PR PHOTOS)

The realism of *Breaking Bad* comes impressively to the fore in the last act of this episode. Tuco is a big, strong guy who has been snorting extraordinarily pure crystal meth all day, and it still hurts like hell when he gets shot. There's none of the grunt-and-go-on so common with police dramas and action flicks; Tuco *screams* in pain. The final shoot-out between Hank and Tuco as Walt and Jesse cower in the desert, terrified of being discovered, also partakes of this kind of graphic realism. These are both men who actually do understand firearms, and know full well that a bullet doesn't care who you are. The first exchange of fire is wild, both trying to fill the air with enough lead to keep the other guy down, and maybe get a lucky hit. It's only when Hank takes a deep breath, calmly sets himself, and takes an aimed shot that the battle suddenly comes to an end. It's a powerful moment, and sublimely filmed. The hydraulics in Jesse's tricked-out car have been going off. It finally stops jumping, and everything is silent as Hank stands over the man he has killed. Then Tio's bell, hard and pure, rings out, reminding us all that there are more Salamancas out there.

LAB NOTES

HIGHLIGHT

WALTER: "Oh, so my life is not the priority here, because I'm gonna be dead soon?"

JESSE: "Uh . . . *yeah!*"

DID YOU NOTICE

- Walt's full name is Walter Hartwell White.
- Hank tacks Tuco's headshot on the DEA's bulletin board, over the "head" of a human silhouette target, indicating that he is the central object of their case. In an excellent juxtaposition, Hank kills Tuco by shooting him in the head at the end of the episode. Hank's tradition of tacking a headshot over the "head" of a human silhouette target will be referenced again in later episodes.
- Note Skyler's detailed collection of information when she talks to the detective. She always tries to be organized and to cover every possible base, but she can never think of absolutely everything.
- The missing posters featuring Walt's face are a nice echo of Tuco's headshot as posted up by Hank in the DEA office.
- Hank and Marie carry on a hilarious nonverbal conversation over and around Sky when Marie reveals Hank's concern with the second cell phone. Betsy Brandt and Dean Norris pull this off perfectly, and realistically portray the kind of idiosyncratic "language" that develops between people who have been in a relationship for a long period of time.

SHOOTING UP

- The cold open in this episode is what we call one of Gilligan & Co.'s "the beginning is the end" sequences, where the viewer is tantalized by quick glimpses of a situation without being given enough evidence to figure out what is going on, details that are filled in by the end of the episode. Viewers saw this back in season 1 with "Crazy Handful of Nothin'" when Walt-as-Heisenberg is walking away from the bombed building in the cold open.

- Again the setting is the desert, which now evokes an almost immediate sense of danger and criminality for the viewer. Interestingly, the lingering shots of the detritus of human habitation actually make the area look more deserted, not less. These odds and ends speak of failure and abandoned lives long forgotten. None of these objects have any meaning or memory, despite being exactly the kind of objects that should have both. Nothing good can come of being in this place.
- The use of quick flash-cuts, close-ups, and shots taken under and around the bouncing car, are very nicely done, providing teasers as the viewer sees the car in parts, suddenly identifying it as Jesse's with the "Cap'n Cook" vanity plate, and the quick glimpse of what may be a body on the other side of the car.
- As he approaches Walt's Aztek to check it for clues, Hank's face is seen reflected in the bumper. Gilligan & Co. play with reflections from time to time, and nicely set up the idea of Hank and Walt being mirror images of one another.
- Sound plays a big part in the episode, particularly the squeaking thump of the hydraulic system in Jesse's car and Tio's bell.

TITLE "Grilled" can refer to interrogations, particularly of Tuco's questioning of Walt and Jesse as compared to Hank's of Jesse's mother. It is also a reference to the platinum dental-appliance that Tuco wears.

INTERESTING FACTS
- Tuco's grill (which we're going to guess wasn't actually platinum) was encased in Lucite and given to Raymond Cruz, who so brilliantly portrayed Tuco, after his departure from the show.
- During the shoot-out at Tuco's, both Hank and Tuco appear to be terrible shots. They're within 25 feet of one another, yet neither is even grazed. However, with adrenaline pumping on both sides, this is how most firefights actually play out. It's estimated that thousands of shots are fired for every person killed in combat during wartime. Unlike the movies, it's hard to keep your head when people are shooting at you, no matter who you are.

SPECIAL INGREDIENTS

LOJACK TECHNOLOGY

Hank uses the LoJack system installed in Jesse's Monte Carlo to track it to the desert. While putting an expensive tracking system on a late '80s model Monte Carlo might seem silly, car theft is big business in the United States and the cars most favored by thieves aren't the ones you probably think they are. While flashy, pricey, new models can be targets for thieves, the three most common stolen cars are the 1994 Honda Accord, the 1995 Honda Civic, and the 1991 Toyota Camry. All three cars are popular for street racing and all three pre-date modern anti-theft technology, such as microchips that prevent a copied key from being used to start the car. (And hey, Jesse spent good coin on those hydraulics.)

The LoJack (opposite of "hijack," get it?) was founded in the late 1970s with a simple idea. Rather than installing an alarm to alert a car owner and scare off a thief, the LoJack system works to recover a stolen car. The LoJack system works through a small transceiver hidden in the car that is activated when the theft is reported. Police then follow the silent radio signal to track and recover the car.

CARTELS VERSUS MEXICAN LAW ENFORCEMENT AND THE MEXICAN ARMY

When Felipe Calderón was elected president of Mexico by a razor-thin margin in 2006, his top priority was getting the country's drug cartels under control. To accomplish this ambitious goal, he has relied heavily on the Mexican Army, which is thought to be less corrupt than the local and national police forces. Results have been, at best, mixed.

The cartels are highly organized and very well funded. They include the Sinaloa (aka the Pacific Cartel and the Golden Triangle Cartel) organization, which operates out of the western Mexican states and has been linked to meth Superlabs. This cartel is led by Joaquín Guzmán ("El Chapo" aka "Shorty") Loera, whose fortune is estimated at $1 billion. Guzmán is allied with Ismael Zambada García and they are considered by drug enforcement officials to be two of the top drug kingpins in the country.

Shootings, beheadings, and torture have been used to terrorize the Mexican population and send a message that once you're in the drug trade, you're in for life. Unfortunately, the Mexican military's response hasn't exactly been stellar. Roughly a quarter of the army has been engaged in the violence that continues to consume Mexico. In 2008 alone, more than 6,000 Mexican nationals died in the drug violence. (Hard numbers are difficult to come by, since people have a way of just disappearing.) Mass graves have been discovered that have been filled by the cartels, the state and federal police, and even the Mexican Army.

MEXICAN METH SUPERLABS

There's a lot of money to be made in the meth trade — that's why Walt gets into this in the first place. In early 2012, the Mexican Army made an unprecedented seizure of 15 tons of pure meth with an estimated street value of $4 billion U.S. — in a single bust. This was equal to half of all meth seizures worldwide in 2009. While Mexico is certainly not the only site of such Superlabs, large busts of meth and the component ingredients are disturbingly common. For example, in December 2011, Mexican authorities seized 675 tons of methylamine that was headed to Guatemala.

Interestingly, however, the meth produced in Mexican and Central American Superlabs is often inferior in quality to American-made meth. The director of the Tennessee Methamphetamine and Pharmaceutical Task Force, Tom Farmer, points out that most U.S. meth is made with pseudoephedrine, which is banned in Mexico and restricted in the U.S. Pseudoephedrine creates a more powerful high in the resulting meth, making U.S. meth the "preferred brand" among users.

B it by a Dead Bee

2.03

Original air date: March 22, 2009
Written by: Peter Gould **Directed by:** Terry McDonough

"What's changed, Jesse?" — Walter White

Walt, Jesse, and Hank deal with the fallout from their final encounter with Tuco. Meanwhile, Walt's lies get bigger and more complex, but Skyler's not buying them anymore.

So how do you explain a two-day disappearance to your family without revealing that you spent those days as the prisoner of a psychotic drug lord who was killed by your brother-in-law because you decided that becoming a meth cook was a good idea? If you're Walt, you don't explain anything, you just kick the lies into high gear. The problem is that Walt's big lie winds up being told to people who aren't as gullible as he needs them to be, and, as usual, he didn't see that coming. Anna Gunn is exquisite in this episode, giving us a Skyler who wants desperately to believe her husband, but is becoming less and less able to do so in the face of mounting inconsistencies.

"Bit by a Dead Bee" also begins a major arc for a fan favorite: Hank. Despite all of his bravado and bluster, Hank shows signs of regret over killing Tuco. Tuco was a thug, a criminal, and a violent psycho, and Tuco shot first, leaving Hank no choice but to defend himself. Hank knows all of this, but it isn't enough. Gilligan & Co. don't flinch from the reality that, for most people in the world, no matter what training they may have received, killing another human being is a difficult thing to live with. And so it should be.

Dean Norris's portrayal of Hank has been remarkably nuanced from the beginning of the series, but he really begins to shine as Hank tries to deal with having killed a person, even though he acted in self-defense.

And Walt? Walt's not having an easy time of it either, but he's a better rationalizer. Emilio was self-defense, as was Krazy-8 — kinda. As for Tuco, Walt wound up not having to kill him after all . . . but he was willing to. As he does in every episode, Bryan Cranston brings his skills to bear with breathtaking mastery. Without Cranston's craft, Walt would quickly degenerate into a predictable caricature, but Cranston continues to create a complex, complete character; while we get so damn pissed at him for making the choices he does, we can never quite give up hoping that he'll start making some different, better ones. Walt is despicable in so many ways, and becomes more so as the series progresses, but he is also achingly human.

In any event, things are beginning to heat up for all of the characters. Walt discovers that you really can't go home again after pulling some of the stuff he has, no matter how you justify it. Jesse is now squarely in the DEA's — and Hank's — sights. Skyler is watching her husband go crazy and her family fall apart, yet she doesn't know the reason for any of it. And Hank is moving into that long darkness at 3 a.m. and trying to figure out the whys of himself. To mangle the great Irish poet Yeats, things are falling apart, and the centers cannot hold.

LAB NOTES

HIGHLIGHT

JESSE: "You still want to cook . . . *seriously?*"

DID YOU NOTICE

- Jesse and Badger (Matt Jones, who has also made appearances on *Community*, *Reno 911!*, and *How I Met Your Mother*) still haven't figured out that the best way to move a heavy barrel is to roll it along the ground.
- There are recurring shots of the print on the wall in Walt's hospital room, which shows a man rowing away from his family who stand on the shore. Metaphor much?
- The scene with Walt looking in on Skyler and Walter Jr. as they comfort one another is heart-rending, and a brilliant placement of Walt on the outside of the family circle, looking in. It's a position he has chosen to put himself in.
- Jesse's father won't pick him up after the DEA lets him go. Jesse's poor relationship with his parents will prove significant.
- Hank's still looking at the security video from the chemical warehouse robbery. He's tenacious and determined.

SHOOTING UP

- The POV from the bottom of the hole opens the episode as Walt and Jesse bury Tuco's gun, a visual metaphor for the fact that Walt and Jesse keep burying themselves deeper and deeper in this dangerous new world.
- The camera work as Jesse and Walt make their way to the highway is worth watching. The camera gets farther and farther away, giving the viewer a sense of both the vastness of the desert and the smallness of the two figures in it. Then, suddenly, the camera is at or a little below ground level, and Walt and Jesse are backgrounded, huge but out of focus, still lost despite their nearness.

- The use of color in Wendy's hotel room is a recurring element, and makes her room seem almost unreal, submerged, somehow insulated from the hard light and life outside.
- Time-lapse photography of the desert and sky is used to good effect to denote the passing hours.

TITLE The title "Bit By a Dead Bee" comes from Howard Hawks's famous 1944 film *To Have and Have Not*. The film is known for being the place where Humphrey Bogart met Lauren Bacall, but that's not the key to this episode's title. Walter Brennan's character, Eddie, goes around asking people the first line of a joke, "Was you ever bit by a dead bee?" The joke is finally completed when he meets "Slim" (Bacall), and he finally explains to her, "You got to be careful of dead bees if you're goin' around barefooted, 'cause if you step on them they can sting you just as bad as if they was alive, especially if they was kind of mad when they got killed. I bet I been bit a hundred times that way." In Walt and Jesse's case, Krazy-8 and Tuco are both still biting them, even after they're dead.

MUSIC As Walt waits for the bus to take him back to the hospital the music is "Waiting Around to Die" by the Be Good Tanyas, mirroring Walt's own condition as he waits on his cancer to kill him.

INTERESTING FACTS *Buffy the Vampire Slayer* fans will recognize Walt's shrink in this episode as Harry Groener, aka Sunnydale's Mayor Richard Wilkins.

SPECIAL INGREDIENTS

FUGUES AND FUGUE STATES
Let's start with what a "fugue" is musically because the term was used in that manner for centuries before the headshrinkers got hold of it. While there are many variations, in a strict fugal form, a theme is stated, then repeated in a different pitch by a second voice, and then a third. The key is the different voices in a single piece.

In the world of psychiatry, a fugue state is a dissociative memory disorder. To relate it back to the musical fugues, it's as if another voice is singing the person's song on a different pitch from the original. It's fairly rare, but is more common in people (such as combat veterans) who have experienced traumatic events or natural disasters. For example, in a documented case a man who was a Vietnam veteran walked between the Twin Towers only minutes before the first plane struck on September 11 and later experienced a fugue state and disappeared from his law office in Westchester County, New York. Six months later, he was found living under an assumed name in a homeless shelter in Chicago with no memory of who he was or how he'd gotten there.

A fugue state can last a few hours or several months, and often is not diagnosed until the person has emerged from it and remembers his or her identity. A fugue state isn't amnesia, which is associated with damage to specific parts of the brain. A dissociative fugue state has no known physical cause. Triggered by a traumatic life event, the person enters the fugue state and, somehow, cannot retrieve memories associated with the event — as if the brain is protecting the victim from a reality too traumatic to comprehend. Fortunately, when the person emerges from the fugue state, the person can once again access these "lost" memories, although memories of events that happened during the fugue may remain a mystery. A fugue state is a truly puzzling and frightening condition and yet more proof that the human brain is both a marvelous example of unparalleled beauty, and just as nutty as a cage of squirrels.

GRILLS, OR GRILLZ DENTAL APPLIANCES

One of Tuco's most distinguishing characteristics has to be his platinum "grill," which winds up in a block of Lucite as a grim souvenir. Grills (aka "grillz") are cosmetic dental appliances usually made of costly metals such as gold or platinum, although silver may also be used. Grills are often custom-made to fit snugly over existing teeth and are removable. While cosmetic dentistry is an ancient practice (wealthy Mayans were known to drill bits of jade into their teeth), in modern times the trend really caught on with the rise of hip-hop. Eddie Plein is often credited with being at the forefront of the trend with his creation of simple gold caps in the 1980s for musicians such as Flavor Flav and Big Daddy Kane. Gradually, Plein's creations became more and more complex, often incorporating gemstones into the design. Murray Forman, a professor at Northeastern University specializing in the study of hip-hop, posits that the conspicuous display of wealth indicated by elaborate grills is an obvious symbol of financial success.

Tuco's elaborate and expensive grill is thus a mark of his status as the cartel-connected king of meth distribution in ABQ. Its transformation into a grisly trophy recalls ancient war-trophies like shrunken heads, which were visible symbols of the possessors' power, prowess, and potency.

Down

Original air date: March 29, 2009
Written by: Sam Catlin **Directed by:** John Dahl

"Why are you like this? *Why?*" — Mrs. Pinkman

Jesse's lifestyle undergoes a sudden and rapid change. Elsewhere, Walt discovers that he doesn't have as much control over people as he thinks he does.

Like season 1's "Cancer Man," "Down" focuses on families. This time, however, it's about how families can be torn apart. Jesse's parents play a major role in this episode, having finally reached a breaking point. Again, it is tempting to cast Mr. and Mrs. Pinkman as callous and uncaring jerks who make their son homeless in order to save their own necks, but it's not that simple. Jesse is an addict, and has been for several years. At the beginning of the episode he is broke, but when evicted from his house, the viewer sees a box full of pot and a pile of crystal or coke on a large mirror at the foot of his bed. The bills Jesse desperately tells Walt about in the opening scene begin to seem more fantasy than reality. Drug addiction does not merely affect the user, but also everyone around him, and the addict will manipulate, con, steal, and abuse every relationship he or she has in order to feed his addiction. Gilligan & Co. are well aware of this, and the attitudes and actions of Jesse's parents are those of a couple who have lived with an addicted child for years, and who have, quite correctly, determined that if they do not let go of Jesse and his addiction, he will take them down with him.

Viewers are sympathetic towards Jesse because they know he's a good kid at heart, but it is also made clear that Jesse has made the particular bed in which he's now lying. His house isn't, and never really has been, his. For all of his talk, there is more than a little doubt about the extent to which Jesse took care of his aunt as she was dying from cancer. In the 72 hours between being told to leave the house and actually being evicted, he has done absolutely nothing to try to deal with the situation. Finally, he sets up a lab to produce precursor for crystal meth in the basement of his house, thus, as his parents' lawyer rightly points out, risking the seizure of the land, the house, and everything that's in it by federal law enforcement. Jesse has screwed things up royally, and is now facing the consequences of his actions.

The worst part of this process is Jesse's growing realization that he is alone. Some of his friends have started families, who understandably don't want a homeless junkie in their lives. Other friends will party with him, but don't hang around with him afterwards. At the beginning of the episode we see Jesse gently responding to the homeless guy's greeting outside the convenience store, and for the rest of the episode the audience watches him come closer and closer to joining that man on the sidewalk. Jesse hits bottom in this episode, and it is a difficult journey to watch. It is, however, very real.

Meanwhile, Walt's life is also quickly flying out of his control. His lies are starting to catch up with him and he just can't keep his mouth shut. Skyler is *almost* convinced, *almost* lulled back into trusting him . . . and then Walt explains the second cell phone again. Walt believes he's a master manipulator, but in reality he's a terrible liar. To expect that Skyler would believe that he couldn't figure out how to work a cell phone is ridiculous, and more than a bit insulting. Sky doesn't take it lying down either, giving Walt a dose of his own medicine and proving that there is only one true master of passive-aggressiveness in the White household, and it's not Walt.

However, Walt's biggest problem in this episode is his utter inability to listen to anyone. Jesse tries again and again to get Walt to understand that his problems are not only major, but affect both of them. Walter Jr. tries to get his dad to understand that his CP makes it really hard to drive with one foot instead of two, but Walt won't hear it, insisting that his son's legs are fine, when the truth of the matter is that they aren't. Finally, Walt won't listen to Skyler as she confronts him about everything that's going on and gives him an opportunity to come clean and tell the truth, right now. Walt doesn't take advantage of the chance, however, believing that Skyler won't actually do anything about it, despite all evidence to the contrary. Walt refuses to listen, because his pride in being able to control everyone and everything around him won't let him, and only Jesse's desperate half-serious physical attack breaks through that shell.

LAB NOTES

HIGHLIGHT

> **SKYLER:** "Okay, so talk, Walt. Shut up and say something that isn't *complete* bullshit!"

DID YOU NOTICE

* Jesse's full name is Jesse Bruce Pinkman.
* The last item in the line of evidence bags in the cold open is a pair of eyeglasses that look like Walt's.
* It was Hank's visit with Jesse's mom that brought on the sequence of events leading to Jesse's eviction.
* When someone stole Jesse's scooter, they got through the U-lock that Krazy-8 never could.
* When Walt finally splits the money with Jesse, he keeps the overage. Not quite a 50-50 partnership after all.
* Meth isn't the only thing Walt cooks. In this episode, he makes omelets "New Mexico Christmas style" (with red and green chilies) for breakfast with "Flynn," the new name Walt Jr. is trying out. After the fight with Jesse, he asks his partner, whom he's just called a "pathetic junkie," if he wants breakfast. An olive branch with eggs.
* The look of sheer disgust the lady in the parking lot gives the pregnant Skyler as she lights up a cigarette adds a realistic touch to the scene.

SHOOTING UP

* This is the second black-and-white opening of the season, tying into the cold open of "Seven Thirty-Seven."
* The black-and-white cold open is the most stylistic element of this episode. Again the only bit of color is the shocking pink of the burned teddy bear in the pool, but this time there is a sense of being upside

down in the water, with everything confused. This sequence gives the viewer just a little more information than the first, but still leaves a tremendous amount of mystery.

- After their tussle, Jesse and Walt are seen lying exhausted on the floor of the RV from a POV somewhere well above where the actual ceiling of the RV would be. This is another of the straight-down POV shots that *Breaking Bad* uses again and again.
- The episode begins and ends outside of the same convenience store. Gilligan & Co. use this kind of circular structure regularly.

TITLE The titles are building: "Seven Thirty-Seven . . . Down . . ." Gilligan & Co. will complete the sentence as the season progresses.

INTERESTING FACTS

- The homeless man at the convenience store calls Jesse "Captain America," an apparent non sequitur, but both Cap and his alter ego, Steve Rogers, often drove a motorcycle, so the connection between Jesse on his scooter and Cap on his bike may not be quite as out there as it first appears.
- Walt is playfully flabbergasted to discover that neither Junior nor Skyler know who "Boz" Scaggs is. For those who may be in the same boat, William Royce "Boz" Scaggs is perhaps best known for his years as guitarist and sometime lead singer in the Steve Miller Band. His greatest solo successes were the albums *Silk Degrees* (1976) and *Middle Man* (1980). In 2003, he released *But Beautiful*, a collection of standards that debuted at number one on the jazz charts. Scaggs continues to tour, and also owns a vineyard and winery in Napa Valley, California.
- The name of Jesse's old band is Twaüghthammër. The video for "Fallacies" by Twaüghthammër was made as a webisode and is available online and on the season 2 DVD set.
- Fans have responded to Junior's many breakfast scenes by making them something of an obsession. There are drinking games, internet memes, video games, and incessant jokes all revolving around the fact that Junior is so often seen eating breakfast, and so rarely seen eating any other meal.

● MARIE AND THE COLOR PURPLE

No, not the Alice Walker novel. Purple is a color that has long been associated with wealth and royalty — the dye to create purple cloth was devilishly expensive to obtain, so it was reserved for the rich and powerful. Seldom has a character been so tied to one particular color as Marie Schrader, who is often seen dressed in shades of purple ranging from lavender to royal. On the AMC website devoted to *Breaking Bad*, Marie even has a blog post about her passion for purple. If you bother to point out her obvious preference for a color so closely aligned with luxury and wealth, Marie would probably just stare at you. Of course that's what she surrounds herself with! Marie likes the rare and difficult to obtain, so purple is the natural choice for her. While Marie may put on airs (or perhaps even be a touch delusional), she knows what she likes. And she likes purple. In addition to her wardrobe, purple is associated with Marie in other ways. For example:

- In "Sunset" (3.06), when Marie calls Hank, viewers see numerous purple accents in the kitchen.
- In "One Minute" (3.07), Hank has done some shopping for Marie and he is carrying a purple gift bag and a bouquet of flowers (including some purple ones), wrapped in purple paper.
- In "Box Cutter" (4.01), the master bedroom of Hank and Marie's house is decorated in purple, including the bedcovers.
- In "Thirty-Eight Snub" (4.02), a delivery man comes to the door of Hank and Marie's house wearing a purple uniform.
- In "Open House" (4.03), Marie's reusable grocery bags are purple.
- In "Rabid Dog" (5.12), even Marie's luggage is purple.

Since Gilligan & Co. have been so careful to associate Marie with this color, it's especially interesting that in a later episode, Hank puts a framed picture of the Schraders on his desk with Marie dressed in yellow with a background of yellow flowers — the complementary color of purple.

2.05

B reakage

Original air date: April 5, 2009
Written by: Moira Walley-Beckett **Directed by:** Johan Renck

"You need me more than I need you . . . *Walt.*" — Jesse Pinkman

Walt and Jesse reexamine their business model. Meanwhile, Jesse finds a new place to live, and Walt tries to figure out how to deal with Skyler.

Insanity has been defined as doing the same thing over and over again and expecting different results. Walt and Jesse's initial foray into meth cooking led to Walt killing two people, Jesse becoming an accessory both before and after the fact, and extensively gory damage to Jesse's house. Their second attempt led to some significant income. It also led to them being kidnapped and almost killed by a psychotic drug lord with a platinum grin. After each of these misadventures, both Walt and Jesse swore off cooking to a greater or lesser extent, but eventually they felt they had no other choice but to return to it to meet their financial needs. This time around is no different. Walt's chemotherapy is racking up some $4,400 a pop, and with half of their take seized by the DEA, Jesse and Walt are broke, so they go back into the desert. Because this time things will be different. Right?

Walt's lies and pride are costing him as much as the cancer. Having told Elliott and Gretchen that his insurance will cover the treatments after all, and having assured Skyler that Gretchen and Elliott are paying the bills, Walt is in deep. To 'fess up, he'd have to admit that he needs help, has been lying to everyone, and has been paying for things to this point. Still, he could get out of the meth world at this point with minimal fallout, but his pride won't let him. Perhaps too, there is an element of shame. Walt is a killer, and no matter how he justifies his actions, he is a changed man. He has moved from a nonviolent man to one capable of taking violent action in self-defense to one who is willing and able to premeditate the murder of another person. Whether he can admit it to himself or not, Walt is no longer just Walter White — husband, father, and teacher — he is also Heisenberg — drug-maker, killer, and liar.

One of the most fascinating things about this state of affairs is the contrast between Walt's newfound attitudes and those of Hank. Despite his usual Billy Badass, DEA agent bluster, Hank is obviously shaken to his core by the act of killing Tuco. Yet Hank is also lying to those around him, refusing to admit to any sign of "weakness," and becoming even cockier and more cheerful in his mannerisms around others. But he cannot take his eyes off of the grisly memento of his actions: Tuco's dental work, or grill, in its Lucite cube. He even tries repeatedly to cover it up, but this sardonic smile won't go away. He can't bring himself to explain to Marie why he's started taking days off work, or waking up at sudden noises in the middle of the night sweating and with his gun instantly in hand. He certainly doesn't believe he can tell anyone about the abrupt, disorienting anxiety attacks he's been having lately. Hank believes that to admit any of this would show a most unmasculine, and therefore unacceptable, weakness. So he tries desperately to keep everything tightly bottled up, to "cowboy up" and just get through it all by himself. "Breakage" is important for several reasons, but this parallelism between Walt and Hank is most definitely a big one. In many strange ways they are finding themselves in similar situations, and they are even dealing with them in the same ways to some extent. They are, however, two different men, and despite what the viewer has been led to expect, it is Hank who turns out to have more trouble dealing with the violence he encounters.

Jesse is also moving into new territory, both literally and figuratively. The infusion of cash from Walt has allowed him to find a place to live, and he is even beginning to sober up and take on some responsibilities. He makes sure to pay Badger's cousin what he owes him for the RV, demonstrating a new concern with being "a man of his word." As he organizes his friends into street-level dealers for "Blue Magic" meth, he lays down rules against anything going down in his house, and strict guidelines for the operation of a new distribution scheme with himself at the top. It looks like Jesse is large and in charge, until Skinny Pete (Charles Baker, known for his roles in the 2008 thriller *Splinter* and Terrence Malick's *To the Wonder*) gets robbed. At news of this, Walt demands that Jesse become something like Tuco, even giving him a gun and all but telling him to find and kill the junkies who stole their product. As Walt berates, belittles, and shames Jesse into thinking that he has to do it, the viewer is well aware that Walt himself couldn't do what he's asking of Jesse. Walt's willing to have murder committed, as long as someone else is doing the deed. In trying to be the vicious Heisenberg, Walt reveals himself to be, at bottom, a coward who would much prefer to have others do his killing for him, and who wants nothing to do with the business side of things until he thinks Jesse's not doing things right. Walt is pushing things. Like always.

LAB NOTES

HIGHLIGHT

SKYLER: "Perhaps I smoked them in a fugue state."

DID YOU NOTICE

- The direction the men in the cold open are moving is left uncertain. The viewer generally assumes they are crossing from Mexico to the U.S., but considering the distance Hank throws the Lucite-encased grill at the episode's end, they may be going the other way: *into* Mexico, *from* the U.S.
- The empty chair at Walt's chemo where Skyler usually sits underscores her absence and their troubles at home.
- Jesse's new ride — a beat-up Toyota Tercel — is a big downgrade from the Cap'n Cook–mobile.
- Jesse really doesn't know who Jesse Jackson is.
- Jesse's speech to Walt about their division of labor (partially quoted at the top of this entry) is the first time he calls Walt by his first name, instead of calling him "Mr. White."
- The name of Hank's homebrew brand is "Schraderbräu."
- Unlike Walt, when Marie is finally cornered by Skyler, she actually admits she shoplifted the tiara and apologizes to her sister. Marie

would rather admit something shameful than lose her family. This attitude is fundamentally different from Walt's.

SHOOTING UP

- This episode is full of some incredible camera work, beginning with the cold open waterline POV of the two men crossing the river.
- The extreme close-up of Walt's chemotherapy IV fluid mixing with the backwash of his blood is an example of a shot *Breaking Bad* will use a lot. The show likes to play with perspectives: near, far, up, and down.
- There are several long takes of objects here, which work to imbue things with significance and to visually drive the story: the empty chair at the chemo center, Walt's *long* bill printing out, and Tuco's grill on Hank's desk.
- Time-lapse photography is another technique used so well and often that it becomes a hallmark of the show, in this case during Walt's chemo treatment, while Jesse and Walt cook, and while Jesse and his crew deal meth. When used properly, as it is in *Breaking Bad*, time-lapse is an effective way to show the passage of time, present a montage, and compress narrative events.
- During the meth-dealing sequence, the lighting takes on a sickly greenish tint, similar to but more diffuse than the green of Wendy's room at the Crystal Palace.
- The close-up of the tubing for Hank's home-brew operation is a nice transition shot, and neatly subverts the viewer's expectation that the tubes mean another meth cook.
- A straight-down POV of Jesse pouring chips into a bowl is a reversal of the usual bottom-up POV the show has become so associated with.
- The episode opens and closes with the men in the river, a circular frame for the story and another Gilligan & Co. trademark.

TITLE Jesse explains "breakage" as a part of doing business, a kind of write-off for unavoidable loss that is often allowed for by a business. If you deal in delicate glass sculptures, for instance, some are going to break before you can sell them. However, "breakage" can also mean an unexpected profit earned by the failure of an individual or business to redeem money already spent.

When you buy a gift card, but never redeem it, that's a positive breakage for the issuer.

MUSIC The music playing over the dealing montage is "Peanut Vendor" by Alvin "Red" Tyler, providing a great beat for the time-lapse montage, and making an interesting connection between dealing meth and selling any other kind of product.

INTERESTING FACTS

- "Breakage" marks the first appearance of Jesse's neighbor, Jane Margolis, played by Krysten Ritter (whose other roles include *She's Out of My League*, *What Happens in Vegas*, *Confessions of a Shopaholic*, and *Gilmore Girls*).
- This episode was "dedicated to our friend Kim Manners." Vince Gilligan and Manners worked together on the *X-Files* from 1997 to 2002, and Manners was co-executive producer from 2000 to 2002, while Gilligan was the show's executive producer. Manners died of lung cancer in Los Angeles on January 25, 2009.

SPECIAL INGREDIENTS

ANXIETY AND PANIC ATTACKS

Hank is suffering from extreme anxiety in the aftermath of shooting Tuco, to the point that he is beginning to experience panic attacks. While anxiety is a normal part of being human, it can become a disorder when the anxiety rises to the level of being uncontrollable and excessive. Anxiety is characterized by worry; panic is characterized by fear. Panic attacks usually begin very suddenly and start at a high level of intensity; in fact, many people experiencing a panic attack for the first time confuse the symptoms with those of a heart attack.

Those who have experienced a panic attack often describe it as the most intensely frightening and upsetting event of their lives. Symptoms of a panic attack can include chest pains, hyperventilation, faintness, tunnel vision, and a strong urge to flee. Interestingly, while the person experiencing the panic attack often feels that their body is breaking down, the body is actually protecting itself from the perceived harm. The fact that there actually is no imminent danger doesn't matter one whit to the sympathetic nervous system, which has pumped adrenaline (epinephrine) into the body to give it the energy to fight or flee. In turn, this leads to an elevated heart rate (tachycardia) and rapid breathing (hyperventilation) as the body prepares for confrontation or escape. The release of so much adrenaline restricts blood flow to the head, which causes dizziness and a feeling of lightheadedness.

Effective treatment for panic attacks does exist. Selective serotonin reuptake inhibitors such as Paxil, Prozac, and Zoloft as well as benzodiazepines such as Klonopin, Valium, and Xanax are all commonly prescribed medications; however, the most effective long-term treatments involve cognitive behavioral ("talking") therapy, including breathing exercises to rebalance the oxygen and carbon dioxide levels in the bloodstream.

CHEMOTHERAPY TREATMENT

Chemotherapy (also called "chemo") has been used to treat cancer since the 1950s. It can be an extremely effective treatment, but it is undeniably harsh. Chemotherapy is used for a variety of reasons, including killing cancer cells, slowing the growth of tumors, and shrinking tumors prior to surgery or radiation therapy. Most often, chemotherapy is given as a mix of drugs to both better target the cancerous cells and to prevent the body from becoming resistant to a single chemo drug. Cancer cells grow and divide quickly, and chemo works to stop or at least slow that growth. Chemo drugs are extremely powerful and aren't especially good at distinguishing between the harmful fast-growing cancer cells and healthy fast-growing cells, like the ones in your hair roots, which is why hair loss is a common side effect to chemo treatment. Hair loss can range from simply thinning to total baldness (including eyelashes and eyebrows). Usually, the hair loss reverses a few months after chemo is complete, although the new hair growth might be a different texture or color — straight blond hair can regrow as curly and brown.

Chemo can be taken in a number of ways, including as pills or as a topical cream, but it is most commonly given through an intravenous (IV) line. People undergoing IV chemotherapy often take their treatment in either an outpatient facility in a hospital or in a doctor's office. About three-quarters of American patients receive their treatment in a doctor's office (as Walt does) and studies have shown that treatment given in such a setting is considerably cheaper than treatment given in a hospital setting, although the reason for that has not been clearly determined. It might be that hospitals see more severe, complex cases, or it might be that hospitals, having more resources such as scanning equipment on hand, use those resources more often, which increases the cost of treatment. Either way, Walt is being a smart consumer by having his chemo administered in the oncology clinic.

Peekaboo

2.06

Original air date: April 12, 2009
Written by: J. Roberts, Vince Gilligan **Directed by:** Peter Medak

"You have a good rest of your life, kid." — Jesse Pinkman

Jesse gets to the bottom of Skinny Pete's mugging. Meanwhile, one of Walt's biggest lies comes home to roost.

"Peekaboo" is a hard episode to watch. To their credit Gilligan & Co. take the time to show the viewer the realities of meth addiction, and they don't pull any punches. The junkies' house is okay from the outside, just a bit run-down. Inside it's pure filth. Trash litters the floor, remains of takeout rot where they have been left, and there is absolutely nothing of value whatsoever. But the heart-ripping part of the episode isn't the squalor of the house, or even the scabrous condition of the two junkies. It's the silent, nameless, little redheaded boy who lives in the middle of it all. He's an innocent in hell, and this hits the viewer like a sledgehammer to the gut.

Awakening to find a pistol-waving, tweaking Jesse in his home, and his parents nowhere to be seen, the child is completely unfazed. He gets up from his filthy little mattress on the floor and turns on the TV, his face grime-smudged, his underwear and T-shirt unchanged for who knows how long. This is his life, waking to strangers while not knowing where his parents are, and sleeping in a room that can be locked from the outside. His silence speaks volumes. In this life, the best chance for survival is to remain small and silent, and going unnoticed is often the safest thing one can do. The viewer gets the

(COURTESY MICHAEL SLOVIS)

sense that he generally *does* go unnoticed by his putative parents — Spooge and an unnamed woman — who are wretched scum living only for the next fix, and who are willing to do anything, up to and including murder, to get it.

This cycle of addiction, desperation, criminality, and violence is what Jesse and Walt are actually producing in the RV, and what the viewer is complicit in as the audience roots for the two protagonists. This is the end result of their various misadventures: the creation of a hell on earth that snatches up innocents along with willing users. Jesse teaches the boy to play peekaboo, and the viewer gets the devastating sense that this is the first time anyone has ever actually played with the child. Certainly, the only parental attention he gets during the episode is when he's pulled onto his mother's lap as a shield against Jesse's gun. To his credit, Jesse is horrified and deeply offended by the kid's situation, and instinctively reaches out to the boy, making his eyes light up. Perhaps most chilling is the boy's reaction to his mother clubbing Jesse on the back of the head after he has come out to get Jesse to play peekaboo again. He flinches, but he doesn't cry or cry out. He has seen this kind of sudden violence before, seen his parents tweaked out of their minds and insane. He remains quiet and very, very still, lest their madness turn on him next. "Peekaboo" is a horror story made more terrible in that it is happening every single day. The scenes are well played by actors David Ury (who has had guest roles on *Community*, *Raising Hope*, *Heroes*, and the *Young and the Restless*) and Dale Dickey (*True Blood*, *Winter's Bone*, and 2008's *Changeling*).

Giving the viewer a break from this hell is an interesting confrontation between Walt and Gretchen as she discovers his massive lie about how she's paying for his cancer treatments. When his soft-spoken manipulation fails, Walt gets angry and the audience gets a look into his past with Gretchen. Somewhere along the way, on a visit to Gretchen's family, Walt got angry and walked away in a huff from Gretchen, Elliott, and Gray Matter. Did he think they wouldn't succeed without his brilliant input, only to find out that he wasn't as necessary, as *special* as he thought? It would explain a lot about Walt's motivations. The fact that he may well be blaming Gretchen and Elliott for his own mistakes fits in well with Walt's apparent need to feel like he must get even with the world.

Jesse, however, takes an interesting turn in this episode when he does what he can to save the kid from the life of abuse and neglect he's been subjected to. Between the early childhood traumas the boy has experienced and the overloaded government children's services agencies and foster programs in the United States, the chances he will wind up in a good, supportive home and get the help he needs are slim. Even so, Jesse's actions at least give the kid a shot, as small as it may be, and in doing so may save Jesse too. Consider this in contrast to Walt's choices, both present and past, which throw away his future.

LAB NOTES

HIGHLIGHT

SKINNY PETE: "I can't be all about . . . *spellin'* an' shit!"

DID YOU NOTICE

* Despite trying to act all big and bad, Jesse is fundamentally not a killer. He doesn't even want to hurt the beetle that he runs across in the cold open, and is a bit perturbed when Skinny Pete steps on it.
* Perhaps the ultimate sign that one is in hell: the only channel the TV in the junkies' house gets is the Home Shopping Network, and they're selling knives.

- Subtle bits of luxury and wealth surround Gretchen: her hands-free car phone that is crystal clear and picks up her voice perfectly; the almost total lack of road-noise in the interior of her expensive Bentley; the elegant restaurant where she and Walt meet for lunch with the table so carefully placed away from other people.
- Gretchen's vanity license plate reads "GRAYMTR."

SHOOTING UP
- The opening shots of the episode give the viewer an increasingly high viewpoint: from a ground level shot, to the bug's POV, to a human-level view as Jesse and Skinny Pete talk.
- We get a fridge's eye POV in this episode too, making the audience a "Pepper." Another POV seen repeatedly in *Breaking Bad* is the business end of the gun muzzle, the "victim" perspective. This shot will return several times, and in a big way.
- When Jesse wakes up from being brained by the junkie, he's on his left side, face mashed to the floor, a favorite framing for wake-up shots. This is the first time that Jesse is seen this way. Up until now it has been Walt waking up like this ("The Cat's in the Bag" ". . . And the Bag's in the River").

TITLE "Peekaboo" most obviously references the game Jesse plays with the kid, but it also may refer to Gretchen's discovery of Walt's lies. On another level "Peekaboo" also gives the audience a look into the horrific reality of meth addiction and the lives that get ruined by simply being on the edge of it.

INTERESTING FACTS The little boy in the episode is actually played by twin brothers Dylan and Brandon Carr.

SPECIAL INGREDIENTS

H. TRACY HALL
Walt's right: the physical chemist H. Tracy Hall did create the first synthetic diamond while working for General Electric in 1954. Ever since diamonds were discovered to be a pure form of pressurized carbon in 1797, people had been searching for a reliable way to create artificial diamonds. Occasionally, a

researcher would claim to have found the secret, but their work could never be reproduced.

Hall joined GE's "Project Superpressure" in 1953. He'd previously worked with a high-powered pressure chamber that leaked so much water from its hydraulics that he had to work in rubber boots. GE was in the process of purchasing a massive press and denied Hall the $1,000 and time in the GE machine shop he requested to build his own. He persuaded a friend in the shop to do the work in his off-hours and a former supervisor persuaded GE to purchase an expensive component (tungsten carbide dispersed in cobalt) that Hall's process required.

There were a few false starts, but on December 16, 1954, Hall created the world's first artificial diamonds. The experiment was repeated with identical results, and on Valentine's Day, 1954, GE announced that it had created synthetic diamonds. However, the news release implied that the diamonds had been made in GE's expensive new press, not in Hall's invention.

Hall's work, which became the basis of a multi-billion-dollar industry (synthetic diamonds are used for industrial cutting and machining, as well as having applications in laser technology and electronics), was worthy of the Nobel Prize. Instead, GE gave him a $10 savings bond.

Disheartened, Hall left GE — where thanks to the company's connection to Hall's childhood hero Thomas Edison, he had dreamed of working since he was in the fourth grade — and landed at Brigham Young University. Eventually, he and two colleagues started Novatek in Provo, Utah, which utilizes other processes and presses invented by Hall to create artificial diamonds for industrial use.

METH MOMS

Hoo, boy. The mom in "Peekaboo" is not an exaggeration. Meth causes people to do horrible, reprehensible things. Children are not immune from the violent, crazed actions of those high on meth. Just three examples illustrate this, but we could easily list hundreds:

+ December 2011 — in Albuquerque, a mother currently stands accused of stabbing her eight-year-old son with a screwdriver while high on meth.
+ January 2012 — in Fresno, California, a mother used an iPad to record herself smoking meth a few hours before she went on a killing spree,

shooting her two young children, her husband, and a cousin before turning the gun on herself.

* March 2012 — in Atlanta, a mother "forgot" to give her child food and water while she smoked meth in the apartment. When the police arrived, everyone scattered, leaving the baby behind.

2.07

Negro y Azul

Original air date: April 19, 2009
Written by: John Shiban **Directed by:** Félix Enríquez Alcalá

"Bonds are what hold the physical world together — what hold *us* together." — Walter White

Jesse is shaken by recent events, but Walt sees them as an opportunity. Meanwhile, Skyler goes back to work and Hank begins a new job.

As the opening after the credits hints, this episode is really all about bonds: how they're made, and how they're broken. With their relationship strained, and Walt refusing every opportunity to tell Skyler what's going on, she moves a bit further away from him by going out and finding a job. Not an unreasonable thing to do, after all, since she doesn't know of Walt's grand scheme to secure the family fortune. Sky is able to use her connection to Ted Beneke (Christopher Cousins, best known for his 17 years as Cain Rogan on *One Life to Live*) to get her old job as company bookkeeper back. Walt's none too happy about the situation, especially since Sky didn't tell him about her plans. Again, in Walt's mind, Skyler having to work is a sign that he's failed as a provider, and this is only exacerbated by the fact that he is beginning to pull in some serious cash, yet is unable to tell her about it. Skyler seems to be done with allowing herself to be manipulated, and there's really not a damn thing Walt can do about any of this.

With control of his family slipping out of his hands, Walt turns to Jesse. He tries to take back his command that Jesse "take care of" their breakage problem, and insists that he didn't mean that anyone should be killed, but this sounds more than a bit hollow, and comes too late. Jesse himself is shaken by what he has seen in "Peekaboo," particularly by the sight of the male tweaker, Spooge, having his head crushed by an ATM machine. As usual, Jesse has turned to drugs to run away from his feelings. Just witnessing an act of deadly violence has shaken him to his core and literally sickened him. He is incapable of rationalizing things away as skillfully as Walt, and wants only to retreat from the violence around him. Walt will have none of this, however. Upon learning that people believe it was Jesse who crushed Spooge's head, and that this reputation has elevated Jesse's stature on the street, Walt immediately reinforces the story and pep talks a deeply stoned Jesse into expanding their business by moving into new territory and raising their prices. Blinded by sheer greed, Walt ignores Jesse's warnings of the dangers of such a move.

Those dangers are brought home in a big way as Hank begins his new job in El Paso, and joins a combined DEA/*Federales* task force operating on the Mexican side of the border. Hank is out of his element in his new job, seemingly outclassed by the DEA agents in El Paso, unable even to speak fluent Spanish as they do. It seems that Hank's good-ol'-boy act won't be getting him anywhere in this new environment. As is often the case with Hank though, first appearances are deceiving. The viewer has to think that Hank is more than a little right when he gets tired of buying tidbits of information from "Tortuga" via the *SkyMall* catalog, and starts demanding information. Also, though his fellow agents make fun of him in Spanish in the field, it is Hank who first spots Tortuga in the scrub desert. It is also Hank who is first on the scene. Though he is ridiculed by his fellows for being sickened by the sight of Tortuga's severed head fastened to the tortoise, it is worth noting that if the agents had been paying more attention to their jobs than making fun of the new guy, they might have spotted the booby trap that ultimately kills several of them and maims the DEA agent who thinks so little of Hank. Again Hank is quick in a crisis. Though deafened and stunned, he has his belt off and applied as a tourniquet above the severed leg of his wounded colleague within seconds, likely saving the man's life. Hank may not be immune to human frailties, but he can always, *always* be counted on, especially when things go from bad to completely FUBAR.

Finally, we see the beginning of something between Jesse and his neighbor

Jane. Their love story is charmingly innocent, with Jesse rushing around to just "bump into" Jane, and the two of them are as awkward as a pair of teenagers in their approach to one another. Indeed, the connection they make in front of the audience is not sexual, or even as passionate as a kiss. Instead Jane hesitantly reaches out to take Jesse's hand as they sit before his new TV, the message "searching for signal" pulsing across the screen. From the very beginning this is something different, something special — and another bond is created.

LAB NOTES

HIGHLIGHT

> **BADGER (ON ANSWERING MACHINE):** "Hey, it's Badger, man."
> **SKINNY PETE:** "Don't use your real name!"
> **BADGER:** "That's not my real name."

DID YOU NOTICE

- Walt is being much sneakier with his new "second cell phone."
- While Walt doesn't want Jesse calling him, he certainly expects Jesse to pick up the phone when he calls.
- From the very moment they meet, Jane refuses to be manipulated by Walt.
- The show emphasizes the looks, especially from women, that the very pregnant Skyler gets as she applies for a job at Beneke. This is a nice comment on the continuing disadvantages women face in finding employment, especially if they are mothers, or likely to become mothers while working.
- Ted Beneke is the same man in the photograph that Skyler stares at so wistfully in "Seven Thirty-Seven."
- At the Atomic Bomb Museum as Walt leaves from his meeting with Jesse's crew, having led them to believe that Jesse killed Spooge, there is the sound of an air-raid siren and a bomb blast. When Jesse meets them in the same place later, there is a faint but clear bit of museum voiceover: ". . . headed by Werner Heisenberg."
- The message on Tortuga's tortoise: "¡Hola DEA!" (Hello, DEA!).
- The shirt Jesse is wearing while he holes up in his apartment displays

a jack-o'-lantern face — something that looks scary, but is really just a hollow gourd.

- Turns out that Marie was right when she made that comment about the cartels and severed heads in "Breakage."
- As Jane takes Jesse's hand, there are church bells ringing in the distance.

SHOOTING UP

- The cold open includes Los Cuates de Sinaloa's performance of "Negro y Azul" and is filmed in the style of a music video, complete with opening and closing credits. The cold open in this episode does more than introduce the viewer to *los narcocorridos* (drug ballads, see below), it also serves nicely to give the viewer some exposition, letting the audience know that Walt and Jesse's efforts have not gone unnoticed by the Mexican drug cartels, especially now that Heisenberg's Blue Magic has crossed the border, and the cartels aren't getting a piece of the action. The legend of Heisenberg has grown as well, and that may not be a good thing for Walt.
- The beautiful, panoramic cinematography in the Mexican desert gives the viewer a sense of the vastness, and emptiness, of the land.
- The light in the Mexican desert is different too — harsher, more yellow — a subtle effect to let the viewer know that we're not in New Mexico anymore.
- There's another floor-up POV as Jesse and his crew bump fists in the Atomic Bomb Museum.
- The muted screaming in the background as the camera focuses on the silhouette of Hank's profile against a gorgeous sunset is incredibly well done, bringing together horror and beauty in an eerie moment of the sublime.

TITLE "Negro y Azul" (which translates to "black and blue") alludes to Walt/ Heisenberg's dark coat and hat, as well as the mystery of his face, and to the meth he makes, Blue Magic. It also refers to what he will look like if the cartel gets to him.

INTERESTING FACTS

- "Negro y Azul" is written and performed by Los Cuates de Sinaloa

("The Sinaloa Buddies" is one translation), and the musicians featured in the cold opening are the members of the band.

♦ In the lyrics to "Negro y Azul," Albuquerque is called "Duke"; "Duke City" is a longstanding nickname for Albuquerque. The city was named in honor of Don Francisco Fernández de la Cueva y Enríquez de Cabrera, who was the viceroy of New Spain (now Mexico and much of the American Southwest) from 1653 to 1660, and who also held the title of Duke of Albuquerque, a town in the Extremadura region of Spain.

♦ About 11 seconds into the music video that forms the cold open of this episode, there is a shot of Los Cuates de Sinaola foregrounded against the RV, and in the midground to the viewer's right is a figure dressed as Walt/Heisenberg, who is facing away from the camera. In the midground to the band's left is another figure standing under an open umbrella. This is the only time this figure is seen in the video, and fans have been unable to identify the figure's significance, or which character it might represent.

♦ Tortuga is played by Danny Trejo, the voice of Enrique on *King of the Hill,* and a veteran "bad guy" of 30 years boasting such films as *Machete, Grindhouse, Once Upon a Time in Mexico, Heat,* and *From Dusk Till Dawn.*

SPECIAL INGREDIENTS

NARCOCORRIDOS (DRUG BALLADS)

The song "Negro y Azul" is an example of a type of music known as a *"narcocorrido,"* which translates into "drug ballad." The band singing "Negro y Azul," Los Cuates de Sinaloa, take their name from the Mexican state of Sinaloa, a narrow strip of land in northwest Mexico that is home to the notorious Sinaloa drug cartel as well as being the hideout of Jesús Malverde (discussed below). According to band manager José Juan Segura, a *corrido* is a real-life story set to music. While some *corridos* deal with migration or smuggling, *narcocorridos* tell the stories of the drug trade. Often, actual events, dates, places, and people are woven into the lyrics of the songs and singer Gabriel Berrelleza has called *narcocorridos* "the nightly news set to music."

Narcocorridos date back to the 1930s. Some critics equate *narcocorridos* to gansta rap, claiming that the lyrics of the *corridos* celebrate, if they do not actually glorify, the drug trade and those involved in it. However, unlike gangsta rap, which has a relatively narrow fan base, *narcocorridos* are approaching the musical mainstream. The songs are wildly popular among a broad range of age groups, and plenty of *narcocorridos* fans have no link to cartel or drug activity. The popularity of the drug ballads stems in part from the fact that some drug traffickers and cartel kingpins become quite popular due to their business acumen and their willingness to challenge a government that is notoriously corrupt. Also, some, like the infamous Colombian cartel boss Pablo Escobar, take very good care of the people in their employ, as well as the broader community, all of which engenders a sense of loyalty. Taken together, these factors can produce folk heroes who are celebrated through song. These are mythologized through the *narcocorridos* much like the American criminals and murderers Jesse James, Billy the Kid, and John Wesley Hardin were in North American folk music.

SAINT JESÚS MALVERDE

First off, Jesús Malverde isn't really a saint — not according to the Catholic Church, anyway. The Church has very strict guidelines that must be met before a person is canonized as an official saint and Malverde hasn't made the cut. Nevertheless, Malverde is treated as a sort of "folk saint" in parts of Mexico (and, increasingly, in parts of the United States as well) and has become the unofficial patron saint of drug traffickers.

Born in the 1870s, Jesús Malverde watched his parents work themselves to death (some accounts claim they actually starved to death) trying to make an honest living. The experience left him bitter and none too sure that there was any benefit to staying on the straight and narrow path of righteous labor. Following the death of his parents, he hid out in the hills of Sinaloa, Mexico, and became a thief. Not just any thief, though — Malverde became a Robin Hood figure, using some of his ill-gotten booty to help the poor, who didn't care too much how he came by the money he was distributing to aid them. He was captured and hanged by the authorities in 1909.

Shortly after his death, stories began circulating of Malverde appearing to help the desperate poor. One especially moving story credited Malverde with showing two thieves the location of their lost pack mules (who just happened to be lugging stolen gold). From this point on, Malverde became the go-to guy for religiously minded criminals. The cult of Malverde has grown to the point that shops selling religious items such as medallions and candles report having a hard time keeping Malverde items in stock. Furthermore, not everyone who prays to Malverde is involved in the drug trade — he's quite popular among many marginalized groups. However, the DEA and other branches of law enforcement have added Malverde items to the list of "things to look for" in determining which vehicles, places, and persons it would be wise to suspect of involvement in drug dealing and trafficking.

2.08

Better Call Saul

Original air date: April 26, 2009
Written by: Peter Gould **Directed by:** Terry McDonough

"Seriously, when the going gets tough you don't want a criminal lawyer, all right? You want a *criminal* lawyer. Know what I'm sayin'?" — Jesse Pinkman

Walt and Jesse deal with Badger's arrest. Meanwhile, Hank struggles to deal with what he experienced in Mexico.

While the cold open sets up the episode's central storyline, the opening after the credits picks up where "Negro y Azul" left off, only Jesse's flat-screen has now picked up a signal, as have Jesse and Jane. The audience does not see any graphic depictions of sex, but only comes in during the afterglow, to see two very happy people who are really just starting to get to know one another. Aaron Paul plays this perfectly, showing us that Jesse is falling hard for this girl, and when he lets the gangsta persona fall away, what is left is a really sweet young man who wants very much for this new relationship to start off right. As for Jane, she may be a bit more skittish, but she's there too, and a bit of her backstory is revealed with her Narcotics Anonymous chip marking 18 months of sobriety.

The main story, however, focuses on Walt and Jesse trying to handle Badger's arrest, and this brings in what has to be one of the most interesting secondary characters in television: Saul Goodman (Bob Odenkirk, a writer for *Saturday Night Live* and best known for his comedy on *Mr. Show with*

Bob and David). Saul is rude, crude, tasteless, sleazy, tacky, and as crooked as a mountain switchback road. His bread and butter are the scum of the earth, and he's always sure to get his money first, as he demonstrates in his meeting with Badger. He's also one hell of an attorney. Despite being the quintessential shyster, Saul doesn't even consider backing down when confronted by Hank and the DEA, and quickly gives back better than he gets when Hank tries to tell him off.

Walt doesn't think much of Saul to begin with, and goes in to meet him with the thinnest of cover stories about being Badger's uncle. He misreads Saul badly, and tries to bribe him, but that's not Saul's game. Again and again in this episode Walt tries to control things by force. He tells Jesse to rule by fear, but that leads to Skinny Pete and Combo (Rodney Rush) being afraid to tell him about Badger's arrest. He tries to intimidate Saul through kidnapping and threats, but winds up as Saul's client instead. It is also Saul who shows the viewer just how out of their league Walt and Jesse really are. After all, killing Badger to keep him from spilling to the DEA really makes the most sense, but Jesse won't even entertain the idea, and Walt quickly agrees. The plan the three of them do eventually agree on is much riskier and, to Walt's frustration, much more expensive.

Walt is not the only one facing difficulties, however. Hank is badly shaken by his recent experiences in Juárez: holing up in his bedroom, eyes shut, fists clenched, barely holding himself together in the face of the horrors he witnessed. Oddly enough, it is Walt who manages to break through his bluff and bluster and bring Hank back around to at least a semblance of normal. Walt has danced this line before, usually enjoying playing dangerous word games with his DEA brother-in-law, but now Walt speaks powerfully from his recent experiences and tells Hank to move through his fears and get on with things.

It is a strange reversal. In the first episode of *Breaking Bad*, Hank is Mr. Macho Toughguy while Walt is Caspar Milquetoast, yet now it is Walt who is giving a version of a "cowboy up" speech to Hank, and it works. Not entirely, as Hank seems to be suffering from a pretty severe post traumatic stress disorder (PTSD), as his panic attack in the elevator demonstrates. He is more or less able to hold it together in public, and while his colleagues are congratulating themselves on busting the infamous Heisenberg at the end of the episode, Hank is unconvinced. Ironically, Walt has buttressed the one man who is not only a brilliant detective, but also becoming increasingly obsessed with finding and busting Heisenberg. As usual, Walt isn't nearly as smart as he thinks he is.

LAB NOTES

HIGHLIGHT
SAUL: "So if you want to make money, and keep the money you make — Better Call Saul!"

DID YOU NOTICE
- Badger's bench in the cold open is plastered with one of Saul's ads.
- Right now, Blue Magic is selling for $175 for 1/16 of an ounce (a "teenth").
- Skyler's wearing low-cut dress as she heads to work on the weekend.
- Saul's loan out (see below), "Ice Station Zebra Associates" takes its name from the 1968 film *Ice Station Zebra*, a Cold War military/spy thriller largely driven by successive plot twists.
- Badger's real name is Brandon Mayhew.
- There's a lovely bit of Three Stooges–like physical comedy as Jesse and Walt can't get the car door open after warning Badger, so Jesse has to dive in through the open window.
- Walt and Jesse again make a crucial decision based on the "sacred" coin flip.
- The ridiculous pom-pom topped ski masks are back.

SHOOTING UP

- The bright colors of Saul's ad on the bench during the cold open are matched by the equally bright, primary colors of the playground in the background. Both reflect Badger's view of the world, and dealing as some kind of great game, and also subtly reinforce the realities of exactly where meth gets sold.
- The floor-up POV of Hank in the elevator during his panic attack provides a distorted angle to work with the sickly green lighting during the attack. When the doors open and Hank is back in his 'Everything's Okay' mode, the elevator walls are revealed to be a soothing blue instead of that sickly green, a nice contrast.

INTERESTING FACTS

- Saul compares Walt to Fredo Corleone from the 1972 film *The Godfather*, directed by Francis Ford Coppola. Fredo (played by John Cazale) is the second son of Don Vito Corleone (famously played by Marlon Brando). Unlike Vito who went from a penniless immigrant to enormously wealthy head of a ruthlessly successful mafia family, Fredo is almost comically inept in his attempts at criminality.
- Getz, the APD undercover officer who busts Badger in the cold open is played by DJ Qualls, who appeared regularly on *Memphis Beat* as Officer Davey Sutton, and has also appeared on *Lost*, *The Big Bang Theory*, and *Supernatural*, as well as several films.
- Saul has a website at www.bettercallsaul.com.

SPECIAL INGREDIENTS

ATTORNEY-CLIENT PRIVILEGE

In a hilarious scene, the kidnapped Saul tells his abductors to stick money in his pocket so attorney-client privilege is invoked. Does privilege really go that far? Sort of, but it's not the cash that creates the privilege. Attorney-client privilege is more sacred than any of Walt and Jesse's coin flips. In fact, it's one of the cornerstones of the American legal system. What you tell an attorney who is acting as your attorney (casual conversations at a crowded cocktail party don't count) is pretty much inviolate. With very few exceptions, the attorney cannot be compelled or voluntarily disclose matters communicated in confidence by the client.

The underlying justification supporting the concept of attorney-client privilege is sound — if a person seeking legal counsel doesn't feel certain that whatever is discussed in the attorney's office is confidential, the person is likely to withhold crucial information from the attorney and no one benefits from such a system. Clients are free to waive the privilege, in which case the attorney is free to discuss whatever has been waived. Absent that, generally an attorney has to keep their trap shut, even after the death of the client.

The most notable exception to the privilege restriction is the crime-fraud exception, which states that the privilege is moot when the communications between the attorney and the client are made to further a crime or fraud, which pretty much wipes out Saul's entire practice. This has led to some tough, tough moments for attorneys, as the privilege remains intact if the crime has *already been committed* before the attorney knows about it. In other words, if a client comes into Saul's office, dumps a bloody knife on the desk and says, "The body's three miles out in the desert. What now?" Saul cannot, under promise of disbarment, tell law enforcement anything. Saul can, however, refuse to take the case and strongly encourage the client to go voluntarily to the police, an unlikely scenario at best, given his clientele.

LOAN OUT

Saul Goodman may be a sleazy example of the underbelly of the legal profession with truly horrible taste in office decor, but he's good at what he does. Saul instructs Brandon's family to pay the retainer fee to "Ice Station Zebra Associates," which is a "loan out" corporation. Loan outs are quite common in the entertainment industry as well as in the legal profession. The advantages to loan outs are why you see so many actors and recording artists set up their own production companies.

Here's how it works. An individual (let's call him "Saul") wants the protection of a corporate entity. Saul sets up a corporation that is solely owned by him and the resulting corporation hires Saul as an employee, "loaning out" his services. In return for providing Saul's services, the corporation collects the expenses and fees generated by Saul's work, which can then be paid for and deducted at the corporate level while the rest of the loan out's income is paid to Saul as salary.

It seems complicated and it is. The Internal Revenue Service doesn't like loan outs very much because they can generate sizable tax savings by using deductions and tax shelters that wouldn't normally be available. Also, by being an employee of a corporation, Saul can only be sued for his corporate assets, not his personal stash — an advantage Saul no doubt likes quite a bit. Therefore, it is very important that Saul keep excellent records, including an employment agreement between himself and Ice Station Zebra. In this matter, Saul's records are probably current up to the minute.

Days Out

2.09

Original air date: May 3, 2009
Written by: Sam Catlin **Directed by:** Michelle MacLaren

"Yo, lie much?" — Jesse Pinkman

While waiting for the results of a test that will determine the efficacy of his cancer treatments, Walt and Jesse head back into the desert for an extended cook.

Family is again a significant part of this episode. Walt's entire family, including Hank and Marie, are on hand for the PET/CT scan that will reveal the effects of his cancer treatments, despite knowing that they won't get the results for a week. Every one of these people has taken the time to be there for and with Walt, because they love the guy. This close-knit family is what Walt is tearing apart with his lies, but he can't see that. In fact, all that he is prepared to see is confirmation of his imminent death. Despite not knowing one thing about reading PET/CT scans, Walt thinks he knows enough to interpret a shadow on his lung, and immediately jumps to his own conclusions.

After lying to Skyler about where he'll be, and to Jesse about why they need to cook, Walt and Jesse head back out into desert. The episode now becomes a study of the strange and growing bond between Jesse and Walt. Walt's health is not good, and his coughing fits are getting worse, but he pushes through most of the cook. Meanwhile, Jesse steps up as a true partner in the process rather than just a menial, not-very-talented assistant. He and Walt work together as a team, professional and efficient, and when Walt is totally exhausted, he shows his confidence in Jesse by letting him finish the cook. Jesse has come a long way from his Cap'n Cook days in season 1, and he and Walt have begun to develop a mentor-mentee relationship, both where the chemistry of meth is concerned, and in more personal ways. Jesse is pleased to be learning and to be considered a good student by Walt, while Walt is equally pleased to be teaching him. Throughout the series there have been glimpses of Walt in the classroom that reveal his true ability and joy as a teacher, and this comes through clearly and rather sweetly in his interactions with Jesse during this episode. Walt turns even their last-gasp attempt to jumpstart the RV into a teaching moment as he constructs makeshift batteries, a moment Jesse flubs by confusing "wire" with an element.

For all of Jesse's progress, however, he remains more than a little hapless and helpless. Besides cooking, Jesse can't seem to do anything right in this episode as his mistakes mount and each one leaves the two of them in more and more desperate straits. Their troubles become so grave that Walt is forced into actual honesty as he finally reveals his cancer to Jesse, and even, nearly delirious from dehydration, admits that all of his rationalizations about doing this for his family are ultimately hollow because "all I ever managed to do was worry and disappoint them. And lie." In a reversal of their usual roles, it is now Jesse who gives Walt a pep talk, demanding that he use his scientific knowledge to figure a way to start up the RV, and refusing to allow Walt to give up and give in to self-pity and despair. The two men grow very close in this episode, though perhaps only temporarily so, and the strange nature of their relationship is highlighted: Walt and Jesse are both really bad for each other and really good for each other. Which way things will fall out between them on any given day is a toss-up, like flipping a coin.

To top off Walt's long weekend, he gets his test results back and — remission. What should be the most joyous news he's ever received is instead worse than the death sentence he was expecting. In the closing scene, Walt washes up and then, after staring at his reflection in the stainless steel of the paper-towel holder, slams his fist into it several times. His excuse, his justification for everything he's done, is gone. If he doesn't have terminal cancer then there's no reason to continue cooking. On the other hand, if he doesn't have terminal cancer, then he can no longer ignore the rules and constraints of his life. Death set him free, but living? For Walter White, *that's* become the cage.

LAB NOTES

HIGHLIGHT

JESSE: "C'mon you bitches! Hear me now!"

DID YOU NOTICE

- The episode begins and ends in the clinic bathroom with plentiful running water, yet in the middle of the episode, lack of water is the primary problem.
- Skyler says goodbye to Walt at the airport with tenderness. It seems that things could really be okay for the two of them, and she obviously still loves Walt deeply, despite his lies.
- The RV has gone from being a jury-rigged setup to a rather slick, high-tech mobile meth lab.
- Walt and Jesse burn up during the day, but have to bundle up for warmth at night, a realistic portrayal of the difficulties of surviving in the desert where there is rarely cloud cover or vegetation to prevent the day's heat from dissipating when the sun goes down.
- 42 lbs. of meth at $40,000/lb. = $1,680,000. If Walt and Jesse are netting $672,000 each after costs (including 17 percent to Saul), then their costs (supplies and gas?) are $50,400, while Saul stands to make $285,600 on the deal.

SHOOTING UP

- Time lapse is used a lot in this episode, and is combined with montage sequences when Jesse and Walt are driving into the desert and while they are cooking. When they become stranded, there is a lot of camera work from ground-level up, emphasizing the vastness and emptiness of the desert, and how far out Jesse and Walt really are.
- The trademark up-from-the-bottom POV appears as Walt and Jesse pour liquid meth into a Pyrex dish for cooling.
- Walt and Sky's bedroom is dark and shadowy, done in dark blues and dark wood. Jesse and Jane's bedroom is filled with bright sunlight and warm yellows. Sky and Walt's relationship is in a dark place while Jesse and Jane are in the light, happy honeymoon period.

- A contrail from a passing jet is also used well to indicate the passage of time as it slowly fades and dissipates in the sky above the RV.

MUSIC The tune backing the cook montage is "Good Morning Freedom" by Blue Mink.

INTERESTING FACTS This episode includes another reference from Francis Ford Coppola's *Godfather* trilogy, this time from *The Godfather, Part III*. Upon hearing the news of Walt's remission, Hank leans forward and says "Just when I try to get out, they pull me back in!" This is a line said by Don Michael Corleone (Al Pacino) as he is forced to return to criminal activity just as he was about to take the family businesses legitimate.

SPECIAL INGREDIENTS

PET/CT SCANS
"4 Days Out" takes place as Walt and his family are waiting for the results of a PET/CT scan. Positron emission tomography (PET) and computerized tomography (CT) scans are state of the art imaging tools that physicians use to make treatment recommendations for patients. While the two scans are usually done at the same time, they accomplish two completely separate goals. A CT scan can detect changes in the anatomy of the body — in Walt's case, this scan would show the exact location and size of his lung cancer. A PET scan is different in that it allows a doctor to distinguish between benign and malignant growths at the molecular level. Since the CT scan gives a detailed picture of the body's internal structures and the PET scan shows disorders at the molecular level, the combined PET/CT scan is a powerful tool in any physician's arsenal in treating diseases such as cancer.

HOMEMADE BATTERIES
It's happened to all of us. We've left our keys in the ignition and drained the battery on our mobile meth lab, leaving us stranded in the trackless desert. What to do? Well, if you're knowledgeable enough about chemistry to make "poison out of beans," a dead battery is only a minor inconvenience. What Walt does could actually work, so let's step through building a mercury battery.

Walt, in full-out McGyver mode, sends Jesse off to collect coins, galvanized metal, and the brake pads from the RV. As he explains, a battery is simply an anode and a cathode separated by an electrolyte. Walt uses a polypropylene container (a common plastic dish) to hold everything. The cathode is the positive terminal of this one-cell battery — where the supply of current flows out from. Walt creates this with mercuric oxide and graphite taken from the brake pads. The anode is the negative terminal — this is where the resulting current will flow into from the cathode. Walt's is made from zinc, such as that found in the galvanized coating of household hardware. Walt uses a handful of nuts, washers, screws, and pocket change.

Walt's cut-up sponges soaked in potassium hydroxide (an ingredient used in meth manufacturing, as well as having less nefarious uses) supply the electrolyte separating the cathode and the anode. Walt uses copper wire as the conductor. Once they have assembled six cells and run the wire through each, Walt gingerly attaches the jumper cables to the anode and the cathode and — it's just enough to jumpstart the RV. At least on television. While Walt's construction of the batteries would indeed generate current, it is unlikely that they would produce enough juice to jumpstart the RV.

2.10

Over

Original air date: May 10, 2009
Written by: Moira Walley-Beckett **Directed by:** Phil Abraham

"Stay out of my territory." — Walter White

Walt tries to adjust to life sans cancer and cooking. Meanwhile Jesse's relationship with Jane is tested, and Skyler is thinking of greener grass.

Walt is really shaken by the news of his remission. He can no longer justify or rationalize cooking meth, or continuing to lead the double life he has been for the past few months. Things are back to normal, or should be. And Walt can't stand that. Walt's feelings about his pre-cancer life have been made clear over the course of seasons 1 and 2 as he has gone from powerless nobody to feared drug lord. His partial confession to the hospital psychologist in "Bit by a Dead Bee" made his view of his life clear: colleagues surpassing him, low salary, son with cerebral palsy, etc. In Walt's view his old life was insufficient, wasted, and worst of all, small. Now he is expected to return to it, and for most of this episode he tries to do just that . . . sort of.

Walt is not a man who can do nothing, so he finds something to occupy his time and to try to anchor himself in ordinary life. His home improvement project quickly becomes an obsession, as finishing it means a full return to his old life, high school chemistry class and all. Skyler goes from telling him to stay home and rest to rather sharply demanding to know when he's going back to work. Walt is not happy to be cancer-free. Skyler, Junior, Hank, Marie, and even Jesse are all thrilled, but Walt just can't deal with it. Walt has

tasted something even more addictive than meth: power, pride, and respect. He has no reason to cook, but oh how very much he wants to. This unfortunate headspace leads to Walt earning the Worst Father of the Year Award, as he turns the party celebrating his remission into a booze-fueled pissing contest with Hank, with Walter Jr. as the playing field.

The viewer is familiar with Hank in the role as Junior's surrogate father, and has seen him do right by his nephew *and* his brother-in-law again and again. Here Hank's "we're all guys, so have one and don't tell your mom" attitude quickly shifts as Walt keeps pouring straight tequila into Junior's cup, and all but forcing him to drink. Walt tries to escalate the situation while Hank tries to calm things down, again emphasizing that both of these men are not who they appear to be at first glance. Walt taunts Hank, deluding himself into acting like the badass that Heisenberg's reputation purports him to be, and is likely only saved from an ass-kicking by Junior suddenly throwing up in the pool. Walt actually smirks as Skyler and Hank are distracted, as if he's proven something. Perhaps, in a very twisted way, he has, if only to himself, and only in his own mind. He has fooled himself into thinking that he has stood up to Hank and faced him down. It is a small and very personal delusion of grandeur, but perhaps a signal of things to come. Junior's apology and desperate desire to be acknowledged for having kept up with Walt and Hank the next morning is just heartbreaking, and provides a solid jolt of reality for Walt, but one he is unlikely to remember for long.

Skyler too is having trouble adjusting to Walt's remission, because things are just refusing to return to normal, and since her husband is still shutting her out and keeping secrets, she turns to someone else for sympathy, at first relatively innocently, but then with progressive premeditation. Her work clothes become tighter and lower cut, and she begins luring Ted Beneke into her office with practiced helplessness. To this point, Skyler has been largely a sympathetic character, doing the best she can by her family and a husband who is lying about something every time his lips move, but she is now approaching a moral line herself. If Walt's breaking bad is a stone thrown into the still pond of their lives, then Skyler is one of the people most affected by the ripples he has caused, and the audience begins to expect more ripples to come.

Interestingly it is the growing relationship between Jesse and Jane that provides the most hopeful aspect of the episode. Their first major fight and subsequent reconciliation through comic book character sketches is just lovely, and provides a great reversal of traditional gender roles as Jesse tries to define their relationship and Jane denies that such a thing even exists.

LAB NOTES

HIGHLIGHT
JESSE: "I was a kid when I drew all of these. It was like . . . four years ago."

DID YOU NOTICE
+ The water is rusty as Walt shaves. The water heater has been a problem from season 1, a nice, long setup.
+ Walt's confrontation with Hank over Junior takes place around the pool, where Walt tends to retreat when things aren't going the way he wants them to.
+ The continuing portrayal of Jesse and Jane's relationship as something strangely pure and innocent. This is something good and clean, and that's important to Jesse and the story.
+ The transition from Skyler knocking over her pens to lure Ted in to

Walt using a power drill to put a screw in the wall is a brilliant use of an old-school Freudian visual metaphor for sexual intercourse.

- Walt is buying Kilz in the home improvement store. Kilz is a primer paint specially formulated to kill and cover up evidence of mold and other discolorations. In other words, Kilz gets rid of everything bad and whitewashes the situation until it appears nice and clean — on the surface. The parallels with Walt and his home-improving jag are telling.

- The wannabe cooks Walt confronts in the parking lot are a bald guy and some skinny gangsta wannabe who have a camper. There's something familiar about them . . .

MISCALCULATIONS By and large, *Breaking Bad* doesn't give us a chance to use this category very often, but they deserve to be called on something in this episode. As Walt pays cash for the water heater, he comes across a bloody bill and quickly hides it. Unfortunately, the blood, which is supposedly dried, is much too bright and much too red. It should have been a dark, rusty-brown color. It probably wouldn't have shown up as well on camera, or been as easily identifiable by the viewer, but it would have been more accurate.

SHOOTING UP

- A new black-and-white cold open culminates in a view of the smashed windshield of Walt's car and two filled body bags in his driveway. It is worth taking the time to return to the previous cold opens of "Seven Thirty-Seven" and "Down" to see how each builds on the next, giving the viewer a bigger and bigger look at something really, really bad.

- The opening establishes continuity with the ending of the previous episode as the camera lingers on Walt's badly bruised knuckles. It's a nicely subtle indicator that some, but not much, time has passed between episodes.

- The transition shot that leads into Walt's remission party is a great misdirect, focusing in close on a pile of crystals that turns out to be margarita salt rather than the expected crystal meth.

- The bottom-up POV from Jesse's frying pan is one of our favorites in the whole series. The pan actually turns out to be made of clear glass, making this shot something of a nod to fans of the show, and a nice tongue-in-cheek recognition by Gilligan & Co. that this has become the show's signature shot. It's also a play on the old anti-drug ad that compared a frying egg to "your brain on drugs." Nice, especially coming from Jesse.

- ◆ The transition shot from the rusty water around the bottom of the water heater to the same colored tea in Skyler's cup at the office is very nicely done.

TITLE The third in the series: "Seven Thirty-Seven . . . Down . . . Over . . ."

INTERESTING FACTS "Over" features the first appearance of Jane's father, Don Margolis, played by John de Lancie, of *Star Trek: The Next Generation* fame.

SPECIAL INGREDIENTS

STRIKER STRIPS OR MATCH HEADS?

While at the home improvement superstore, Walt comes across a wannabe meth cook who is busy giving whole new meaning to the phrase "one-stop shopping." Walt offers some unsolicited advice about not buying everything in one place and he also points out that not all matches are suitable for a meth cook.

Really? A product that can include lye and brake fluid and now's the time to get picky?

Well, yes. As we've detailed earlier, the "red, white, and blue" method of meth manufacture involves red phosphorous, which is found in matches, but not in match *heads* — at least not in the heads of safety matches, which are the most common ones found nowadays. "Safety matches" separate the igniting materials into the heads and the striker strips to prevent unintentional combustion. When you drag the match head over the rough striker strip, the friction generates enough heat to convert some of the red phosphorous in the strip into white phosphorus, which then ignites upon contact with the air. (Those "strike anywhere" matches are different and do contain phosphorus in the match heads. That's why you can ignite one of those on a belt buckle or boot heel or other Wild West accessory.) Since safety matches only have phosphorus in the striker strip, Walt's right — it's better to buy a ton of individual matchbooks so the potential cook winds up with many more striker strips for the cook.

M andala

Original air date: May 17, 2009

Written by: George Mastras **Directed by:** Adam Bernstein

"This game we playin'? We don't have the street cred to survive it." — Skinny Pete

Walt's plan to push Jesse's crew into new territories leads to serious trouble, but Saul may have an answer. Meanwhile, Jane makes a choice.

The cold open to this episode gives the viewer a look at the street-level reality of Jesse and Walt's meth-dealing operation, beginning with a tour through some rough barrio streets. Combo's fate is a hard reminder of the real world of drugs, gangs, and kids, and also of just how ill-prepared Walt and Jesse are to function in that world. In pushing into another gang's territory, Walt and Jesse have moved into a realm where deadly violence is commonplace and life is frighteningly cheap, and though they themselves and the people they love remain separated from these dangers, they are all still affected by them.

Walt is at least spared the existential crisis that faced him in the previous episode. He has made the decision to continue his criminal activities, and the high price of the operation to remove his cancer once and for all gives him all the excuse he needs. He fairly jumps at the chance to cook again, agreeing to have the operation without even pretending to consult Skyler, though she's sitting right beside him at the time. Therefore, he's all the more flummoxed when Combo's murder throws a wrench into his plans. Walt's self-centeredness shines through in this episode. He doesn't even know who Combo was, and doesn't even have the decency to hide that fact when Jesse calls to give him the news. Blocked one way, Walt is all too eager to make a hook-up with the mysterious distributer Saul offers to set him up with, possible consequences be damned.

Jesse, on the other hand, has lost a friend, and as usual when under stress, he turns back to the pipe. Only this time, he doesn't go alone. The audience learned in "Negro y Azul" that Jane is 18 months sober, and apparently a member of a 12-step program. Now she is faced with a choice. Leave the suffering Jesse to his self-pity and meth, or join him, comfort him, and use again. Gilligan & Co. don't back away from showing that Jane makes a deliberate choice here. This is not some innocent being lured into trouble by bad company, this is a recovering addict who knows the consequences of using again, and who chooses to do so anyway. The results are staggering. Jesse's apartment, which has slowly become comfortably if sparely furnished, and has always been neat and bright, is transformed into a pigsty with empty bottles, food containers, and cigarette butts strewn across the floor, and the entire place seems smaller, darker. Jesse has been painted as an addict, but his condition is relatively new. Jane, on the other hand, is a full-blown addict, and once she picks up, she's all the way back out there, and focused only on one thing: the next, better high. Ironically, it's Jane who introduces Jesse to something new, showing up one night with her "works": a couple of needles, a spoon, surgical tubing, and some heroin. Jesse and Jane's relationship — in fact their entire future — has gone from bright and hopeful to dark and dirty in a matter of days.

Walt, however, is focused only on his own desire to move up in the meth business, forcing a meeting with Saul's contact even after being turned down because of Jesse's habit earlier in the episode — which brings us to Gustavo Fring: businessman, fast-food entrepreneur, philanthropist, and a real-live drug kingpin. Played with absolute brilliance by Giancarlo Esposito (whose credits include *Revolution, South Beach, Do the Right Thing,* and *NYPD Blue*), Gus is cold, controlled, and utterly ruthless, facts that Walt fails to truly appreciate as he tries to go into business with him. His obsession with Gus comes at the expense of his family, as he shows up late for Skyler's latest ultrasound because of his meeting with Gus early in the episode. But even worse, Walt is so focused on the deal that, when the time comes, he ignores the progressively urgent calls and texts from Skyler telling him the baby is coming, and makes a choice of his own: drugs over family. His newborn partnership over his newborn daughter.

LAB NOTES

HIGHLIGHT

SAUL: "Let's just say I know a guy who knows a guy . . . who knows another guy."

DID YOU NOTICE

- Gus runs a very successful fast-food chicken chain called Los Pollos Hermanos, which translates into "The Chicken Brothers."
- Giancarlo Esposito can change Gus's expression from professional courtesy to snake-cold killer with just a slight shift of his eyes or a tiny change in the tone of his voice.
- Now it's Jesse who's trying to get Jane interested in going to see the Georgia O'Keeffe Museum.
- Jesse uses the scales on Saul's statue of Lady Justice as an ashtray, a nice visual demonstration of both Jesse's contempt for authority and Saul's repurposing of the law as an aid to criminal activity.
- Ted Beneke spends a great deal of his time on the phone, apparently explaining late payments and unfulfilled orders.
- Skyler makes her own choice in this episode when she goes back to work for Ted after discovering his embezzlement.
- Skyler is more worked up after her Monroe-esque rendition of "Happy Birthday" than Ted is.

SHOOTING UP

- The quick edits from bicycle POV to wider shots of the kid riding through the barrio (and the focus on the child's brightly colored shoe-laces) serve both to give the audience a tour through the neighborhood as well as focusing our attention on the kid as being important.
- As Jane is debating on whether or not to leave while Jesse smokes up, she pauses with her hand on the inside doorknob of his apartment door. The camera lingers on her hand, showing the viewer her choice.

The light shining in from outside through the drawn shade over the door's glass creates a remarkable effect. The angle allows the audience to see beyond the shade, to where bright, clean daylight pours in through the glass. The bright light also casts the shadows of the mullions between the glass panes onto the shade, shadows that seem like bars from the inside of the apartment. Jane's deliberate choice thus becomes between light and dark, between freedom and the prison of addiction.

- ◆ The ceiling-down shot of Jesse floating upwards on his first heroin high is unique in the series. Though other higher-than-the-ceiling views have been and will be used, this is the only time that a character rises with the camera almost in the fashion of a mannerist painting. It is a tremendous use of camera work to show the euphoria of the drug and the accompanying madness.

TITLE Mandala is Sanskrit for "circle." Buddhist and Hindu religious artwork often depict mandalas as sacred spaces, and such figures are sometimes used as focal points for meditation or signifiers of sacred spaces. In this case, the title seems to refer to a larger circular framing within the story of *Breaking Bad*, one that begins here but ends a couple of seasons down the line.

SPECIAL INGREDIENTS

HEROIN AND WORKS

Jane introduces Jesse to heroin, a powerful opiate that can be smoked or snorted, but is most powerful when injected straight into a vein. Jane, like many addicts, has a near-ritual associated with her use of the drug and takes a few safety precautions (HIV is common among intravenous drug users due to sharing needles, for instance), but don't be fooled — there's no safe way to use heroin. One of the obvious dangers is that heroin, like all street drugs, is often cut with other substances, some of which aren't nearly so wholesome as Jesse's signature chili powder. After all, who's a junkie going to complain to about substandard quality control in their stash?

A careful junkie cleans her spoon with alcohol before placing the heroin in it. A touch of water is added to the spoon, which is then heated from below with a lighter to cause the heroin to dissolve into the water. Next, a tiny bit of cotton is dropped into the mixture to absorb it. A (hopefully clean) hypodermic needle is then used to pull the heroin through the cotton fibers into the (also hopefully clean) syringe. In theory, the cotton filters out germs and impurities. The junkie finds a vein that isn't too collapsed from repeated injections, cleans the site with alcohol, and then injects the mess into a vein, praying that she hit the vein and didn't puncture it or miss it entirely. How can you tell? By inserting the needle, then pulling the syringe plunger up just a bit to see if blood is being drawn up — blood equals vein. Then push down the plunger and hope for the best. If the needle is dirty from being shared, the user may also be putting HIV, hepatitis B, or hepatitis C into their bloodstream along with the drug. Many heroin addicts report overwhelming feelings of warmth, safety, and euphoria, even if they've taken the drug on a freezing rooftop. Many users also report immediate vomiting, coughing fits, and constipation.

Yeah. Tons of fun.

12-STEP PROGRAMS

When Jane shows Jesse her 18-month chip, it establishes that Jane is an addict who has attained sobriety through a 12-step program. Millions worldwide have found long-term sobriety through 12-step programs, which began with Alcoholics Anonymous in 1935 and have since expanded to other programs based on AA's 12 steps, such as Narcotics Anonymous and Cocaine Anonymous.

What all 12-step programs have in common is the requirement of total abstinence from the addict's "drug of choice" — there are no Super Bowl exceptions for alcoholics — paired with an admission that the addict has to find something bigger than the drug. That said, 12-step programs are spiritual in nature, but definitely not religious. (Although religious groups have borrowed from 12-step programs to create faith-based recovery programs.) People in recovery most often work the 12 steps with a mentor (known as a "sponsor") who has worked the steps before them. Addicts are unpleasant people who have usually wrecked their lives and the lives of those around them by being master manipulators who will lie, cheat, and steal to get what they want, when they want it, so being accountable to a sponsor is a unpleasant change of pace. The system works because the addict's sponsor knows all the addict's tricks; after all, the sponsor has pulled them too.

Twelve-step programs don't work for everyone. But it worked for Jane for a year and a half, which is no small accomplishment for an addict, who literally can't imagine going for a single day without using. In keeping with *Breaking Bad*'s unflinching stare into the horrors of drug use, we noticed that Jane is never shown talking to her sponsor. It may be that she thinks she's beyond that, and that after a year and a half, she's strong enough now to handle life all by her lonesome.

She's not. And she should have pushed that door open and walked into the sunlight.

2.12 **P**hoenix

Original air date: May 24, 2009
Written by: John Shiban **Directed by:** Colin Bucksey

"Wanna see what your daddy did for you?" — Walter White

Walt makes a big score, but can't tell anyone about it. Meanwhile, Jesse and Jane's downward spiral accelerates.

"Phoenix" is one of several landmark episodes in *Breaking Bad*. Since the pilot episode, Walt has justified everything he's done, everything he's been through, and everything he's put the people around him through, by saying that it was all for the good of his family. First to provide financial security for them after he died from cancer, and most recently in order to pay for a lung lobectomy that will remove his cancer once and for all and thus allow him to be there to provide for his family's future in person. To this point, Walt has had an excuse, no matter how flimsy, for each of his actions. No more. The last gasp of that excuse is his choice to make the biggest drug deal of his short career rather than attend the birth of his daughter. Even insulating his house with $1.2 million can't obscure the fact that providing for his family is not what's really driving Walt.

This is the point where Walt's real troubles begin to manifest. *Breaking Bad* is largely about families, and "Phoenix" provides a good look at Walt's without beating the viewer over the head with it. Walt Jr. is changing diapers and taking care of his newly arrived sister, manning up in a very real way (and one that has nothing to do with matching his dad and uncle drink for drink).

127

Above and beyond that, Junior has created a website to help raise money for his dad's cancer treatment, a website that is extraordinarily touching and clearly reveals Junior's love for his father. Hank and Marie are thrilled to have a new niece to cuddle and spoil, and the entire family is united in wanting to celebrate Holly's arrival into the world, up to and including a poolside feast from Los Pollos Hermanos. Every single member of Walt's family is glad to step in and work together to see the White clan through. Marie and Hank will help with childcare, Skyler's gone back to work, and beyond the website, Junior's going to try to find an after-school job to help out as well. This family may have its problems, but they are all dedicated to each other and willing to support and work for each other's happiness, no matter what. It can sometimes be hard to step back from one's life and see what's right in front of you, but it's glaringly obvious that this is one hell of a good family, and that's no small thing.

Except to Walt. Walt can't stand it. He sees Junior's website as begging, charity as a dirty word, his son and wife working as a failure on his part. With Walt, everything is about him, and he cannot see or accept acts of support and love from his family as anything but evidence of his own failure. What's worse is that these efforts are all unnecessary because Walt has provided. In his mind he has gone out there and risked everything to make sure his family is secure, and it absolutely galls him that he simply cannot tell them about it. Their love and support don't matter, not if it comes as a result of them thinking that he can't provide for them. Of course, his family doesn't actually think that; it's all in Walt's head, which is becoming an increasingly scary place. He's proud of what he's done, and furious that he can't crow about it from the rooftops.

Meanwhile, Jesse and Jane have entered the darkness. Their little world collapses suddenly when Jane's father discovers that his daughter is using again, and in a scene strongly reminiscent of the one between Jesse and his mother in "Down," Don Margolis cries "Why — why do you do it?!" In the throes of a desperation only an addict can know, Jane manipulates her father, Jesse, and even Walt into getting an out: Jesse's share of the meth money. Jesse and Jane rhapsodize about the new life they could have with all that money, but even they don't really believe what they are saying.

In one of the most quietly powerful moments of the entire series, Walt

(ANDREW EVANS/PR PHOTOS)

and Don meet randomly in a bar. Walt has stopped in on a whim on his way home from delivering Jesse's money and (maybe) buying Jane's silence. Don's there to wonder about his daughter's promise to go back into rehab the next day. Don tells Walt never to give up on family and makes it clear that, in his mind, nothing else really matters. This message from one father to another resonates with Walt, so he goes back, not to his family, but to Jesse, full of righteous intentions to make him do the right thing. In the process, he murders Jane. This is not self-defense; this is murder, as cold and cruel as can be. Walt knows what to do if someone is vomiting while on their back: you turn them on their side so they don't aspirate on it and choke to death. He showed Marie how to put a towel under baby Holly's back in her crib to prevent exactly the same thing. Walt knows immediately what he should do, and instead of doing it, he stands over Jane and watches her die. It can be argued that there are other moments in the series that can be singled out as the one in which Walt became irredeemable, but for our money, Jane's murder is the single instant when the viewer knows that there is no going back.

LAB NOTES

HIGHLIGHT

WALT: "Cyber-begging, that's all that is. Just rattling a little tin cup to the entire world."

SAUL: "Yeah, there's no deep-seated issues *there*."

DID YOU NOTICE

+ Despite having chosen a drug deal over being at Holly's birth, Walt has the gall to get pissy when he learns that Ted brought Skyler to the hospital.

+ When Jane and Don attend the 12-step meeting, the recovering addict picking up a one-year chip shares how he did whatever he had to in order to stay clean, even staying away from certain people. Jane made a different choice.

+ When Jesse and Jane shoot up, Jane calls him "baby," and tells him to lie on his side in case he throws up. A nice harbinger of things to come, and a connection with baby Holly and Walt.

+ The heartbreaking scene where Jane cons her dad into letting her get better "tomorrow" is one of the most realistic scenes in the series. Gilligan & Co. don't skimp on the realities of addiction and addicts here.

+ Don Margolis is seen at the 12-step meeting both with and without Jane in this episode, and is also seen drinking a beer after confronting Jane and Jesse. It is unclear whether or not he is also a recovering addict. If so, he would most likely not be drinking alcohol, as 12-step programs such as Alcoholics Anonymous, Narcotics Anonymous, and Cocaine Anonymous all consider alcohol use to be breaking sobriety. If not, it is somewhat unusual for Don to be attending the meeting in the first place. Of course the beer could be his own slip after confronting Jane and Jesse, or his overprotectiveness of Jane might extend to making sure she goes to meetings by going with her.

SHOOTING UP "Phoenix" is largely free of stylistic camera angles, concentrating instead on direct storytelling. However, the use of the abandoned De

Anza Motor Lodge returns again to an empty place without memory, a place on the edges of things.

TITLE Jane was born in Phoenix, but the title has another meaning as well. The phoenix is a mythological creature, a beautiful bird who can sense when its own death is near. The phoenix then builds a funeral pyre and throws itself into the flames to die. However, the phoenix is also reborn from the very fire that destroys it. What will rise from the ashes of Jane's death?

INTERESTING FACTS

- The De Anza Motor Lodge seen in the cold opening is named for Juan Bautista de Anza (1736–1788). De Anza was born in the Sonora province of New Spain, and from 1774 to 1777 he led an exploratory expedition into California on behalf of the Viceroy of New Spain, during which he discovered the first land route to San Francisco Bay. He served as the governor of the province of Nuevo Mexico (New Mexico) from 1777 to 1787, campaigning successfully against the Native tribes of the province, including the Comanche.
- Junior's website for Walt actually exists, and until late 2013 when AMC disabled the link, the "donate" button redirects readers to a page collecting money for the National Cancer Coalition. See it at www.save walterwhite.com.

SPECIAL INGREDIENTS

IS JANE'S DEATH MURDER?

Okay, we'll admit it. Legally, it would be tough to prove that Walt's actions regarding Jane rise to the level of "guilty beyond a reasonable doubt" to get a murder conviction — especially if you're looking at his actions from the point of view of first degree, premeditated murder. What Walt does is different from waiting in the bushes to pounce on someone and beat their brains in with a baseball bat, which would be classic first degree murder. However, Walt is nonetheless responsible for her death by both his actions and his inaction. Usually, not taking action cannot be legally held against someone — there is a notable exception if you are in a position of protecting the public, like a lifeguard at a public pool, for instance. However, there are exceptions and we believe this is one of them.

Walt starts the ball rolling when he goes charging into the apartment and begins shaking Jesse. At that point, Jesse and Jane had been sleeping in spoon fashion on their sides, but when Walt starts shaking Jesse, Jane rolls over flat on her back where she could choke on her own vomit. (A truly disgusting way to shuffle off this mortal coil, by the way.) Jane begins choking and we see Walt — who, it's been clearly established, *knows what to do* — decide to do nothing. In some jurisdictions, such indifference to human life resulting in death could be charged with the poetically named "depraved-heart murder."

Regardless of whether the legal system considers Walt guilty, morally he's got Jane's blood on his hands.

COMPUTER ZOMBIES

Saul has a plan to use computer "zombies" to launder Walt's drug money using Junior's website. The fact that Junior created the site to legitimately raise money for Walt's cancer treatment makes Saul's plan especially slimy, but could it actually work? Short answer? Oh, yes.

"Computer zombies" are created when a hacker takes over a computer (or a dozen, or a hundred, or a thousand, or many, many more) and uses the computer(s) to conduct illegal activities without the knowledge of the computer's actual owner(s). Saul's scheme involves a hacker using many, many computers to funnel Walt's drug money into Junior's charitable website through small "donations." This converts the dirty money to clean funds, with no one being the wiser. (There's more on money laundering in the season 3 part of this book, if you're interested in the fine details.) You may have been the victim of a "zombie attack" yourself and not even have known it since the legitimate owner can still use a zombie computer although he may wonder why the computer is running so slowly.

While Saul's scheme seems fairly sophisticated, many hackers who create zombies aren't all that proficient at writing script or code. They don't have to be. All they really need is a trusting computer owner with email or an internet connection. The first stage of the process is to get the installation program to the "victim computer." Often, this is done through email or through a regular website. The hacker disguises the program with an innocuous name to fool the victim into opening the file. Once the victim has the file, it must be activated. Usually, the file is disguised, since very few people are going to open a file called "Beware — Dangerous Zombie Software." Often, hackers make the zombie file appear to be an innocent picture file of cute kittens. Another common tactic is a pop-up ad with a "No Thanks" button. When the victim clicks on the "No Thanks" button (or the picture file of the cute kittens), the malicious zombie software is activated, although nothing seems to happen. All too often, users think, "Hmm, bad file," and forget about it, when they should run all the anti-virus and anti-spyware software they have.

The now-activated file attaches itself to some element of the victim computer's operating system and now, every time the victim turns on his computer, the program becomes active. Usually, these programs either allow the hacker to directly control the user's internet activity or they simply have instructions for the now-zombified computer to carry out a task at a particular time, such as making a $50 donation to the "Save Walter White" fund from an electronic bank account, in this case one controlled by Saul and Walter.

ABQ

Original air date: May 31, 2009
Written by: Vince Gilligan **Directed by:** Adam Bernstein

"Ask anyone . . . he's a great father, a great teacher. He knows everything there is to know about chemistry, he's patient with you, he's always there for you . . . he's just — *decent*." — Walter White, Jr.

Walt deals with the fallout from Jane's death. Meanwhile, his choices seem to take on a life of their own, like falling dominoes.

In "ABQ," Jesse is shattered, and it's heartbreaking. Walt, never one to listen to others when they say something he doesn't want to hear, especially Jesse, didn't realize the depth of Jesse's feelings for Jane, or what her murder would do to his partner. Just a few episodes ago, Jesse and Jane were playing in the sunlight, and now there's nothing but death and broken dreams. Jesse has hit bottom, blaming himself for Jane's death and seeking his own in the utter squalor and despair of a drug house. Found by Walt, Jesse clutches him with agonizing grief and Walt begins to realize that he didn't just remove an obstacle from his path or a bad influence from Jesse's life when he watched Jane choke to death, he also killed someone incredibly important to his very young partner.

Walt, of course, believes that everything can be fixed and that he is the guy to do it. With the money they've made from meth, Jesse gets checked into a luxury rehab that puts Dr. Drew's to shame. In spite of his surroundings, something in Jesse seems permanently broken. His agony is wrenching, and Aaron Paul brings pain, grief, and hopelessness to the screen with enough force that the viewer can hardly bear to watch it. Jesse is something close to an automaton in this episode, too traumatized to do or think anything beyond what Walt and Saul's cleaner tell him to do. Perhaps even more frightening, the audience is left with the impression that Jesse really just doesn't care anymore — about anything.

Jesse's not the only thing that Walt is trying to fix in this episode. As Saul's plan for using Junior's site to launder Walt's money picks up speed, Junior and Skyler are overjoyed at the apparent response they're getting, and the money that's coming in. Walt, on the other hand, is furious. That's money that he earned, and he has to pretend that it all came from the goodness of strangers and that he had nothing to do with it. Worse, the local news media gets wind of the story (thanks to busybody Marie) and he finds himself forced to sit beside his son as his tale of woe is told and Junior receives praise for the site. Walt's self-centered bubble is burst however, when he hears Junior praise him to the skies, lifting him up as a tremendous moral role model — this, just days after he murdered a young woman and shattered Jesse's world.

Jesse's world isn't the only one destroyed by Walt's actions. John de Lancie's portrayal of a devastated father just trying to muddle through a newly empty world is one of enormous and gentle power. He shows up at his daughter's apartment to take her to rehab, only to find ambulances and a coroner's van. Too stunned to even answer questions, his expression says it all, and the viewer can just imagine the self-torture he's putting himself through. If only he had forced Jane to come with him last night! In this episode, for the first time the viewer gets to see the inside of Jane's half of the duplex and it's the bright, clean home of an artist, with a vibrant mural on the wall featuring a woman who looks very much like Jane dancing in the sky. Her father is there to pick out a dress for Jane's funeral — one with long sleeves, to cover the track marks on her arms. Tragedy upon tragedy, and Gilligan & Co. aren't done yet.

Jesse and Don's lives have shattered, and now it's Walt's turn. Addled by drugs before his lobectomy, he admits to the second cell phone, and a few weeks down the line, Skyler is packing the bags and the baby and tells him to be gone when she gets back. Walt goes into full damage control mode, but Sky's done her homework, and every single lie Walt has told her is revealed, one after another, and she doesn't want to hear anything else from him. Period. Walt is left alone, a man who just a few hours ago believed he had everything: money, family, even health. Now he has nothing, and everything he did "for his family" has led to losing them. Worse, Walt's actions are rippling out as Don Margolis, Jane's dad, goes back to work, still grief-stricken, still more than a little stunned, and really in no shape to do his job as an air traffic controller.

The black-and-white cold opens of the season come together in the last moments of the episode as two planes collide, right over Walt's house, and Walt finds himself in the path of, and the ultimate creator of, a literal rain of death.

LAB NOTES

HIGHLIGHT Gus dropping a few dollars into the jar for Walt that Hank has set up at the DEA office.

DID YOU NOTICE

- The van that pulls away from the camera in the suddenly colorized cold open has NTSB painted across its roof: National Transportation Safety Board, which investigates aviation accidents.
- The people from Office of the Medical Investigator (OMI) are the ones who investigate deaths, including Jane's, and the vans in the cold open were from the OMI.
- Hank remarks that the "Blue Sky" meth is now being distributed everywhere *except* in New Mexico, as if the cooks have suddenly gotten smarter. Walt's deal with Gus is getting noticed.
- Walt calls Jesse "son" when he goes to get him out of the drug house.
- Jane's incredible self-portrait mural recalls Jesse asking her if she had ever wanted to be a superhero in "Over." Turns out she did, and like Jesse, she drew herself in the role.
- Also in the upper right-hand corner of Jane's mural is a small pink teddy bear, seemingly falling through the sky.
- Gus's trip to the DEA as a sponsor of the annual "Fun Run" shows how cold he is, and how hard he's worked to become a pillar of the community. It also gains him information. He knows Hank works for

the DEA and is Walt's brother-in-law, and he knows Walt has cancer. All of these are things Walt hasn't deigned to tell him.

- Don refers to the call letters of one of the aircraft on his radar-screen as "Jane" by mistake. (It should be "Juliet.")
- The headshot of Walt that Hank has placed upon the donation jar first appears shot from an angle that superimposes it on the human silhouette target on the DEA's bulletin board, in the same position a picture of Tuco was placed during the earlier DEA manhunt for him.

SHOOTING UP

- "ABQ" is packed with exquisite camera work and stylistic framing. The cold open stitches together all three previous black-and-white openings, and adds on a final element, in which the electric pink bear remains the only spot of color until the camera pans back to reveal the White house, bracketed in the background on either side by pillars of black smoke.
- There is a variant of the up-and-through POV shot *Breaking Bad* uses so often and so well. This time the POV is from the inside of a mattress, and the squeaking and Jesse's unmistakable grunting seem to be sexual, but are revealed to be the results of Jesse's desperate attempts to revive Jane by CPR. During the entire course of their relationship, the viewer never sees or hears Jesse and Jane make love, though it is clear they do. This is a brilliant way to keep the relationship innocent in the audience's eyes, and somehow pure, and the linking of sex and death here is more than a bit shocking.
- The surgery scene is free from gratuitous gore and blood, but the audience sees Walt treated like a piece of meat, shoved this way and that, and none to gently as the surgical team performs the lobectomy. Perhaps this is a metaphor for the lack of control that Walt actually has over his life, despite thinking otherwise.
- Arguably the most brilliant POV shot of the series thus far occurs as the viewer gets a teddy-bear's eye view of a fall from thousands of feet in the sky into Walter White's pool, where it is suddenly revealed that Walt's shirt is the same color as the iconic teddy bear's fur.

TITLE "ABQ" completes the season-long sequence: "Seven Thirty-Seven Down Over ABQ." A Boeing 737 passenger jet has gone down over Albuquerque.

INTERESTING FACTS

- ◆ This episode is the first appearance of the ever-skillful Mike, played by Jonathan Banks. While his first role was in a public service movie called *Linda's Film on Menstruation*, you probably recognize him from his roles in *48 Hrs.*, *Beverly Hills Cop*, and *Wiseguy*.
- ◆ Founded in 1926, the National Transportation Safety Board is the federal agency tasked with investigating not only airplane crashes, but also other accidents involving mass transport like buses, trains, and ferries.

SPECIAL INGREDIENTS

LUNG LOBECTOMY

Walt's cancer treatment involves a lung lobectomy, which is serious surgery involving cutting into the body, spreading the ribs, and removing the cancerous portion of the lung, often along with some lymph nodes. It sounds scary and it *is* major surgery, but you have more lung tissue than you probably think you do. The right lung has three lobes (upper, middle, and lower) and your left lung has two (upper and lower). Following the surgery, the patient's lung may leak air and fluid, which can cause the lung to collapse, making breathing difficult. To prevent this, chest tubes are put in during surgery to drain the fluid and air from around the lung and make it easier for the recovering patient to breathe. This is in addition to the stomach tube and catheter that are inserted during the surgery, as well as the heavy-duty stitches and staples. As the body heals, the tubes are removed and the stitches are absorbed. Many patients return home within a week of the surgery and are often back to work within six to eight weeks.

AIR TRAFFIC CONTROLLERS

Don Margolis works as an air traffic controller, a profession that is consistently ranked as one of the highest paid occupations that does not require a college degree. While it is not uncommon for an experienced air traffic controller to make upwards of $100,000 a year, it is also an occupation with an unbelievably high stress level — and that's on a good day.

Air traffic controllers work in control towers and approach control facilities at airports. Total concentration is required and the work is exhausting.

Shifts often involve weekends, overnights, and holidays with very limited breaks. Air traffic controllers have to deal with the complexity of air traffic, working long shifts without a break, and dealing with tricky weather patterns. It is not uncommon for a single air traffic controller to be communicating with 10 aircraft all within five miles of each other and some busy airports handle more than 100 operations an hour — which means nearly two takeoffs and landings per minute.

While Don doesn't work alone, many air traffic controllers working in Federal Contract Towers ("FCT") do. FCTs are the result of the Federal Aviation Administration contracting with the private sector to provide air traffic control services for the smaller, lower-traffic airports. If it sounds scary, it should. Such air traffic controllers are responsible for getting all this done with no backup and may in fact be coordinating simultaneously with up to three facilities at once while they're also talking with pilots in the air wanting to get on the ground and with pilots on the ground wanting to get into the air. The stress level on a routine shift (let alone when storms and other bad weather move in) can be mind-melting. For this reason, the Federal Aviation Administration has mandated retirement for air traffic controllers at age 56.

SPEED KILLS (SEASON 2)

BODY COUNT
Walt: 1 (Jane)
Walt/Don Margolis: 167 (Wayfarer 515 and chartered jet passengers)
Tuco: 1 (No-Doze) (+ an unknown number more)
Hank: 1 (Tuco)

BEATDOWNS
Jesse: 1 (by Hank)

What's Cooking

"BETTER CALL SAUL!"
LAWYERS AND ADVERTISING

In "Live Free or Die," Walt contemptuously calls Saul "a two-bit bus bench lawyer." Leaving aside the fact that Saul's 17 percent cut of Walt and Jesse's enterprise can hardly be termed "two-bit," Saul is, in fact, known for his aggressive advertising, including bus benches. This type of open, in-your-face advertising is a relatively new phenomenon, however. Abraham Lincoln once famously advised a young man who was considering a legal career to resolve to be an honest lawyer, and if he could not do that, then he should resolve to be honest and not bother being a lawyer. It's a lovely story showcasing how important ethics were to "Honest" Abe, but it's worth noting that Lincoln was not above a little judicious self-promotion. He was one of the lead attorneys for the Illinois Central Railroad in the landmark 1855 case of *Illinois Central Railroad v. County of McLean* and how he got there is an interesting story. As the case was heating up, Lincoln first discussed the case with McLean County officials, offering his services in the impending litigation. When that elicited no response, he wrote to officials one county over. Still getting no nibbles for his hook, Lincoln wrote the railroad, making it clear that he was available to advocate for the railroad's position. Four days later, he was retained. While this was acceptable in the 1850s, Lincoln's actions would have been grounds for disbarment during the first half of the 20th century.

For all the jokes about lawyers and ambulance chasing, ethics are a corner-stone of the profession and, let's face it, degrees in law were being awarded while doctors were still using bloodletting to balance the "four humors" of the body and leeches were considered cutting-edge medicine. All jurisdictions in the United States insist that would-be lawyers show competency in understanding and applying established standards of conduct before being admitted to the practice of law. Nearly all states measure this knowledge by the Multistate Professional Responsibility Examination (MPRE), an exam that law students take in addition to the "regular" bar exam.

One element of professional responsibility deals with what is and is not permissible advertising by lawyers. Nowadays, advertising by members of the bar seems ubiquitous, but that has not always been the case. The American Bar Association (ABA) was founded in 1878 and, at that time, regulations concerning how lawyers advertised their services varied greatly from state to state. Concerned that standards for the profession were slipping, the ABA promulgated the *Canons of Professional Ethics*. Adopted in 1908, the *Canons* codified ethical standards for members of the bar.

The membership of the ABA overwhelmingly believed that advertising was crass and undignified for the noble profession of the law, so the *Canons* expressly forbade advertising by its members. It was assumed a lawyer either had an established clientele or that word of mouth regarding the lawyer's quality of work would soon result in one. Lawyers could print business cards and use letterhead stationery and firms were allowed to be placed in law directories (not telephone directories) containing basic contact information, but that was the extent of permissible advertising, and that's where things stood for nearly 70 years. No billboards, no TV ads, no bus benches, and no direct mail to your house after getting a speeding ticket. The reasoning behind this ban was elitist at best. If you were from a social class that utilized lawyers (for real estate transactions or drawing up wills and trusts, for example), you probably already had your "family lawyer," but if you were not from that social class, finding an attorney could be difficult and intimidating, and often you didn't even know what your rights were, due to the lack of available information. Imagine living in a rat-trap apartment and feeling sure that your landlord was supposed to be responsible for fixing the stopped-up plumbing, but not knowing how to reach an attorney who knew the issues of landlord-tenant law.

The situation began to change in the early 1970s when two young lawyers, John Bates and Van O'Steen, were admitted to the State Bar of Arizona.

After a couple of years working for the Legal Aid Society, Bates and O'Steen went into practice together. They decided their firm would focus on a large volume of uncomplicated cases, such as uncontested divorces, name changes, and adoptions. However, in order to create the volume of cases they needed, Bates and O'Steen realized that they needed to get their names out to the general public, so in February 1976, they placed an advertisement in the local newspaper. By any standard, the ad was discreet and tasteful, simply stating the types of matters the firm would take on, a basic price list, and contact information, including the firm's address and phone number, all under the heading "Legal Services at Very Reasonable Fees."

However, the newspaper ad, no matter how restrained, was guaranteed to bring the two young attorneys to the attention and scrutiny of the State Bar of Arizona, due to the very specific restriction of Arizona Disciplinary Rule 2-101(B) which read in part: "A lawyer shall not publicize himself . . . through newspaper or magazine advertisements, radio or television announcements, display advertisements in the city or telephone directories, or other means of commercial publicity, nor shall he authorize or permit others to do so on his behalf." The State Bar of Arizona promptly suspended both Bates and O'Steen's licenses to practice law. Bates and O'Steen, who had paid attention in the constitutional law classes, sued, claiming that the total ban on advertising violated the free speech guarantee of the First Amendment to the United States Constitution. When the case reached the United States Supreme Court, Bates and O'Steen prevailed on the free speech claim. The Court ruled that a total ban on advertising served to "keep the public in ignorance" and "inhibits the free flow of information." States were allowed to regulate lawyer advertising to ensure that the information contained in the advertisement was true and did not mislead the public. With *Bates v. State Bar of Arizona*, the floodgates opened. The ink was barely dry on the Supreme Court's decision when the California firm of Jacoby & Meyers placed a print advertisement in the *Los Angeles Times*. The firm also became the first in the United States to use television to advertise their services. Saul's billboards and late-night TV commercials are a direct descendant of the *Bates* decision.

Not all advertising is okay, though. *The Model Rules of Professional Conduct* of the ABA (which New Mexico adopted in 1986) prohibit direct contact with potential clients and insist that written, recorded, and electronic communications that are attempts to solicit employment for the lawyer be clearly identified as "advertising material." Although restrictions vary somewhat from state to state, activities that smack of "ambulance chasing" are generally off-limits, including restrictions on direct solicitation of victims of ferry crashes and other major disasters. (Saul manages to find ways to get around these barriers: remember his ad seeking injured people to join his class action lawsuit following the tragic Wayfarer crash in season 2?) Saul is an excellent example of the very outer limits of lawyer advertising. He uses billboards and outrageous television and internet ads to get his face before the public; even his office is decorated in an over-the-top way to suggest that only he, Saul (McGill) Goodman, understands your pain and will fight to get you justice, whether your case involves workplace injury, drunk driving, or emotional distress caused by a disastrous plane crash. Of course, if you've gotten yourself into a little trouble involving a misunderstanding of criminal law, Saul's willing — for a reasonable fee, of course — to assist you in that matter as well.

To a degree, advertising is a question of taste and lawyer ads run the gamut from discreet and elegant to in-your-face and ridiculous. Alexander & Catalano, a firm in upstate New York, made a series of ads depicting its attorneys as possessing superhuman speed to reach a distressed client, towering over downtown office buildings, and even counseling space aliens. When New York attempted to change its advertising rules, this firm seemed to be in the bull's-eye, since part of the new state rules prohibited advertising that relied "on techniques to obtain attention . . . including the portrayal of lawyers exhibiting characteristics clearly unrelated to legal competence."

The Court of Appeals ruled in favor of the law firm, although they did agree that Alexander & Catalano do not actually represent space aliens. "It is true that Alexander and his partner are not giants towering above local buildings; they cannot run to a client's house so quickly that they appear as blurs; and they do not actually provide legal assistance to space aliens. But given the prevalence of these and other kinds of special effects in advertising and entertainment, we cannot seriously believe — purely as a matter of *common sense* — that ordinary individuals are likely to be misled into thinking that these advertisements depict true characteristics."

Common sense and the law? Well, it seems that those two seldom keep company these days. But it can be entertaining.

3.01

N o Más

Original air date: March 21, 2010
Written by: Vince Gilligan **Directed by:** Bryan Cranston

"Self-hatred, guilt, it accomplishes nothing. It just stands in the way." — Group Leader

Walt deals with the fallout from his actions last season. Meanwhile, Jesse wrestles with his own demons, and something wicked begins to move north from Mexico.

Breaking Bad's third season seemingly begins out of context. The cold open of "No Más" takes place well away from Walt and Jesse, from Albuquerque or any place the viewer is familiar with. The image of poor people grimly crawling through dirt and heat with utterly focused determination looks medieval, like some group of extreme penitent-pilgrims marking the Stations of the Cross, and this interpretation isn't far off. Joining the crawl, but moving far more quickly, are two wealthy-looking young men who wear silver death's-heads on the toes of their expensive, hand-tooled cowboy boots. Their destination is a shrine to Santa Muerte (Saint Death) and their purpose is to lay upon the shrine a crudely drawn picture of Walter White in his Heisenberg hat and glasses. Throughout, neither of the men, who are apparently twins, says a word. They are intent, intense, and absolutely terrifying. Rarely has a television show introduced a season's "big bad(s)" with such terrifying power. The viewer is left with the impression that things have become dangerously serious for Walt. He is swimming in shark-infested waters, and the sharks are hungry.

Walt, meanwhile, is trying desperately to deal with, and distance himself psychologically from, the 167 deaths caused when air-traffic controller Don Margolis, grief-stricken over the loss of his daughter Jane, mistakenly directed two airplanes into the same air space at the same time, causing them to collide almost directly over Walt's house, killing everyone aboard both planes. Of course, Jane was dead because Walt killed her, and so this particular chain of falling dominoes begins with him.

The advice quoted above is offered by the 12-step group leader to Jesse and the other addicts at the recovery center, but it is the core of the entire episode. In terms of recovery from addiction, it signifies that the addict must move beyond self-hatred and guilt in order to positively change his life. Amends will need to be made, but nothing at all can be accomplished by wallowing in either emotion, lest they become excuses to avoid change and use again. For Walt, though, these words serve only to help him rationalize his level of responsibility for all those deaths and his current family situation. Walt tries to downplay the extent of the disaster to the students and faculty at the high school where he teaches, as well as to himself. He desperately tries to shift blame for the accident elsewhere, going so far as to tell Jesse that he blames the government. Most of all, he tries to forget about it, but he can't. His refrain is about moving on and surviving, but he's not having much success with that, particularly when it comes to his family life.

Walt genuinely seems to think that — somehow — things can and should go back to "normal," the way they were before his cancer diagnosis. He honestly can't seem to understand Skyler's reaction to his lies, and to the shocking revelation that he is a meth "manufacturer." In Walt's world — or the world as Walt would very much love to make it — his actions were all about his family, and he should be respected and praised for having done so much for the people he loves. Any reaction other than gratitude just confuses the hell out of him. Again, he tries to get out of the meth game, even turning down an offer of $3 million for three months' work with Gus. He is searching for something that will magically make all of his mistakes disappear and get things back to where they should be, especially his "happy family." Fundamentally, Walt doesn't want his choices to come with consequences, except for those he views as positive. At most, his is willing to concede that negative consequences might be temporary problems, but never lasting effects. Above all, and despite his refusal of Gus's offer, Walt does not want to change. Indeed, he sees no reason to do so. This comes out most poignantly in his dealings with the now sober Jesse, who blames himself for Jane's death, and also in part for Wayfarer 515. The audience knows that Jesse shares some responsibility for Jane (the two of them did choose to use, after all), but that her death was actually an act of murder by Walt. Walt can never admit this to Jesse, of course, and so he tries to jolly his partner along, while allowing Jesse to believe in his own guilt.

LAB NOTES

HIGHLIGHT
PAMELA: "Do you feel you have a good understanding of you and your husband's financial situation . . . ? You'd be amazed at what I've seen partners hide from one another."

DID YOU NOTICE
* As Walt almost burns his cash the matchbook has an ad for Saul Goodman's law office on the cover.
* There is a makeshift marker of flowers and crosses on the corner of Walt's house in memoriam of Wayfarer 515.
* Walt is playing dangerous games around Hank again, this time telling him the truth about having $500,000 in cash in a duffel bag.
* Walt cuts the crusts off his PB&J, just like he did when making sandwiches for Krazy-8.
* The student who suggests automatic A's in light of the Wayfarer 515 crash is the same kid who was trying to get Walt to change his chemistry test grade in "Negro y Azul."
* Walt uses euphemistic language when confronted by Skyler about his meth making, distinguishing between "dealer" and "manufacturer."
* The twins communicate with one another without ever speaking.
* In the wake of Wayfarer 515, most people wear blue ribbons or pins as a gesture of remembrance, but Walt does not.

MISCALCULATIONS When Jesse's group leader tells the story of his daughter's death, he gives the date as July 18, 1992, and says he was leaving his house to get more vodka because the ABC store closed at 5 p.m. However, July 18,

1992, was a Saturday, and the ABC stores in Portsmouth, Virginia where the group therapy leader says he was living at the time, stay open until 9 or 10 p.m. on Saturdays.

SHOOTING UP

- The cold open and border crossing scenes are filmed using a different light filter, making a hard, yellow light that not only suggests heat, but also is a subtle indicator of location: Mexico, rather than the U.S.
- When the twins exchange their tailored suits for the clothes of the poor farmer, they obviously terrify the farmer and his wife, particularly as they loom over their little girl. For the latter shoots, the camera is positioned either above the twins' shoulders and angled steeply down, or at the level of the little girl canted steeply upwards, both angles emphasizing the difference in size between the girl and the twins, and increasing the viewer's sense of dread.
- Breaking away from the flash-forward type of cold open used in previous seasons, Gilligan & Co. nonetheless link the cold open and closing scene as the wounded truck driver crawls away from the twins in the dust, just as the worshippers of Santa Muerte crawled in the cold open.

TITLE "No Más" is Spanish for "no more," likely referring to Walt's apparent attempt to get out of meth cooking, Jesse's newfound sobriety, and Skyler's attitude towards Walt.

INTERESTING FACTS

- Marla Tellez, Jeff Maher, and Dana Cortez, the local TV anchors featured in the episode's opening sequence about Wayfarer 515, were all regional news personalities in and around Albuquerque when the episode originally aired.
- This episode features the first appearance of Jere Burns as Jesse's group therapy leader. Besides a recurring role on *Breaking Bad*, Burns also plays Wynn Duffy on the FX series *Justified*.
- Jesse's group leader says he used to live in Portsmouth, Virginia. Not coincidentally, Portsmouth is the hometown of Vince Gilligan's girlfriend. Gilligan himself was also born and raised in Virginia.

- The group leader confesses that he hit and killed his six-year-old daughter with his truck on his way to the ABC store. Viewers living in one of the 18 "control states" in the U.S. got this reference immediately. In control states, the state government has a monopoly over the wholesaling and/or retailing of alcoholic beverages, which means the state sells alcohol (usually distilled spirits, such as the vodka the group leader was rushing to get before the store closed) in state-run "Alcoholic Beverage Control" stores, which are known as "ABC stores" for short.
- This episode also marks the first appearance of the mysterious twins, played by real-life brothers Luis and Daniel Moncada. Originally from Honduras, both brothers have trained as Muay Thai fighters.

SPECIAL INGREDIENTS

SANTA MUERTE

The worship of the skeletal Santa Muerte ("Saint Death") is both old and new. Mesoamerican societies held a certain reverence for death, seeing it as merely the other (and necessary) half of life. This reverence is seen today in mainstream Day of the Dead celebrations in which entire families gather in graveyards to pray for friends and family members who have died. It is a lighthearted, festival atmosphere; in fact, a traditional Day of the Dead treat is chocolate formed into the shape of a human skull.

The European Christian tradition also used skeleton figures, but in a different, more somber, way. Skeletons and skulls were used to symbolize human mortality and during epidemics, such as the Black Death, skeletons were often decked out with crowns and scepters to signify the triumph of death. So when the Catholic faith arrived in the New World, elements of the old and new faiths began to merge and synthesize. Santa Muerte is one result of this clash of cultures. Worship of Santa Muerte has undergone a boom in the last 30 years, especially among the poor and the outcasts of Mexican society. As such, shrines and altars are beginning to be seen in public places, although most shrines to Santa Muerte are still kept clandestine.

While never an official saint of the Catholic Church, Santa Muerte is reputed to be very powerful, having the ability to grant favors that other saints cannot, such as causing someone to fall in love with the petitioner or bring misfortune or even death to the petitioner's enemies. It should be noted that Santa Muerte will only grant such desires if the petition is made with "clean hands." In other words, the petitioner must be both in the right and continue to live that way. In seeking her intercession, petitioners make offerings to Santa Muerte. These often include both traditional gifts such as flowers, incense, and candles, and less common gifts such as cigarettes, cash, and liquor.

As the patron saint of outsiders, Santa Muerte is also very popular with criminals, including drug traffickers. Occasionally, images of Santa Muerte are found alongside images of Jesús Malverde, who is regarded as a "narco saint" (see page 103). However, due to the extreme jealousy attributed to Santa Muerte, many worshippers isolate her image from any other religious icons.

TENERIFE AIRPORT DISASTER

At the high school assembly following the Wayfarer crash, Walt attempts to minimize the disaster by invoking the most dreaded event in the history of aviation disasters — Tenerife, as Walt explains, was much worse. He's right — the 1977 tragedy at Tenerife is the worst aviation disaster in history. To this day, the very name gives pilots and air traffic controllers cold sweats. What makes this tragedy even more unbelievable is that it happened on the ground.

Tenerife is the largest of the Canary Islands and a popular vacation spot. When a terrorist bomb caused the Gran Canaria Airport to close, aircraft were diverted to the smaller Tenerife Airport. A dense fog rolled in, greatly reducing visibility. Among the aircraft that were diverted to Tenerife were two Boeing 747 jumbo jets — KLM Flight 4805 and Pan Am Flight 1736.

Once Gran Canaria reopened, the flights left quickly without waiting for the fog to lift, as passengers and crew were frustrated by the delays. The KLM flight taxied out first. The Pan Am jet was scheduled to take off after KLM 4805 and was supposed to turn off the main runway onto a taxiway to free up the runway for KLM 4805. Due to the fog, the Pan Am pilot missed the designated turn from the runway to the taxiway and was still on the runway, searching for the next turning.

KLM 4805 powered up to takeoff speed (the pilot mistakenly thought he'd been cleared for takeoff), only to emerge from a fogbank to see the

Pan Am flight stopped squarely in the middle of the runway. The Pan Am crew opened the jet's throttles and sharply turned left to avoid a collision, but the KLM flight was traveling too fast. Unable to stop, the KLM flight collided with the Pan Am jet at a speed of approximately 160 miles per hour. Both jets were ripped apart by the impact and the full load of fuel on KLM 4805 ignited. The heat of the fires was so intense that it cleared the fog for approximately half a mile around the crash site. All 234 passengers and 14 crew members aboard the KLM flight were killed, along with 326 passengers and nine crew members aboard the Pan Am flight. Fifty-six passengers and five crew members aboard Pan Am 1736 survived.

● THE CARS OF *BREAKING BAD*

You can tell a lot about somebody by what they drive. Or what they choose to cook meth in, but we'll leave the Fleetwood Bounder (aka the "Crystal Ship") for another discussion.

Walt begins the series driving a Pontiac Aztek in a yawner shade of sorta-green. The Aztek was designed to appeal to the Gen X crowd, but instead was such a disaster that it caused General Motors to shutter the Pontiac brand. In 2007 *Time* magazine called it one of the worst cars of all time and in 2010 placed it on a list of "50 Worst Inventions of All Time." The Aztek was designed as a "crossover" car — one that had some of the desirable elements of an SUV (such as a large cargo capacity and elevated seating) but was never really intended for off-road driving. In other words, it's a whole handful of nothing, much like Walt at the beginning of *Breaking Bad*. He's a frustrated school-teacher who yearns to be more than he is, but just isn't designed for it. Also, in Walt's case, the windshield of his Aztek is often cracked, symbolizing the toll his hidden life is taking on the things and people around him. Later, Walt sells his oft-repaired Aztek for $50 to the mechanic who has kept the car on the road for him. Walt then leases a spiffy new Chrysler 300, a vehicle that has become quite popular within the gangster culture. Leasing such a flashy car fits with Walt's growing embrace of his Heisenberg persona.

Jesse also begins in one car and ends in another, although it's the inverse of Walt's car choices. At the beginning of season 1, Jesse is driving a tricked-out Monte Carlo with vanity plates and "look at me, bitches!" hydraulics. It's the car of a drug dealer and Jesse's playing the part to the hilt. Later, though, Jesse drives a rusted-out Toyota Tercel — the car of a workaday slob just trying to make it from payday to payday. It's an anonymous car, unlikely to draw the attention of anyone — including the DEA.

Speaking of anonymous cars, Gus drives a solid, sensible Volvo sedan: a cautious car for a cautious man. The Volvo might be the perfect example of hiding in plain sight. It's a nice enough car, but it lacks flash. It's quiet, which is Gus all over. Interestingly, Walt acquires a Volvo during season 5. Based on events, it seems Walt might be stepping into Gus's more ruthless habits, but not his more cautious ones.

At 16, Junior wants a car. Badly. Very quickly, he gets two. In a fit of generosity, Walt gets him a Dodge Challenger, the modern muscle car. Appalled at the ostentation (this doesn't fit the story, Walt!), Skyler insists that Walt return the car. Instead of the power and sex appeal of the Challenger, Skyler gives her son a PT Cruiser, a safe, solid car that pretty much wipes out any cool points Junior may have accumulated in his entire life. Junior, who is a loving, caring son, does his best to hide his disappointment from his mother, who he knows was trying to do a good thing. When Walt jumps from his Aztek to the Chrysler 300, he also gets his son another Challenger and, at this point, Skyler just lets it happen.

Skyler drives an old Jeep Grand Wagoneer — the kind with wood panels on the sides. She's had this car for a long time and the feeling you get is that the Jeep, much like the Whites' house, was intended to be a short-term, temporary stop on Walt's rising path of upward mobility. But then reality set in and the starter house has been home for Junior's whole life, and it's likely the Jeep has been there just as long.

Hank also drives a Jeep, but his is a late-model Jeep Commander. It's a solid car for a solid man. Nothing too flashy, but dependable.

Marie drives a Volkswagen Beetle in royal blue (she must not have been able to swing a purple paint job). It suits her — it's a nifty little throwback of a car, but is often considered to be prone to mechanical problems. In a similar fashion, Marie can be cute as a button, with many good qualities (loyalty being chief among them), but she borders on crazy from time to time.

Both Saul and Mike drive big land yachts of cars: Saul's is a shiny white Cadillac DeVille with vanity plates, which is perfectly suited for a criminal lawyer; Mike's is an old, tired Chrysler that you'd never look at twice. Perfect for a man who makes a very comfortable living as a "cleaner." At the very end of his road, Walt will also drive a large car with a very sizable trunk — he needs the room.

Caballo Sin Nombre

Original air date: March 28, 2010
Written by: Peter Gould **Directed by:** Adam Bernstein

"I can't be the bad guy" — Walter White

Walt deals — poorly — with his anger issues. Meanwhile Jesse finds a new place to live.

Walter White not only thinks he's smarter than he is, but as this episode demonstrates, he also thinks he's more important than he is, which may be an even more dangerous delusion. Certainly, no one else seems to think Walt is all that special, including the New Mexico State policeman who pulls him over for his busted windshield. Walt's frustration and angry attempts to manipulate the cop out of giving him a ticket wind up getting him pepper-sprayed and hauled into jail. Worse for his ego, he has to call Hank to help get him out, listen as Hank gives a sob story about Walt's recent life to the arresting officer, and then abjectly apologize for his behavior.

One might expect this experience to take Walt down a peg or two, but in fact he continues to insist on what he sees as his due, while indulging in toddler-like temper tantrums such as throwing pizza on the roof of his house or grabbing his genitals while yelling at his answering machine. No matter how he tries, no matter what he does, Walt just can't seem to make his life go back to the way he wants it to be and he refuses to even consider that perhaps it can't, and even shouldn't. His attempts at control and forced reconciliation with Skyler serve only to make things worse, particularly for Walter

(IZUMI HASEGAWA/PR PHOTOS)

Jr., the true innocent who's caught in the middle of all this. Junior is hurt, angry, and confused, and made more so by the fact that neither Walt nor Skyler will tell him what the hell is going on, especially why their marriage has suddenly fallen apart. As we've seen many times before, Junior sees his dad as infallible, so he takes out all of his frustration on his mother in alternating fits of rage and brutal silence. RJ Mitte carries out his role beautifully in this and subsequent episodes, making the viewer's heart hurt for a young man trapped in such a wrenching, seemingly inexplicable, situation.

It is Skyler, however, who may be in the most uncomfortable position. As Saul points out to Walt, she really cannot reveal what's going on to anyone for fear that it would destroy her family, which it would. Hank would be ruined, Junior shattered, and Skyler would potentially face accessory charges. So she has to stay silent, deflecting Hank and Marie's questions and taking every single thing Junior dishes out at her to protect him from the truth. Walt makes a tremendous amount of noise about all he does for his family, but it is Skyler who is willing to actually sacrifice for that family, and who is willing to risk alienating her only son in order to protect him. Skyler possesses tremendous strength, and she is less and less afraid of using it as time passes. Unfortunately Walt also recognizes the truth of Saul's analysis, and so he forces his way back into his house, determined to stay, arrogantly heedless of the consequences.

These consequences are not merely dire, but deadly, as the mysterious twins from the previous episode make it to Albuquerque and go to visit none other than Héctor "Tío" Salamanca, who uses a Ouija board to spell out Walt's name for them. Chillingly, the viewer has yet to hear either twin say a single word, and perhaps they don't need to: their chrome-plated axe is eloquent in and of itself. The scene of the two of them silently sitting on the foot of Walt and Skyler's bed, waiting patiently for Walt to get out of the shower, is utterly terrifying. Walt will never know how close he came, or how much he already owes Gus Fring for a simple text message reading "Pollos."

Jesse is getting back out into the world again as well, but finds that despite being sober for 45 days, his past still haunts him, and his father is unwilling even to let Jesse into his aunt's house where he used to live, which is now extensively remodeled and on the market. There is something new to Jesse, however. In "No Más" he told Walt that he had accepted that he was the "bad guy," and the viewer now sees a new hardness to him as he calculatedly goes about getting what he thinks of as his house back from his parents. He doesn't rant, rave, or make a scene, he just figures out what to do, how to do it, and then goes about getting it done. Jesse now owns his house outright, and can shut his parents out of it instead of the other way around. This is a darker, more serious man than the viewer has previously seen. Perhaps Walt is not the only person who's breaking bad, after all.

LAB NOTES

HIGHLIGHT

SAUL: "Some would call that fraud in the service of concealing a felony. I myself am more open-minded . . . How about it, counselor? Do you concur?"

DID YOU NOTICE

* Jesse has a 45-day sobriety chip hanging from his rearview mirror.
* Saul's vanity plate reads "LWYRUP," advice his clients should take in their involuntary dealings with law enforcement.
* Ted Beneke's rationalization for embezzling from his own company is that he did it for his family, the same excuse Walt makes.
* The address of Jesse's house is 9809 Margo Street.
* The pizza Walt flings onto the garage roof is not sliced.
* Mike calls someone besides Saul about the twins and the threat they pose to Walt.

- Walt's doing laundry again in this episode, only now it's clothes instead of money.
- Walt stops to fish a Band-Aid out of the pool, always trying to control his world.
- Walt is scarred by his experiences, literally, as the lobectomy scar is clearly visible as he showers. His outer body is beginning to reflect his inner condition.

SHOOTING UP

- Time-lapse photography of the desert is used again in the cold open, hinting that some time has passed between this episode and the one before.
- The use of downward and upward camera angles is again used to great effect with the twins, particularly at the nursing home in their brief encounter with the puzzle-solving elderly women.
- When Walt wakes up from his bender after the failed pizza-night, he is on the floor, facing left, with his face smashed against the floor, a pose and shot used repeatedly throughout the series with different characters.

TITLE "Caballo Sin Nombre" is Spanish for "A Horse With No Name," the title of a song by the band America, which is heard playing on Walt's car radio as he drives through the desert in the cold open, and which he is singing in the shower at the end of the episode. The song's lyrics reference the vast emptiness of the desert, something *Breaking Bad* also demonstrates over and over again.

SPECIAL INGREDIENTS

LOS ZETAS

Hank speculates to his DEA coworkers that the truck explosion looks like "high-end cartel work," the sort of thing you'd expect to see in Juarez, rather than north of the border. Los Zetas might do this sort of job. Coming to prominence in the late 1990s, Los Zetas are relatively new players in the cartel wars, but they have quickly catapulted onto the center stage of global drug trafficking and control the largest territory of any of the Mexican cartels.

Los Zetas ("the Zs") take their name from the radio code name of high-level Mexican officers. It is believed that Los Zetas were primarily formed from ex–army commandos who deserted the ranks of the Mexican military to work for the Gulf Cartel; around 2010, they broke away from the Gulf Cartel to form their own organization. They are highly organized, well trained, and have been defined by the DEA as being "the most technologically advanced, sophisticated, and dangerous cartel operating in Mexico." It's an apt description for what amounts to a group of Green Berets deciding to run a drug cartel.

Los Zetas are known for brutal tactics to secure drug routes, control of product, and loyalty. Using weapons such as assault rifles and grenade launchers, Los Zetas have carried out attacks on both rival cartel targets and civilian populations with death tolls numbering in the hundreds. Members of Los Zetas have been arrested in connection with some of the worst atrocities in Mexico's bloody drug war, including the massacre of 72 migrant workers headed to the United States in 2010, the burning of a casino that killed 52 in 2011, and the slaughter of 49 people whose decapitated and dismembered corpses were found dumped on a highway in 2012.

POLLEROS (COYOTES) AND "CHICKEN RUNS"

For any number of reasons — including fleeing the ongoing drug-related violence in Mexico — many people are unwilling to go through the long, drawn-out process to get the proper documentation to immigrate into the United States. Often, these desperate people seek out the services of a *pollero* ("chicken herder," also often called a "coyote"), someone specializing in smuggling people across the border from Mexico into the United States on what is known as a "chicken run." It makes sense, since smuggled people are often crammed into dark and tiny compartments, much like transporting poultry to market.

Such illegal border crossings are hazardous at best and lethally dangerous at worst. Coyotes may sneak immigrants across the border in trucks with false compartments or guide them across the desert at night. Due to the danger, coyotes demand high fees, paid up front. An ethical *pollero* takes pains to make sure the crossing is as safe as possible — ensuring the car trunk can be unlocked from inside, plenty of water is available, and so on — but others aren't so picky. Stories of coyotes robbing, abandoning, or sexually assaulting their clients are common, and roughly 150 to 250 people die trying to cross the desert into the United States every year.

Despite the danger, thousands of immigrants still feel it's worth the risk to reach the United States.

3.03

.F.T.

Original air date: April 4, 2010
Written by: George Mastras **Directed by:** Michelle MacLaren

> "All that I've done, all of the sacrifices that I've made for this family, all of it will be for nothing if you don't accept what I've earned." — Walter White

Walt moves back into his house, Jesse ponders what to do next, and Gus holds a meeting.

After his talk with Saul in the last episode, Walt has decided that he is holding all of the cards when it comes to his family and living situation, and so he has moved himself back in. In a masterpiece of psychological dominance, control, and manipulation, he doesn't even try to stop Skyler from calling the police — and he wins the gamble because the only way she can have the cops remove him is to inform them about his meth business, an act that would tear the family apart and drag them all down with him. Walt has drawn a very tight box around Skyler and her only escape is the one she can't take. Walt sees his action as a step in restoring their marriage and life together to "normalcy," a victory after which he can afford to be magnanimous. Skyler, on the other hand, sees it as reducing her role in her marriage, her home, and her family to one that is, at best, marginal. That having been said, Skyler really does have a choice here. She *could* reveal Walt's activities to the police and deal with him once and for all. There would be personal and public consequences to her action, but in all likelihood, Skyler, Junior, Hank, and Marie would be strong enough to survive them. Like Walt, who could get out of the drug business by turning himself in and going into witness protection, Skyler is faced with a choice that would solve her problems, but one that she is unwilling to take.

Walt even comes all the way clean with Skyler, revealing the duffel bag full of cash that he has earned, and he is very intent on her understanding that he has *earned* this money. In Walt's mind, the money is proof of his rationalization about doing everything for the family, proof that he has *provided*. To Walt, the fact that he has brought home enough money to secure the family through Junior's and even Holly's college tuitions should completely make up for every lie he has told, every criminal act he has perpetrated, and even for forcing his way back into Skyler's life against her will.

Skyler, however, isn't buying any of it. At this point she sees the money for what it is: an attempt to buy her off. Walt has severely underestimated his wife and by forcing her into the tightest of corners and imposing his will on her, he has merely activated qualities in Skyler that mirror his own. In the midst of preparing another elaborate family dinner, with Walt chattering on like everything in the world is all right, Skyler drops her bomb. In seducing Ted she has hit Walt in his most tender spot: his pride. He can force her to allow him to live in their house, and he can pretend that everything is going to be all right, but in the end all of that is meaningless, because he can't make her love him. Skyler's affair may be petty and spiteful, but it is also viciously effective. "I fucked Ted." She guts Walt with three words, and then cheerily calls the boys to the dinner table. Walt has met his match, and her name is Skyler.

Jesse is also back in a house that is now unquestionably his, though his entire decor consists of a sleeping bag and an ashtray. In one of the most heartbreaking sequences of the entire series thus far, Jesse repeatedly calls Jane's phone number, again and again and again, just to hear her voicemail message. Until, finally, the number is disconnected and, all alone in his empty house, Jesse has to face the fact that Jane is really gone, and that he will never again hear her voice. After rehab, Jesse is much changed, and perhaps not for the better. His affect is flat, and fundamentally he just doesn't seem to care about anything anymore. His split with his family now seems to be permanent. His bond with Walt is tenuous at best. His friends are largely of the fair-weather variety, and Jane is dead. So Jesse does the one thing he knows how to do: he cooks meth.

Family and psychological troubles are not the only dangers faced by Walt and Jesse. Gus Fring is dealing with much larger troubles for everyone concerned. The murderous twins, now revealed not only to be cartel assassins but also Tuco's cousins and Héctor "Tio" Salamanca's nephews, were the ones who were supposed to drive up from Mexico to pick up Walt and Tuco in "Grilled." Now they and Héctor have sworn a blood feud with Walter White. Gus, the regional boss for the Mexican cartel, can hold them off momentarily, but as Juan Bolsa (Javier Grajeda), Gus's superior in the cartel, reminds him: the cousins are not reasonable men. Walt's game has moved into extraordinarily high-stakes play, and he doesn't even know it.

LAB NOTES

HIGHLIGHT

WALT: "Honestly is good, don't ya think?"

DID YOU NOTICE

* Mike works for Gus, though Saul doesn't know this.
* Juan paints a message on Tortuga's gift: "¡Hola DEA!" We've seen this tortoise in "Negro y Azul."
* Denied the master bath, Walt pees into the kitchen sink, but there is another bath in the house, so he's just peeing in the sink out of sheer spite.
* Walter Jr. and his friend Louis (Caleb Landry Jones, recognizable from the TV series *Friday Night Lights*) are watching *Aqua Teen Hunger Force* while Sky and Walt have their talk in the kitchen.

SHOOTING UP

* A hard yellow light is used again for the cold opening, indicating that the scene takes place in Mexico.
* Rather than flashing forward or back to details directly connected to the action in the episode, this cold open fills in a little detail of the recent pasts of several secondary characters. It's a really nice touch, and helps to make the characters three-dimensional, giving them a "life" outside of the main storyline that goes on whether the audience sees it or not.

TITLE "I.F.T." is short for Skyler's "I fucked Ted."

INTERESTING FACTS

- Hank's DEA boss is known by his title's acronym: "ASAC," or Assistant Special Agent in Charge.
- "I.F.T" is dedicated to "our friend Shari Rhodes." Shari Rhodes was casting director for the first two episodes of *Breaking Bad*, handling local casting in Albuquerque and New Mexico. Born in 1938, Rhodes's first credited role was as a member of the casting department for Steven Spielberg's *Jaws*, and she acted as Spielberg's casting director for his 1977 film *Close Encounters of the Third Kind*. Her one acting credit in a career that spanned 37 years was a small role in "I.F.T." She plays the "Bingo Lady" whose van is stolen by the cousins for Héctor. Rhodes died in 2009 in Santa Fe, New Mexico, after a long struggle with cancer.

SPECIAL INGREDIENTS

INDUSTRIAL CHICKEN FARMING

As the owner of a chain of chicken restaurants, Gus Fring operates a large-scale poultry farm in the desert outside of Albuquerque. While we suspect that no other chicken farm is used as a meeting place for cartel discussions, other unsavory business is conducted at such farms on a regular basis.

If you think of chicken farming as involving kindly Old MacDonald spreading grain for the chickies to peck at, E-I-E-I-O, then you have no idea what your supermarket chicken goes through. Plenty of books and articles are out there to explain just what is involved with getting your shrink-wrapped chicken tenders to the refrigerated shelves in the market, but we'll point out a couple of items.

First, no one — and we mean *no one* — would go into an industrial chicken house for fun. The smell alone will knock you off your feet. The term "chickenshit" might be used to refer to something small and essentially worthless, but if you pack (as many industrial operations do) thousands of birds into a small space, very strong odors result. While life is possibly worse for egg-laying birds (battery cages are a horror that have been banned in a number of European countries), the six-week life of a broiler chicken is hardly a romp on the farm.

In the industrial system, broiler chickens are raised in "growout houses," where often 20,000 birds are stuffed into each 400-foot-long house. That means each bird spends its entire life in less than a square foot of space, which isn't enough room to stretch out its wings. While these structures provide protection from predators, such crowded conditions also mean that ammonia from the chicken manure poisons the air, causing damage to the chickens' respiratory systems, eyes, and feet. Some growout houses have walls that can roll up to permit fresh air and light to enter, but many do not. Broilers are fed a diet of corn and soybean meal with powerful antibiotics added to cut down on the spread of diseases that are rampant when so many animals are crammed into such limited space.

Of course, not all broilers are raised in growout sheds. Some farmers use a movable coop known as a "chicken tractor" or an "ark," which is a covered, floorless framework. Think of it as a cage with grass as the floor. Once the chickens forage one area clear, the chicken tractor is moved to another foraging spot and the first spot has time to regrow using the chickens' manure as natural fertilizer. The mesh allows sunshine and fresh air to circulate while also protecting the chickens from predators such as foxes and hawks. However, this is a more expensive method for raising poultry, since more birds can be crammed into the area of a growout house.

Green Light

Original air date: April 11, 2010
Written by: Sam Catlin **Directed by:** Scott Winant

"I don't believe fear to be an effective motivator. I want investment." — Gustavo Fring

Walt's efforts to control his life aren't working out. Meanwhile, Jesse is cooking again, and Hank has a decision to make.

It's a brand new Jesse Pinkman who opens this episode. Cool, charming, confident, he doesn't even blink when a cop walks in as he's holding out a 'teenth of Blue Magic to the young cashier. Jesse is trying hard to live up to his self-proclaimed role of bad guy and there's more than a little bit of the snake in the Garden of Eden as he convinces the innocent salesgirl to take meth in lieu of money for gas and smokes. The question is whether this is actual confidence or just a side effect of ceasing to give a shit. Judging by Jesse's behavior since he returned from rehab, it is likely the latter.

Walt, on the other hand, is anything but calm and collected. His marriage is on the rocks, Sky's sticking it to him by having a fling with Ted, and when Walt tries to prove that two can play the cheating game, his pass at the beautiful high school principal is laughable and rebuffed with shock and disgust. Walt may have wormed his way back into his house, but his life there isn't turning out the way he planned. Skyler may not have the ability to force him out, but she can make his life there a living hell. Even Walt's fumbling attempt to reclaim his male pride by confronting and beating up

Ted is foiled by a too-heavy potted plant and good solid Plexiglas. Walt spends much of this episode throwing one long tantrum — even after being picked up by Mike and having to sit through a come-to-Jesus talk with Saul, he petulantly taunts Mike as the cleaner removes all of the surveillance devices that he planted in "Caballo Sin Nombre." He also manages to rupture his relationship with Jesse after the latter comes to him with a batch of meth he has cooked using Walt's recipe. Jesse shows off his product to Walt, desperate for validation from the one man who has been something like a mentor to him recently, and Walt crushes him like a bug. Not because Jesse's

(ALBERT L. ORTEGA/PR PHOTOS)

product is inferior, but because it *isn't*. With his marriage and his job in the toilet Walt can't stand the thought that someone might be able to cook meth as well as he does. The fact that he is the best meth cook in the country is the one thing he has left, and even that turns out to be a fallacy.

Meanwhile, Hank has some real problems. He is struggling with his own sense of masculine identity, to the point of provoking fistfights in biker bars, and his panic attacks seem to be getting worse, not better. His boss has arranged for him to go back to El Paso, but that's the last thing Hank wants to do, only he hasn't figured out how to tell Marie that, much less ASAC George Merkert (Michael Shamus Wiles, recognizable from guest spots on *Monk*, *Criminal Minds*, and *Justified*). Hank is looking for an excuse and finds it in the reappearance of Blue Magic out in the county. Hank jumps on the find like a drowning man going after a life preserver, because the Heisenberg case might just be large enough to allow him to justify staying in New Mexico — not just to justify it to his boss, but to himself as well. Dean Norris shows his chops as he gives the viewer a Hank who is wrestling with himself, trying to figure out how and why he doesn't seem to be the guy he always thought he was, and what to do about that fact. It is an exquisite portrayal of a strong man learning to deal with real fear and fundamental uncertainty while still holding onto the things about himself, his job, and the world that he believes are righteous. It's between Jesse's don't-give-a-shit carelessness and Hank's considerable skills as a detective that Hank gets the first big lead in the case: pictures of the RV. When forced to respond to the offer of El Paso, Hank is man enough to be honest with himself and with his boss. He can't go. Hank is an honest man, and no matter how much he might like to avoid certain truths, he just can't — he doesn't allow himself that luxury. He is not Walt.

And behind the scenes is Gus, who makes Walter look like a naked babe when it comes to manipulating people and events. Despite his refusal to work with junkies, Gus buys Jesse's meth. With Mike on his payroll he knows all about Walt's current problems and preoccupations, and the viewer gets the sense that Gus is a man who does not do anything without thinking it through. He is working an angle with this buy, and that can only lead to trouble for Walt.

LAB NOTES

HIGHLIGHT

SAUL: "Speaking as your lawyer, I'm always looking for billable hours, but speaking as your business associate, I'm strongly advising that *you get your shit together!*"

DID YOU NOTICE

- Mike's expression while Saul and Walt talk is like a man who is herding kindergarteners.
- When Marie drops Hank off at the airport it's at the entrance for Wayfarer Airline, the same airline involved in the mid-air collision at the end of season 2.
- Saul's working on a class-action suit around the Wayfarer 515 disaster.
- Gilligan & Co. do a good job of showing the realities of police work. Hank doesn't work like Sherlock Holmes. He does the legwork, going so far as to make a list of "M" names and tracking down every single possibility.
- There's a chalk-drawn scythe on the street in front of Walt's house.

The scythe is symbolic of Santa Muerte, showing that the cousins have not given up on their vendetta yet.

- When taking a phone call in his car, Hank signals and pulls off to the side of the road. The man takes the law (and safety) seriously.
- Walt has a new windshield on his Aztek.

SHOOTING UP

- The cold open relies heavily on handheld camera work, emphasizing the tension as the cop approaches the counter where Jesse holds out the meth to the salesclerk.
- Skyler and Ted's brief sex scene is shown via a distorted reflection among pictures of Ted's estranged family, a shot that creates a nice remove for the viewer while still noting the adulterous aspect of the scene, and sets up Skyler's growing dissatisfaction with the affair.
- Sickly green lighting is again used during Hank's panic attacks, managing to convey a mix of nausea and wrongness.
- The ATM camera's POV of Hank is a great shot, and underscores that while diligence and patience play a role in police work, Hank's intelligence and observational skills do so as well.

TITLE "Green Light" can be seen as having multiple meanings. It may reference the actual green lighting of Hank's panic attacks, the go-ahead to chase down the lead of the RV, or Walt's getting a green light to go back to cooking meth. Or all of the above.

INTERESTING FACTS The groundbreaking David Lynch series *Twin Peaks* (1990–1991) prominently featured a traffic light changing from red to green and back again. Like the traffic light in this episode, there was something ominous about it, as if some power was giving the go-ahead to someone for something to happen. It allowed the viewer to put his own meaning on the swaying light.

SPECIAL INGREDIENTS

CLASS-ACTION LAWSUITS

Saul may be many things, but he's not a lazy man. In addition to providing legal representation to Duke City's prime meth-maker, he's also involved in a class-action lawsuit stemming from the Wayfarer disaster. A class-action lawsuit occurs when multiple plaintiffs have been injured (physically, financially, etc.) from the same cause of action. In a perfect world, a class action allows the little guy to band together with other little guys to take on the Big Bad Corporation who caused the harm in the first place. While one single little guy can't hope to match the resources of a major drug company, or restaurant chain, or airline, a class action allows the playing field to be leveled. A class-action lawsuit has to be certified as such by a judge, who must be persuaded that there are enough plaintiffs to make it practical to proceed down the class-action road. Once that happens, all potential members of the class (in other words, everybody who may have been harmed by the defendants' actions, product, etc.) must be contacted so they have the opportunity to either stay in the class or "opt out" of it. This explains all those "did you take Drug X and were you injured?" commercials on television. If you choose to opt out, you have the right to bring your own lawsuit, but you have no claim on any settlement reached by members of the class action, since you "opted out" of being a member of the class.

Brown v. Board of Education (1954), in which the United States Supreme Court ruled that racial segregation of public schools was unconstitutional, is probably the most well-known class-action lawsuit in America and it was actually the result of five separate class-action lawsuits being consolidated into one.

M ás

Original air date: April 18, 2010
Written by: Moira Walley-Beckett **Directed by:** Johan Renck

> "What does a man do, Walter? A man provides for his family
> . . . a man *provides*. And he does it even when he's not appre-
> ciated, or respected, or even loved. He simply bears up — and
> does it. Because he's a *man*." — Gustavo Fring

*The split between Walt and Jesse widens. Meanwhile, Hank's obsession with the RV
grows, and Skyler has second thoughts about Walt's new career.*

In the cold open to "Más" the RV gets a little bit of its own backstory.
This is entirely appropriate, as the mobile lab has quietly become a character
over the past 24 episodes. The RV is now more than a convenient backdrop
for Walt and Jesse's antics — it has been imbued with meaning and some
very personal history. It is where Walt's descent into darkness and murder
began. It is where Jesse, homeless and alone, crawled for shelter and rest
against the collapse of his world. It has been the scene of desperate bonding
and shattering animosity, and in "Más" the audience learns how it was lifted
from obsolescence in a backyard to become a strange and vital part of Jesse
and Walt's lives, and an iconic feature of the show itself.

Skyler undergoes an interesting near-conversion in this episode. Her affair
with Ted is paling quickly, particularly in the face of his growing insistence
that it become something more permanent and meaningful. As with Jesse
and Jane's big spat in season 2, Gilligan & Co. do a nice job of playing with

gender roles here. It is Ted, not Sky, who is becoming emotionally attached, and Sky, not Ted, who is using the affair to satisfy her various desires, with little or no thought for how those desires might affect him. It's a nicely played role reversal, and as with Jesse and Jane, it works because it's not belabored. In both cases it is exactly how the viewer would expect the characters involved to react.

Skyler is becoming increasingly uncomfortable with things, not least because she finds herself enjoying things like Ted's heated-tile bathroom floor, likely bought with some of the $1 million he embezzled from his own company. Ill-gotten gains can be seductive though, especially if there might be a way to put them to one's own uses, a thought that begins to grow and eat at Skyler more and more after she finds a duffel bag filled with long green bills in the nursery closet. Skyler is traveling her own path of corruption, beginning with her vengeful affair, and now her principles are beginning to weaken under the siren call of all that money. Anna Gunn carries this off with true brilliance, giving a subtle performance that shows all of the pressure beginning to work on Skyler.

Corruption is a common theme in *Breaking Bad*, but the show also has a few incorruptibles, like Hank, who is becoming increasingly obsessed with finding the RV and breaking the Heisenberg case. In fact, doing so has become incredibly important, as Hank sees it as the only way he can redeem himself in the eyes of his coworkers, bosses, and family for his inability to face going back to El Paso. Hank is still falling apart, and still desperately trying to find something to latch onto. Unfortunately, like Walt, he overlooks what's right under his nose: Marie. The snarky, bitchy, klepto of seasons 1 and 2 has become something more. There is no mistaking her love for Hank and the genuine worry she feels for him. Hank has convinced himself that he let her down by leaving the fast track to promotion, but in reality what Marie cares about is him, not a condo in D.C. Betsy Brandt deserves high praise here, as perhaps no character on the show has grown so much and so organically as Marie Schrader. Alongside Dean Norris, Brandt has given the audience a real marriage, with all of the rough edges, laughter, and tears, backed with a titanium core of love, respect, and commitment.

In the end, of course, it is Walt who drives the show, and Gus Fring who knows exactly which buttons to push to get Walt to cook for him. Despite Walt's cocky protestations to the contrary, he is completely driven by pride, and Gus knows exactly how to use that to drive him. At the end of the day, it's not the money or the incredible new underground Superlab that brings Walt back into the game. Rather, Walt's motivation is sheer masculine pride, and Gus plays on that need of Walt's with a maestro's virtuosity. Walt makes a terrible mistake thinking that he is Gus's equal in any way, shape, or form, or that Gus is in any way transparent. Walt has effectively burned all of his bridges with Jesse, perhaps his one true ally in all of this, and has even moved out of his house and signed the divorce papers. Walt is cutting strings just when he is putting himself in a position where he will likely desperately need them to stay alive.

LAB NOTES

HIGHLIGHT

PAMELA: "I'm half as qualified and twice the price of a therapist."

DID YOU NOTICE

- Walt's production quota for Gus is 200 pounds of Blue Magic per week. This is for a three-month contract, so that's roughly 2400 pounds of meth.
- Skyler allows Walt to take care of Holly for the first time since he forced his way back into their house.
- Jesse takes care of Walt's new windshield, reducing it once again to a spider web of cracks, just like after Wayfarer 515.
- Hank finds a picture of Jesse, Skinny Pete, and Combo in Combo's old room from the night at the strip club seen in the cold open.
- Combo's real name was Christian Ortega.

NITPICKS Pamela, Skyler's lawyer, makes her last appearance in this episode, and appears to have simply been a device to let the audience hear what Skyler is thinking about everything going on in her life. Though the scenes between the two of them are well played by Anna Gunn and Julie Dretzin (who has been on *30 Rock* and *Six Feet Under*), the use of this device is unusually clumsy for Gilligan & Co.

SHOOTING UP

- The cold open combines both a flashback that fills in some backstory, and a setup for the clue Hank finds at the end of the episode, making it a cousin to the circular episode structure used so often by Gilligan & Co. in season 2.

- ♦ The lovely scene of Walt in the Superlab is superbly done. The scene's almost Disney-like soundtrack of Peder's "Timetakesthetimetimetakes" combines with truly loving camera work as Walt, a kid in a candy store, explores the place. With this sequence, the Superlab is firmly established as an important place.

TITLE "Más" is Spanish for "more," acting as a counterpoint to the season opener "No Más" (no more), and also referring to Walt's return to the meth trade.

INTERESTING FACTS "Más" was dedicated to Gwyn Savage, who created the company FilmSavage, LLC, specializing in bringing local New Mexico talent and services to film and television shows filming in the area. She worked in the casting department for extras on *Breaking Bad* for seasons 1 and 2, though her work was uncredited. She died in 2010 at age 44.

SPECIAL INGREDIENTS

HEATED FLOORS (BACK TO ANCIENT ROME)

At first, the heated floor in Ted's bathroom signals luxury to Skyler. However, as her discomfort with the affair progresses, she tries to remove herself from this sign of opulence by tossing a towel on the floor to provide a terry-cloth barrier between her bare toes and the illicit extravagance.

Humankind has always sought ways to stay comfortable and warm. Engineers living during the Roman Empire came up with a fairly dependable system of underfloor heating that wasn't all that different from modern systems. Considered a necessary part of any wealthy Roman household (especially those located in the colder reaches of the empire, such as in Britannia), these hypocausts kept socially important Romans toasty warm. As the villa was being constructed, brick pillars were used to support the floor and spaces were left inside the walls to allow hot air from the furnace to circulate both beneath the floor and through the walls. The furnace was manned by slave labor whose task it was to keep the home fires burning and also to keep the system clean, as soot buildup could easily ignite. Since such systems were so labor-intensive to build and maintain, they were very expensive. Therefore, having such a system in your house was seen as a sign of immense wealth and devotion to personal comfort. Interestingly, once the Roman Empire ended, this technology seems to have simply been abandoned, bitterly cold British winters notwithstanding.

3.06

Sunset

Original air date: April 25, 2010
Written and directed by: John Shiban

"Name one thing in this world that's *not* negotiable."
— Walter White

Walt starts a new job and Jesse starts a new business. Meanwhile, Hank follows a hot lead, and Gus holds a meeting.

The Salamanca cousins may have taken a break last episode, but, as the cold open to "Sunset" reveals, they are still very much out there, still focused on killing Walt, and utterly vicious. Perhaps even more frightening than killing anyone who gets in their way, including cops, is the cousins' willingness to push Gustavo Fring. Their stillness and silence match his own, and their message is clear: they are not going away, and they will have their vengeance for Tuco's death.

Still blissfully unaware of all of this, Walt has moved into much nicer, newer digs, complete with furniture, and he's excited about his first day at work. As the cherry on top of the Superlab cake, Gus has provided him with a dream assistant in Gale Boetticher (David Costabile who has been in the movie *Lincoln*, and on *Suits*, *Flight of the Conchords*, and *The Wire*). Gale is a man who shares Walt's passion for chemistry, is eager to put himself under Walt's tutelage, can talk to Walt on his own intellectual level, makes fantastic coffee, has excellent rationalization skills, and even inspires Walt to read poetry. If Walt could have designed the perfect person to mentor, it would have been Gale, and they get on famously, working together as a well-honed team on the very first day and even managing to play some chess between steps in the cook. This is, without the smallest doubt, the ultimate working environment for Walt. The Superlab is cutting edge, safe, and well removed from the harsher realities of the drug world. Walt is working with someone who marches to the beat of the same drum he does, and he's making millions of dollars for his work to boot. It is Walt's perfect job.

Unfortunately, it may already be in danger of blowing up in his face.

Cast out by Walt, Jesse still has the mobile lab in the RV and he's already proven that he can make Walt's recipe, so he's back in business with Badger and Skinny Pete, promising them that this time, things will be different. The RV is still parked on the lot owned by Clovis (Tom Kiesche, recognizable from roles on *Monk*, *Big Love*, and *Weeds*), and Jesse has learned enough to keep low and be cautious. Unfortunately, he throws all of that to the wind when he hears that Walt is going to destroy the RV and tears off to stop him — with Hank following close behind. This sets up one of the most nail-biting standoffs of the series, with Walt and Jesse inside the RV, Hank's SUV blocking it from behind, and Old Joe (Larry Hankin), the inexplicably helpful junkyard-lawyer, making sure that Hank gets a warrant before he busts into the vehicle. Just when it looks like Walt and Jesse's criminal careers are over, Walt gets the truly despicable inspiration to call Hank's cell with a fake message about Marie being badly injured in a car accident.

As planned, the message sends Hank screaming away to get to the side of his presumably injured wife. The interesting thing about this is that Walt probably wouldn't do the same thing for Skyler. After all, he has already chosen meth over his family when he missed Holly's birth in order to make his first deal with Gus in "Mandala" and "Phoenix." Unlike Walt, Hank tears out of the junkyard as fast as he can, everything else instantly relegated to unimportance next to Marie. Walt may talk about being a family man, but Hank acts like one. The terror, relief, and fury that flow across Hank's face as he enters the hospital, can't find Marie, and then gets a call from her and realizes he's been played are incredible, and Dean Norris makes every second real. Walt has saved his own hide once again, but at what cost? He who pokes bears with sticks is likely to get eaten eventually.

With Hank away, the RV and all the evidence it contains can be destroyed in a lovely montage as Walt and Jesse look on, more than a little sadly. Indeed, before Jesse and Hank's arrival, Walt had taken a quiet moment to pause and run his hands over the equipment, smiling slightly, saying goodbye, as do we. The scene is filmed with obvious care and affection, saying a lingering farewell to a favorite character. The end of the RV marks a fundamental change for *Breaking Bad*. Things can never be the same again. Finally, as the sun sets over the remains of the RV, Gus and the cousins meet for a parley in the desert, and Gus makes them an offer they can't refuse: Hank.

LAB NOTES

HIGHLIGHT
SAUL: "Even the starship *Enterprise* has a self-destruct! I'm just sayin'!"

DID YOU NOTICE
- The Native American police officer has a tag hanging from his rearview mirror that reads "Homeland Security" on one side and on the other has an old sepia-tone photograph of Native American warriors above the words "Fighting Terrorism Since 1492."
- Things tend to go "ding" around the cousins. The flagpole and wind chimes in the cold open, and the fryer bell as they wait in Los Pollos, are all subtle reminders of Don Héctor's invisible presence.
- Jesse has become protective of his house, going so far as to tell Badger to stop marking up the floor with his *Riverdance* imitation.
- The cousins have set up an altar to Santa Muerte in the house they've occupied.
- The cousins speak for the first time in this episode, in answer to Gus's question, "What do you want?" One says, *"Tu sabes,"* which means "You know."

SHOOTING UP
- Again a hard yellow light is used in the cold opening, although this time the scene is in the U.S. It is possible that the scene takes place on one of the many Native American reservations around Albuquerque, and therefore, at least theoretically, in "foreign" territory.
- During the killing of the police officer, the camera focuses on the closer cousin, reducing the axe-swinging one and his victim to blurred

images in the background, cushioning the violence for the viewer somewhat while still making it perfectly clear.

- That trademark *Breaking Bad* "shoot up through something clear" POV shot is used to shoot up through Jesse's clear glass coffee table as he talks business with Badger and Skinny Pete.
- The montage showing the wrecking of the RV has already been mentioned above but it is worth noting, particularly the choice to eliminate the crushing sounds in favor of superimposed music, removing the sequence somewhat from reality and adding to the melancholic nostalgia of the entire scene.

TITLE "Sunset" is another title with multiple meanings, referencing both Gus's meeting with the cousins and the end of the RV era of *Breaking Bad*, which also takes place at sunset.

INTERESTING FACTS

- The use of the familiar form of the second-person singular when Leonel (Daniel Moncada) addressed Gus, *"Tu sabe,"* may be significant. The *"tu"* is a familiar form of address that may indicate a subtle insult to Gus, coming from someone who is his subordinate in the cartel structure. The more formal *"usted,"* however, is rarely used anymore in Mexico and Hispanic Central and South America, so this may be reading too much into things.
- Gale quotes a line from the Walt Whitman poem "When I Heard the Learn'd Astronomer," which is all about the dichotomy of studying something versus wondering at the marvel of it:

    When I heard the learn'd astronomer;
    When the proofs, the figures, were ranged in columns before me;
    When I was shown the charts and the diagrams, to add, divide, and
        measure them;
    When I, sitting, heard the astronomer, where he lectured with much
        applause in the lecture-room,
    How soon, unaccountable, I became tired and sick;
    Till rising and gliding out, I wander'd off by myself,
    In the mystical moist night-air, and from time to time,
    Look'd up in perfect silence at the stars.

SPECIAL INGREDIENTS

PROBABLE CAUSE FOR SEARCHING VEHICLES VERSUS SEARCHING RESIDENCES

In the United States, the Fourth Amendment to the U.S. Constitution requires that a search warrant be issued before law enforcement can start rifling through a person's house, clothing, or possessions. There are very specific rules for how and when a search warrant is issued, one of which is that the warrant has to describe specifically what is to be searched, and what (or who) is to be seized. Like all constitutional guarantees, this one isn't absolute — there are certain circumstances in which law enforcement can act without a warrant. The biggest exception is if you freely consent to the search; in that case, no warrant is necessary. But Walt and Jesse, crouched in the RV in the junkyard, certainly have no intention of consenting to Hank's search.

As *Breaking Bad* shows, the rules are stricter for searching a person's "domicile" than they are for searching a person's "vehicle." The reasoning behind the different rules is that you have more of an "expectation of privacy" in your home (that's your "domicile," by the way — you only have one permanent domicile, even if you have multiple "residences") than you do in your vehicle, since you (usually) don't live in your car. Also, since a motor vehicle can easily move, there is reason to allow the police to begin the search more quickly, before any evidence or contraband can be moved out of their jurisdiction. For a search of a vehicle, police have to have probable cause, but don't necessarily need a formal warrant.

So which is an RV — a vehicle or a residence?

Like most legal answers, it depends. Is the RV being used as living quarters? Is it hooked up to utilities? Is it licensed? Is it mobile or is it up on blocks? In other words, is it being treated like a residence? These questions came up in the 1985 Supreme Court case *California v. Carney* and the court found that a readily movable motor home is subject to the lower standard of vehicles.

Maybe Hank should have gone ahead and entered.

WALT WHITMAN

Gale Boetticher quotes "When I Heard the Learn'd Astronomer" which is contained in Whitman's *Leaves of Grass*. Walter "Walt" Whitman (1819–1892) was called "America's poet" by Ezra Pound and his influence on American poetry is undeniable. Whitman is often given the title of "father of free verse" to acknowledge his mastery of this poetic form, which does not rely on traditional meter or rhyme, yet often retains a sense of structure through the use of repeated phrases and punctuation. Whitman's best-known work (hopefully more for its enduring poetic qualities than for being obscene in its depiction of sexuality, as it was called upon its publication in 1855), *Leaves of Grass*, uses these techniques. Whitman paid for the first printing with his own money and continued to revise this epic up until his death nearly 40 years later.

Scholars and researchers debate Whitman's sexuality, with many finding evidence of homosexuality or bisexuality in his writings. Whether or not Whitman was what would commonly be considered "gay" may never be a settled issue, but without a doubt, his brilliance in capturing the delight brought about by living continues to resonate with readers.

One Minute

3.07

Original air date: May 2, 2010
Written by: Thomas Schnauz **Directed by:** Michelle MacLaren

"La familia es todo." — Héctor Salamanca

Hank has a series of very bad days. Meanwhile, Walt and Jesse make a deal.

In another flashback, the cold open of "One Minute" gives us a look into the past and reveals the driving motivations of the mysterious and terrifying cousins. In his brutally delivered lesson, a much younger Héctor Salamanca gives the pre-teen cousins a chilling reminder of what is at the core of *Breaking Bad*: family. This explains the Salamanca family's vendetta against Walt and his own family: a vendetta that Héctor widened to include Hank, whose picture is now placed on the grown-up cousins' altar to Santa Muerte in place of Walt's.

Career-wise, however, Hank is pretty much taking care of ending things all by himself. The audience has previously seen Hank worried, afraid, irritable, happy, and angry, but never has the viewer seen him in a truly out-of-control rage. His beat-down of Jesse is vicious and unexpected, and all the more effective for being so. Gilligan & Co. do an outstanding job of portraying violence realistically, particularly its suddenness. Real fights where at least one opponent's objective is to seriously injure or kill the other are rarely long, drawn-out affairs. It takes frighteningly little time to really hurt someone, as Hank demonstrates in the opening scene.

However, unlike the show's criminal characters, including Walt and Jesse,

Hank — having come to something approaching his right mind again — does not attempt to hide what he's done or flee the scene. Instead, he calls the police, the EMTs, and his boss, and stays through the ensuing investigation. Hank takes responsibility for his actions, even when the consequences aren't in his favor.

This episode marks a turning point for Hank in many ways, but most especially, it shows him finally accepting and dealing with his fears and the reality that he isn't the man he thought he was. In two incredible scenes, Dean Norris and Betsy Brandt bring the strength of Hank and Marie's marriage to the screen. When Hank is at his lowest, Marie is right there, holding him tightly as he finally loses it in the elevator, in her arms, away from prying eyes. Later as Hank prepares to give his final statement, he tells her that he isn't the man he thought he was, but he doesn't seem too upset at being the man he actually is: "I swear to God, Marie, I think the universe is trying to tell me something and I'm finally ready to listen." He goes in to the meeting, tells the absolute truth, and again accepts the consequences, coming out a lighter, freer man, looking forward to going home and surprising Marie with flowers and making up for his attitude over the past weeks. Of course, he never gets the chance. The final shootout with the cousins is incredibly intense, but despite PTSD, sheer terror, and confusion, Hank demonstrates a level of courage and tenacity that is truly staggering, and the cousins meet their match.

Though Hank's storyline is central to the episode, Jesse's runs a close second. Hank has truly messed him up and he's had enough. Aaron Paul turns in a tour de force performance in this episode. The two furious monologues he delivers to Walt serve as damning indictment of Walt's pride and arrogance. Jesse bears some responsibility for his choices, but he is correct in laying the blame at Walt's feet for the way his life has turned recently. Though he doesn't know it, when he tells Walt that he is more alone than ever, he is snapping at the right person because Walt murdered Jane. Finally, he dismisses Walt utterly by condemning him as being driven only by selfishness and self-centeredness. Behind all of this is the wounded rage of a young man who is desperately seeking some kind of validation from a father figure. Jesse put his trust and hope in Walt and has been utterly betrayed without hesitation or compunction. Astonishingly, Jesse's tirades actually get through to Walt, and the man *apologizes*. As much as he can, anyway, admitting that

Jesse's meth is as good as his own, which, for Walt, is no small thing. Their partnership is restored at the expense of Gale, who is so innocently confused at Walt's sudden turn that it's like watching a puppy being kicked. The consequences of Walt's actions, as well as the number of people affected by them, continue to increase.

LAB NOTES

HIGHLIGHT

SAUL: "You're now officially the cute one of the group. Paul, meet Ringo. Ringo, Paul."

DID YOU NOTICE

◆ *"La familia es todo"* means "Family is all." This is one of the major themes of *Breaking Bad* and recurs again and again as the motivation behind one character after another.

◆ In the cold open, the young Marco takes Leonel's action figure and breaks the head off. In the final scene, Hank's last desperate shot effectively blows off the adult Marco's head.

◆ Also in the cold open, a younger, virile Héctor Salamanca is seated in a wooden chair decorated on the sides and back with carved wheels, foreshadowing his eventual confinement in a wheelchair.

◆ After Jesse's call to Walt accepting a renewed partnership, the scene fades out with him gazing at the cartoonish image on the pain chart for "the worst pain imaginable."

SHOOTING UP

◆ The cold open is filmed using a different yellow lighting from the lighting that is usually used for *Breaking Bad* scenes taking place in Mexico. While it does serve to set the scene as taking place outside of the U.S., this softer yellow light is more reminiscent of the blue lighting used in Walt's grad-school flashbacks in ". . . And the Bag's in the River." The softer quality signals the viewer that the scene is taking place in the past.

◆ There are several instances of the now familiar up-and-through POV in "One Minute." As Héctor is drowning Marco, the camera looks up through the bottom of the metal tub that holds Héctor's beers, and the young Marco's head is slammed against the bottom, which is transparent to the camera. The upwards POV is seen again as the adult Marco opens and removes his axe from the trunk of his car in the final moments of the episode.

• After Hank receives the ominous call warning him that he has "one minute" before the cousins come for him, Gilligan & Co. actually take a real-time minute to ratchet up the tension as Hank calls his partner Gomez, looks around the parking lot, and starts sweating. It's a brilliant buildup, and one of the longest minutes in television.

• At the end of the episode, two elevated shots are used to move the viewpoint from being relatively close to Hank and Marco's bodies to a point showing the entire parking lot and the sprawled, blood-surrounded forms of Hank, Marco, Leonel, and an unlucky passerby.

TITLE "One Minute" refers not only to the mysterious warning call that Hank receives before the cousins' attack, but also references Héctor's words while drowning young Marco: "How much longer do you think he has down there? One minute?"

INTERESTING FACTS The brothers Marco and Leonel Salamanca are played by real life brothers Luis and Daniel Moncada. While Leonel was Daniel Moncada's first role as an actor, Luis Moncada began his acting career in 2002 as Smiley of the Fighting Fridas on *American Family*. The actors that play the younger versions of Marco and Leonel, Ruben Munoz-Soto and Victor Munoz-Soto, also appear for the first time on TV in this episode.

SPECIAL INGREDIENTS

JHPS AND THE WINCHESTER "BLACK TALON"
The cousins need to go shopping for a few things — among them, two military-level bulletproof vests. They are dealing with a seller who swears he can get his hands on anything, including "Black Death" ammunition. This appears to be a fictionalized version of jacketed hollow point (JHP) bullets

and the name suggests that the model is the Black Talon, which was one of the most notorious JHPs put on the market.

What makes hollow point bullets so deadly is a tiny dent in the tip. When such a bullet enters a soft target (like a human body), pressure is created in the dent that forces the metal of the bullet around the inside edge of the dent to expand outward, at incredibly rapid speed. This expansion decreases the distance the bullet travels (so there's less chance of the bullet exiting the body and hitting someone else), but it also causes extreme tissue damage. A jacketed hollow point bullet is coated in a harder metal, such as copper-coated steel to increase the strength of the bullet. In short, such ammunition is designed to do maximum damage to the human body.

Black Talons were manufactured by Winchester Ammunition from 1991 to 2000 and were available for both the law enforcement and civilian markets. While in all major respects, Black Talons were a fairly standard JHP, an urban legend developed around them. According to this legend, Black Talons were designed to rip up your innards with their expanding razor-sharp claws. While not inherently worse than any other JHP bullets (all of which cause horrific injuries when fired into a human body), Black Talons would not remain on the civilian market for long.

In 1993, Black Talon bullets were used in mass shootings on each coast of the United States. The first was on July 1 at a San Francisco law office. Eight people were killed and another 15 were shot. The second took place the same year on December 7 on the Long Island Rail Road commuter train in New York. Six people were killed and another 19 injured by the shooter. Black Talons were removed from the public market, although they continued to be sold to law enforcement until 2000.

UNIVERSAL PAIN ASSESSMENT TOOL

Hospitals often use "pain charts" to have patients communicate their level of pain and one of these is seen hanging in Jesse's hospital room. More properly called the "Universal Pain Assessment Tool," these charts have cartoon faces grimacing as the pain becomes more severe and unbearable. Often, the faces are printed in different colors, with green indicating no pain and a deep red indicating severe pain. The idea is that a patient can simply point to the appropriate cartoon to get across just how much pain they are in at a given moment. These charts can be very useful, as people have vastly different tolerance levels for pain. Still, the idea of self-assessment based on pointing at a cartoon frowny-face seems to go against the current trend in American medicine for treatments that are often centered on high-tech and quite expensive machines that go *ping*!

CREATING THE PERFECT ICE CREAM SUNDAE:
AN INTERVIEW WITH MICHAEL SLOVIS

Michael Slovis served as the director of photography for 44 episodes of *Breaking Bad*, beginning in season 2. He also directed four episodes of the show — "Kafkaesque" in season 3, "Cornered" in season 4, and "Live Free or Die" and "Confessions" in season 5. Mr. Slovis was kind enough to sit down with us to talk about working on the show.

GUFFEY: How did you come to be involved with *Breaking Bad?*
SLOVIS: I came on at the beginning of the second season. My friend, Adam Bernstein, had directed episodes two and three of the first season and Vince Gilligan went to him and asked him whose name he would throw into the list for this job. He put my name in and fortunately for me, I got the job. The film industry is really based on personal recommendations. That's really how it works: it's really just a word of mouth industry and it's not very big, so people know what's going on.

GUFFEY: You do some amazing stuff — of course there's the famous POV shots that have become the show's trademark, especially "the up-and-through" where you get either a bottom-level POV or you're actually shooting up through what would be a solid, opaque bottom in reality. But in an interview you mentioned that you are not necessarily a great big fan of

these trademark shots, so how do you balance between becoming too cheesy with that and doing it right?

SLOVIS: Well, it's not that I'm not a big fan of them, it's that I'm not a big fan of using them *too often*. And I think that they lose their potency when you use them too much. I don't like doing them gratuitously. I love the shots, it's just that I like to use them judiciously and to an end, whether that end is emotional or poetic story, I like using them for a purpose rather than just because it's a neat shot. I don't like doing any shot that draws you out of the story too much and doesn't emotionally move the story along, and that shot could be a very simple close-up, or a wide shot, or one of the POV shots. I just don't think that the shots should draw that much attention to themselves, to the point of pulling you out of the story. I want people to feel that it was the best way to tell the story at that moment.

That's really what I look for in any shot. When I was shooting very early on, at *CSI*, a young director came to me and he had designed this big old techno-crane shot and we were gonna move all over the place and he said "Isn't it a great shot?" and I said "Yes, it's a wonderful shot but does it tell the story?" There are shots that we've done that did not end up in the show or were designed in pre-production that did not end up in the show. Vince [Gilligan] has this analogy that the show is like an ice cream sundae. A beautiful ice cream sundae [contains] a little chocolate sauce and some nuts and some whipped cream and a cherry on top. But if you take a scoop of ice cream and you cover it with marshmallow and you cover it with pineapple and you cover it with nuts and syrup and you cover it with chocolate and you take that and cover that with fresh pineapple and whipped cream and more of everything, you have a sloppy mess, as opposed to a beautiful, wonderful, nice, delicious, gorgeous looking ice cream sundae.

GUFFEY: One thing I've always enjoyed throughout *Breaking Bad* is that nothing really gets in the way of the story.

SLOVIS: Well, I thank you for that because when people tell me that, that is the nicest compliment ever and, if you really look at the show, I mean, really study it and look at the shots — the shots are very simple. There's very little that is a fancy, fancy shot. What *is* great about the storytelling — and I call it the storytelling because it's not the photography, it's not the writing, it's not the acting, it's not the performances, it's not the art direction stuff, the makeup, it's the amalgam of everything — is that sometimes it's all in place and every single stone is supporting the arch like a wonderful, philharmonic that's doing some great piece of music, and it just all comes together and that's when the sum of the individual elements is much greater as a single entity.

GUFFEY: You can tell you are passionate about your art, about what you're doing, and about telling the story. While in looking at it and just breaking it down, the shots themselves may not be super fancy, but the compositions that you use convey so much information visually that it would take much longer to convey through verbal exposition.

SLOVIS: Well, we only have 44 minutes to tell the story, and eight days to shoot the show, so every single shot has to advance the story. Vince has given us the power to tell the story as best we can and as we see it. He does an amazing job of letting us know what the story is at that moment and then he says, "Go ahead and tell the story of these two people at this moment as best you can."

GUFFEY: Who would you cite as your influences as a cinematographer?

SLOVIS: I really, really like the work of Caleb Deschanel a lot. [Deschanel has been nominated five times for the Academy Award for Cinematography, including nominations for *The Right Stuff* in 1983 and *The Natural* in 1984. He's also the father of actresses Emily and Zooey Deschanel.] And there's not a cinematographer working in film or television or commercials or anything that doesn't owe a great deal of gratitude to Gregg Toland, who in *Citizen Kane* broke open American artistic film storytelling. I think that, for me, Caleb Deschanel brought a European aesthetic to American filmmaking. Lots of people carried on after, but British and American cinematographers have attained such a high level of artistry and technique at this point that we just have very few limits on us. The limits that are there right now are purely budgetary and schedule. In terms of what it is that's available for us to tell story, the film stocks right now — if you're lucky enough to be shooting film — are the best that they've ever been and the stories, especially in television, are just getting great. Right now [television has] been invaded by people who want to tell great stories if they can and there's a lot of them out there.

GUFFEY: I know that the house you had been originally using for Jesse Pinkman's, or his aunt's house, was sold and that you had a lot of input into designing the set during season 3.

SLOVIS: Yeah, it was my idea to build that. They were going to try to go to location because what ends up happening on a show like Breaking Bad, our budgets are very tight; it's not a show that was flush with money. Everybody has to function on a budget. There's nothing wrong with that; it's a good thing, actually, and it helps to generate creativity — limits are not bad. However, they were planning on going in a different direction. We generally don't build sets for things we're only going to use once. When we were designing that party scene [in "Thirty-Eight Snub"] for [director] Michelle MacLaren there was just no way we could have shot that as effectively as we did in the location. So, when I asked them what was coming down the pike and they thought that we would be in Jesse's house more — and indeed we were in there quite a lot in subsequent episodes — I said we shouldn't be building this other thing, we should absolutely build the Pinkman living room. We did and it was a lifesaver, it really was.

GUFFEY: You get so many different angles and points of access with that set.

SLOVIS: Let me tell you something about that — there's a name that's almost never mentioned in any of the publicity that I read and he is the foundation, cornerstone, *angel* of our set and his name is Mark Freeborn, the production designer. I get credit for things that Mark does. Mark is a genius. Mark knows so well how to design something so that it looks beautiful on film, maybe not even when you're standing there, but when it's on film. Mark designed that living room. Mark designed the Superlab. Mark designed the DEA office that we used in the last two seasons. Mark designed Gus's office at Los Pollos Hermanos. The guy is remarkable. He's probably more responsible for shows getting done beautifully and on time and on budget than any other person around there. Mark redesigned the interior of the Winnebago so that it was more effective and more efficient to shoot. Everything you see coming up in sets for the last eight [episodes], Mark did. The greatest compliment to Mark Freeborn that I've heard was that most people think that we shoot that entire show on location, and we don't. The White house was a set. Gus's office was a set. Pinkman's was a set. The Superlab, obviously, was a set. All the interior hospitals after season 2 were a set. The interior of the car wash down by the register is a set. Previous to Mark, Rob Wilson King also did a beautiful, beautiful job. The interior of Jesse's apartment in season 2, where Jane dies, that was a set. The interior of the Winnebago was a set, designed by each of those production designers. The basement below Walt's house is a set. The closet where he digs a hole and finds the rotten wood is a set. These are all created spaces by Mark Freeborn and his predecessor, Robb Wilson King. Robb designed the White house, the interior White house. It was a great space to shoot. I loved shooting in that space.

GUFFEY: You said you don't use fancy shots very much but in "Over," when Jesse is getting his first shot of heroin from Jane and he floats up and up and up, above ceiling height, it's a wonderful shot that works so well because it's one of the few times where the shot goes into a kind of weird fantasy element. Then in "Cornered" when Walt's framed in the trap door space and there's that wonderful heartbeat sound, you just pull up and up and up and up, again, beyond what would be the height of the ceiling, to make that a well-like space.

SLOVIS: Well, the truth of the matter is they were not simple to execute but they are not very difficult shots. The one coming up through the closet and you're looking down on [Walt] underneath the floor — the biggest problem with that, and the reason that camera bounces around a little bit, is that we had to have a piece of truss that came down. The camera was looking straight down on the truss and pulling straight up with chain winches, that's it. With Aaron [Paul] being pulled up out of the bed, that was a very simple shot as well. We actually built a rig that Aaron laid on and we hoisted him up to the ceiling of the studio, looking straight down with the camera rigged right over him. Those are very good examples of what I was talking about before; they're not difficult shots to execute — it's basically a close-up of a guy as we drift up — but they are so well-conceived for that moment in time that you don't even think about the fact that you see the set when Aaron drifts up. It fits the story perfectly and it's a great example of what we were talking about earlier, they're perfect examples. The only thing that's different about them is that other people haven't done it and that comes directly as a result of the encouragement and support of Vince Gilligan, Sony, and AMC. I'm telling you that you need all the elements. You need the script and you need the support of the network and the production company and all the executives and your showrunner. All those elements have to come along, for somebody like me to go, "Hey, this is what we'd like to do."

Breaking Bad was kind of a perfect storm. AMC was building a brand. They were ex-filmmakers so they all thought cinematically. TVs were getting bigger. When we started, TVs were these big 60-inch side-lit LEDs so, before that you couldn't use high-resolution to tell the story. You needed to go in close or else people couldn't see what was going on. So, here's this perfect storm of the story we wanted to tell and the vehicle for telling it, all coming together, all at the right time. We were totally conscious of the changes in technology. Most showrunners and networks will tell their people that are out in the field making their TV shows, "Don't come back without coverage." Vince said, "I don't care about the coverage; don't come back without the wide shots."

GUFFEY: And you mentioned earlier that you were shooting with film stock.
SLOVIS: Yep. All film. For specialty shots, we would sometimes use specialty cameras; sometimes digital, but 98 percent to 99 percent of the show is shot on Kodak film and that's another change I made, actually when I first got

there. The first season was shot on Fuji film. I thought that Kodak was a much better match and we seemed to have been right on that call. Here's another advantage to film: right now, Sony is retransferring every frame of all five seasons into 4K for the TVs that are coming up in the future. You can't do that when you shoot digitally unless you originate 4K or 6K [Editor's Note: "4K" and "6K" are also known as "Ultra High Definition" cameras and TVs. The names come from the number of vertical pixels in the resolution, approximately 4000 or 6000 respectively. For a sense of what the numbers mean, at the time of writing most standard HDTVs have a vertical pixel resolution of 1080, or 1K], but they can take film and transfer it to any technology that's coming down the pike.

GUFFEY: Something I definitely wanted to talk to you about is the power in the empty spaces of the scrub desert around Albuquerque. There are images of this wonderful big sky, huge landscape, and these tiny people doing stuff in the wide open, but it's the only place they can do this truly horrific criminal behavior and not be observed.

SLOVIS: You also have to realize that if you ever go to this area of the country, it's vast and civilization is in little pockets. That's what really strikes you about that place: the size of the sky and the color of the desert.

GUFFEY: It comes through so well with what you've done. There are several places filmed where it's abandoned human habitation; the desert has slowly taken over but there's a doll here, an old bicycle there. How much of that is props and set work?

SLOVIS: That's another function of the art director, production designers. They go out and they literally find these places. That was a found location that was tweaked into what it was by adding the car and the clothesline, but the hole that they fell into was already there. The story can start to take shape based on what they really find in these locations and the writers are certainly not against adapting it.

GUFFEY: You often use different lighting to indicate different places. Particularly, in "Salud" when Gus finally gets his revenge after 20 years; the light is harsher and yellower. Was that a deliberate choice, to indicate "we're in a different country, different place," different style?

SLOVIS: Yep. Exactly. I filter the cameras. The cameras are all filtered when we shoot. There's a palette that I use, a specific filtration exterior in Albuquerque, a different filtration that I use in Mexico, and then in urban Albuquerque I use none. What I'm able to do is to go against that and jar you out if I want to, if I care to. We always do that. The show is handheld, but if we decide to go very static people get uncomfortable and they realize, "Oh, my goodness, something's different about this." These are all parts of visual language that we use.

GUFFEY: Some of your most marvelous shots, in my opinion anyway, are very simple. You're focused on Bryan Cranston, or Aaron Paul, or Anna Gunn, and it's just them and the camera and they are so good, even when they don't say anything.

SLOVIS: I totally agree. My favorite shot is of Bryan Cranston deciding to let Krysten Ritter die in "Phoenix." It's just a close-up of a guy and it's my favorite shot of the series.

GUFFEY: What's next for you after *Breaking Bad*?

SLOVIS: I'm gonna spend the next nine months just directing and not shooting at all because, after Breaking Bad it's very difficult to find something that's not a letdown, for me at least. I'm very, very appreciative.

3.08

See You

Original air date: May 9, 2010
Written by: Gennifer Hutchison **Directed by:** Colin Bucksey

"I'm told the assassin who survived is gravely injured. It's doubtful that he'll live. Now thank me and shake my hand."
— Gustavo Fring

Marie, Walt, and the rest of the family wait for news about Hank's condition. Meanwhile, Jesse waits to start cooking in the new lab.

There are few hells as existential as a hospital waiting room when someone you care about is undergoing an extensive emergency procedure. There is something inescapable about it, and no matter how much one really doesn't want to be there, not being there is worse. This is the hell Walt's family, especially Marie and Walter Jr., inhabit for the entirety of this episode. Overwhelmed by grief, Marie desperately looks for someone to blame, and finds a handy target in Steve Gomez and ASAC Merkert. She then turns on Walt, actually finding the absolutely correct person to blame, but since she never knows it, she apologizes for lashing out at him. Betsy Brandt again delivers an exquisite performance. She's so scattered with grief, her mind desperately trying to focus on something other than Hank, but everything she latches onto always leads back to him. RJ Mitte really delivers in this episode as well. Junior is barely holding himself together because, after all, for the past few months, Hank has been more of a consistent father figure to him than Walt. In one of the most touchingly realistic moments of the entire episode, Junior has Walt bring him Mark Bowden's book *Killing Pablo*, because Hank gave it to him, explaining that it is important to know about the guys who worked to bring down Pablo Escobar because "good guys never get ink like the bad guys do." This hits Walt where he lives, because he's really been enjoying breaking bad. He loves the attention, the respect, the power that he thinks his criminal status and cooking abilities give him, but he's definitely not one of the good guys, and he knows it. More importantly, he knows that Hank is the kind of man his son could look up to, but he is not, and that burns.

Of course family is not Walt's only, or even primary, concern in this episode. Indeed, he is the last to find out about Hank's injuries when Jesse, who's enjoying a schadenfreude-high at Hank's expense, delivers the news in the lab. For much of this episode, Walt is doing what he does best — lying: to Gale about why he doesn't want to work with him; to Gus about why he's not in the lab cooking; to Skyler about who is paging him to the courtesy phone. Though to her credit, Sky stops that particular lie aborning with a beautifully eloquent look. Unfortunately for Walt, all of his lies fly apart when none other than Good Citizen Gustavo Fring drops by the hospital with food for both the family and waiting police, and a reward offer of $10,000 for information about the assassins. Gus knows all, and Walt's lies are revealed to have been transparent at best.

The real powerhouse in this episode is Giancarlo Esposito, who brings one of the coldest, most controlled villains in television history alive. Gus is completely comfortable mixing and mingling with literally hundreds of police, with offering rewards and displaying tremendous sympathy for a horrific crime that *he set in motion*. Most chilling of all is how perfectly everything appears to have worked out — for Gus. The cousins, too uncontrollable by far, have been removed from the picture. The DEA agent who is most interested in Blue Magic and who is also the brother-in-law of his new master chef has also been put out of action, and, best of all, Walt is left with no illusions as to who the boss is, and the utter futility of lying to Gus. Walt *thinks* he's a criminal mastermind. Gus actually *is*, a fact he demonstrates by taking care of another loose end in this episode — his superior in the cartel, Juan, who is gunned down only moments after threatening Gus with dire consequences for daring to use the cousins for his own ends. Gus is playing an altogether different game than Walt and Jesse, and on a much grander field.

LAB NOTES

HIGHLIGHT

JESSE: "Oh shit! This is the *bomb!*"

DID YOU NOTICE

* Jesse is still suffering from the effects of Hank's beating, wincing even at the feel of a T-shirt on his skin.
* Jesse also continues to develop a more hardened exterior, taking great delight in Hank's injuries.
* Walt's determined shimming of the uneven table leg in the waiting room. This is a lovely bit of character business again exposing Walt to be someone who thinks he can control and/or fix everything around him.
* Walt showing why so many people care about him as he comforts Marie and reassures her worries about the cleanliness of the hospital.
* Leonel Salamanca is last seen alive as the viewer first saw him: crawling, but with a deadly purpose.
* Mike drops an empty needle into the sharps disposal container as hospital staff and cops rush into the room in response to Leonel's coding into cardiac arrest.

SHOOTING UP

* A patient's POV is used when the EMTs and ER docs are rushing Hank through the hospital.
* Gilligan & Co. subvert audience expectations by showing an intense ER scene of doctors and nurses working frantically, desperately trying to save . . . Leonel Salamanca, the surviving cousin.
* Time-lapse photography is used outside the hospital to indicate the passage of time.
* The scene in the hospital when Leonel catches sight of Walt through the window in his door is incredible. Daniel Moncada's portrayal of rage and hate is visceral and every element of the scene is carefully crafted to reinforce it — again all of it without a word from Leonel, not even when the stubs of his freshly amputated legs hit the floor,

leaving behind a trail of blood as he crawls across the floor towards Walt.

TITLE "I See You" is a homonym for ICU, which is itself an acronym for "intensive care unit," referencing where both Hank and the surviving cousin are in the hospital. The title also references the cousin's reaction when catching sight of Walt through his room's window, and Gus's ability to see right through all of Walt's lies.

MUSIC The tune playing over the scenes of Jesse amusing himself in the Superlab is a cover of Ol' Dirty Bastard's "Shimmy Shimmy Ya" by Prince Fatty.

SPECIAL INGREDIENTS

PABLO ESCOBAR

Pablo Emilio Escobar Gaviria (1949–1993) — the subject of the book Junior is reading — was *the* Colombian drug lord. He was born into poverty and was determined to achieve wealth, power, and respect. The Medellín drug cartel provided him with the means to achieve his goals. Beginning in the mid-1970s, Escobar began patiently building a cocaine empire that, at its height, moved 15 tons of cocaine per day to the United States and was responsible for 80 percent of the global cocaine market. So much money was generated that $2,500 per month was spent just purchasing rubber bands to wrap around the stacks of money and 10 percent of the haul (somewhere over a *billion* dollars per year) was written off as "spoilage" (what Jesse would no doubt term "breakage") when the money became moldy from rainwater or was eaten by rats.

Prior to Escobar, there weren't really drug cartels, although there were kingpins of a sort. With Escobar, the manufacture and distribution of cocaine became industrialized, organized, and mechanized. Escobar was ruthless in his efforts to expand his empire, utilizing a strategy referred to as *plata o plomo* — "silver or lead," meaning "take the bribe or become a target." Escobar was responsible for the deaths of hundreds of police, state officials, and civilians who got in the way. At the same time, he carefully cultivated a Robin Hood image among the most desperately poor of Colombia, sponsoring soccer leagues and donating to hospitals and schools.

In 1991, the Colombian government convinced Escobar to surrender. In return, he would be imprisoned in La Catedral, a prison that Escobar personally designed with his own comfort in mind. He would not face extradition to the United States and would serve a term of no more than five years. Escobar accepted the deal, but from within his gilded cage he also continued his criminal activities (including having disloyal lieutenants brought to La Catedral to be tortured and killed). When he discovered that the government planned to transfer him to another jail, he planned a successful escape and thereby launched a massive manhunt.

In 1992, the United States joined the hunt for Escobar, helping to train a special Colombian police task force. Escobar was discovered hiding in a middle-class neighborhood in Medellín on December 2, 1993, and a firefight ensued. Escobar and his bodyguard tried to flee over the rooftops, but at the end of the battle, Pablo Escobar was dead. The Medellín cartel quickly unraveled.

La Catedral, built to be perhaps the world's most luxurious prison, is now a monastery.

K afkaesque

3.09

Original air date: May 16, 2010
Written by: Peter Gould, George Mastras **Directed by:** Michael Slovis

> "Somehow, something tells me that Hank is here because of
> you — and I'm *not* forgetting that." — Skyler White

Walt and Jesse are up and running at the Superlab. Meanwhile, there are some problems with Hank's insurance coverage, but Skyler may have a solution.

The cold open gives the audience an idea of the sheer scale of Gus's operation. As Walt and Jesse start churning out over 200 pounds of Blue Magic every week, the product is broken down into smaller batches, sunk in plastic containers of Los Pollos Hermanos fried-chicken batter, marked with a blacklight stamp, and shipped out in a seemingly never-ending series of trucks throughout the Southwest, all under the cold eye of Gus himself. This is meth production and distribution on an industrial scale and, according to Jesse's calculations, Gus stands to gross about $96 million on a three-month run for which he's paying Walt and Jesse $1.5 million each. Not a bad deal for Gus at all.

This is the point at which Jesse begins to get stupid. He claims he wants more money, but he's also looking to feel in control of his own destiny. After all, cooking meth has turned into a daily grind, a repetitive job with a schedule, a quota, and layers of management, and Jesse is just hired help. In other words, Jesse has found himself in another damn job working for The Man, and he can't stand it. This is the gist of the reasons he's giving to himself and his friends, but there may be something darker under this explanation. As the

season has progressed, Jesse has begun to care less and less about what happens to him, and his new business model relies on skimming some of the product he and Walt make for Gus, and then selling it at Narcotics Anonymous (NA) meetings, which in and of itself is pretty despicable. Jesse may not be the sharpest knife in the drawer, but he's not an idiot either, and he knows the drug business. Stealing from someone like Gus is never healthy, but perhaps that's the real point. Jesse may be looking for the only way out he can see: death.

It's a way out that Walt seriously flirts with as well. In a further progression into moral bankruptcy, Walt has figured out Gus's orchestration of the cousins' shootout with Hank, and actually congratulates him on the outcome. Worse, Walt claims that he would have done the same thing if their positions had been reversed. With a single raised eyebrow, Gus makes clear his amusement at the idea that Walt considers himself to be his equal. Gus's reaction to this meeting is to offer Walt an open-ended contract at $15 million a year. Walt doesn't say yes, but he doesn't have to; he drives away more deeply involved in the meth trade than ever, and it's almost more than he can stand. For a guy who likes to think he can control everything, Walt's entire life is singularly uncontrolled and uncontrollable, and even his suicide attempt is an act of releasing control by putting the pedal to the floor, closing his eyes, and letting go of the wheel. He pulls back in the end, but his control may be more illusory than anything else.

"Kafkaesque" also sees Gilligan & Co. return to the problems inherent in the American healthcare system, as even Hank's federal insurance plan through the DEA proves incapable of covering the care he truly needs if he is to stand a chance of walking again. In an incredible scene, Skyler spins a tale about Walt's gambling problem that, while awful, has left them wealthy. Her story spins lies from elements of truth: Walt's double life, his fugue state, him being too proud to take charity, etc. It is a masterful lie, so much so that even Walt is left slack-jawed at its coherence, detail, and ingeniousness. Lest Walt think she's come all the way over to the dark side, however, Sky lets him know in no uncertain terms that she's pretty damn sure this is all his fault, and with that being the case, it's only fair that he pay for it. In more ways than one.

LAB NOTES

HIGHLIGHT

> **JESSE:** "What good is being an outlaw when you have responsibilities?"
> **BADGER:** "Darth Vader had responsibilities. He was responsible for the Death Star."
> **SKINNY PETE:** "Yeah. Two of them bitches."

DID YOU NOTICE

- Hank is really not interested in work anymore, which is a big change for him.
- Gus provides a veggie tray for his meeting with Walt — not the first time we've seen social niceties being followed in tense meetings in *Breaking Bad*.
- The NA group leader is the same guy who was Jesse's "Group Leader" in rehab.
- The topic of the NA meeting is "triggers." In recovery-speak this refers to pretty much anything that triggers a psychological craving for the addict's drug of choice. In terms of the series as a whole, and Jesse in particular, "triggers" have a much more ominous meaning, as choices and actions "trigger" chains of events that unalterably change the lives of Jesse and Walt and everyone close to them.
- Jesse uses the NA meeting to actually be honest and talk about the stuff he's dealing with, especially his job, although he does it without getting specific. Growing out of the bond he feels with the group leader from rehab, this will become an occasional habit for Jesse.

- The cold open blends a very realistic commercial for Los Pollos Hermanos and the industrial meth production and distribution also going on at Pollos, linking both with the wonderful tagline: "Yes, the old ways are still best at Los Pollos Hermanos, but don't take my word for it. One taste, and you'll know." Just brilliant stuff.
- The NA meeting is carefully lit so that the circle of the group is within a bright, well-lit space that is surrounded by darkness, a lovely metaphor for the hope provided by the meeting against the darkness of addiction.

TITLE The word "Kafkaesque" comes from the writer Franz Kafka (1883–1924) and the recurring themes of his fiction, which often revolved around nightmarishly surreal situations. In Kafka's writings, the characters often have no real control or even understanding of the forces that are moving them and shaping their lives. In terms of the episode, this applies particularly to Walt, who, despite being the most controlling character in the series, is now seemingly just moved here and there at the whims of other people and of events that he neither understands nor has any say in. Gus, Jesse, Skyler, Marie, even Hank are all actively doing something in the episode, but not Walt.

INTERESTING FACTS In almost every American film, chickens — either live animals or depictions of the bird — are featured at least once. We don't know why and we don't really think it's a Hollywood conspiracy, although it'd be one of the cooler ones. In fact, it is staggering how often chickens appear once you start looking for them. *Breaking Bad* is no exception. From Gretchen's kitchen to the Los Pollos Hermanos commercial, the ubiquitous chicken is there.

SPECIAL INGREDIENTS

GAMBLING ADDICTION
Skyler explains that they are in a position to help with Hank's medical bills due to Walt's supposed gambling problem. While almost everyone gets a little rush from the idea of buying the winning lottery ticket, for compulsive gamblers, it's a whole different story. The *Diagnostic and Statistical Manual of Mental Disorders* (DSM) is the standard handbook of mental disorders in

America and is used daily by government agencies, researchers, and health-care providers. In the fourth edition of the DSM (DSM-IV), pathological gambling was classified as an impulse control disorder, while the newly released DSM-V classifies pathological gambling as an addiction. Regardless of its DSM status, problem gambling wreaks devastation on the lives of both the gambler and those who care for the gambler.

A compulsive gambler knows that their gambling is hurting themselves and their loved ones, yet is still unable to control the impulse to do it. No matter the consequences, a gambler will place just one more bet, sure that this time Lady Luck will bestow one tiny smile upon them. It is estimated that between two and five percent of the people who gamble qualify as having some degree of problem with gambling. More men than women suffer from pathological gambling and men tend to develop problems with gambling earlier in life. That said, gambling addictions in women tend to escalate much more quickly and with greater consequences. Men seem more attracted to interpersonal forms of gambling, such as poker or black-jack, while women seem more attracted to more solitary types of gambling such as slot machines or bingo.

Treatment for problem gamblers often involves 12-step programs and/or cognitive behavioral therapy. There are medications that have shown some success in reducing the urge to gamble, including some mood stabilizers and antidepressants, but psychotherapy seems to be more positive in the long term.

MONEY LAUNDERING

Simply put, money laundering is the process of taking money from Source A and making it look as if it comes from Source B. Criminals launder money to disguise illegal activities because, if law enforcement can connect the money to illegal activity, the cash can be linked to the criminals and the money can be seized. We've talked about this a little back in season 2 with Saul's plan to launder money using computer zombies, but let's examine it a little more.

For Walt, laundering the money he's paid by Gus for his meth making is crucial. Large amounts of cash are suspicious and can quickly draw the eyes of law enforcement. Plus, cash is heavy — much heavier than the stolen diamonds, pilfered documents, or illegal drugs that the criminal got the money for in the first place. Money laundering has three basic steps: placement, layering, and integration.

Placement: The "dirty" money has to be inserted into a legitimate financial institution. Often, this takes the form of cash deposits to a bank, but that's high risk, as banking regulations in the United States require that cash deposits over $10,000 be reported to the government.

Layering: In this step, the dirty money is sent on a merry journey to make it hard to follow. This step might involve bank-to-bank transfers, wire transfers between different accounts in different names (and maybe different countries), changing the currency, and purchasing high-dollar items such as houses, cars, or gemstones to change the form of the money. This is the most complex step and it has the sole purpose of clouding the trail, thus making the dirty money very difficult to trace.

Integration: In this step, the money re-enters the economy in some sort of legitimate-looking form. It now appears to come from a legal transaction. Perhaps the final bank transfer sends the money into the account of a local business in which the money launderer is "investing" for a percentage of the businesses' profits, or maybe a house bought in the layering step is now sold. At this point, the launderer can use the money, which appears to be legitimate and clean.

Among the more popular money-laundering schemes is the use of overseas banks in countries with bank secrecy laws, which essentially allows anonymous deposits and "smurfing," in which large amounts of cash are broken up into smaller, less-suspicious amounts that are then deposited into multiple accounts either by one person over time or by multiple people at once (these are the "smurfs"). Money launderers also may use shell companies that take the dirty money as payment for goods and services that are not actually provided, but create the appearance of legitimate transactions through fake invoices. Lastly, money launderers may place dirty money in legitimate businesses to clean it. Usually, these businesses either deal in so much money (like a casino) that the dirty money easily blends in or they may use small, cash-intensive businesses such as bars, strip clubs, and car washes. While a shell company only exists to launder the dirty money, these types of "front businesses" may actually supply a good or service, but the business either reports higher revenues than it's actually earning to account for the infusion of dirty money or the dirty money is simply folded in with the legitimate funds.

3.10

Fly

Original air date: May 23, 2010
Written by: Sam Catlin, Moira Walley-Beckett
Directed by: Rian Johnson

"It's all contaminated." — Walter White

A fly gets into the Superlab, and as Walt and Jesse chase it, they have a brutally frank discussion.

This is perhaps the most purely psychological episode in the entire run of *Breaking Bad* and there is more than a little debate among fans as to the meaning of the fly and Walt's obsessive pursuit of the insect. For us, "Fly" is all about Walt trying desperately to find a new rationalization for everything he's done and what he's continuing to do. The old reasons aren't holding water anymore. Walt repeatedly claims to be engaging in illegal activities for the benefit of his family, but now he's signed divorce papers and moved out. If that justification is now revealed to be completely hollow, then how can he live with what he has caused, including the deaths of several drug dealers, the outright murder of Jane (and indirect cause of the deaths of the passengers of Wayfarer 515), and the sequence of events that led to Hank's suspension and crippling shootout with the cousins? Dehydrated and miserable in the desert in "4 Days Out," Walt had a moment of clarity where he realized that he *hadn't* been helping his family; all he had really done was "worry and disappoint them, and lie." Now though, he has pushed his family to the point of dissolution, and his actions are spilling over to cause death and misery to more and more of the people he cares about. Worse, every choice he has made has served only to dig his hole a little deeper, and now he's made a deal with Gus to live this life for an indefinite period, maybe until he dies, one way or another.

"Fly" is Walt's long night of the soul, a point of psychic and spiritual pain that ensues when he is no longer able to believe his own bullshit, and a period of time when he desperately attempts to ignore this pain by obsessively focusing on a single task to the exclusion of all others: killing a fly that has found its way into the lab. The fly is merely an excuse to avoid cooking, to avoid thinking, and to avoid feeling or facing the realities of his choices. The episode has all the ingredients to be incredibly difficult for the viewer to endure, but Gilligan & Co. manage to make this dark night palatable by brilliant use of comic relief. Bryan Cranston draws on his remarkable talent for physical comedy, which he demonstrated so often in *Malcolm in the Middle*. His increasingly frustrated attempts to swat the fly have him clomping along with one shoe on, accidentally turning things on and then slapping at them to turn them off, and in one of the best moments of the episode, actually having Jesse hit him in the head with the improvised fly-swatting pole-arm he has created. At no time does the anguish of Walt's inner turmoil get lost, but the external results are remarkably funny.

The metaphor, potentially heavy-handed, is also nicely treated through the use of Walt's obsession with the fly. The fly is unkillable, easily avoiding every attempt to trap, smash, or otherwise obliterate it, and coming through seemingly unsurvivable encounters with Walt and Jesse's fly-killing spree with incredible agility. No matter what Walt tries, he cannot kill his fly, just as no matter what Walt tries, he cannot kill his conscience, or put it to rest with some perfect explanation. Exhausted and drugged by Jesse, Walt gets sloppy and almost reveals that he killed Jane. He even apologizes to Jesse, albeit in a slurred whisper, and likely in a blackout. However, he ends this episode the same man he was when he started, unable to take a single action to try and alter his situation, or to make his family less vulnerable to the fallout of his choices. Walt is supposedly always about control, but, as "Fly" demonstrates, he has actually always been about the *illusion* of control. He's a man running on marbles: it's possible to keep your feet for a while, but you've got to dance like crazy to do it and eventually, you slip. Walt has no plan, no master scheme. He's just been scrambling from disaster to disaster and every time he manages to keep his balance, he finds more marbles under his shoes.

Despite all of Walt's power tripping and bluster, it is in fact Jesse who manages to kill the fly in the lab after Walt falls into a drugged slumber. Jesse has inner turmoil of his own, but none of Walt's deep-seated guilt, so he can squash his problems more easily. This is a simple, powerful statement about relationships, and the possibilities inherent in an honest bond between these two men. Jesse discards this possibility at the end of the episode, however. As for Walt, safe in his bed once again, the fly is still there. Buzzing.

LAB NOTES

HIGHLIGHT

JESSE: "You want me to get it? I'm just gonna need your swatter thing."
WALT: "Make it count."
JESSE: "Oh, I'm gonna make it count, all right."

DID YOU NOTICE

- Jesse talks about watching a nature program the night before, harking back to "Phoenix" when Walt watched a show about elephants before heading over to Jesse's apartment the night he killed Jane.
- This time it's Jesse who is intent on getting the cook done and making their quota.
- Walt wonders how his meeting with Jane's father the night of her death could be coincidence. Another interesting suggestion of a guiding force.
- Exhaustion and drugs bring out the (often self-pitying) talker in Walt. He blabs about the second cell phone before his operation in "ABQ," he becomes honest and maudlin in "4 Days Out," and in "Fly" he almost tells Jesse that he killed Jane.
- Walt's speech about when he should die contains hints about his relationship with his own father and mother, and his father's death.

SHOOTING UP

- There is a tremendous amount of stylistic camera work throughout "Fly." In part this is an effect of the majority of the episode taking place in one, confined space, like a play rather than a multi-camera television show. The movement of the camera, the different angles and shots, from high and low, from above and beneath, through the tangle of the Superlab's equipment, and so on, help to keep things from becoming static. It's a technique that was used by Sidney Lumet for the 1957 film *12 Angry Men*, where all the action takes place in a single room, and is also used brilliantly in "Fly" by episode director Rian Johnson (director of psychological thrillers *Brick* and *Looper*) and series cinematographer Michael Slovis.

- Sound and silence are carefully used in "Fly" as well. When Walt is lying in bed during the cold open, the sound of Skyler singing "Hush Little Baby" (from "Phoenix") is heard. This comes back later in the episode when Walt determines that was the moment when he should have died.

- When Walt gets to work after his sleepless night, there is a long shot of him sitting in the car in absolute silence, without even any sort of ambient noise, until the moment when Jesse knocks on the window, at which point all the noise of the real world comes back. A lovely setup of Walt's mental state. He's not really in the world.

- POV shots are used extensively in "Fly." The fly's POV is seen several times, including a dizzying shot where the fly flips upside down to land on the ceiling. The viewer also sees things from the POV of the scrub brush Jesse uses to clean the tank, the bottom of the bag full of fly catching equipment, the ceiling down, and even Walt's as the fly lands on his glasses.

- Close-ups and mid-range shots are used to good effect, as is the switching of the camera's focus, such as during the scene where Jesse is telling Walt about the possum that lived under his aunt's house. The actors are mostly static, staying in the same place, but the camera first has Jesse in sharp focus and Walt blurry, and then shifts to bring Walt into sharp focus, thereby blurring Jesse. It's a neat trick to provide movement without any actual movement.

INTERESTING FACTS In filming "Fly," Gilligan & Co. made a virtue out of necessity. When the episode was filmed, the entire season was over budget, meaning that any and all means had to be found to cut production costs. Creating an episode that used only one set and minimal cast was an elegant solution, and the quality of the episode reveals that financial constraints are not always a bad thing.

SPECIAL INGREDIENTS

CONTAMINANTS FOUND IN CRYSTAL METH

Walt wants to make the purest meth ever known to hit the market. To that end, he insists on pure ingredients, rather than the brake fluid and match-striker plates that are routinely used in a "dirty cook." Adulterants of all sorts are commonly used to stretch out the yield of a product — Upton Sinclair wrote about truly disgusting adulterants in the meat packing industry in his 1906 novel *The Jungle*. The production of illicit drugs is no different. Tales abound of cocaine being cut with white flour to increase the weight of the product, for example.

With meth, the problem lies in the production itself. Sometimes cooks want their product to stand out (remember Jesse's signature was chili powder). Sometimes ingredients are added to give color to the final product — Strawberry Quik drink mix has been known to be added to a cook to give meth a cheerful pink tinge. While a cook like Walt is concerned with the purity of the final product as a point of pride, most cooks just want to get high and don't care all that much for clean room standards. Therefore, the equipment isn't particularly clean and traces of some really bad stuff can remain in the meth. Consider that components that frequently go into a meth cook include Freon (linked to lung damage), ether (known to cause respiratory failure), muriatic acid (can generate toxic vapors leading to burns), red phosphorus (which is unstable and flammable), and acetone (known to cause reproductive disorders), and you realize just how dangerous this drug really is.

Walt makes an extremely dangerous product and even with the purest of ingredients and the cleanest of labs, his blue meth might kill you and almost certainly will cause you to lose everything you care about. And that's without the junk that most street cooks use.

COMMON HOUSEFLY

Quick — what's the most dangerous animal on earth? Lions and tigers and bears (oh, my!) have all been known to rip people apart, and tangling with a king cobra is not to be recommended. Moreover, the tiny box jellyfish can kill a person as thoroughly as a great white shark. Nevertheless, more people are killed per year by the common housefly than all these other fanged and poisonous critters combined.

In many ways, the housefly is the Rodney Dangerfield of the animal world — it just don't get no respect. In its short (20- to 30-day) lifespan, an adult housefly can reproduce like mad, explaining why the housefly is found in practically every spot on the globe. Far more than an annoying pest, the housefly can transmit a host of diseases, including typhoid, cholera, dysentery, and anthrax. Cleanliness helps, but as Walt found out, flies can be hard to kill.

The housefly transmits diseases in three ways. First, the bristles on its six legs carry trace amounts of whatever the curious fly has landed on, which often includes raw food and manure, both of which can be teeming with disease. Second, flies aren't particular about where they defecate (they don't care that their bathroom is your arm) and their feces can carry diseases. Third, houseflies can only feed on liquids. So when they explore a bit of spilled food or a crumb, they saturate the food with fly spit and digestive juices (read: vomit) until the potential meal dissolves and they can suck it up.

Get the swatter.

3.11

A biquiu

Original air date: May 30, 2010
Written by: John Shiban, Thomas Schnauz
Directed by: Michelle MacLaren

"Never make the same mistake twice." — Gustavo Fring

Jesse's business plan proves more difficult to put into practice than expected. Meanwhile, Skyler wants in on Walt's business.

Any business can get unexpectedly complicated — especially the drug business. In this episode, Walt and Jesse both find themselves faced with complications that, while seemingly not as deadly as other situations they've been in, nonetheless throw some pretty large wrenches into their plans. For Jesse, his plan to sell to people in NA meetings begins to crumble when Badger and Skinny Pete can't bring themselves to do it, and falls apart completely when the girl he picks out as an easy mark turns out to be a real person with a little boy. After Jesse's experiences with his own little brother Jake and the redheaded kid in "Peekaboo," the existence of Andrea's son Brock (Ian Posada) changes everything. Despite his recent negative attitude, Jesse is fundamentally a good, caring guy, and he is much more aware of the realities of the meth world than Walt has ever been. After all, Jesse was probably very much like his younger brother Jake once upon a time; he knows what happened in his life to change that, and he's seen the horror that can become "normal life" to the child of tweakers. There is something in Jesse that truly rebels against the destruction of innocents, especially children. Believe it or not, Jesse is now becoming the conscience of the show and its moral center.

For Jesse, there are certain things that cross an unacceptable moral line. And his sense of loyalty and knowing right from wrong come out in a big way as he discovers just exactly who killed Combo.

He's also aware that people aren't perfect, and that sometimes you just do the best you can. Hence, after Andrea (Emily Rios, recognizable from *Men of a Certain Age* and the TV series *Friday Night Lights*) suggests smoking up, Jesse is able to come down from moral condemnation to an understanding, admitting that he was out of line for suggesting they use in the first place. With Jesse's delightful interactions with Brock, the viewer is treated to another recurring oddity of the show: Jesse is good with kids. He is patient, attentive, and sensitive to their needs and emotions. Some of this comes from Jesse's own youth, but he also genuinely cares for their welfare. His new relationship with Andrea is vastly different than what he shared with Jane — less intense, more grounded — but the audience can now begin to hope that, against all odds, Jesse will eventually be okay, and will find some modicum of happiness if he can. As Walt sinks ever deeper into the moral pit he has dug for himself, the viewer's affection for him is slowly moving over to Jesse, who is now so much more than the junkie gangsta wannabe of season 1.

Elsewhere, Walt's world is spinning even further out of control. Skyler has decided that she wants in and in a big way. Concerned with how Walt is laundering the money they're giving to Hank and Marie, she insists on meeting Saul, who makes a predictably bad impression. Sky now begins to show just how alike she and Walt really are. Skyler is every bit as apt to think she knows more than she actually does and to think she's smarter than everyone around her, including Walt. This is a dangerous character trait that she shares with her husband. Further, Skyler also displays the same failure to listen to other people, even when they have more experience with something than she does. While she has a point that a car wash makes more sense as a business Walt would buy into, her insistence on it despite difficulties reveals a desire — much like Walt's — to control things, coupled with an equal or greater arrogance about her own capabilities. Walt may very well be right in doubting the wisdom of making her a part of his meth business, but he can't quite say no.

LAB NOTES

HIGHLIGHT

HANK: "Pain is my foot in your ass, Marie!"

MARIE: "Hey, if you can get your leg up that high, I say go for it!"

DID YOU NOTICE

* In "Fly," we see a lipstick-stained cigarette butt in the ashtray in Jesse's car. Its origin is explained in this episode's cold open.
* Hank is in really bad shape, and his frustration and anger are equal-opportunity abusers.
* Hank's progress in physical rehabilitation can be used as a rough indicator of the amount of time passing between episodes.
* Walt is now seen holding baby Holly regularly.
* The White family dinner dynamic is much more normal and happy in this episode.
* Saul finds props to illustrate his "this is money-laundering" lecture just like he did with Jesse in "Kafkaesque."

SHOOTING UP

* The cold open is a backstory, giving the viewer a look at Jesse and Jane's visit to the Georgia O'Keeffe museum in Abiquiú, New Mexico. Their lovely conversation in Jesse's car afterwards is heart-rending.
* An up-and-through POV shot of Jesse cracking meth is used again for the cooking montage, and an upward-looking POV from the bottom of Skyler's pasta pot transitions to the White family dinner scene.
* Again the NA group is shown as being a pool of light surrounded in darkness, a darkness into which Jesse and Andrea disappear after he picks her up for the first time.

TITLE Abiquiú is a small, unincorporated township in New Mexico about 53 miles north of Santa Fe. The American painter Georgia O'Keeffe lived there for over 30 years. The O'Keeffe Museum that Jesse and Jane visit is in Santa Fe, but the paintings of the door they discuss were all done in Abiquiú. The title also is a homonym for the way one would pronounce "ABQ," the abbreviation for Albuquerque and the title of the episode in which Jane died.

MUSIC Walt and Jesse pack and weigh their cook to the tune of Son of Dave's "Shake A Bone" — blues music for blue meth.

INTERESTING FACTS Abiquiú has become something of a destination for film crews in recent years, and parts of *Indiana Jones and the Kingdom of the Crystal Skull*, *Cowboys & Aliens*, *City Slickers*, *Red Dawn*, *Wyatt Earp*, and *The Last Outlaw* were all filmed in and around Abiquiú.

SPECIAL INGREDIENTS

GEORGIA O'KEEFFE AND THE DOOR PAINTINGS

Jesse and Jane discuss Georgia O'Keeffe's series of door paintings following their visit to the Georgia O'Keeffe Museum in Santa Fe. O'Keeffe (1887–1986) is one of America's best-known artists and, although she was born in Wisconsin and began her career on the East Coast, she is closely associated with the American Southwest. She felt that the wide-open desert spaces and saturated colors of the Southwest gave her what she needed to break free of European confines of visual art, and by the late 1920s O'Keeffe began spending part of every year working in New Mexico. She permanently relocated there in 1949. While many would find the remote areas of the Southwestern desert bleak and empty, O'Keeffe adored the space, referring to the area by the lyrical name of "the faraway." In fact, following her death in 1986, her ashes were scattered over "the faraway."

O'Keeffe found beauty in nontraditional places and subject matter, including sun-bleached bones and yes, doors. From 1946 through the 1950s, she made the patio wall and door of her Abiquiú house frequent subjects of her work.

Why did she paint the door over and over? Jesse thinks she was trying to capture perfection, while Jane says no, she was trying to make a good feeling last. Either interpretation might explain why Jane's lipstick-stained cigarette still sits in the ashtray in Jesse's car.

MARITAL PRIVILEGE

To convince Walt that she should be cut in on the action, Skyler mentions that spouses can't be compelled to testify against each other, citing the so-called marital privilege. Skyler's right about this one, although, as is often the case with legal concepts, it's not quite that simple.

The marital privilege is designed to protect confidences exchanged within a married relationship. Like all other privileges (doctor-patient, clergy-penitent, lawyer-client, etc.), the idea is to encourage full disclosure within certain specified relationships. However, no privilege is total. If you're seeing a therapist and you tell your shrink you're going to kill your wife at dinner tonight and your doctor thinks you mean it, in most states, the therapist has a duty to warn authorities before you have a chance to act. In the same way, the marital privilege isn't a complete blanket either.

Broadly stated, the privilege means that in a criminal case, a spouse cannot be compelled to testify against the other spouse. (Civil cases, such as those involving child custody in which the spouses are suing each other, are different.) In a criminal case, much depends on the jurisdiction — in some, the spouse is simply barred from testifying; in others, the spouse can waive the privilege. Some federal courts have created a "joint participation in crime" exception to the privilege, in which case Skyler might not be on firm ground here. Further, if the communication is made to either plan or commit a crime, the privilege may not hold, which would create more potential trouble for Skyler.

Timing is also important. In order to qualify for the privilege, the conversation must have occurred during the marriage — not before and not after. Generally, to assert the privilege, the couple must be legally married; a common-law marriage is insufficient to claim the privilege, as is a completed divorce. However, a divorce (or even death) can still bar a spouse from testifying against the other about events and communications that occurred during the marriage.

Also, the communication must have occurred in private for there to be a reasonable expectation of privacy. Witnesses dissolve confidentiality, so either the spouse or the witnesses could testify about the conversation or events in such a case. Skyler and Walt need to find a quiet place to talk about these things and even then, they might not be as far out of the woods as they think.

alf Measures

Original air date: June 6, 2010

Written by: Sam Catlin, Peter Gould **Directed by:** Adam Bernstein

"It's not 'just delivering hamburgers.'" — Wendy

Walt and Jesse deal with the threat posed by Gale. Meanwhile, Marie tries to get Hank to come home.

"Half Measures" is an odd kind of morality tale where no one involved is anywhere near to being a paragon of virtue. The cold open gives the viewer a montage day-in-the-life of Wendy the Meth Whore, which is a horrifically repetitive round of blow jobs in front seats followed by Scope mouth-rinsing, cheap sodas, cheap food, cigarettes, meth — an endless parade of strange men in strange cars, again, and again, and again. The perpetual degradation is highlighted by the relentlessly cheerful tune "Windy" by the Association. Wendy is what she is: a meth addict who prostitutes herself in order to feed her habit, pay for her shitty room at the Crystal Palace, and supposedly take care of a son viewers never meet named Patrick. A model citizen she ain't.

Then there's Jesse, a recovering addict, meth cook, and self-proclaimed "bad guy," who somehow has become the moral center of the show. To Jesse, things are pretty clear. Combo was his friend and employee, and Tomas (Angelo Martinez) was a kid manipulated by gangbangers into doing their wetwork and being their front man. To Jesse, these gangbangers — the kind that use kids to do their crimes — need to be killed as a simple act of justice and right. Not because they stand in the way of Jesse and Walt's business,

(JAKES VAN DER WATT/PR PHOTOS)

or complicate their lives in any way, but simply because using kids crosses a line with Jesse, as does killing someone to whom Jesse owes loyalty and friendship. Of course, Jesse is no paladin, and his use of Wendy as a delivery method for ricin-laced burgers is, in a way, just as despicable as the street-dealers' use of Tomas.

This is vastly different from Walt, who reacts to Jesse's plan with hypocritical (and insincere) shock and weak protests that neither of them is a murderer. For Walt, killing must serve a concrete, immediate end: saving his life when Emilio was trying to kill him; semi-self-defense against an unforgiving Krazy-8; self-preservation against the psychotic Tuco; even the twisted logic of removing a blackmailer and complication in Jane. Walt's kills have all been in the service of theoretically solving some pressing problem, not serving a kind of moral code. He truly cannot understand Jesse's need to kill the street-dealers, particularly as they are apparently members of Gus's larger organization. Walt has just barely gotten things settled down after Hank's beating of Jesse and the subsequent shootout with the cousins, and now Jesse is threatening to rock their already precarious boat, if not punch a hole straight through it. Not to mention that Walt's marriage has become a business deal in which he trades agreeing to Skyler's plan to launder his drug money for four dinners with the family a week and keys to the house. Walt, the smart guy who thinks way too highly of himself, decides that if it works for his marriage, negotiation can solve anything.

It turns out he's wrong, at least in part. In an astonishing turn of events, Gus Fring, a man who can orchestrate the deaths of cartel capos, DEA agents, and professional killers without raising his voice, is told "No" by Jesse — loud-mouthed, inept, cowardly Jesse. Is there just the barest hint of surprise and grudging respect in Gus's eye as Jesse squares off with him? We think so. Still, Gus's will is law, and everything seems settled, until it devolves into a dead kid. With nothing left to lose, and only really possessing the principle that some things just aren't right, Jesse marches out to get himself blown away in some *High Noon*–style shootout, only to have Walt, the real killer of the duo, brutally and efficiently burst upon the scene and kill the street-dealers where they stand. His Heisenberg hat on his head, Walt neither hesitates nor trembles. He is as cold and remorseless as Gus himself. There are some who view this as an almost redemptive, heroic moment for Walt, as he acts to save his partner and surrogate son figure. The problem with this view is that Walt — unlike Jesse, who had to nerve himself up for his actions by getting high for the first time all season and who was visibly trembling and unsure as he approached his putative targets — is filled with nothing but focus and purpose. Walt just kills without a qualm. He has crossed a line somewhere deep within himself. Murder is no longer even a regrettable necessity. It's now just a problem-solving option, as valid as any other, and that's terrifying.

LAB NOTES

HIGHLIGHT
MARIE: "If I can get the groundhog to see his shadow . . . you check out of here."

DID YOU NOTICE
* In the cold open, notice the framing of the shot with Wendy and the sign reading "Friendly Service."
* Skyler is reading up on money laundering on Wikipedia. So much for her condescending insistence to Saul that she knew what it was.
* Walt uses a variant of the "name one thing that's not negotiable" line

again. This time it's with Skyler, but very similar to the line he used with the realtor in "Sunset."

- Junior is in almost every scene with Hank in the hospital, and is obviously spending a lot of time visiting his uncle and surrogate father figure.
- Hank gives Junior some pretty serious hell after their card game, but Junior lets it roll off his back. He's showing some hard-earned wisdom and patience here. Hank's not the only one whose body doesn't work right, after all.
- In this episode Walt's much more accepting of Junior's two-footed driving than he was in "Down."
- This episode is the second time Gilligan & Co. have shown a hand job being used as a reward or motivation, going back to "Pilot/Breaking Bad" with Skyler's gift to Walt on his birthday.
- Hank gives Marie "one minute" to try to arouse him, recalling "One Minute," the title of the episode where he was shot.
- Walt plays with the scales of Justice in Saul's office, the same statue that Jesse used for an ashtray in "Mandala."
- Mike gives up some of his backstory in his conversation with Walt. Interestingly, in the story he is driven by the same sense of right and wrong that is currently driving Jesse.
- At the meeting with Gus at the chicken farm, there is no veggie tray and no coffee, a sign that this is a dangerously serious get-together, employer to employee.
- Walt knows the answer to the Whitman question on *Jeopardy* because, thanks to Gale, he's been reading *Leaves of Grass*. See, kids? Poetry is useful!
- The blood pulsing in Walt's ears drowns out all other conversation, similar to the ringing effect in "Pilot/Breaking Bad," "Cancer Man," and "4 Days Out."
- Jesse uses meth for the first time this season as he cranks himself up to confront the gangbangers.

SHOOTING UP

- To indicate the effects of the meth on Jesse's system, the director uses a series of jump cuts and jerky camera work.

- The use of montage in the cold open with Wendy has already been mentioned, but it's worth remarking on again as an exquisite way of filling in the backstory of yet another secondary character, and as a way to compress time.
- An up-and-through POV from the bottom of one of the large stainless-steel tanks in the Superlab is used as Jesse and Walt cook.
- The saturated neon-green lighting in Wendy's room is a constant throughout the series, allowing the viewer to immediately recognize the location, and also emphasizing the sleaziness of Wendy's existence.
- Tomas's colorful shoelaces have been used as a constant identifier since his first appearance in "Mandala," another use of color to help the audience quickly identify and remember a character.

TITLE Besides tying the moral of Mike's story to Walter, "Half Measures" also refers to how Walt has been acting for much of seasons 2 and 3, just doing things by halves, without looking towards the possible consequences, and kicking potential problems down the road instead of solving them as they appear.

SPECIAL INGREDIENTS

BONNIE AND CLYDE

As Skyler is reading up on money laundering and bouncing baby Holly on her lap, she references "Bonnie what's her name." No doubt Bonnie Elizabeth Parker (1910–1934) would be disappointed that Skyler didn't remember her name. A sometime writer like Skyler, Bonnie Parker teamed up with Clyde Chestnut Barrow (1909–1934) as part of an outlaw gang that led a two-year crime spree during the Great Depression. From the time Bonnie met Clyde, she was devoted to him and, while there is no evidence that any of the bullets she fired ever hit anybody, Parker was an accomplice to more than a hundred felonies during her time with Barrow, including eight murders, seven kidnappings, and six bank robberies, in addition to countless car thefts and assaults.

By all accounts, Barrow's life as a petty criminal changed forever in April 1932 when he was involved in the murder of a store owner during a robbery. Knowing that being taken into police custody now meant facing murder charges, he vowed to never get caught. That summer, he killed a police officer.

Bonnie and Clyde skyrocketed to national infamy after a March 1933 shootout. They had been hiding (not very quietly) at a house kept by Clyde's brother and sister-in-law. When the police came to investigate reports of loud parties and gunfire, the gang shot their way out, killing two police officers in the process. Left behind were: a virtual arsenal of guns, a poem Bonnie had written, and several rolls of film showing the gangsters apparently living a merry and glamorous lifestyle, including shots of Bonnie holding a pistol and smoking a cigar. When the photos and Bonnie's poem hit the newswire, overnight Bonnie and Clyde went from being Texas outlaws to the most infamous duo in the nation.

In May 1934, Parker and Barrow met their end in a hail of bullets as they drove into a carefully laid ambush. After the now bullet-riddled car crashed, the lawmen took no chances and continued to pump dozens of bullets into the car. A crowd quickly gathered to seek souvenirs, gathering up shell casings and splintered glass, even going so far as to cut off bits of the dead outlaws' clothing and locks of Bonnie's bloody hair. The official report stated that Clyde's body had 17 entrance wounds and Bonnie's had 26. Both had suffered multiple fatal shots to the head and Clyde's spinal column had been severed by gunfire. The bodies were so badly shot up that the local undertaker had a hard time preparing the bodies for burial, as the embalming fluid kept leaking out. The blood-splattered car became an instant tourist sensation and can still be viewed in Primm, Nevada. The "death car" is now kept behind glass, so you can no longer sit in the shot-up seats or stick your fingers into the bullet holes, as you once could.

Bonnie had often passed the time writing poetry and she gave "The Story of Bonnie & Clyde" to her mother the last time they met, just two weeks before the fatal shootout. The fatalistic poem contains some lines Skyler might want to ponder a bit:

The road gets dimmer and dimmer;
Sometimes you can hardly see;
But it's fight, man to man,
And do all you can,
For they know they can never be free.

From heart-break some people have suffered;
From weariness some people have died;
But take it all in all,
Our troubles are small
Till we get like Bonnie and Clyde.

F ull Measure
3.13

Original air date: June 13, 2010
Written and directed by: Vince Gilligan

"I saved your life, Jesse. Are you gonna save mine?"
— Walter White

Walt and Jesse deal with the fallout from the previous episode.

Breaking Bad isn't known for being static, but the changes taking place at the end of season 3 are enough to give the viewer whiplash. After spending most of the season either desperately trying to keep things from falling apart or just dazedly letting other people make all the decisions around him, Walt has finally taken decisive action, and for perhaps the first time all season he is fully present. That doesn't mean that all is well, though. Far from it. The most interesting thing about Walt's meeting with Gus, Mike, and Victor (Jeremiah Bitsui) the morning after Walt kills two of Gus's street-dealers is that all three of his interrogators now look at him with something approaching respect, and also wariness. For the first time, we see him searched thoroughly by Mike, and he meets Gus's hardness with his own.

Yet this respect is the type that one holds for an unpredictably dangerous animal, or a volatile mixture one has to handle. Walt is nitroglycerin. The weirdest things can set him off. Through his hardness, however, Walt is doing what he always does: negotiating from what he believes is a position of strength. Walt thinks he's irreplaceable. Jesse knows his recipe, but Gus is highly unlikely to call upon him to cook his meth. Walt views himself as a linchpin without

which the entire structure of Gus's meth empire would fall apart. He is almost right.

Interestingly, as the episode builds to its incredible climax, Gilligan & Co. choose this time to give the viewer some more back-story and some new subplots. A younger Walt and Sky buy what they think of as a "starter" home some 16 years earlier, with Walt talking big about the future — a future that never materialized. However, from the bare and empty space seen in the cold open, the White house has become a warm and inviting place, where people live, where they have history, where dreams change but never quite die, and where new dreams are built. It is a marked contrast to the deserted scrub-desert farm in the opening act, a place abandoned and forgotten, without even the capability of dreaming. The White house may not have been the springboard to the career of the Nobel Prize–winning, enormously wealthy chemist Walter White, but it is the place where he and Skyler built a family. Walt and Sky's life didn't turn out the way they thought it would, but their home seems to suggest that it turned out pretty well overall. Walt just can't ever quite seem to see that.

The audience also gets to see a bit more of Gus's business, and much more of Mike in this episode. He eliminates a cadre of cartel hitmen with little more than balloons from the zoo, a Desert Eagle semi-automatic, a generally phlegmatic world-weariness, and a definitely unconventional skillset. The scene is a lovely bit of badassery, lightened by the humor between Mike and Gus's Chinese bookkeeper and a very upset secretary. More, however, the scene sets up a new storyline, right here at the end of the season, letting the audience know that more is to come and that Gus's strike against Juan was far from the last word in his argument with the Mexican cartel.

At the core of the episode, however, are Walt and Jesse, and Walt's attempts to kill Gale before Gus kills them. For all of his strong talk in the opening, Walt finally finds himself desperate and alone, begging Mike and Victor not to kill him, and offering to give them Jesse if they'll just let him live. There is some question about whether or not the offer is genuine, but many fans believe it actually is. Walt may have saved Jesse in "Half Measures," and may even feel a kind of fatherly affection for him, but Walt's cancer is gone and these days he desperately wants to live, no matter what. So Walt becomes the very thing he has most recently killed: a thug who uses an "innocent" to do his killing. As Jesse faces down Gale, both men slowly weep, both tremble, both having come to this point by the strangest of routes. Gale, the lover of the magic of chemistry, of books and musicals, and who owns a turntable but not a TV; and Jesse, wannabe gangsta in too deep, who found and lost his great love, who found there was a line he could not cross and live with, but who now crosses a different one in defense of a man who may well not be worth defending.

LAB NOTES

HIGHLIGHT

WALT: "You said 'no half measures.'"

MIKE: "Yeah. Funny how words can be so open to interpretation."

DID YOU NOTICE

- The windshield of Walt's Aztek is spider-webbed with cracks for the third time this season.
- Gus has changed the locks to the lab, just like Skyler changed the locks to Walt's house.
- Gus's face is utterly immobile and cold until Gale hits the "right" number of cooks he needs before he can confidently take Walt's place, at which point Gus's eyes light up and he smiles.
- Walt keeps track of favors owed to him, but he's not so good with favors he owes to others.
- Jesse is hiding out in the same laser tag place that Saul tried to get Walt to buy as a cover for money laundering.
- Gale and Walt both beg their respective killers with the same line: "Please don't do this."

- The slow pan starting with the fireplace and unlit Duraflame log in the cold open is repeated exactly in the opening of the fourth act, giving the viewer a before and after look at the space that becomes the White house.
- A handheld camera is used in the car as Walt waits to meet with Gus, giving the audience a sense of nervousness, immediacy, and physical closeness.
- Walt and Mike are silhouetted against a big sky as they meet in the middle of the field in the opening, a very classic Western shot.
- The final POV shot of the season is Gale's, as he stares down the muzzle of Jesse's gun.

MUSIC This episode features an eclectic mix of music: the background for Mike's elimination of the cartel hitters is "Shambala" by the Beastie Boys; the tune Gale is listening to when Gus comes to visit is "Crapa Pelada" by Quartetto Cetra; and when Jesse comes to see him, Gale's phone is drowned out by "Man Chang Fei" by 張帆.

INTERESTING FACTS Dillwyn, Virginia, where Saul leads Mike to believe Jesse is hiding, is the closest town to the geographic center of the state of Virginia, Vince Gilligan's home state.

SPECIAL INGREDIENTS

METALLIC BALLOONS AND POWER LINES

Mike deliberately uses a bunch of Mylar balloons to short out the power in this episode. It works. In fact, it only takes a single metallic balloon making contact with energized power lines to cut electrical power to thousands of consumers. The balloon's shiny surface is the result of a metallized nylon that is quite good at conducting electricity. When it comes into contact with a power line, the balloon creates a short circuit leading to an overload of current and thus to power outages, downed power lines, and fires. If you see balloons tangled in power lines, don't try to knock them loose, and if you have metallic balloons, don't turn them loose outside.

DESERT EAGLE PISTOLS AND SILENCERS

In addition to balloons, Mike also uses what appears to be a silenced Desert Eagle pistol to take care of business. When this gas-operated, semi-automatic pistol was first introduced in the early 1980s, Hollywood took notice. The Desert Eagle is a big, imposing-looking handgun — really big. With a six-inch barrel, a Desert Eagle is just under a foot long. Compare that to a Beretta 9mm semi-automatic pistol, which has a barrel length of 4.9 inches and overall length of 8.5 inches and you start to understand the sheer size of the thing.

First seen in 1985's *The Year of the Dragon*, the Desert Eagle and its variations became the go-to big gun for movies and television, making hundreds of appearances in films such as *RoboCop* (1987), *Black Rain* (1989), *The Last Action Hero* (1993), the *Matrix* trilogy (1999–2003), and even *Austin Powers in Goldmember* (2002), as well as television shows such as *Miami Vice*, *Firefly*, and *Fringe*. It's basically a gun for badass characters, so it seems right that Mike is using one.

SPEED KILLS (SEASON 3)

Body Count
Walt: 2 (Gus's street-dealers)
Salamanca Twins: 11 (truckload of illegal immigrants, driver, 2 elderly ladies, reservation cop, random guy in parking lot, Tortuga, etc.)
Gus: 1 (Juan Bolsa) + Unknown Others
Hank: 1 (Marco Salamanca)
Mike: 5 (Leonel Salamanca, 4 cartel hitters)
Jesse: 1 (Gale)

Beatdowns
Jesse: 1 (by Hank)

What's Cooking

"THIS HO HAS TO GO!!!!!!!"
FAN HATRED OF SKYLER WHITE

There is a segment of *Breaking Bad* fans that see Walt as doing what he has to do to provide for his family. To some of these fans, Walt's choice to cook meth and establish a drug empire is viewed as courageous, as his actions involve great personal risk. In turn, these fans view Skyler as a disrespectful, shrewish wife who does not appreciate Walt's efforts. A Facebook page called "Kill Off Skyler White" provides these fans with a forum to vent their frustration with Skyler, as do a number of other such sites. And their frustration often gets ugly, as a sampling of posts illustrates (all quotes verbatim from the site, including grammatical errors):

- "She makes me want to punch women."
- "She is a cunt and needs to die."
- "Why didn't they leave her in the pool?"

Other posts express the wish that Skyler's end involve pain, torture, and rape. A corresponding "I Hate Marie Schrader" page is similar, where some fans have expressed sentiments such as:

- "I don't no which bitch I hate more??..It's a conundrum"
- "i hate this bitch so much i cant wait until shes dead"
- "Cheers to a Marie free episode last night!"

As sisters, it's hardly surprising that both Skyler and Marie share some personality traits, including being strong, outspoken women. For this, both characters earned heaps of disdain from some fans, with a certain segment actually rooting for the violent death of both sisters. However, the vast majority of the contempt is directed at Skyler rather than Marie, so Skyler will be the primary focus of this discussion.

Fans who see Skyler as an annoyance that must be put in her place with violence and quite possibly murder are seeking to punish her independence and silence her voice, although the fans themselves often don't see that as what they're advocating. Over and over again, what is expressed on these sites is a rage that Skyler simply "doesn't know her place." Interestingly, Walt is generally given a pass for his behavior, which includes drug manufacturing, poisoning a child, and multiple murders. Sky, on the other hand, is being marked for death because she (a) had an affair, (b) used Walt's money to pay off her lover's tax debt, and (c) isn't willing to just let Walt do as he pleases. It's likely that (c) annoys these fans more than the other two reasons, which is the truly disturbing part.

Misogyny and hatred of strong female characters is hardly new to television or to social media (see Betty Draper on *Mad Men*, Carmela Soprano on *The Sopranos*, Rita Morgan on *Dexter*), and deep at its corroded heart is the desire to control women, which implies that women have power that must, at all costs, be corralled. It can be argued that Skyler is acting with power and agency and that independence is the "crime" for which she must be punished with assault, violence, and death. But it can also be argued that Skyler *lacks* power. Certainly the deliberately uncomfortable-to-watch bed scene in "Madrigal" indicates a powerless Skyler — and let's not even discuss the kitchen sex scene that winds up with her avocado face mask smeared on appliances. To a misogynist, it's not enough for a woman to be robbed of agency to act as she pleases, for that might mean she doesn't obey. No, a woman cannot even have the *appearance* of defying a man. And that is what is at the heart of Skyler-hate — a mere woman is keeping Walter Hartwell White from having his way. Vince Gilligan has called early-season Skyler "the voice of morality on the show" and he has expressed dismay that people view her as a "killjoy" when Walt's the one cooking drugs and murdering people. But it must be said that Skyler is not without her flaws, so let's examine them in terms of why some *Breaking Bad* fans feel Skyler must be punished.

Skyler needs to be punished because she slept with Ted. Okay, not defending infidelity here. It is true that Sky breaks her marriage vows and she does this very deliberately, fully intending to inform Walt of her transgression.

So why does she do something so hurtful and cruel? Well, it could be to even the scales a bit. At this point, Sky knows that Walt's money is coming from his venture into the meth-manufacturing business. Wanting to protect the family, Sky consults a lawyer about filing for divorce from Walt. Walt refuses to leave the house, so Sky takes this course of action to push him out. Reprehensible, yes. But not worthy of a slow, painful death. Also, hardly anyone says that Ted ought to be strung up for fooling around with Sky. In fact, Ted is shown to have a deeper emotional commitment to the affair than Skyler has. The sin for which Sky is being punished under this scenario is her behaving in a masculine way by undertaking an extramarital affair devoid of emotional ties. Bad Skyler, bad!

Skyler needs to be punished because she used Walt's money to pay off Ted's debts. Now, this one really doesn't make a lick of sense. On top of being willing to fool around with the very married Skyler, Ted has been cooking the books and the IRS has caught up with him. Sky's name is all over those official tax documents and if her involvement comes to light and the IRS begins sniffing around the Whites' financial records, there's going to be hell to pay. Sky does what Walt would do and concocts a complicated scheme to get the money to Ted so he'll pay the debt and end the inquiry. But Ted gets greedy and things get wildly out of hand. The difference is that no one winds up in a barrel or with red laser sights tagging their chests. The sin for which Sky is being punished under this scenario is acting too much like Walt. Bad Skyler, bad!

Skyler needs to just shut up and take it. This is the core issue. Here, the fans are honest enough to not bother disguising their misogyny. Under this theory, Skyler needs to shut her trap and be grateful that Walt is willing to go to such dangerous lengths to provide for the family. This theory is particularly ugly, for it puts forth the concept that, as a man, Walt should be praised for his willingness to support his family, despite the horrors that may entail when one supports one's family through large-scale drug dealing, manipulation, and wholesale murder. By voicing her opposition to Walt's actions and by demanding that he stop, she is a buzzkill who must be punished. Bad Skyler, bad!

In all of these scenarios, Skyler's sins pale when placed side-by-side with Walt's. This is not to say that Skyler is a saint — far from it. Skyler can be manipulative, sly, and dishonest. She crafts elaborate lies and insists on controlling the story that gets told. She even suggests that Jesse should be killed to protect the story. In short, she and Walt are an excellent pair. The problem is that very few couples can exist for long with two alphas fighting for dominance. To a misogynist, this is unnatural in the extreme — man is innately superior to woman, upending that status quo is wrong, and the transgressing female must be severely corrected for daring to step out of line.

At the beginning of *Breaking Bad*, Walt is a weakling of a man, married to a woman who is so dismissive of him that she's not really paying attention even as she's servicing him sexually. Yet she also cooks breakfast for the family every morning and uses his birthday bacon to spell out "50" on his plate. As Walt's choices have made him a less honorable husband and father, viewers became confused. We rooted for him to succeed by not only beating the cancer, but also to "show them all" what a worthy man he is. Then as his choices turn darker and the bodies begin to pile up, Skyler is left to confront the harsh truth that her once-pathetic husband has become a stranger to her, and a stranger who is willing to use force and violence to attain his goals. Skyler has a physically challenged son and an infant daughter to protect from a man she scarcely recognizes these days and what she does see scares her to the marrow of her bones. She's trying hard to find a way to live in this bed she's made and she deserves better than to be wished a violent, painful death for calling Walt on his unending stream of bullshit.

Anna Gunn, who plays Skyler, actually took the extreme step of writing an op-ed piece in the *New York Times* about these issues and the concern it caused her, not just as an actress, but also as a person. She states in the piece, "Because Skyler didn't conform to a comfortable ideal of the archetypical female, she had become a kind of Rorschach test for society, a measure of our attitudes toward gender." Gunn saw that Skyler was a lightning rod for some people who disliked strong female characters who were strong even when that meant behaving in opposition to male characters. According to her, some folks were confusing the role of Skyler White (whom they hated) with the actress Anna Gunn (whom they did not know) to the extent that she had to obtain bodyguards to protect herself against the death threats she was receiving.

Threatening an actor because you don't like the character she plays on television? Even Badger has more sense than that.

Still, it must have made that 2013 Emmy win especially sweet.

EPISODE GUIDE

SEASON FOUR

4

B ox Cutter

Original air date: July 17, 2011
Written by: Vince Gilligan **Directed by:** Adam Bernstein

> "We're all on the same page . . . the one that says, 'If I can't kill
> you, you'll sure as shit wish you were dead.'" — Jesse Pinkman

*Gus violently demonstrates his displeasure at the death of Gale. Meanwhile, Skyler
tries to find Walt.*

Season 3 ended with the viewer looking down the business end of Jesse's
pistol, but that's not when Gilligan & Co. choose to pick things up in the first
episode of season 4. Instead, the cold open to "Box Cutter" is a flashback, set a
month or two earlier as Gale Boetticher and Victor are unpacking equipment
and setting up the Superlab beneath Gus Fring's industrial laundry. There's
a lot of exposition going on here and most of it is very, very subtle. The
biggest surprise is that the Superlab was never intended for Walt. Instead,
it was *Gale* who was originally chosen to be Gus's master chef. Indeed, it is
Gale's very honest assessment of Walt's product that causes Gus to change
his mind about working with Heisenberg. When Gus first takes Walt to see
the Superlab in "Más," he allows him to assume that this has all been done for
him, although he never actually says so, knowing that Walt's pride and ego
will do the rest. The cold open to "Box Cutter" reveals is that Gus is playing
a long game. A *very* long game.

The suspense of season 3's cliffhanger is finally alleviated as the first act
of "Box Cutter" picks up right where "Full Measure" left off. In one of the

most incredible sequences of the entire series, Giancarlo Esposito, Bryan Cranston, Aaron Paul, Jonathan Banks, and Jeremiah Bitsui give simply astounding performances as Gus enters the room, methodically removes his coat, and puts on a jumpsuit. Gus's silence, stillness, and meticulous neatness are more terrifying than any raging speech could be, and the tension is almost bone-breaking as Walt desperately justifies himself and tries to convince Gus to let them start cooking. When Gus suddenly kills Victor, everyone, including Mike, is horrified, yet Gus remains calm, even as he pulls Victor's head back so that his blood will splatter Walt and Jesse, who have no choice but to watch Victor die gurgling. The message is clear: Victor is a trusted and capable member of Gus's organization. In fact, he has been watching Walt so carefully that he can duplicate his recipe for meth. But Victor screwed up when he let himself be seen at Gale's apartment, so he is now a serious liability. To this point Gus has seemed to be rather reasonable for a drug lord, but this brutal act makes it absolutely clear that if Gus's operation is directly threatened by anyone — no matter how trusted or long-serving — Gus will do *whatever* it takes to deal with that threat. Further, he will act without hesitation or regret, and he won't even get his shoes dirty as he bloodies his hands.

Something very interesting and unexpected happens here. As Victor is slaughtered, Walt pushes himself as far back in his chair as he can, turning his head away from the gruesome spectacle, and his mouth and throat work to suppress his terrified nausea. Jesse, though, leans forward and *meets Gus's eyes*, unflinching and unafraid. Something fundamental has shifted in Jesse and Gus sees it. This transformation is reinforced when Walt and Jesse talk over breakfast later, with Jesse eating heartily. Walt is scared out of his wits, trying to figure out what to do, but Jesse is matter-of-fact. Gus has just told them that, sooner or later, they're dead men, and Jesse has accepted that. The status quo following the deaths of Gale and Victor is quite clear, and since Jesse has already crossed the ultimate moral line when he murdered Gale, in his eyes, death is the next logical consequence. After Jane and Gale, that's all right by him, at least for the moment. Walt, on the other hand, is confused. Nothing in his master plan worked out as he had intended. Instead of Gale's execution putting him in an unassailable position of power, he finds himself confronted with his own powerlessness, and he doesn't know what to do next. Walt is afraid, again, and when Walt's afraid, dangerous things follow.

LAB NOTES

HIGHLIGHT

SKYLER (ON THE PHONE WITH SAUL): "He carpools to work — in a meth lab."

SAUL: "Hey! Whoa! You're breaking up there — I didn't quite catch that last . . . Whoo! You're a Chatty Cathy today!"

DID YOU NOTICE

- Gus and Gale's conversation in the cold open about the purity of Walt's meth and Gus's statement that he doesn't consider Walt to be professional places the flashback during the season 2 episode "Mandala."
- Skyler finds the glass eye that fell from Wayfarer 515 in Walt's apartment. Though not as prominently displayed as in season 3, the eye continues to be a reminder that Walt's past is always with him, and despite all of his rationalizations, cannot be erased.
- Walt and Jesse are much more confident and competent with using hydrofluoric acid to dispose of Victor's body than they were with Krazy-8 and Emilio way back in season 1.
- Referring to Gale, Walt tells Gus, "I'd shoot him again tomorrow." Walt's quick to take credit for what he didn't do.
- After they leave the lab, Walt and Jesse are dressed in matching cheap slacks and T-shirts from some big box store because the clothes they had been wearing were covered in Victor's blood. Again, as in ". . . And the Bag's in the River," this is very similar to the scene in Quentin Tarantino's *Pulp Fiction* (1994) when Vincent and Jules are wearing cheap T-shirts and shorts after accidentally shooting Marvin (Phil LaMarr) and splattering themselves with gore.
- On the coffee table in Gale's apartment there is a notebook clearly labeled "Lab Notes."
- Gale's best meth is 96 percent pure, while Walt's is 99-plus percent pure. Those numbers will be important later on.

SHOOTING UP

- The now familiar POV shot appears early in the cold open as the viewer gets an inside-the-box perspective while Gale cuts away the straps. Later, it's a view from inside the hydrofluoric acid–filled barrel with Victor's remains as his gun and the eponymous box cutter are tossed in.

◆ Simple primary colors dominate the scene of Gus killing Victor. Walt is in blue, Gus is in a red hazmat suit, and the bright yellows of the containers in the background create a very simple color palette. These are "happy" colors that are often used in playgrounds and elementary schools because they're bright and cheerful. Here they serve to underscore the shock and horror of Victor's death for the viewer because such an act is even more unexpected against such a background.

◆ As Gus silently looks around the lab for the box cutter, the camera is above the lab, looking down, a God's-eye-view of the proceedings that gives the viewer a sense of the space and of everything happening at once.

◆ There is a lovely transition shot from a floor-up POV of Jesse mopping up Victor's blood to a plate-up POV of him using a French fry to mop up some ketchup at Denny's, giving the viewer the same kind of visceral connection between murder and breakfast that makes Walt so shocked that Jesse can eat. It is also strongly reminiscent of a similar linking of gore and food with Emilio's liquefied remains in ". . . And the Bag's in the River" and the grill-up POV of barbecue chicken cooking in "Cancer Man."

TITLE The title is obviously connected with the actual box cutter used by Gale and Gus, but it may also indicate that Walt and Jesse's actions at the end of season 3 have opened up a new and much more dangerous life for them in season 4.

INTERESTING FACTS

◆ "Box Cutter" marks the first appearance of Saul Goodman's security guard Huell, played by stand-up comic Lavell Crawford.

◆ As Walt changes the channels on the Aztek's radio, a DJ references Albuquerque's "330 days of sunshine a year." Duke City is in the so-called "Sun Belt," a name given to the lower third of the United States. Roughly described as the area south of the 36th parallel, the Sun Belt is known for having a moderate climate with relatively mild winters and extended summers. The Albuquerque area has well over 300 sunny days per year, with low humidity and little rainfall (about nine inches per year). However, New Mexico is also prone to some extreme weather, including blizzards, drought, and high winds — and *Breaking Bad* viewers know that the New Mexico desert is a harsh and unforgiving place.

SPECIAL INGREDIENTS

ROCKS AND MINERALS

Hank now collects minerals and he makes a point of correcting anyone who claims that he collects rocks. In an interesting echo of Walt's precision towards all things chemical, Hank is touchy about the difference and he gets exasperated with those who don't understand that minerals are purer than rocks. Simply put, the difference is that rocks are composed of various sorts of common minerals all mixed in together, while minerals are the building blocks of rocks. If a rock is a baked chocolate chip cookie, then minerals are the chocolate chips, flour, eggs, sugar, etc. that make up the cookie; the ingredients themselves. Minerals are often identified by their crystalline structure, meaning that Walt, the "master of crystallography" ("Gray Matter"), and Hank share an obsession.

Minerals are also classified by their resistance to scratching (their hardness), which is measured by the Mohs scale. The softest mineral (with a ranking on 1 of the Mohs scale) is talc, while the hardest (with a ranking of 10) is diamond. A mineral can only be scratched by an object with a higher Mohs score, which explains why only diamond can scratch diamond.

The study of rocks is called "petrology" while the study of minerals is called "mineralogy." While rocks fall into three broad classifications — igneous, sedimentary, and metamorphic — there are over 4,000 distinct minerals. So if Hank wants a complete collection, he's going to need a bigger house.

4.02

Thirty-Eight Snub

Original air date: July 24, 2011
Written by: George Mastras **Directed by:** Michelle MacLaren

"You won, Walter. You got the job. Do yourself a favor and learn to take 'yes' for an answer." — Mike Ehrmantraut

Walt schemes to deal with Gus while Skyler plots to buy Bogdan's car wash. Meanwhile, Jesse and Hank struggle with their recent violent encounters.

"Thirty-Eight Snub" is about pain — not so much physical pain (though Hank is surely experiencing more than his fair share of that) but psychological pain, which no amount of physical therapy can help heal. Walt's murderous plotting runs throughout the episode, but it is Jesse and Hank who form the story's heart this time around. Gale's murder is beginning to come home for Jesse, who is skimming Gus's product and using again. After an afternoon with Badger and Skinny Pete, he realizes that his new, insanely powerful sound system, the meth, and his buddies' hyper zombie video game arguments still aren't enough to distract him from himself. "It's quiet," he says, and Jesse just can't have that right now. If things are quiet, if there's nothing to focus his attention or blur his mind, then he has to think about Gale, and remind himself that he is now a cold-blooded murderer. Facing that is terrifying, and living with it is even worse, so Jesse desperately opens his house to any and all comers for a meth-fueled, multi-day, continuous house party. Jesse doesn't care who's there, or why; all he wants is noise, people, booze, drugs, and absolutely anything but to be alone with himself.

When he finally does find himself alone, he turns up the decibels and slumps down right against the speakers, head in hands, eyes wet, as if it is all he can do to hold himself together.

Meanwhile, Hank's mineral collection has become an obsession. Unable to sleep and unwilling to face his own anger and frustration over the disabling gunfight with the Salamanca cousins in "One Minute," Hank stays up into the wee hours turning his minerals over and over, examining, cataloging, categorizing, reading, distracting himself as surely as Jesse is doing. Unable to turn off his usual exuberant bonhomie with his physical therapist (PT) or other outsiders, he reserves all of his anger for Marie, who is doing everything she can for him, from unflagging support and cheerleading to hand-scrubbing his bedpans. It's a vicious cycle for Hank. He sees what he's doing, sees what a selfish, angry bastard he has become, but he just can't stop. If he does, like Jesse, he will have to face the fact that he will probably never walk without difficulty again, that he has no job and no real prospects, and that his career may be over. Becoming totally dependent on his wife for everything from paying the bills to wiping his ass is the ultimate emasculation for tough guy Hank, so he lashes out at Marie, and hates himself a little more for it every day.

The two portraits are an incredibly moving depiction of human suffering and untreated post-traumatic stress disorder (PTSD). *Breaking Bad* refuses to look away from the consequences of what Jesse and Hank have been through, and the sheer emotional agony each man is experiencing reaches out from the screen and grabs the viewer with instantly recognizable human truth. Aaron Paul and Dean Norris use their craft to exquisite effect here, creating a level of emotional realism that goes right to the hearts of viewers. Gilligan & Co. are dedicated to bringing an evolving show and characters to the screen, and one of the most fundamental ways human beings grow and change is through pain. The kind of inescapable suffering that Jesse and Hank are experiencing is something that, in one way or another, most viewers have gone through, and that makes them "real." Perhaps most real of all is the fact that in life, actions and choices have consequences, and we all have to live with them — every day.

The ripples of Hank and Jesse's pain are beginning to affect those around them as well. Marie is Hank's rock, but she's not made of granite. She's as fragile as one of Hank's precious geodes, and just as liable to fragment if handled too roughly. She knows better than anyone else what's going on with Hank, but being the constant target for Hank's self-pitying rage is taking its toll. Marie is trying to hold everything together, from house to bills to her family to her job to Hank himself, and it's more than she can bear. Jesse's girlfriend Andrea is also caught in the waves, even as Jesse tries to make things right between them, and better for her and Brock. Jesse is withdrawing, pushing her away, and not telling her why. Yet he is also providing for her and her son, sending conflicting messages, at best. In the end, it is the relationships that make *Breaking Bad* the best show on TV, and the truth of relationships, sad to say, is sometimes pain, confusion, and heartbreak — three things Gilligan & Co. portray very well indeed.

LAB NOTES

HIGHLIGHT

BADGER: "Think on it bro: they're not just zombies, they're *Nazi* zombies!"

DID YOU NOTICE

- Badger and Skinny Pete's meth-fueled babble about zombies is apropos. Before they came in, Jesse was completely zombied out himself, staring into the flashing lights of his new stereo.
- Badger provides an explanation for the uncut pizza seen in "Caballo Sin Nombre" when Walt threw a tantrum and hurled a huge uncut pie onto the roof of his garage.
- Mike, heretofore unflappable, is visibly upset when he finds a dried spot of Victor's blood on his cuff.
- The delivery guy dropping off minerals at Hank and Marie's house is wearing Marie's favorite color: purple.
- Walt's carefully lined up bullets on the breakfast counter mirrors Marie's Splenda packets.
- The deliberate contrast between the quiet, sunny, cheerful suburban world outside of Jesse's house, and the dim, dirty, violently loud world within it.
- The debris and trash from Jesse's party is starting to pile up, mirroring his earlier apartment when he and Jane began using meth and heroin.

- Skyler doesn't seem to see anything wrong with taking Holly along for the ride as she lays her own schemes.

SHOOTING UP
- Primary colors are used as an ironic counterpoint to and underlining of what's going on as we see the lights from the sound system playing across Jesse's face as he stares blankly at the system.
- The POV shots from the perspective of the fireplace and the Roomba make Jesse's living room seem larger than it actually is.
- During the party, the camera is again in God's-eye mode, and again placed above the point where the ceiling would be.

TITLE The gun Walt buys from the dealer is a .38 caliber "special" snub-nosed revolver, meaning that the barrel length on the pistol is three inches or less. Accurate only at close range, this type of pistol has long been preferred by undercover or plainclothes police because it is easily concealable. Likewise, criminals have also found the .38 snub to be a handy accessory.

INTERESTING FACTS
- The illegal gun dealer Walt buys the pistol from is played by Jim Beaver, also well known for his roles as Whitney Ellsworth on *Deadwood*, Bobby Singer on *Supernatural*, and Shelby Parlow on *Justified*. Beaver began his career in 1977 in an uncredited role in the Burt Reynolds and Kris Kristofferson football film *Semi-Tough*.
- Between seasons 3 and 4, the actual house that had been used for Jesse's house in earlier seasons was sold, necessitating the construction of a set duplicating the interior. Series cinematographer Michael Slovis argued for — and got — a specially constructed set of Jesse's living room that was both larger than the original, and designed to allow Slovis to capture shots from multiple angles and positions throughout the set.

SPECIAL INGREDIENTS

"NEW MEXICO IS NOT A RETREAT JURISDICTION": STAND YOUR GROUND LAWS
It is often said that a man's home is his castle and that certainly is the case

when it comes to self-defense. Under the common law, self-defense allows a non-aggressor the right to use force (even deadly force) if that person reasonably believes that such force is necessary to protect himself from imminent use of unlawful force by the other person. Under this law, a person is required to retreat if he could do so safely before resorting to deadly force, but there is an exception if the attack is in the non-aggressor's house or on his immediate property — your home is your castle.

However, many states, including New Mexico, have enacted so-called "stand your ground" laws. These laws essentially do away with the "retreat" element of a self-defense claim. The common law permits a person to "stand his ground" against attack within his own house, but these laws expand that. While many states require that the person asserting the self-defense claim must have a right to be at the location where the altercation occurred, New Mexico's law simply states that the person must have been "threatened with attack." In Walt's line of work, that covers a lot of territory.

O|pen House

Original air date: July 31, 2011
Written by: Sam Catlin **Directed by:** David Slade

"For what it's worth, getting the shit kicked out of you — not to say you, uh, get used to it, but you *do* kinda get used to it."
— Jesse Pinkman

Jesse continues his downward spiral. Meanwhile Marie goes house hunting, and Walt and Skyler become allies in an attempt to acquire the car wash.

In "Open House," Walt may be front and center in Gustavo's meth operation, but he isn't the one in control. To watch Walt's every move, Gus has installed cameras in the lab and they are not set on some kind of automatic sweep, but are apparently staffed — and all Walt can do is flip off the person watching. Even at his apartment Walt can't get away from being interrogated, as Skyler badgers him about his black eye. Walt, of course, frames his encounter with Mike in "Thirty-Eight Snub" as a "fight" rather than a one-punch takedown, and intimates that Mike's advanced age kept Walt from responding. Lying has become as automatic as breathing and this petty attempt to make himself look tough to Skyler simply underlines Walt's current impotence. Between the two of them, it is Skyler who now leads the way, easily manipulating Walt's masculine pride to convince him that they must purchase Bogdan's car wash and no other, simply as an act of petty revenge.

In fact, "Open House" fully reveals that Skyler is just as manipulative, underhanded, and selfish as Walt. She has set her mind on getting Bogdan's

car wash, having spent weeks doing exhaustive research and getting her numbers together, but when Bogdan Wolynetz (Marius Stan) won't sell she refuses to accept it. Skyler wants what she wants and is willing to go to almost any lengths to get it, including committing felony fraud. Faced with two petty, vindictive, and petulant clients, Saul comes through, but he's becoming increasingly aware that Walt and Skyler are making his life dangerously difficult. Both have left reason far behind, and after the successful scam to trick Bogdan into selling, Skyler skewers Walt over the small things, like a bottle of champagne, carefully overlooking the fact that they just spent $800,000 on a car wash. Skyler is so intent on the devil in the details that she is missing the big picture.

Meanwhile, Marie has finally cracked. In an incredible sequence of vignettes, Betsy Brandt gives the viewer an incredible portrait of a woman trying to escape the hard realities of her current life, even if only for a little while — not only the responsibilities that she has had to shoulder since Hank's shooting, but also the never-ending flow of derision, anger, and belittling comments from her hurting, angry husband. It's not just escape Marie wants, though: it's rescuing. She finds solace once again in shoplifting, only this time she ups the ante to petty theft by taking things from people's homes. The things she steals are ridiculous: a Hummel figurine, a collectible spoon, a silver frame. Each is a memento of the imaginary life she creates for herself as she visits various open houses, lives that had their troubles, but were healthy and happy, where she was loved by husbands and children and where things were good. Once again Marie's stealing is a cry for attention. But where before she wanted to pull the attention away from a pregnant sister with a sick husband and get her own spouse to spend more time with her, this time it's an attempt to compel Hank to notice she exists. When Hank is forced to finally respond to her positively by getting her out of trouble, she finally lays out everything. Her breakdown is devastating to watch, because the viewer has seen where she's been, and knows exactly what she's been doing. She's done everything she could think to do, been the kind of spouse everyone wishes they had, bent over backwards to support and love Hank, and all she's gotten is his grief, anger, and pain. Of course she breaks; who wouldn't?

Something comes from Marie's grief besides relief, however. Hank's friend, APD Detective Tim Roberts (Nigel Gibbs who's also had roles on *House M.D.* and *The Shield*) brings him a copy of the complete case file on Gale's murder. Roberts knows exactly what Hank needs and knows that Hank won't get it from either minerals or Marie. Hank needs a puzzle to solve and criminals to catch. It's what the man does, after all, and despite all of Hank's protestations to the contrary, he's not near done with being a cop. It's who he is. The episode ends on another sleepless night for Hank, only this time it's not minerals he turns to, but the lab notes of Gale Boetticher.

LAB NOTES

HIGHLIGHT

SAUL: "I mean — just so we're on the same page here — you're saying that we 'make him an offer that he can't refuse?'"

DID YOU NOTICE

- Walt is still enjoying coffee from Gale's elaborate setup in the Superlab, and as he does so, the reality of Gale's murder comes home to him — for a moment.
- Jesse's having none of Walt's manipulation this season and he turns Walt's questions about what's going on with him right back around.
- Not only is Jesse starting to scratch like a tweaker, a nervous clawing at the back and side of his neck, but his house is beginning to take on the look of the tweakers' home that we saw in "Peekaboo." Jesse's becoming the sort of person he despises.
- Saul is still trying to get someone to use the nail salon as a money laundering cover, like he did for Jesse in "Kafkaesque."

- Tim Roberts is the same APD detective who handled Walt's missing persons case in "Over."
- The haunting, almost chant-like music playing over Jesse's go-kart and homecoming montage is "If I Had a Heart" by Fever Ray, and adds to the emotional jaggedness and out-of-place feeling that surrounds Jesse.

SHOOTING UP

- The camera work in "Open House" is subtle, and the only trademark POV shot used is from the surveillance camera in the Superlab.
- A montage of jump cuts (where two sequential shots of the same scene or person are taken from just slightly different positions) is used for Jesse's go-kart driving and homecoming, lending the scene a sense of disjointed timelessness and rage. Again primary colors from the stereo system in Jesse's house are used to light his face as he settles into the wild and violent drug party that his house has become. The strobing red, green, and yellow lights add to the disjointed and out-of-place feeling of his living room, again complemented by flash cuts (very quick views of different scenes or different elements within a scene) to various instances of sex, violence, slam-dancing, and graffiti going on around Jesse as he, paradoxically, finally relaxes.

TITLE "Open House" refers not only to the real estate showings Marie visits (and the fact that she treats them as if the contents are open for the taking), but also to Jesse's house, which he has thrown open to all of the dangerous and chaotic forces of the outside world.

SPECIAL INGREDIENTS

EPA CAR WASH INSPECTORS?

Skyler may be a manipulative felon, but she does her homework. Bogdan *should* be concerned about the Environmental Protection Agency (EPA). Commercial car washes use water and chemicals to remove dirt and grime from vehicles. The resulting waste-water can be harmful to the environment and is highly regulated in the United States. In addition to plain old dirt, contaminants in car wash waste-water can include oil and grease (which can contain hazardous materials such as herbicides, benzene, chromium, and arsenic, to name only a few), detergents, phosphates, and chemicals used in cleaning and maintaining the machinery of the car wash.

The Clean Water Act requires car washes to route waste-water to either water treatment facilities or state-approved drainage facilities. Filtration of the waste-water is recommended so that fewer solids are present in the discharge to a sanitary sewer system. Once filtration has taken place, the car wash has a "sludge" that has to be disposed of, also in accordance with particular regulations and laws. All of this is designed to prevent soil and groundwater contamination. Having your business shut down to deal with these issues is both hugely inconvenient and costly. No wonder Bogdan is eager to sell.

Bullet Points

4.04

Original air date: August 7, 2011
Written by: Moira Walley-Beckett **Directed by:** Colin Bucksey

"God, I wanted to get this guy — me personally, I wanted to be the one to slap the handcuffs on him . . ." — Hank Schrader

Skyler and Walt get their story straight, but family dinners remain problematic. Meanwhile, Walt tries to figure out if Jesse left any clues behind at Gale's apartment.

Skyler has her car wash, but her schemes aren't complete until she can create the perfect cover for how they got the money to buy it, so she's been working on expanding her off-the-cuff gambling story from "Kafkaesque" into a full-fledged explanation. Although she pretends to be doing all of this because she has to, she's also really enjoying the process. After all, as "Pilot/Breaking Bad" revealed, Skyler is a frustrated fiction writer, and this is the most important tale she has ever constructed. Unfortunately, just as with the champagne in the previous episode, Skyler's obsession with the details blinds her to the truth that the simpler a lie is, the better. Skyler wants more than a return to a semblance of normalcy; she wants the satisfaction and credit for being the one to make that happen. Her pride and ego are every bit a match for Walt's, only where Walt's self-image is tied up in being the world's greatest meth cook, hers is invested in being the fixer and the author of perfect fictions.

The family dinner at Hank and Marie's is arguably more important in and of itself than any of Skyler's plots. This marks a seeming return to normalcy for both families. Such dinners were the norm up until Hank's shooting and subsequent retreat into self-pity and rage. Now Hank seems much more himself: clean-shaven, fully dressed, genuinely glad to see the Whites, and eager to share not only his mineral collection but also the real reason behind his attitude change — Gale's notebook. The unusual opportunity to get inside the mind of the kind of person he is so good at tracking down has brought Hank at least somewhat out of his angry spiral into depression. Hank's biggest skill as a detective, however, is that he notices things that most everyone else misses. Walt should be terrified that Hank has Gale's notebook, and he is, but for all the wrong reasons.

Once again jumping to conclusions without any supporting evidence, Walt assumes that the fingerprints found at the scene are Jesse's, and that without them, Hank will have nothing to go on and won't be able to make a case. While Hank sees Walt as the ultimate harmless egghead, Walt sees Hank as just another dumb cop. Their continuous underestimation of each other is one of the driving tensions in *Breaking Bad*, and perhaps Gilligan & Co.'s greatest plot of all.

On the upside, Walt's frantic visit to Jesse gives the viewer the opportunity to see Jesse's house from an outsider's perspective. The place is completely trashed. An unconscious body blocks the door, the walls are covered with graffiti, and people in various states of undress and consciousness sprawl, sit, stand, or dance in their own filth, all lit by the cycling lights of the sound system and backgrounded by the paranoid monologue of one skinny tweaker who always has something to worry about and expound upon. The transformation of Jesse's home from place of refuge from the outside world to a chaotic condensation of all the worst elements of that world is complete. In the middle of it all, Jesse seems to have found some sort of unstable peace, which Walt immediately tries to destroy by making him remember every second of Gale's murder, the very thing from which Jesse has been so painfully escaping. Jesse has Walt ejected and returns to his cocoon of noise and drugs, where he has finally become numb and achieved the relief of not caring about anything, up to and including whether or not he lives or dies — making it the perfect time for a road trip with Mike.

LAB NOTES

HIGHLIGHT

SAUL: "My name never comes up with these guys, does it?"

DID YOU NOTICE

+ When Walt's "gambling problem" is revealed, Walt Jr. thinks his dad is a stud, and Skyler doesn't like that at all.
+ Walt's story about his black eye has changed. Now Mike sucker punched him, the implication being that that was the only way Walt could get beat up by an older man.
+ Jesse grabs a hot young thing and takes her up to his bedroom to . . . play video games. He's not as numb as he thinks he is: he still needs simple companionship.

SHOOTING UP

+ The first shot of the cold open is beautifully done, both aesthetically and as deliberate audience misdirection. The apparent smoke against the black background recalls the *Breaking Bad* opening credits, and thus the exhalation of a meth smoker, but it turns out to be Mike's breath chilled by his sitting in the refrigerated truck. Both gaseous swirls emanate from a deadly source, however, as the rest of the scene demonstrates.
+ The use of Gale's touristy, apparently made-in-Thailand music video of "Major Tom" by Peter Schilling is a wonderful use of a film-within-a-film — or *mise en abyme* — technique, and creates an impressive mix of humor, shock, and sadness. It also adds an interesting element to Gale's character. You can see the complete video at: http://www.tinyurl.com/GaleMajorTom.
+ The end of the episode sees the return of another trademark *Breaking Bad* shot: the wide angle shot of desert and sky that emphasizes the emptiness of the desert spaces around Albuquerque, which the viewer has by now been conditioned to see as being without memory and where dangerous and deadly things happen.

TITLE "Bullet Points" refers not only to Skyler's outline for their gambling addiction story, but also to the holes punched into the back of the truck by the hijacker's bullets during the cold open.

INTERESTING FACTS

* Peter Schilling's "Major Tom" (1983) is a retelling of the classic David Bowie tune "Space Oddity" (1969).
* Hank and Walt briefly mention the film *The French Connection* (1971) and Jimmy "Popeye" Doyle (Gene Hackman). In the film, Doyle is an NYPD narcotics detective, chasing a major drug distributor, a Frenchman named Charnier. Despite Walt's claim that Doyle never catches "the guy," the ending of the film is much more ambiguous. Interestingly, "Popeye" Doyle wears a hat that is strikingly similar to the one worn by Walt in his Heisenberg persona.

SPECIAL INGREDIENTS

THE KELLY CRITERION

Skyler's been reading up on gambling strategies, particularly one system known as the Kelly Criterion, which is named for its creator, J.L. Kelly. Kelly began developing investing strategies based on probability theories, and posited that his system was suitable for a "long game" in which the investment is repeated over and over, always with the same probability of winning and the same payout ratio.

Kelly's system has been applied to game theory, as well as the stock market. Keep in mind that the Kelly Criterion can't guarantee a win; rather, it guarantees that you (1) won't lose all of your money, and (2) maximizes your profits when you win. The system maximizes growth rates by using a mathematical formula to determine the percentage of a player's bankroll that should be bet at a particular stage of the game.

The trick is that, in order to use the Kelly Criterion successfully, the player must be able to estimate three items: the odds, the probability of winning, and the probability of losing the bet. In a game such as blackjack that has only two outcomes (losing the entire bet or winning the bet amount multiplied by the payoff odds), card counting helps. Mathematically, the Kelly Criterion looks like this:

$$f = (bp - q)/b$$

Where:

f is the fraction of the player's bankroll that should be wagered,

b is the odds the player receives on the bet,

p is the probability that the player will win the bet, and

q is the probability the player will lose the bet.

It's complicated, messy, and requires great attention to detail. No wonder Skyler likes it.

Shotgun

Original air date: August 14, 2011

Written by: Thomas Schnauz **Directed by:** Michelle MacLaren

"Since when do vegans eat fried chicken?" — Hank Schrader

Mike takes Jesse for a ride. Meanwhile, Walt tries to confront Gus, and talks too much at another White-Schrader family dinner.

The cold open to "Shotgun" is loud and frenetic, starting the episode off at a fever pitch and seemingly setting the stage for a grand confrontation. After the credits, however, all of Walt's tire-screeching sound and fury winds up signifying nothing, as Gus continues to elude him and Walt's control over his situation continues to disintegrate. He thinks he's being a man of action, but what he is actually doing is drawing attention to both himself and Los Pollos Hermanos — a tactic not likely to amuse Gus. Most frightening to Walt is the realization that he has lost control over Jesse. Throughout the preceding three seasons, Jesse has, for the most part, been the person most susceptible to Walt's manipulations. Walt has used his status as a father figure to con Jesse into everything from approaching Tuco with a business proposition to murdering Gale. Now, however, Jesse is moving away from Walt. Indeed, Jesse has been moving away from everyone and everything, including himself, since the beginning of this season. Walt's aborted confrontation with Jesse in "Bullet Points" has proven that Jesse just doesn't care, and he won't hesitate to have Walt thrown out of his house. Now, Jesse seems equally

uncaring that Mike has taken him deep into the desert for some unknown purpose, and Walt is more lost than ever.

While Walt spends most of the episode flailing about, Jesse enjoys a strange, mind-numbingly boring sort of adventure as he and Mike spend the entire day driving from point to point to make pickups of money at six different, abandoned spots. Though Jesse claims not to care what happens to him, he nonetheless arms himself as best he can as they arrive at the first drop point, unsure yet as to what's happening and to what Mike's real motives are. It seems he might not be quite as fatalistic as he's been acting. By the end of the day, Jesse has assumed the role of Mike's guard, and despite Mike's exasperated assertions that Jesse isn't "the guy," Jesse has assumed responsibility for watching Mike's back anyway. Mike has given Jesse a purpose and it doesn't seem to even matter that it's a false one, with Gus pulling strings behind the curtain. In "Shotgun," Jesse starts pulling himself out of the hole he's been trying to bury himself in since Gale's murder.

It's not all gloom and doom for Walt though. As he and Skyler finally reconcile, it's worth noting that this too occurs under false circumstances, with Sky misinterpreting Walt's frantic call from the cold open as a thoughtful, honest declaration of love. With the one thing he has desperately wanted since the beginning of season 3 within his grasp, Walt's pride makes him hedge when Skyler offers to let him move back in. He has to make her wait, and wonder, but only for a little while. Walt has reached the point where all of his relationships are games built around his supposed ability to manipulate other people's emotions to his own benefit. The sweet, kind guy of earlier seasons has all but disappeared.

Walt blows any chance he has at retaining Jesse's loyalty by suggesting to him that he is not important enough for Mike and Gus to take an interest in him. Fundamentally, Walt still sees Jesse as a loser. In making this clear to Jesse, Walt pushes him further away, undermining his own ability to control Jesse.

His manipulation of Jesse is not the only thing Walt royally screws up in this episode either. After more than a few too many glasses of wine at another extended family get-together, Walt disagrees with Hank's belief that Gale was Heisenberg and suggests that the mysterious genius is still at large. This time, perhaps because he is actually telling the truth, Walt is thoroughly convincing. Walt's flaws are many, but pride is by far his favorite deadly sin. Something in Walt can't abide the thought that Gale, his *lab assistant*, might go down in history as the master crystal meth cook Heisenberg. Blue Magic is Walt's formula, Walt's genius made manifest, and he is incapable of letting the credit go to someone else. To make matters worse, Walt mixes his extraordinary hubris with a continued underestimation of Hank's abilities as an investigator. Walt is undoubtedly brilliant, but that very fact often makes him blind to the brilliance of others.

LAB NOTES

HIGHLIGHT

MIKE: "You're not the guy. You're not capable of being the guy. I had a guy, but now I don't. You are *not* the guy."

DID YOU NOTICE

* Jesse's newly shaved head and darker wardrobe give him more than a passing resemblance to Mike.
* Hank is wearing a DEA "Fun Run" T-shirt as he and Tim Roberts discuss Gale's case. Hank first met Gus when he toured the DEA

offices as a major sponsor of the Fun Run in "ABQ," and it is indirectly because of Gus that Hank will likely never run again.

- Junior doesn't really like coffee, but he drinks it to bond with his dad.
- Jesse is drumming out "Fallacies" by his former band TwaüghtHammër while waiting for Mike.
- Gilligan & Co. had to be careful in filming Anna Gunn this season, particularly when it comes to the sex scene between Walt and her in "Shotgun." Ironically, during season 2, when Skyler was heavily pregnant with Holly, Anna Gunn had to endure extra makeup and prosthetics to simulate pregnancy, while in season 4 she had to go through the opposite, as costuming, makeup, and clever camera angles attempted to mask the fact that Gunn was actually *very* pregnant during filming.
- The yellow shirt worn by Gus during his meeting with Mike echoes the yellow hazmat suits worn by Walt and Jesse in the Superlab.
- Walt and Jesse's montages are set to Ana Tijoux's fantastic "1977," a perfect complement to the accelerated motion and quick cuts used in the filming.

MISCALCULATIONS Not to get too nitpicky, but exactly how dangerously does one have to drive in Albuquerque to attract the attention of the APD's traffic division? In the cold open Walt is driving the Aztek like he's entirely lost his mind. There's just no way that doesn't get noticed by a cop, or that some ticked-off driver doesn't call in Walt's plate number.

SHOOTING UP

- There is some superb cinematography in this episode, particularly in the montage of Jesse and Mike's day. In a nice take on the familiar stop-motion filming *Breaking Bad* has used so effectively throughout the series, accelerated motion is now used to capture Jesse's movement during this very long day.
- There are some great POV shots in Walt's cooking montage, particularly from Walt's viewpoint inside the filter mask, a bottom-up POV from one of the tanks, and several object POVs as Walt struggles with the cook.
- Walt and Sky's makeup sex scene is nicely done. Beginning with a

ceiling-down shot as the two of them fall into bed, things progress through a distorted view shot through the lenses of Walt's glasses on the bedside table, which blurs things without hiding what's going on.

SPECIAL INGREDIENTS

DEAD DROPS

Mike takes Jesse on a series of "dead drop" pickups during this episode. In a "live drop," two or more people meet face-to-face to exchange information, cash, or other items of interest. A dead drop is used to pass items without the need for an in-person meeting. Generally, an innocuous signal is used to indicate that a dead drop has been made — convicted spy Aldrich Ames, for instance, left chalk marks on a mailbox to indicate to his Soviet handlers that a dead drop had been made. The trick is to make sure both the signal and the drop itself are located in places that the average person would simply overlook. There's even a travelers' game version of dead drops called "geo-caching" in which the dead drop contains anything from small prizes to clues to find the next drop.

Cornered
4.06

Original air date: August 21, 2011
Written by: Gennifer Hutchison **Directed by:** Michael Slovis

"No. No. This whole thing, all of this — it's all about *me*."
— Walter White

Walt's lies continue to come undone. Meanwhile, Jesse starts a second job helping Mike, and Skyler takes Holly and makes a fateful choice.

Gilligan & Co. like circular structures, and the cold open of "Cornered" brings the viewer right back to the cold open of "Shotgun," with the steaming breath of two guards in the back of a Los Pollos Hermanos truck. This time, however, things don't work out so well for Gus's men. The hijackers have gotten smarter, and much more cold-blooded. Taken together, the two cold open sequences are evidence of things happening in the larger narrative world beyond just Walt and Jesse, things that are both utterly out of their control, and inescapably closing in on them. Something big is happening, and the lunch-stealing assassins are just the tip of the proverbial iceberg.

As for Walt himself, "Cornered" sees him fumble every relationship he has in an effort to reassert control over the people around him. Skyler figures out that his "I love you" message wasn't a sweet thought, but a terrified, self-centered goodbye that had something to do with Gale's murder, making their reunion the product of yet another lie. Skyler can also clearly see what Walt refuses to: things are quickly spiraling out of control and they are all in danger.

In one of the iconic monologues of the series, Walt tries to convince her that she has it backwards, that, in his words, "I *am* the danger!" This is both true and false, of course, and to her credit, Skyler realizes that Walt is no longer just lying to the people around him, but also to *himself*. Walt actually *is* the danger to Skyler, her children, and everyone around him, and he has either killed, planned to kill, or threatened to kill nearly everyone who has posed a threat to his family. But he's not Vic Mackey, Tony Soprano, or Don Draper, despite many critics aligning him with those antiheroes; Walt is flawed, impulsive, proud, and makes rash decisions. He believes he *is* the danger, when in

(ANDREW EVANS/PR PHOTOS)

fact he more often *causes* the danger. To this point, Skyler has been treating Walt's criminal activities as some kind of game by which she herself can gain some control over her life, but with this latest testosterone display, she finally gets a sense of the deep waters she is swimming in. In the smartest move she has made since the end of season 2, Skyler grabs Holly and leaves.

With Skyler and Holly in the wind, Walt lashes out at Junior because he simply can't *stand* the idea that his son thinks he's an addict. Like turning Hank back onto Heisenberg, Walt's pride won't allow him to stay under-cover. The irony is that Junior is once again completely on Walt's side. Once he's really hurt his son's feelings, Walt tries to fix things with a day off from school and a brand new, tricked-out Dodge Challenger. To be fair, Junior guilts him into it, and why not? After all, Junior has been caught between two of the most selfishly manipulative people on the planet for almost a year now, and Walt and Sky have taught him well that adults get what they want by manipulating other people's feelings. Junior, however, is more honest about things — he knows damn well Walt is buying him off and isn't afraid to call him on it.

Finally, Walt figuratively *hurls* Jesse away from him by refusing to believe that Jesse is capable of being an asset to Mike and Gus, and insisting that since Jesse is worthless, all of his new jobs must have something to do with Walt himself. With this little display of self-absorption, Walt's true character stands utterly revealed: he cannot see beyond himself, or even entertain the thought that there are things that have absolutely nothing to do with him. In spite of his earlier angry protestations to Junior, Walt is acting very much like an addict with his utter selfishness and self-centeredness. He couldn't have driven Jesse more firmly into Mike and Gus's corner if he had tried. Even people Walt doesn't know get burned by his selfishness as, out of a fit of petulant spite, he involves three immigrant workers with the Superlab, an act that ends with them being deported by Gus. Walt has become a kind of anti-Midas: his "brilliance" destroys everything it touches.

As for Skyler, she makes an interesting, and fateful, choice. After driving for most of the day, she winds up at the intersection of four states. Echoing the "sacred" coin flip from "The Cat's in the Bag", Skyler tries to let fate decide. Only when the flipped quarter gives her an answer she doesn't like, she cheats and changes it. In her own twisted way, Sky is as bad as Walt, believing just as strongly that she has the power to fix everything and protect the people she cares about. Even with something as simple as a coin toss, Sky can't leave anything to fate. Yet this is selfishness and self-centeredness as well. Skyler actually *can* protect the people she cares about. She can get out, report Walt to the feds, and get herself and the kids into the Federal Witness Protection Program. Will there be some fallout, especially for Hank and Marie? Sure, but it doesn't look like Hank's going to be able to go back to the DEA anytime soon anyway, and face it, Hank and Marie, despite all of their failings, are the two most stable people in the show. Instead, Skyler goes back into the mess, and assumes a mantle of righteousness to rival Walt's.

LAB NOTES

HIGHLIGHT

MIKE: "I guess we'll go with Plan A then."

DID YOU NOTICE

- The UV stamp marking the "special fry batter" from the cold open of "Kafkaesque" comes back into play in this episode.
- Victor's replacement, Tyrus Kitt (Ray Campbell, recognizable from *The Shield*), is named for the first time.
- While he *is* being a bit of a jerk, Bogdan actually tells Walt some truth about the realities of being "the boss." Walt will have opportunities to recognize this truth as the series progresses.
- Junior's been doing research into Gamblers Anonymous (GA) and gambling addiction. His concern about his dad, and the way he's been acting, comes out in all of these subtle ways.

SHOOTING UP

- Again, the first shot of the cold open echoes not only the previous episode, but the opening credits of the show itself. Very meta.
- The same God's-eye, top-down POV is used for Skyler's coin flip as was used for Walt and Jesse's in "The Cat's in the Bag."
- The shovel-blade's POV as Jesse lures the meth head out of his house is brilliant, and adds both humor and an underlining of the skewed reality of a meth high, as well as highlights the importance of the shovel itself.

TITLE "Cornered" refers not only to Four Corners, where Skyler makes her choice, but also to Walt and Skyler themselves, both of whom feel progressively cornered in their lives and relationships.

INTERESTING FACTS

- Series cinematographer Michael Slovis directed "Cornered." He also directed "Kafkaesque." This might explain the resonance between the two episodes, particularly with Walt's shower sequences.
- Jesse gets knocked out by the tweaker who is played by Damon Herriman, a character actor appearing in TV and film regularly since 1976. Recently, Herriman played Bruno Hauptmann (one of the Lindbergh baby kidnappers) in *J. Edgar*, and he has a recurring role as Dewey Crowe on FX's *Justified*.

SPECIAL INGREDIENTS

FOUR CORNERS

When Skyler drives to the Four Corners Monument to decide her fate, she enters into a legally ambiguous place that both is and is not part of the United States. The Four Corners Monument is the only place in the U.S. where four states — Arizona, New Mexico, Utah, and Colorado — intersect at a single point. The monument site is located in the Navajo Nation, which is a semi-autonomous Native American–governed territory, meaning that it is and is not part of the United States. Crimes committed within the Navajo Nation may fall within the jurisdiction of the federal government, the state government, or the tribal government, depending on the nature of the crime and the race of the victim and perpetrator. The Navajo Nation covers more than 25,000 square miles of northern Arizona, southeastern Utah, and northwestern New Mexico — it's almost the size of West Virginia. The Four Corners Monument is in a particularly remote area of the Navajo Nation and one perfectly suited for the sort of deep thinking Skyler needs to do.

Problem Dog

4.07

Original air date: August 28, 2011
Written and directed by: Peter Gould

"The thing is, if you just do stuff and nothing happens . . . what's it all *mean*? What's the point?" — Jesse Pinkman

Jesse begins to climb back into the daylight from his journey through his own personal heart of darkness. Meanwhile, Hank's been working things out.

"Problem Dog" is one of the most exquisite episodes of *Breaking Bad*, and provides a mirror image to "Cornered." The cold open reveals that Jesse has begun to clean up his house, and with it, his life. Several bulging bags of trash sit on the empty living room floor and he has added a large-screen HDTV to his existing sound system. As he plays a first-person shooter game, complete with a plastic, gun-shaped controller, he flashes back and forth from the game to memories of shooting Gale. He is pale, panting, and sweating as he plays, but when his character in the game dies, and he has a chance to quit, Jesse instead restarts the game. Unlike Walt, who has been desperately denying the reality of his situation and his own responsibility for it, Jesse is putting himself through a very rough sort of therapy by directly facing his psychological demons. He plays the game *because* it forces him to face Gale's murder, and to face himself and his own actions.

Jesse's house echoes this journey. It becomes cleaner and cleaner as the episode progresses, with the order of his place echoing the order of his mind and soul, just as his home's disorder for most of this season has mirrored the chaotic psychological place he's been in. Gilligan & Co. do a very careful job with these details, up to and including how the graffiti on Jesse's walls can't be entirely washed away or even covered up by a single coat of paint. Like everything Jesse has experienced, the marks on the walls will always be there, underneath. Jesse also returns to his NA meeting, the one place where he has been able to be truly honest, if nonspecific, since going to rehab. In sharing his story about his "problem dog," and confronting the group leader, Jesse lets out his pain and rage, loosening their hold on him. Yet he also believes that he deserves to pay for what he has done, that he deserves both pain and punishment. Aaron Paul delivers what may be his most powerful performance in the series in this scene (for which he would win an Emmy in 2012), and Jesse's bloody rawness is heartbreaking to watch. Again, Jesse is facing himself and taking responsibility for his choices, a powerful and painful process, and one that Walt consistently refuses to go through.

In fact, Walt spends this episode throwing one kind of childish fit after another. When Sky insists that the expensive car go back to the dealership, Walt blows it up after wrecking it while doing donuts in an abandoned parking lot. He whines to Saul about his life even as Saul is knocking down Walt's charges to an amazing "misdemeanor trash burning," and he cooks ricin in the Superlab because it makes him feel like he's getting away with something. All in all, Walt has turned into a 12-year-old boy who is having a bad day. He's also made the leap to believing that murder is the solution to all his problems, and just like the last time, he tries to manipulate Jesse into doing the dirty work for him. Walt's attempts to manage Jesse are so blatant, however, that Jesse calls him on it, although he agrees to kill Gus if he gets the chance. Jesse's loyalty to Walt is weakening, largely because of Walt's attitude towards him, as well as the increasing level of trust both Mike and Gus are placing in him, up to and including arming him and letting him take a small part in upper-level organizational goings-on. As Walt is regressing, Jesse is growing up and beginning to make his own choices.

Finally, there is Hank. Amazingly on his feet and walking with only the assistance of a cane, he comes face-to-face with Gus in a brilliant scene where each man is gaming the other, but only Hank knows it. It's an interesting parallel between the two characters. Both have laser-like focus, play the long game with tremendous patience, and can lie with utter sincerity. The difference is that Hank feels deeply and is capable of love, while Gus is an utter sociopath, his emotional range having been burned out of him long ago. Hank's even back in the DEA, and laying out a case against Gus that he's built piece by piece from home, while also busting his ass in rehab and putting his marriage back on firmer ground. For the first time, Hank's true genius is fully on display as he confidently lays out his evidence, each piece carefully researched, every rock diligently turned over; a frightening, dogged intellect stands revealed under all that good-ol'-boy attitude. Hank's study of minerals, the building blocks of rocks, has paid off in his investigation, where all the individual pieces that make up the mystery of Gale's murder have yielded the key to the entire case.

LAB NOTES

HIGHLIGHT
WALT: "Please, one homicidal maniac at a time."

DID YOU NOTICE
- Marie's new, truly happy attitude about Hank when Skyler asks after him. It's a small bit, but brilliantly done by Betsy Brandt.
- Hank is once again being the surrogate father to Junior that Walt seems incapable of being, while still careful not to undercut Walt as he goes about it.
- The tinnitus-like ringing sound effect as Jesse makes his choice about poisoning Gus is the same effect used throughout the series at moments of great personal stress, going all the way back to Walt's cancer diagnosis in "Pilot/Breaking Bad."
- The cartel's representative is the same guy who led the hijackers in the cold open to "Cornered."
- The soundtrack to Walt's donut-searing, axle-busting ride in the Challenger is "Boots of Chinese Plastic" by the Pretenders, a great classically rebellious rock tune by a band who's managed to stick together and stay in the business for decades — a nice commentary on Walt's teen-like-spite fit.

MISCALCULATIONS Skyler's failure to find out exactly how much money she is supposed to launder and how often plays into her obsession with details to the detriment of the larger picture, but it's also a staggeringly stupid error, and Skyler is *not* dumb.

SHOOTING UP

+ "Problem Dog" uses a lot of close-ups, from Jesse's screen-lit face in the cold open, to the ricin cigarette, to the dripping coffee at Gus's meeting.
+ The iconic up-and-through POV is used as Jesse preps the ricin cigarette and the audience gets the view up through the coffee table.

TITLE "Problem Dog" refers to both Gale and Jesse, the former as described by Jesse at the NA meeting, and the latter as he begins to climb up out of his own personal darkness.

INTERESTING FACTS

+ In this episode, viewers learn that Steve Gomez made "GS-14," which is a high-level pay designation for United States civil service jobs. The "GS" stands for "General Schedule" and there are 15 levels: GS-1 to GS-7 are generally entry-level positions, while GS-8 through GS-12 are mid-range and GS-13 to GS-15 are top-level positions, such as mid-level supervisors or high-level technical specialists. A GS-15 is roughly the equivalent, pay-wise, of an army colonel or a navy captain, so Gomez's promotion puts him high on the pay scale. In 2011, when "Problem Dog" aired, this meant that Steve had a base pay of $84,697.
+ The use of the video game *Rage* in this episode deserves a special mention. The game had not yet been released when it appeared in *Breaking Bad* and the game's appearance in the show served to start a fair amount of excited internet chatter. In what is a truly unusual crossover, players of *Rage* can discover a *Breaking Bad* "Easter egg" surprise embedded within the game — go to Sheriff Black's office and walk past him into the next room and on a shelf, you'll find Tuco's Lucite-encased grill from season 2.

SPECIAL INGREDIENTS

RAGE AND PRODUCT PLACEMENT IN AMERICAN TELEVISION

When Jesse is seen playing *Rage*, or when Junior guilts Walt into buying his silence with a sharp new car, *Breaking Bad* engages in a tradition as old as television itself: product placement. When television first arrived on the entertainment scene, it was common for companies to sponsor entire shows, which was a holdover from radio. Gradually, production costs made it prohibitive for one company to sponsor a complete show, so the idea of advertisers buying blocks of shows came into being.

Product placement is slightly different. While sponsored advertisements occur outside of the show's parameters, in product placement, branded goods or services are placed within the show itself, most usually in exchange for payment by the company for the placement. Product placement can form deep and lasting relationships between companies and consumers, a non-tangible asset companies long to achieve. For instance, *The Love Boat* was set aboard the *Pacific Princess*, which was part of Princess Cruise Lines. The show ended in 1986, but the company used the slogan "It's more than a cruise, it's the Love Boat" until 2002. And let's not even talk about *Knight Rider* and the Pontiac Trans Am.

● VEGGIE TRAYS

Throughout *Breaking Bad*, characters show up at gatherings carrying pre-cut, store-bought snack trays. While long a staple of social events, some of the *Breaking Bad* gatherings are the sorts that don't usually make a person think, "What this meeting needs is carrots and ranch dip!" For example:

- In "Gray Matter" (1.05), Skyler sets out a fruit and veggie tray to provide refreshment for those attending Walt's intervention.
- In "I.F.T." (3.03), Gus includes a vegetable tray for his meeting with the Salamanca cousins who have come to town to avenge Tuco's death.
- In "Kafkaesque" (3.09), Gus has a veggie tray for his meeting with Walt because, really, you want to observe the social niceties when making an offer someone can't refuse.
- In "Problem Dog" (4.07), Jesse brings a veggie tray to Gus's meeting with the cartel.

Interestingly, there is no snack tray (and not even any coffee!) at the meeting with Gus at the chicken farm in "Half Measures" (3.12), a sign that this is a dangerously serious get-together, as employees are called on the carpet for substandard performance.

ermanos

Original air date: September 4, 2011
Written by: Sam Catlin, George Mastras
Directed by: Johan Renck

"This is what comes of blood for blood, Héctor — *sangre por sangre.*" — Gustavo Fring

Twenty years ago, Gus was introduced to the Mexican cartel, while in the contemporary storyline, he meets with two enemies: one old, and one new.

"Hermanos" takes the viewer deep into the darkest parts of Gus Fring's heart. Gilligan & Co. have never been content for Gus to be a generic bad guy who sprang full grown from the plot convenience warehouse, and there have been increasing hints that Gus is playing a much larger, longer game than merely running Southwestern U.S. distribution for the Mexican cartel. In fact, Gus has recently received some uncomfortable attention from the cartel. The question is — why? Gus has a good thing going, and is successful on several levels, with a crisply clean cover identity. He's also a man of great patience and control (with seemingly none of the pride, ego, and greed that hamstring Walt) and he is perfectly content to hide his multibillion-dollar light under the bushel of a comfortable middle-class existence. So why would a man like Gustavo Fring rock the boat? Why take chances with an unstable pair like Walt and Jesse? Why arrange the death of Leonel Salamanca and Juan Bolsa in "I See You"? Why go to such elaborate lengths to set up his own mass-meth-manufacturing facility in the Superlab and staff it with the most

brilliant chemists he can find? "Hermanos" provides the answers to all of this and it is magnificently, gloriously chilling.

Once upon a time, in the cold open to "One Minute," Héctor Salamanca referred to Gus sarcastically as "the great generalissimo." As it turns out, that is perhaps the most apt description possible of this cold, controlled monster masquerading under the guise of nerdy fast-food franchisee. The Superlab is an idea over 20 years old, and the search for the perfect chemist to run it has been going on for nearly as long, costing Gus tens of thousands of dollars through the endowment of the Maximino Arciniega Chemistry Scholarship at the University of New Mexico. All of that, however — *all of it* — is utterly beside the point. What has been driving Gus for all these years? Revenge: a vendetta so baroque and brilliant that it deserves an epic poem or a grand opera. At the heart of this blood feud lies the elderly Don Héctor Salamanca, trapped in the prison of a body rendered largely irresponsive by either a stroke or a progressive neuromuscular disease. Gus visits Héctor regularly to keep him informed as he kills the old man's family and friends one by one. Twisting the knife deeper and deeper, Gus always leaves Héctor wondering if the next visit will be the one in which Gus kills *him*. Walt and Jesse, for all of their dangerous instability, have unknowingly managed to bring some of Gus's enemies to him, and even provided the means for their destruction. Gus has always been terrifying, but "Hermanos" takes it to an entirely different level.

Gus may have been getting a bit anxious lately, however, as his meeting with Hank, the DEA, and APD shows. Throughout, he is serenely calm, and utterly convincing to everyone except Hank. Indeed, Hank is the only one who has even a sense of the creature that lies under Gus's mask, but he doesn't have the proof. Despite this unexpected interrogation, Gus's only reaction is the slightest twitching of a single finger as he takes the elevator downstairs *after* the meeting is finished. Fortunately, all of this darkness is broken by the comic interlude provided as Hank, in search of the proof he needs, enlists Walt's help to bug Gus's car. After all, as Hank says, it was Walt's comment about Heisenberg still being out there that got Hank to keep digging. Watching Walt hem, haw, and squirm slides over into the realm of true hilarity when Mike pulls up beside Walt and Hank in the Los Pollos Hermanos parking lot, gives Walt a disgustedly amused look, and begins to read his paper. It's a much-needed laugh-out-loud moment in the middle of a dark, dark season.

LAB NOTES

HIGHLIGHT

HANK: "I mean he's got reasons for *everything*. This guy's *Terms of Endearment* convincing."

DID YOU NOTICE

* As Walt and the other patient wait for their CT scans and Walt is talking about never giving up control, on the wall behind and between the two is a motivational poster urging patients to "stick together" with each other and their support networks, something Walt is progressively doing less and less of.
* The younger Héctor Salamanca is already suffering some type of physical infirmity, and has to use his left hand to raise his right to his mouth so that he can take a drink.
* In trying to convince Don Eladio (Steven Bauer) of the superiority of

274

his product, Max (James Martinez who has had roles in *The Sessions* and *Gravity*) talks about the chirality of the molecules involved, echoing Walt's classroom lecture in "The Cat's in the Bag."

- Max tells Don Eladio that Gus is "my partner and I need him, I swear to God!" An almost word-for-word echo of Walt's claims about Jesse.
- Jesse's house is very neat and clean in this episode.
- The younger Héctor strongly insinuates that Gus and Max are gay. This may be just an attempt to make them angry, but it is also not the first time Gus has been coded as homosexual. Though he mentions "kids" to Walt when he has him over for dinner in "Abiquiu," there is never any evidence that he has ever had children, much less a wife. His grooming is always immaculate, and there is something just slightly effeminate about his attitude, qualities which, on American television, often serve as shorthand for homosexuality. The way he lets his hand linger on Héctor's knee in the cold open is also presented as a deliberate insult and violation of the old man's *machismo*. Certainly his reaction to Max's murder is heart-rendingly emotional, and a blood feud is usually undertaken for family, not friends, no matter how close.
- When it comes to Héctor and Gus, it's all in the eyes, and Mark Margolis and Giancarlo Esposito are masters of making subtle expressions speak in long sentences. Riding the elevator down from his meeting with the DEA, Gus looks up and into the camera at the end of the sequence, and there's nothing but murder there.
- When Gus makes it clear that everything that's happened to the Salamanca cousins and Juan Bolsa is part of a deliberate revenge for Max's death 20 years ago, Héctor violently shifts his eyes away from him. At the end of the episode, Gus tries to get Héctor to look at him, but the old man refuses. It is all Héctor can do, the only action he can take. Refusing to look at Gus is to proclaim him dead.
- As Gus rides the elevator, the only sound is the regular dinging of the bell indicating the passing floors, a sound reminiscent of Héctor's little bell. This effect has been used before in season 3 with the Salamanca twins to foreshadow Héctor's hand in events.
- There are secrets underneath the floorboards in the White house now, and all the normal day-to-day things are taking place on a foundation of dirty money and lies.

SHOOTING UP

- ◆ A hard, yellow filter is used for the flashback scenes in Mexico, again doubling as a cue for the viewer that this is taking place both in the past and outside the U.S.
- ◆ The circular episode structure is back: the episode begins with Gus visiting Héctor in the nursing home intercut with images of blood in a swimming pool, and ending in the same way and with the same images.
- ◆ Again, close-ups are used to underline the importance of certain things, like Héctor's eyes and Gus's hand on his knee.
- ◆ Close-ups also allow for the subtle acting of Esposito and Margolis to have full effect.

TITLE "Hermanos" is Spanish for "brothers," and there are a lot of brothers in this episode. There is Los Pollos Hermanos, "the chicken brothers," both in reference to the restaurant, and Gus and Max. The Salamanca cousins are brothers, and are the sons of Héctor's brother, and Walt and Hank are brothers-in-law.

INTERESTING FACTS Max Arciniega, the name of Gus's tragically murdered friend whom Gus names the chemistry scholarship at the University of New Mexico for in his quest to find the best meth cook, is also the real name of the actor who played Krazy-8 in season 1.

SPECIAL INGREDIENTS

CHILE AND THE PINOCHET JUNTA

Gus, Chilean by birth, blames the Pinochet regime for the lack of official records regarding his early years. Sloppy record-keeping was the least of Augusto Pinochet's crimes. Pinochet was the leader of a military junta that overthrew the socialist government of President Salvador Allende on September 11, 1973. He had been named commander in chief of the Chilean Army just 18 days earlier. Although ostensibly part of a ruling group, in June 1974, Pinochet assumed sole power as president. In the first three years of his rule, over 130,000 people were arrested and many were tortured. A true count is impossible — many people simply "disappeared."

Pinochet did not permit political opposition, but he abided by the terms of the 1981 Constitution and in 1988 a referendum was held to determine if Pinochet would remain in power for an additional eight-year presidential term. He was no doubt surprised by the vote going against him. Free elections installed a new president in March 1990, although Pinochet remained commander of the armed forces until 1998. Due to a provision in the 1981 Constitution, as a former president, Pinochet then became a senator-for-life. If Gus and Max's confrontation with Don Eladio took place about 20 years from *Breaking Bad*'s present, that places it somewhere between 1990–1991, and puts Gus in Mexico for at least a little while before Pinochet lost power.

Things never really seriously unravelled for Pinochet. In 1998 he was detained by British authorities on a visit to London. Under the principle of universal jurisdiction, Spain had requested his extradition in connection with the torture of Spanish citizens in Chile during his time in power. Pinochet was kept on house arrest for two years and was ultimately released on medical grounds without facing trial. In early 2000, he returned to Chile, where the Chilean Congress created the status of "ex-president," which granted him a financial allowance and immunity from prosecution. The Supreme Court of Chile overturned its own precedent-setting decision in 2004, ruling that he was capable of standing trial, but Pinochet always managed to slip out of having to publicly answer for his regime's actions in a courtroom. He died on December 10, 2006, and was never convicted of any of the crimes or human rights abuses of which he had been accused.

B ug

Original air date: September 11, 2011
Written by: Moira Walley-Beckett, Thomas Schnauz
Directed by: Terry McDonough

"Can you walk? . . . Then get the fuck outta here and never come back." — Jesse Pinkman

Jesse gets a new and dangerous job opportunity from Gus, but Walt refuses to help him prepare for it.

For the entirety of season 4, Walt's life has been spinning out of control. Nothing has worked out like he planned, and no amount of lying, scheming, and manipulation has served to get things back to where Walt wants them. He has even found himself made into a double agent for Gus as part of Hank's unofficial investigation into Gus's business. Skyler's car wash is taking off to the point that Walt could get out of the meth business if he wanted, but that's not something his pride will allow, and Gus is unlikely to let him walk away at this point anyway. Even Jesse has moved beyond Walt's control and he continues to evade killing Gus despite having plenty of opportunities.

Meanwhile, the world has changed dramatically for Jesse. To all appearances, he has become a trusted member of Gus's organization and has found a new father figure in Mike. Unfortunately for Walt, Gus and Mike seem to repay loyalty with loyalty more often than Walt does. In "Bug," Jesse is taken all the way in: into Gus's home, and also into the mysterious conflict between Gus and the cartel, which has heated up to a boil. While Walt impotently rages and whines at being shut out of things, Jesse is moving into a position of importance. All the pain and self-inflicted agony and the self-driven crawl back has hardened Jesse and given him a new strength. He doesn't think twice about starting the cook when Walt is late, and he isn't afraid to look Gus in the eye and demand to be seen and heard. Yet his loyalty to Walt remains intact . . . until Walt himself destroys it.

The irony of Walt becoming so furious because Jesse lied to him is thick enough to cut with a knife, and Walt's haughty disdain for Jesse's intelligence, ability, and loyalty finally goes too far. Ever since season 1, Walt and Jesse have regularly fallen into play fights where they roll around, but always wind up lying on the floor or ground, panting, physically and emotionally exhausted, getting up as friends. Not this time. Jesse brutally beats Walt until there can be no doubt in either of their minds that Walt has lost and Jesse is done with him. There is no wrestling away Jesse's anger. It is hard not to cheer at this scene, because with all that Walt has done, including all the things Jesse doesn't know about, this beating has been a long time coming and it is enormously satisfying to finally see it. Walt has managed to lose the one friend he has left in all of this mess and has driven Jesse fully into Gus's arms.

LAB NOTES

HIGHLIGHT

SKYLER: "When I input everything into the Quicken nothing flashed red, so that's gotta mean it's okay, right?"

DID YOU NOTICE

* Hank's USB GPS tracking device uses Google Earth to display Gus's activities, a nice bit of product placement, as is Skyler's mention of "the Quicken" in her interview with the IRS auditor.
* Ted has known about the IRS investigation into his books for months, but has done absolutely nothing about it.
* Skyler plays the blond sexpot perfectly. She may well be a better liar than Walt.
* Gus cooks the same meal for Jesse as he did for Walt in "Abiquiu," and Jesse is seated on the same side of the table as Walt was.
* Los Pollos Hermanos has 14 locations — Gus is doing all right for himself.

SHOOTING UP

- Ground-level close-ups are used repeatedly in this episode, beginning with Walt's broken eyeglasses and moccasins in the cold open, with the same low-angle shot picking up the shoes again after the credits.
- There's a lovely, floor-up POV of blood dripping and splattering in the cold open.
- The slow-motion film and sound around Jesse during the sniper attack is very well done. While Mike's voice is almost inaudible, the strangely hypnotic sounds of the bullets' whip-hissing through the air and impacting around him slams the tension level right through the roof.
- The sniper's POV, complete with the telescopic rifle-scope's crosshairs is seen superimposed on first Jesse, and then Gus.
- As Gus talks to the mysterious caller after the attack, he is framed by deep blackness, and shown in a very small pool of dim light, an extremely claustrophobic shot.
- A floor-up POV is also used for the wince-inducing shot of Jesse slamming Walt into the glass-topped coffee table.

TITLE "Bug" references the GPS tracker, but also harks back to the brilliant season 3 episode "Fly."

INTERESTING FACTS Hank hums the theme from *Rocky* as he and Walt go to retrieve the GPS tracker. Interestingly, in the original film, Rocky wears a dark pork-pie hat when he's in civvies, one that's not dissimilar to Heisenberg's own topper.

SPECIAL INGREDIENTS

THE CID OF THE IRS

Ted's got problems. While not involved in the money laundering business, he's had Skyler keep double books — one for public consumption (such as the IRS) and one that showed the actual income and outflow of his business. He owes the government hundreds of thousands of dollars and he's managed to attract the attention of the Criminal Investigation Division (CID) of the Internal Revenue Service. Prior to 1978, this unit was known the "Intelligence

Unit" of the IRS and has always been remarkable for its dogged investigations of complex financial crimes. Remember — Public Enemy Number One himself, Al Capone, was taken down by the IRS, not rival gangsters. The CID is nigh-inexorable, for its special agents are quite willing to patiently build their case, which probably accounts for a conviction rate in excess of 90 percent — and that dates from the founding of the CID in 1919 to the present. Skyler's name is all over those falsified records and with her car wash enterprise, she is right to be scared.

GPS TRACKING DEVICES WITH USB CONNECTIVITY

Hank has Walt plant a Global Positioning System (GPS) on Gus's Volvo wagon so Hank can see where Gus goes every day. This is a passive tracker in that it tracks, but does not transmit. Instead, the data is recorded and can then be viewed on a computer once the device is removed from the vehicle and plugged into a computer for download, in this case, through the USB port.

While using such a device is perfectly okay if you're a fleet manager tracking where your delivery trucks were during the day, the trick here is that Hank is behaving in an "extralegal" manner — he has no warrant to track Gus's car. Hank's not the only one who does this — these removable trackers are big business. You can easily find these devices for sale on internet "spy gadget" sites for about $200, depending on recording capacity and battery life. Read the language on these sites carefully, as they first cheerfully point out the many useful applications of these trackers (which include getting dirt on unfaithful lovers) and then sternly remind potential buyers that these devices "may not be used to violate the privacy rights of others!"

S alud

Original air date: September 18, 2011
Written by: Peter Gould, Gennifer Hutchison
Directed by: Michelle MacLaren

4.10

"I'm the guy your boss brought here to show you how it's done. And if this is how you run your lab . . . no wonder. You're lucky he hasn't fired your ass. Now, if you don't want that to happen, I suggest you stop whining like a little bitch and do what I say."

— Jesse Pinkman

Walt licks his wounds, and tries to explain some things to Junior. Meanwhile, Skyler tries to help Ted out, and in Mexico, Jesse gets an offer he can't refuse.

"Salud" is the first in the series of climactic episodes wrapping up season 4. Although several characters go through some significant changes during the episode, perhaps the most surprisingly important moments come from Junior. "Salud" begins on Junior's 16th birthday, and for a middle-class kid whose last car was a tricked-out Dodge Challenger, the used PT Cruiser that Sky presents him with is a bit of a comedown; when it comes to afford-able, safe cars, a PT Cruiser is not exactly the thing to fire the heart of a 16-year-old American boy. Junior, however, proves once again that he is fun-damentally a sweet, thoughtful kid, and he swallows his disappointment in the car and does his best to make his mom happy by appreciating the thought behind her gift, if not necessarily the gift itself. His birthday having begun on this kind of semi-sour note, Walt gives his son the gift of taking care of his battered, drug-addled, whining, weeping, tighty-whitey-wearing father for the rest of the afternoon. Walt earns another Worst Father of the Year Award for his performance in this episode (his trophy shelf is getting rather full of them), while Junior once again takes home the coveted Best Son Ever trophy. Because he *does* take care of his dad. Not out of a sense of obligation, not even resentfully, but because, despite all of Walt's bullshit over the past year, for Junior, he still hangs the moon and the stars and the kid simply loves his dad. He even repairs Walt's glasses for him while Walt sleeps it off.

Walt responds in the usual way: selfishly. He never even thanks Junior, and instead makes excuses for his behavior by launching into a monologue, the gist of which is that he doesn't want Junior to remember him as the broken sad-sack of the previous night, but as a strong, dependable father. For the first time since season 1, Walt also reveals a significant chunk of his past when he describes his father's lingering death from Huntington's disease. Walt's problem with that particular piece of his past is not his father's long struggle, but the fact that he can only remember his dad as weak and sick. It's not about his dad, in other words, but about him. In a truly exquisite turn, and underlining which of the two is actually acting like a grown man, Junior calls Walt on his crap, and tells him that he'd rather have the broken and sloppy Walt of the night before than the one he usually gets, because "at least last night you were *real*." Junior just wants his dad, and that's the one thing Walt hasn't been for him since the series began.

Meanwhile, Gus pays off his 20-year blood debt in spades. After Jesse cooks a batch of crystal purer than the Mexicans have ever achieved, Jesse, Mike, and Gus are invited back to the infamous swimming pool of Don Eladio's hacienda, putting Gus in the position to kill *everybody*: Don Eladio, all of his capos, and even the hijacker-sniper supreme, Gaff (Maurice Compte, whose credits include *24* and *All the Real Girls*), who goes down tangled in Mike's garrote. The bloody scenes at Don Eladio's are truly operatic, as the kingpin goes from reveling in victory and decadent excess to floating facedown in the same pool that once collected the blood of Gus's closest friend (and perhaps his one true love). Gus triumphant is a sublime and awful sight as he stands amid the bodies of his enemies offering freedom or death to those who remain. In their subsequent escape, Jesse experiences his life collapsing into a few seconds of action as he lives the video game *Rage*, and he doesn't freeze under fire. Instead, Jesse guns down their last assailant who is also the man who wounded Mike. As the episode ends, Jesse is Gus and Mike's one hope of survival, and he is at last moving with true purpose. With all that Jesse has been through, and all the times he has been (sometimes unknowingly) victimized and manipulated by Walt and others, it is good to see him becoming more assured, even in the service of evil, while fundamentally remaining himself. Something Walt has not managed to do.

LAB NOTES

HIGHLIGHT

SAUL: "I just thought you'd like to know — loath as I am to say: *I told you so.*"

DID YOU NOTICE

- Jesse and Mike are mirror images aboard the plane, sitting with the same posture and position, looking out of opposite windows.
- It's a nice bit of audience misdirection as Saul worries over a client, but instead of Walt walking through the door, it's Ted Beneke.
- Saul is wearing the blue and pink ribbon marking the Wayfarer 515 crash, a necessary accessory for his class-action lawsuit.
- Jesse's cook tests out 96.2 percent pure, which is less than Walt's 99-plus percent best, but also better than Gale's 96 percent as detailed in "Box Cutter."
- Jesse, Gus, Mike, and Gaff are the only men not drinking and playing with the hookers during Don Eladio's celebration.

SHOOTING UP

- Wide shots are used at the beginning to emphasize the isolation and smallness of Gus, Mike, Jesse, and even the huge SUV and small airplane that picks them up as compared to the open emptiness of the desert.
- There are two lovely shots of Junior in this episode. The first shows him supporting the half-dressed Walt with one hand while having to support himself on his crutch with the other, and the second shows him from a distance, standing alone in Walt's kitchen, a young man suddenly faced with an adult's responsibility.

- There is a great use of the trademark POV shot from the nightstand looking up to Junior's face as he sees the pill bottle.
- A yellow filter is used for the Mexico scenes.
- Time-lapse photography is used to show the passage of time outside of the lab, as well as the arrival of more and more people as the day and night go on.
- Gus's reflection is seen in Don Eladio's pool as he stands at the very spot where Max was killed 20 years ago.
- A crane-shot looking down on the pool deck gives a great look at the sheer carnage as Gus, Jesse, and Mike walk through all of the bodies.
- The POV from the bottom of the pool is used to great effect as Don Eladio's corpse falls into the water.

TITLE "Salud" is Spanish for "good health," and is commonly used as a toast. In this episode, the irony of the word is obvious.

INTERESTING FACTS Zafiro Añejo is a fictional, top-shelf tequila. The bottle used in the episode appears to be modeled after those used for the Hardy Cognac Perfection series of liqueurs.

SPECIAL INGREDIENTS

HUNTINGTON'S DISEASE

Walt explains to Junior that his father (Junior's grandfather) died a slow death from Huntington's disease. Huntington's is an inherited disease (Walt mentions his mother had him tested) that causes the progressive degeneration of nerve cells in the brain. It usually results in impairment in both movement and cognitive ability. Symptoms most often develop in a person's forties or fifties, with the most common symptom being some form of uncontrolled movement (sometimes subtle tremors, sometimes a muscular tic) of the head, face, or extremities. Memory, concentration, and the ability to organize and plan are also impacted. Changes in the brain lead to mood swings, anxiety, depression, and sudden anger. Obsessive-compulsive behavior in patients has also been noted.

While medication can help manage the symptoms, there is no effective treatment for the inevitable decline that Huntington's causes. Affected persons commonly live for 15 to 20 years after the initial diagnosis, meaning that Huntington's is cruelly characterized by a long, slow descent into death.

PHENYLACETIC ACID

Jesse is at loose ends in the Mexican Superlab when he is told that they do not have a particular ingredient on hand — phenylacetic acid — since they synthesize their own. Jesse doesn't know how to do that, but rises to the occasion, impressing Gus and Mike with his command of the street vernacular in the process.

For quite a while, small-time meth makers used pseudoephedrine to make their product — *Breaking Bad* references this back in season 1 — but a crackdown on medicines containing the ingredient forced meth makers to go back to their roots, so to speak. Phenyl-2-propanone (also known as P2P) was one answer. While the sale of P2P is closely monitored, it can be easily made. Phenylacetic acid can be transformed into P2P, which can then be made into meth. Keep in mind that meth is a completely synthetic drug — when one source of ingredients dries up due to a legal crackdown, another is sought out. This is what happened with P2P originally, which drove manufacturers first to ephedrine, then to pseudoephedrine.

This switch is showing up in testing of methamphetamine confiscated from Mexico. In 2007, only one percent showed the presence of phenylacetic acid, but by 2009, that number had increased to 16 percent.

C rawl Space

4.11

Original air date: September 25, 2011
Written by: George Mastras, Sam Catlin
Directed by: Scott Winant

"I don't want to talk about it. To you or to anyone else. I'm done explaining myself." — Walter White

Jesse returns from Mexico with a new self-assurance. Meanwhile, Walt tries to get out, but Skyler's already spent the money they need.

"Crawl Space" is definitely a setup episode, but one that achieves a level of brilliance rarely seen on television. For Walt, everything seems to be moving at light speed, completely beyond his control. He can't stop Hank's investigation into Gus's businesses, no matter what he does; he's destroyed his relationship with Jesse; and with Jesse now cooking on his own, the one thing that makes Walt valuable to Gus Fring — the one thing keeping Walt alive — no longer applies. The Walt of season 4 has largely been passive. There have been no brilliant schemes; no last-minute, genius, scientific saves; no easy manipulations of people to achieve Walt's ends; and, as his face — bruised and bloody for much of the season — has shown, no standing apart from the violence of his choices.

To this point in the series there has always been *something* Walt could do to make things better and to maintain the illusion that he is able to control the new life he has chosen for himself. No more. In "Crawl Space," Walt finds himself in the desert and face-to-face with the monster that lives under Gustavo Fring's usual mask of calm civility. This is a creature who will make

Walt's life a desert, who can and will slaughter everyone Walt cares about, up to and including baby Holly, and who will sleep soundly after doing it. Despite the lesson of Victor's death in "Box Cutter," it is only now that Walt truly understands that he is dealing with a man who will, without compunction, do whatever is necessary to ensure his own survival and prosperity.

Even more chilling, "Crawl Space" suggests that Gus may be becoming a full-blown psychopath. He is giving way to his impulses more, and his behavior is far more erratic and less controlled. He cannot resist going to the nursing home to taunt Héctor with what he did to Don Eladio and his minions. Gus even goes so far as to leave Don Eladio's charm against the evil eye with Héctor, a very careless move. Indeed, his confrontation with Walt in the desert, when he lets his true self show, is evidence of this increasing lack of control and of Gus's new need to talk, threaten, and explain. With no more cartel to worry about and conspire against, Gus is, for the first time in over 20 years, operating without constraints, and it is already beginning to change him.

With Saul's help, Skyler funneled money to Ted to cover his tax debts, but Ted refuses to pay, preferring instead to use the funds to finance a lifestyle he can't afford. When direct appeals don't work, Skyler enlists the help of Saul's "A-Team." Their strong-arm tactics do work and the check is in the mail, but a loose rug coupled with a rabbity Ted adds up to disaster, further obliterating Walt's plans.

As Walt's life is coming apart at the seams, Jesse's is knitting back together. His home is fully recovered from the chaos of earlier episodes; Andrea and Brock, whom he had pushed away for most of the season, are now close again; and *Rage* has been replaced by *Sonic the Hedgehog* in what is now a family-friendly place of refuge from the outside world. Indeed, Jesse is determined to keep his place in this condition and shuts out both Walt and his pathetic attempts to manipulate him into saving his life. Jesse has come out of a very dark hole a new man, and everything that has happened this season has served only to make him strong, independent, and confident. He has come into his own, and that leaves Walt truly alone. Finally aware of the reality of his situation, Walt makes a fatal decision, and the lies, assumptions, and omissions between Skyler and him come home to roost in the deadliest way possible. Walt is trapped. Trapped in this new life that was supposed to free him and his family just as surely as he was trapped in his old life — and all of it is his own damn fault. As the reality of the situation hits him like a ton of money bags, Walt laughs and cries maniacally while lying on his back in the crawl space. The episode's incredible final shot symbolizes all of this, and as the camera rises higher and higher, the trapdoor framing Walt seems to get smaller and smaller.

LAB NOTES

HIGHLIGHT

SKYLER: "The whole reason we're in this mess is because you had me cooking your books, so when did 'wrong' become a problem for you?"

DID YOU NOTICE

- Héctor still refuses to look at Gus.
- Saul's "end game" contact from "Bullet Points" comes into play.
- Ted's real problem with Sky's money isn't that it's dirty, but that it's not enough.
- Ted trips over his rug early in the episode, nicely setting up his disastrous fall later.
- The desert ground and the dirt floor of Walt's crawl space look almost exactly alike.
- When Gus comes to visit him, Héctor is watching the 1957 film *The Bridge on the River Kwai*, in the climax to which Alec Guinness sacrifices his life in order to blow up the bridge he has so painstakingly created.

SHOOTING UP

- ◆ There are several trademark wide-angle shots of the desert in "Crawl Space": in the cold open as Jesse comes driving like hell to the field hospital, as he and Gus begin their walk back to the U.S., and as Walt is left alone in the desert after his "interview" with Gus.

- ◆ Back and forth close-ups are used for the conversation between Gus and Héctor, and again the subtleties of Giancarlo Esposito and Mark Margolis's facial expressions carry the weight of the scene.

- ◆ The intricate camera work in the final scene is beautifully done, with the viewpoint shifting from Walt looking up and out from the crawl space into the upper world of life and light, to a ceiling-down perspective of Walt seemingly entombed, framed by the trapdoor opening. The perspective trick of raising the camera far higher than the room's actual ceiling would be while maintaining the walls is used here again to tremendous effect.

TITLE "Crawl Space" here refers not only to the actual crawl space of the episode's ending, but the increasingly limited range of Walt's actions.

SPECIAL INGREDIENTS

"MACHO" CAMACHO

Hank refers to Puerto Rican boxer "Macho" Camacho while he and Walt are on the stakeout at the chicken farm. Born Héctor Luís Camacho Matías in 1962, Camacho was a boxer known for both his flamboyant style and his devastating quickness in the ring. He held major championships in three weight classes: super featherweight (130 lbs.), lightweight (135 lbs.), and junior welterweight (140 lbs.). He also earned minor titles in four other weight classes, making Camacho the first boxer to be recognized as a septuple champion. In 1997, Camacho knocked out Sugar Ray Leonard in five rounds, a bout that sent Leonard into permanent retirement.

A long-time New Yorker (his mother moved there when Camacho was only three), Camacho was also a popular figure in Puerto Rico, and he often appeared on national television shows and media events. Following his retirement, Camacho had run-ins with the law and had trouble with drug use. On November 20, 2012 (after this episode aired), Camacho was shot while sitting in a car parked outside of a bar in his old hometown of Bayamón, Puerto Rico, in an attack that killed his driver. Nine small bags of cocaine were found in the driver's pocket and another bag was open inside the car. After several days in hospital, Camacho was taken off life support and suffered cardiac arrest; he was declared dead on November 24. To date, no one has been charged with the crime.

CHARMS AGAINST THE EVIL EYE

Gus claims Don Eladio's necklace following the bloodbath at the hacienda and gleefully shows his grisly trophy to Héctor Salamanca, who still refuses to look at Gus. Eyes are clearly important here. Whether Don Eladio truly believed the amulet granted him protection is an open question; however, people from many cultures wear or carry lucky charms of one type or another to ward off misfortune. The term "evil eye" ("*mal ojo*" in Spanish) is actually not quite accurate. The belief is that a person who does not necessarily have evil intent can harm you, your property, your children, etc. simply by looking at those people or things with envy. Don Eladio certainly wants to protect what is his and his eye-shaped amulet is a fairly common symbol of protection.

Charms to deflect the evil eye are called "apotropaic" (literally "turns away") talismans and can be found in many cultures dating back millennia. The Bible contains several mentions regarding the perils of the evil eye. Among these talismans are: tiny mirrors sewn into fabric to reflect the evil eye back at the gazer (India); an amulet shaped like a long, gently twisting horn (Sicily); a blue or turquoise bead painted to resemble an eye and often worn as a necklace (Turkey); and eye-shaped seeds fastened to the body with yarn or ribbons (Mexico).

End Times

4.12

Original air date: October 2, 2011
Written by: Thomas Schnauz, Moira Walley-Beckett
Directed by: Vince Gilligan

"I have made choices — listen to me: I alone should suffer the consequences of those choices, and those consequences . . . they're coming." — Walter White

As things begin to fall apart, Walt and Jesse are thrown together again in a final effort to kill Gus.

The cold open to "End Times" begins with the same, almost insect-like sound effect that ran under the final scenes in "Crawl Space," immediately ratcheting up the tension to a fever pitch that isn't helped by the fact that the DEA and Gus Fring's people both drive black Suburbans. Walt is convinced that he is Gus's real target, and that if he holes up at Hank and Marie's with the DEA, he will only be putting them all in danger. The truth of Walt's belief remains somewhat murky, because Walt is not the danger he wants to think himself. After all, Gus has already told him that he will wait to deal with Walt, and threatened to kill Walt's entire family if Walt interfered with his plans to eliminate Hank, whose investigation of Gus's businesses is currently a far greater threat than Walt is. At this point, Hank's aggressive investigation of Gus's businesses is disrupting operations, something that simply cannot continue. Walt is on Gus's list, to be sure, but he may be further down than he thinks he is.

However, in "End Times" Walt maneuvers to get the freedom and space he needs to become a real danger to Gus, in large part by restoring his alliance with Jesse. In an incredibly intense scene, Bryan Cranston and Aaron Paul demonstrate why they are two of the greatest actors of their time, with Jesse more than willing to blow Walt to hell and Walt equally desperate to convince Jesse that he had nothing to do with poisoning Brock, but that Gus probably does. The final showdown between the two ends with Jesse pushing a pistol into Walt's forehead, and Walt himself pulling the barrel against his skull so tightly that the impression of the muzzle can be clearly seen on Walt's forehead afterward. That kind of intense, painful physicality

(DAVID GABBER/PR PHOTOS)

is grueling work for an actor, and the intensity of Cranston and Paul's performances in this scene is phenomenally gripping.

"End Times" also shows Walt, for the first time in season 4, calling on his scientific knowledge and abilities to try to escape the situation he has created by constructing a pipe bomb. It appears that Walt is back in the game at last, but his genius fails him. Gustavo Fring has been waging a long and patient war against a ruthless Mexican drug cartel for 20 years. In all of that time, there has likely never been a day in which his life was not at least theoretically in danger. Yet Gus has not only survived, he has prospered. The careful stillness Giancarlo Esposito brings to the role of Gus is again in evidence as he takes the time to pause and to listen. Gus has developed exquisite survival instincts, and he is not going to ignore those finely honed skills when they start speaking to him. Gus doesn't *know* that anything is wrong — he simply can't know that Walt is watching him several hundred meters away — but somehow, he can sense that things are not what they should be. As he turns and walks away, his guards don't say a word, and certainly don't question him. They just follow.

"End Times" is a masterpiece of grueling anticlimax. Except for an interlude by Walt's pool where he apparently contemplates suicide, the pace is frantic and the tension constantly tightens towards a final showdown . . . that simply doesn't happen. Hank is getting closer and closer, Brock is poisoned, Jesse and Walt are working together again, and Gus is always plotting, always planning, as is Walter White. In the end, however, the viewer is left dangling as Walt's best chance slides by and Gus calmly walks away, nothing resolved. The pressure that "End Times" places on the season finale is therefore enormous, and Gilligan & Co. will not disappoint.

LAB NOTES

HIGHLIGHT
SAUL: "'Honey Tits': I say it's endearing."

DID YOU NOTICE
- Even disabled and at home, Hank manages to manipulate Gomez into furthering his investigation into Gus's organization.
- As Gus walks away, Walt's glasses are pushed up onto his forehead, so without the binoculars, he can't see. This is a nice bit of symbolism, as Walt's vision is often impaired beyond needing corrective lenses. Walt reacts to things far more than he acts to cause them in the first place, so he is often one move behind.
- As Walt spins his .38 snub by the side of his pool, Apollo Sunshine's "We Are Born When We Die" plays in the background, a song that references Walt's apparently suicidal thoughts, and perhaps something more.

SHOOTING UP
- When Jesse confronts Walt in Walt's living room, all the blinds are pulled, making the space deeply shadowed and cave-like. It's an almost claustrophobic setting, perfect for the darkness between the two men, and recalling Plato's "Allegory of the Cave." Saul's office is closed up and shaded as well, creating another cave-like space.
- Time-lapse photography is again used for Jesse's overnight stay in the hospital.

- The framing of Andrea, her mother, and Brock through the ICU doors is carefully done, and Brock looks positively tiny in the huge hospital bed, emphasizing both his innocence and frailty.
- The lighting in the hospital chapel for Jesse's meeting with Gus is incredible. The lighting fixtures are sconces that focus the light downwards, giving the room alternating swaths of light and darkness, with a dark cross lit from the top down seeming almost ominous. In the same scene, Gus, Jesse, and Tyrus are all shown with half of their faces in shadow and half in the light, and Gus and Jesse are lit as opposites, with the left side of Jesse's face in darkness, and Gus's right side equally shadowed.

TITLE Saul tells Jesse that "the end times are here," and the entire episode is laden with a sense that everything is about to be destroyed.

SPECIAL INGREDIENTS

CELL PHONE DETONATED PIPE BOMBS

Walt gets his science groove on in this episode as he whips up a homemade bomb using a cell phone as a remote-controlled detonator. Would this work? The short answer: absolutely. The darker corners of the internet are full of instruction on such evil mischief and, while these sites claim that this is a great way to say, light fireworks from a safe distance, it's a good bet that not all web-surfers are cruising these sites looking for ways to ignite Roman candles.

Face Off

Original air date: October 9, 2011
Written by: Vince Gilligan **Directed by:** Vince Gilligan

"I won." — Walter White

Walt improvises Plan B with an unlikely ally. Meanwhile, Jesse is pulled in for questioning by the police.

"Face Off" picks up just a very few minutes after the nerve-wracking final moments of "End Times." Gus knows something isn't right, but before Walt and Jesse have time to come up with something else, Jesse is pulled in for questioning by the APD about his strangely thorough knowledge of ricin. This sets up one of the most brilliantly funny scenes in the entire series, as Walt confronts Saul's long-suffering secretary Francesca (Tina Parker), and receives one of the more comprehensive reaming-outs of his life from this woman who puts up with Saul's sleaze and is now facing unemployment as Saul skips town due to the depth of the shit piled up by Walt and Jesse.

Francesca is not Walt's only "collateral damage." There was the kindly janitor, Hugo, who was busted and lost his job because of Walt; Elliott and Gretchen Schwartz, who found themselves tied up in some twisted game of Walt's lies; No-Doze, gunned down to serve Walt and Jesse's greed; Bogdan, forced to sell the business he worked for 20 years to create , etc. Walt and Jesse have been cutting a swath through the lives of almost everyone they have incidentally met. Add to this the sheer death and destruction they continue to bring onto the people they are actually close to, and the men begin to look like the embodiments of disaster. Francesca is a solid reminder to the viewer that what Walt and Jesse do has ripple effects that reach far wider than is generally shown from week to week.

In spite of the interaction, Walt's actions in "Face Off" won't be any different. In fact, this episode may mark one of the biggest rocks Walt has ever thrown into the Cause and Effect Pond. Yet, in a way, Walt becomes something of a secondary character as his plan to kill Gus unfolds, and the heart of the story shifts once again towards the touchstone relationship of season 4: Gustavo Fring and Héctor Salamanca. Again, it is impossible to overstate the skill that Mark Margolis brings to his role as Héctor. Despite his severely limited range of motion and expression, Margolis gives the older Héctor a passionate eloquence that never fails to captivate. The final scene between Héctor and Gus is again a study in subtlety: both men so controlled, so powerful. For 20 years Gus has planned his revenge, and has personally made sure that Héctor knows exactly what has been happening and who has been responsible for it all. Worse, Gus has *gloated* in his victory, rubbing ground glass into Héctor's wounds as he oversees the elimination of the old man's entire family. Héctor, trapped in a wheelchair and bound within a body that refuses to respond to his still razor-sharp mind, is helpless against all of this and the only defiance he's capable of is refusing to acknowledge Gus by so much as looking away from him. Until the end. In one of the most memorable moments of television history, and just as Gus is about to finish him once and for all, Héctor looks him in the eye, something he has pointedly avoided all season. At first there is sorrow in his eyes, and pity, but that fades momentarily into an expression so filled with rage and hate that it roars despite Héctor's silence. The ending to this grand vendetta between the two men is fittingly explosive, and Gilligan & Co. may have crafted the greatest death in TV history as, proper to the end, Gus straightens his tie before shuffling off this mortal coil.

After the blazing destruction of the Superlab, done with none of the wistful sadness Walt and Jesse displayed with the destruction of the RV in "Sunset," Walt is left triumphantly independent and the true depths of his depravity, the evil that he has chosen to make his own, is finally revealed in the last few frames of the episode. Walt has become a creature willing to poison, even potentially kill, children in order to serve his needs, manipulate people, and save his skin. Here at the end of season 4, Walt has truly, fundamentally broken bad, and there can be no coming back. Potentially, however, Jesse now has the opportunity to be free of all of this, and to build something like a "normal" life with Andrea and Brock. For Skyler, life has become even more complicated and frightening, now knowingly married to a killer, and potentially an unknowing accessory to murder in her attempts to force Ted into paying his debts. Hank has been proven right, but the death of Gustavo Fring and the destruction of the laundry raise more questions than they answer, leaving him with more work to do. Whatever happens, season 5 promises to be one hell of a ride.

LAB NOTES

HIGHLIGHT
HÉCTOR: "S – U – C – K – M – Y . . ."

DID YOU NOTICE
- Walt doesn't hesitate to send in his partially disabled neighbor (played by Vince Gilligan's mother) in to flush out the bad guys, or get killed.
- Walt is coughing again during all of his running around early in the episode.
- The name of Héctor's nursing home is Casa Tranquila, which translates as "Tranquil House."
- Héctor's final wink to Hank as the elevator doors close on him at the DEA offices.
- There is a framed picture in Héctor's room showing the toddler Salamanca cousins on either knee of a young Héctor, and the preteen Tuco standing beside them, with Don Eladio's charm against the evil eye draped over the picture frame.
- Héctor's bell, to this point in the series always so pure and resounding, is muted by its connection to the explosives.
- Héctor's room at Casa Tranquila is number 303, which recalls "I.F.T." (episode 3.03), where Héctor and Gus are seen face-to-face for the first time in the series.
- Gus's half-normal, half-destroyed face is reminiscent of the season 2 half-charred teddy bear, right down to the missing eyeball.

SHOOTING UP

- Close-ups are used to emphasize objects like the car bomb and the picture with Don Eladio's necklace in Héctor's room, and are used again to cut back and forth between Gus's and Héctor's faces during their final confrontation.
- The episode is laced with humor, including the lovely shot of Walt on the ledge outside of Héctor's window, and the delightedly friendly elderly woman in the next room, who can see him.
- The shot of Gus's walking body is very carefully done. Beginning to Gus's left, it appears that he has miraculously survived unharmed, but this is belied by the horrified expression on the nurses' faces as they come to a sudden halt upon seeing him. As the camera pans around, the viewer is presented with the now iconic image of Gus's half-face as he straightens his tie. This is an exquisite combination of camera work, makeup, and effects.
- As the head-on shot of Gus is finally revealed, behind him in the burned-out room a charred lump of human remains falls wetly from the ceiling.
- The destruction of the Superlab includes a plethora of classic *Breaking Bad* POV shots.
- As Walt and Jesse destroy the Superlab the driving guitars are from the Taalbi Brothers' "Freestyle."
- The music swelling as the lily of the valley in Walt's yard is revealed is "Black (featuring Norah Jones)," by Danger Mouse and Daniele Luppi.

TITLE Beyond the obvious allusion to Gus's grisly end, "Face Off" refers to several different confrontations in the episode: Jesse and the cops, Walt and Francesca, Jesse and Gus's thugs, Walt and Gus, Gus and Héctor, Marie and Hank, and Hank and Héctor, to name a few.

SPECIAL INGREDIENTS

LILY OF THE VALLEY

Lily of the valley poisoning? Turns out that sweet little flower favored by May brides has a nasty sting. One legend associated with the plant is that it sprang from Eve's tears when she and Adam were evicted from the Garden of Eden, which seems to fit, as Walt's actions certainly mark a point of no return to his halcyon pre-meth days. The Victorians attached all sorts of benevolent meanings to the lily of the valley, including purity of heart, humility, love's good fortune, and returning to happiness. Despite all of that, it turns out that every single part of the plant — the stems, the flowers, the berries, and the leaves — are extremely toxic. Ingesting lily of the valley can result in blurred vision, rashes, headaches, vomiting, disorientation, and sudden alterations in heart rhythm. Treatment involves breathing support, IV fluids, and possibly the insertion of a temporary pacemaker to regulate your heart rhythms. And you could still die.

Walt knew *all* of this.

SPEED KILLS (SEASON 4)

BODY COUNT

Gus: 12 (Victor, Don Eladio, and 10 of his capos)

Jesse: 1 (Joaquin Salamanca)

Walt / Héctor Salamanca: 3 (Gus, Héctor, and Tyrus)

Mike: 1 (Gaff)

Gaff: 4 (Los Pollos truck driver, 2 guards, and Gus's man at the chicken farm)

BEATDOWNS

Walt: 2 (by Mike and Jesse)

What's Cooking

BUYING THE HOUSE

PLACE IN *BREAKING BAD*

As a show that relies heavily on history and memory to develop its narrative, *Breaking Bad* uses one of the most fundamental elements of human existence as a framework: our ability to intentionally create meaningful places. The list of created places in *Breaking Bad* is far too extensive to cover in its entirety, so Jesse's house, the RV, the Superlab, and Walt's final, mobile lab, are just a few representative examples examined here. The concepts of "place" and "space" as used here draw upon theories of humanist geography. Humanist geographers seek to realize an idea of place as a universal part of human experience in the day-to-day world. To do so, scholars turn towards phenomenological and existential philosophy to develop a theory that depends upon subjective human experiences to give places meaning. This intentional process of imbuing a given place with meaning is seen as an inherent part of the human experience of the world, and the relationship between human experience and place is encapsulated by such common sentiments as "making a house a home" or "this is where I grew up." In short, it is what we do and the experiences we have that make a particular place meaningful to us.

Of all the places experienced by human beings, home is perhaps the most meaningful, and this may be especially true for Jesse Pinkman and the house at 9809 Margo Street. In season 1, Jesse's home is a place imbued with the personal history of his Aunt Ginny, her struggle with cancer, and her relationship with Jesse, whom she apparently took in when his parents kicked him out of their house for using drugs. Although in seasons 1 and 2 Jesse considers the house to be his place, in reality, it is his aunt's memory and history that predominate. The decor is dark, feminine, and floral; there are delicate knickknacks on the shelves, and doilies on the furniture. Though Jesse undoubtedly inhabits more of the house than when his aunt was alive, even in his upstairs bedroom Jesse's presence remains minimal, and is largely confined to a few possessions strewn atop his aunt's lingering order. The house is therefore in a transitional state. Jesse lives there as he did while his Aunt Ginny was still alive, but is only slowly creating a history and meaning separate from those that he shared with her. Jesse has yet to wholly remake his aunt's place into his own.

The idea of "home" is generally associated with deep meaning, safety, respite, and with being a field of care. In Jesse's case, this idea of home grows out of his experience of his aunt's love. The fact that Jesse has not made any real attempt to modify the decor is evidence of a desire to remember Ginny, and to maintain his home as it was when she was alive, with all the existing associations of safety and security. However, the inevitable and increasing encroachment of Walt and Jesse's criminal activities into their personal and private lives is a major theme in *Breaking Bad*, and this growing domination is often shown by the intrusion of their illegal adventures into their respective homes.

Krazy-8's death, the disastrous attempt to dissolve the body of Jesse's ex-partner Emilio, and the strong, fish-like odor given off by methylamine as it is processed fundamentally change Jesse's home, and what started in the basement has moved into the main areas of the house. The damage to the house, combined with lingering odors, makes it unsalable, and leaves Jesse's home partially destroyed. The memories of his aunt and his life before Walt are being subsumed by these new events, which drastically alter Jesse's experience of place in his own home. Indeed, the show reinforces these memories as the series progresses. In "A No-Rough-Stuff-Type Deal," the camera lingers on the sunlit, empty, support-pole in Jesse's basement — the site of Krazy-8's death. Later, in "Down," Jesse's scooter is stolen, despite having been secured by the steel U-lock that he and Walt had placed around Krazy-8's neck. In each case the viewer is immediately reminded of what happened in Jesse's basement without the need of any further exposition beyond the camera's focus. Moreover, the lab that Jesse and Walt set up in the basement is the immediate cause of Jesse's eviction by his parents in season 2. This reinforcement serves to keep the memory of these events in the basement alive, and to imbue the place itself with a history and meaning that go beyond the diegetic world of the series to become part of the audience's experiential history of that place, and a kind of social memory. Basements thus become a place of death and danger for both the characters and the viewer.

By the time Jesse purchases the house through the efforts of his lawyer Saul Goodman, all traces of him, his aunt, and even his misadventures with Walt have been removed, including furniture, keepsakes, art, appliances, and countertops. Even the walls have been uniformly painted rental white. To everyone but Jesse (and perhaps Walt), the house on Margo Street is no longer a place, but instead is now an empty space, and one that Jesse seems in no hurry to fill. At first, Jesse's sole possessions are some clothes, a sleeping bag, and very little else. Later, some minimal furniture appears: a futon couch, a glass-topped coffee table, and a beanbag chair. Jesse is claiming the space, but is apparently resisting making it into a truly intimate place. This is because, during season 3, Jesse is largely out of place, and resistant to the idea of having a home, a place in the world where he belongs. Unable to find refuge and comfort in his home as a private place, Jesse partially destroys the boundaries between outside and inside, public and private, by turning his living room into the site of a frenetic, ongoing, drug-fueled party where people come and go as they please and at all hours. As this cycle continues, Jesse's psychological state of being out of place, of having transgressed, is given physical expression as the walls of his living room become stained and are covered with graffiti. Leftover pizza crusts and fast-food wrappers mix with cigarette butts, blood, and discarded clothing as Jesse's house becomes polluted by the outside world, just as Jesse himself has been. In abandoning his place to outside forces, Jesse is not turning away from the idea of home as a place of retreat and refuge. Indeed, Jesse is actually seeking refuge *by means of* the noise and constant activity.

As Jesse begins to recover from his downward spiral, his psychological state is again reflected in his efforts to recover his home from the forces he has invited in. The brilliant episode "Problem Dog" opens with Jesse having begun to clean his house, and later in the same episode Jesse is seen carefully repainting the walls of his living room. In a nice bit of symbolism, the graffiti still shows through the first coat of paint, a reminder that this passage too is now an indelible part of the history of this place. By literally getting his house in order, Jesse is also restoring order within himself and in his life. In "Bug" the climax of this process occurs with a violent confrontation in Jesse's living room in which Jesse brutally beats Walt and tells him to "Get the fuck out, and never come back." With this demand, Jesse's house has once again become a place where he controls access, one that is clearly separated from the outside world. By season 5 Jesse has once again found his place, and for the first time since season 1, his home has returned to a traditional state of being a place of respite and care, though he still finds himself unable to completely escape the realities of his outside life.

Walt, on the other hand, never seems quite at home in his house at 308 Negra Arroyo Lane (which translates as Black Stream). The truth of the matter may be that, at least during the series, the only places where Walt ever feels completely at home, completely secure, and completely self-confident are within the series of meth labs he runs. From their first cook in the RV, Walt makes it clear that, in the lab, he is in charge, and Jesse is to obey his rules. The lab is fundamentally Walt's place, for he has mastered its mysteries to a greater depth than perhaps anyone in the country. It is his labs to which Walt seems to devote the most attention, and the most care. Walt's adamantine insistence on respect for the chemistry, for lab procedures, and for an obsessive precision when it comes to cooking, demonstrates a deep concern for the chemistry lab as a very personal place, and for his own self-image as a professional scientist. In his life, the meth lab is the one place where Walt consistently excels, where he is at his absolute best. While he may be losing his wife and his children, his job, and everything else that was once important to him, in the lab Walter White remains in control and in charge.

Walt sets up the first lab himself, converting a 1986 Fleetwood Bounder recreational vehicle (RV) into a mobile meth lab. The RV has become perhaps the most iconic symbol of *Breaking Bad*, and for the first three seasons, takes on such a central role that it can be considered a character in its own right. In terms of place, however, the RV is a complicated study. It is inherently mobile, yet also includes essential elements of home and of permanence. Though moving through the outside world, it provides a sheltered, inside place for anyone within it. The vehicle is designed to allow for the performance of all of the most basic human life experiences, including sleeping, eating, eliminating, and socializing. Though a hotel room provides the same type of space, the RV is personal property, literally the owner's place, and often imbued with rooted memory by various personal possessions and the experiences shared in it. This seeming paradox is humorously demonstrated by Hank's attempt to enter and search the Crystal Ship in "Sunset," which is frustrated by the convoluted legal question of the RV as both vehicle and domicile. For Walt and Jesse, the RV becomes a true place of meaning and care, where their personal relationship is formed and solidified. In "4 Days Out" it becomes their temporary home, shelter from the desert's nighttime cold, and the setting for the deep intimacy of facing death and finding a way out of a dangerous situation together. By the time of the RV's destruction in "Sunset," the vehicle has become an important place to both men, and Walt even takes a lingering moment to caress the equipment in the rear of the Crystal Ship, smiling slightly as he does so, an act that is mirrored in "Felina" when Walt spends his final breath saying goodbye to his final lab.

The second lab in the series, the Superlab created by Gustavo Fring, appears at first to be a place of realized dreams for Walter, emphasized by the wonderful scene in "Más" where he explores the lab to the almost Disneyesque melody of Peder's "Timetakesthetimetimetakes." The candy-red floor, shining stainless steel equipment, and Walt's look of childlike wonder as he explores the place all combine to give the Superlab a dreamy aura. The problem with this wonderful space — at least for Walt — is that in the final analysis, it belongs to Gus. Initially, the Superlab appears to be Walt's place, as Gus allows him a tremendous amount of leeway in terms of his hours, even when it comes to replacing the incredibly overqualified Gale with Jesse, despite the latter's history of addiction and erratic behavior. In the episode "Fly," however, Walt's concept of the Superlab as his place begins to shift. Suffering from a kind of mini-psychic break exacerbated by sleep deprivation, Walt becomes obsessed with destroying a single housefly that has made its way into the lab. Referring to the insect as a "contaminant," Walt desperately tries to remove the fly from the Superlab and to thus restore cleanliness and order to this place as the symbol of his life and ambition, both of which are now spiraling out of his control. The fly-killing quest is ultimately successful, but in a larger sense, Walt's efforts are utterly futile because, when it comes to his own world, and his place in it, "It's all contaminated." The Superlab has become a trap for Walt, a prison of his own making.

When Walt kills two of Gus's street-level dealers, Walt's control over the

Superlab is lost. Gale returns, bringing with him Gus's thugs, who now keep watch on Walt. After Gale's murder in "Full Measure," and Jesse's co-option by Gus and Mike in season 4, the Superlab can in no way be considered Walt's space any longer, and he is progressively out of place within it. Walt's presence in the lab has become largely transgressive, for he is inserting himself into the others' place, and is tolerated only because he remains of some minimal use to Gus. By the time of "Face Off," Jesse too has become a prisoner of the Superlab, and in one scene is literally chained to the place, yet another moment of foreshadowing for his penultimate fate at the hands of Todd in season 5. Though the Superlab has become a place every bit as central to the story as the RV was, its destruction is very different, as neither Walt nor Jesse shows hesitation or regret. This time Walt and Jesse are destroying a place that has taken on meanings that are wholly negative and they act to free themselves not only from Gus's domination, but from the sense of being out of place and out of control.

In their next effort, Walt makes sure to maintain the maximum amount of control over his new lab and over who has a place in it. Indeed, until he retires and allows the lab to pass into the hands of Lydia, Todd, and the neo-Nazis, Walt's control over the mobile meth lab he and Jesse design is almost total. This time Walt *chooses* to be transgressive, using the cover of Vamanos Pest Control's house-covering fumigation tent to set up his meth lab within other people's homes. In a very real way, Walt and Jesse have now become home invaders who violate the most intimate places of people whom they have never even met. The invasive nature of Walt and Jesse's new operation is clearly and chillingly emphasized by the noise of children playing nearby as the toxic gas from Walt and Jesse's first cook is released into the neighborhood and the gas is vented into a backyard full of children's toys and a swing set. This lab is not removed from the everyday places of the innocent. Walt and Jesse are not cooking in the desert anymore, or even underground, but right in the middle of residential neighborhoods. This transgression is not merely against personal place, but also against the larger social space of ordered life. Yet Walt seems immanently comfortable in this new lab and in his role as invader. As we see Walt, Jesse, and later Todd enjoying snacks while sitting on the furniture and watching the televisions in the homes of their unsuspecting customers, it's clear that in Walt's eyes, the lab is now truly his home, and the fact that it regularly changes location is irrelevant.

Wheresoever the lab is, that place is home, *Walt's* home, and the actual owners of the place, and the meanings those people attach to it, are of no consequence. It is perhaps the ultimate act of spatial transgression: the theft of another's place.

Finally, at the end of season 5, the lab, once mobile, has again become stationary, a kind of cut-rate Superlab at the compound of Todd's uncle Jack. For Jesse, the lab becomes a place of torment, of torture, imprisonment, and slave labor, as Todd and the neo-Nazis manage to do what Gus could not, and keep him chained and cooking at their pleasure. For Jesse, the lab goes from a potential source of financial gain and freedom from the law, and becomes instead a place of total subjugation and powerlessness. In the end he is only freed through the actions of Walt, whom Jesse may well hate even more than he does Todd. For Walt, however, the lab is a final trip home before dying, with the reflection of his smiling face the last thing he ever sees on Earth. With everything and everyone else irrevocably lost, the lab is the only thing Walt has left in "Felina," but that's okay, because in a sense he gets to die at home.

EPISODE GUIDE
SEASON FIVE

5

ive Free or Die

Original air date: July 15, 2012

Written by: Vince Gilligan **Directed by:** Michael Slovis

"Yeaaah, bitch! MAGNETS!" — Jesse Pinkman

Walt has a new attitude as he, Jesse, and Mike tie up some loose ends. Meanwhile, Skyler's not too sure about the new Walt, and Hank is back on the case.

Gilligan & Co. have used cold opens to foreshadow the future before, particularly in season 2, but they have never looked as far forward as they do in "Live Free or Die." In Denny's on his 52nd birthday, Walt once again has a full head of hair and a full beard, but instead of looking healthier, he is drawn, pale, and seemingly older, the lines of his face deeper, the flesh of his neck hanging in loose folds. This future version of Walt is so unexpected that it throws the viewer off balance. With no background, the audience is given some quick and confusing exposition, including that Walt's living under an assumed name, apparently in New Hampshire, and that's he's just bought a machine gun and 400 rounds of ammunition, which he intends to use in Albuquerque. Thus the first part of the final season of *Breaking Bad* begins out of context, with the viewer unaware of the history that has led to this scene, which has moved Walt from the confident victor over Gus to the worn fugitive seen in Denny's. Whatever has happened, the cold open promises it's going to be an exceptional season.

After the credits, however, things return to a more familiar normal as the story picks up with Skyler's call to Walt at the end of "Face Off," and continues with the fallout from the assassination of Gustavo Fring. Mike returns from Mexico, and his world-weary cynicism brings some much needed laughter to the episode as he, Walt, and Jesse try to figure out what to do about the records contained on Gus's confiscated computer. Walt begins to construct intricate schemes to access and destroy it, but it is Jesse who finds the best and simplest solution to their problem, albeit one that still requires more than a little elaborate assembly, accomplished with the help of Old Joe, the junkyard owner who helped get rid of the RV in "Sunset." Indeed, the return of people and things from the series' past is a recurring theme in the first half of season 5, beginning with Mike and Joe themselves.

Walt, Jesse, and Mike manage to destroy Gus's laptop while it's in police custody, along with half of the evidence room, and in classic style, Walt is compelled to push things beyond their limit. The giant magnet they have rigged in the truck does the job effectively, but Walt insists on waiting until beyond the last second and on turning the power to the device all the way up, thereby forcing them to abandon the truck, magnet, and everything. Walt is never content with things being adequate; he needs to push everything too far. The extra juice creates an unintended consequence: a picture of Gus and Max that is also in the evidence room is broken, revealing some very interesting numbers hidden beneath the photo. As with Gale's death, the end of Gus meant that Walt was on the verge of walking away unscathed, with the investigation potentially closed. And once more, it's Walt's hubris that opens everything up again. Walt is unconcerned, because the death of Gus has given him a new attitude. Calm, cold, and in control, Walt seems utterly self-assured and frighteningly focused.

The new attitude is not lost on Skyler, nor is the fact that her husband is a murderer. Anna Gunn does a brilliant job at giving Skyler's fears a physical reality. She shies away from Walt, keeps several feet between them when she can, and when she can't, it is all she can do not to shudder and shrink away from the contact. While Walt is reveling in his newfound sense of power and authority, Skyler is beginning to realize that she is living and working with a monster. Walt has truly become the danger, but to whom?

Skyler herself can't claim any truly solid moral high-ground anymore. When she learns that her strong-arm tactics to force Ted to pay what he owed to the IRS in "Crawl Space" resulted in severe injuries from which he is only now regaining consciousness, she rushes to his bedside — to find that Ted is absolutely terrified of her. A surprised and initially guilt-ridden Skyler quickly regains her composure and coldly takes full advantage of Ted's fear. She's learning that problems can solve themselves if people are scared enough of what you might do to them — a lesson Walt has unwittingly taught her.

LAB NOTES

HIGHLIGHT

> MIKE: "You know, I can foresee a lot of possible outcomes to this thing, and not a single one of them involves 'Miller Time.'"

DID YOU NOTICE

- Spelling out "52" with the bacon recalls Walt's 50th birthday breakfast in "Pilot/Breaking Bad."
- There's prominent product/brand placement of Denny's throughout the cold open.
- In the cold open, Walt's car is an old Volvo, the same make of car that Gus drove because of its inconspicuousness.
- Walt is none too happy with Junior's hero-worship for Hank, nor the fact that Hank took Junior along when he was checking out Gus.
- It is once again Hank's observations at a crime scene that leads to the decisive clue, as he puts together the melted camera in the Superlab and Gus's computer.
- Mike poses as Postal Inspector "Dave Clark," as in the Dave Clark Five of British Invasion fame.
- The large legal tome on Saul's desk is a treatise on aviation law, on which Saul must be boning up in preparation for his class-action suit in the aftermath of Wayfarer 515.
- Walt and Jesse are now wearing more "professional" ski masks to pull off the evidence vault heist, ones that lack the top-knot pom-poms viewers saw in seasons 1 and 2.

SHOOTING UP

- The cold open uses a downward shot of Walt's license plate and a trunk-bottom POV as Walt loads his new car, both trademark shots.

- Walt's meeting with the illegal gun dealer (Jim Beaver) is again shot in the mirror, as the two men talk to one another's reflections as they did in "Thirty-Eight Snub."
- There are two more trunk-up POVs as Walt bags the evidence of his bomb-making and the lily of the valley plant in the trunk of the Aztek.
- The shot of Walt playing with Holly in her bassinet is nicely framed by shooting through the rectangle of the master bath's doorway.
- Mirror-shots are prominent in season 5, particularly shots of Walt reflected in his bedroom mirror.
- The shiny new red tricycle in the police evidence vault is an interesting prop. Not only does it show the magnet's effect early by rolling, but it also hints at some very dark crimes indeed.

TITLE "Live Free or Die" is the official state motto of New Hampshire, and in the cold open, both Walt's driver's license and his license plate are from that state. It may also reference Walt's purpose for returning to Albuquerque after apparently having made his getaway.

INTERESTING FACTS
- The waitress calls Walt "Mr. Lambert" as he leaves the Denny's in the cold open. Gilligan & Co. may have chosen this name in "honor" of Dr. Frank L. Lambert, an American professor of chemistry best known for his campaign to change the definition of the thermodynamic principle of entropy from "disorder" to "energy dispersal." In a similar way, Walt's actions in coming back to New Mexico and buying a trunkful of mayhem seem to be his version of taking the total chaos and disorder of his life and turning it into focused energy which is going to be dispersed. Of course, this is a case of using different words to describe the exact same effect.
- When Hank sees the bodies in the burned-out Superlab, he mutters "Fring, you magnificent bastard." The line is a reference to the film *Patton* (1970), starring George C. Scott as U.S. Army General George S. Patton. In the film, as Patton watches American forces routing the German Afrika Korps in battle he shouts, "Rommel, you magnificent bastard! I read your book!" Hank may well have Gale's lab notebook in mind as he paraphrases the line.

SPECIAL INGREDIENTS

"POPCORN" EFFECT ON SUPERHEATED TEETH

During their investigation of what remains of the Superlab, Hank and Gomez find the two bodies, but dismiss the possibility that identification of the corpses can be done, since the bodies are not only burned to a charcoal briquette state, but the teeth are unusable as a means of identification due to the high heat of the fire causing the teeth to "popcorn." But don't crime scene investigators use dental records all the time to identify victims?

Yes, they do. But *Breaking Bad* might have it right here, although teeth don't exactly explode like popcorn. Generally, teeth are a very reliable way to identify a body, since tooth enamel is harder than any other substance in the human body, including bone. Teeth will remain long after the rest of the body has decayed. Teeth can withstand temperatures of more than 2,000 degrees Fahrenheit, although teeth that have been subjected to intense heat (such as the type of heat generated by a chemical fire in a meth Superlab) may become quite fragile and if the teeth are exposed to that level of heat for an extended period of time, they can carbonize.

In this case, the hard part is going to be obtaining the necessary records to compare to whatever remains of the victims' teeth. Having the teeth without records may not be of much use. No family members or friends are likely to come forward and it's doubtful that Gus had a dental plan for his lower-echelon workers. While DNA samples could be taken from the pulp at the center of teeth to aid in identifying the bodies, there has to be something to match the sample to. Those two henchmen might just remain John Doe 1 and John Doe 2.

SAUL AND CLARENCE DARROW

Walt insults Saul by telling him that he's not Clarence Darrow; in fact, Walt refers to Saul's advertising tactics and says that he's nothing but a "two-bit bus bench lawyer." Ouch.

Clarence Darrow (1857–1938) was a firebrand attorney who was best known for defending teenage "thrill killers" Nathan Leopold and Richard Loeb in 1924 and defending John T. Scopes in the famed "monkey trial" in Tennessee. Darrow had a fascinating career beyond these two cases and he routinely chose unpopular clients and causes. Referred to by his friend

Lincoln Steffens as "the attorney for the damned," Darrow ardently believed that everyone, no matter what crime had been committed or what sacred cow had been tipped, had the fundamental right to a zealous defense by a sharp, committed attorney. Thus, Darrow is a model for idealistic lawyers to this day.

Darrow was not without his faults, however. In 1911, he defended the McNamara brothers, who were accused of causing a fire that killed 21 people when an incompetently built bomb went off early. Although he managed to save the brothers from the death penalty, there is strong evidence that Darrow achieved the verdicts by bribing jurors in both trials. If true, Darrow's bribery might mean he and Saul have more in common than Walt thinks.

⦿ WALT & THE BACKYARD POOL

Walt and Skyler's house features a backyard pool, which is Walt's favorite place to retreat and ponder. The pool is also a favorite place for family gatherings. When we first see the pool in the pilot episode, it's a little neglected, with debris floating on the surface. Walt is sitting in a chair, flipping lit matches into the pool as he thinks over a few things. By the end of the series, the pool has taken on a more sinister quality.

- In "A No-Rough-Stuff-Type Deal" (1.07), Walt and Hank retreat to the pool from the noise and fuss of Skyler's baby shower. Hank smokes an illegal Cuban cigar while the two men discuss what is illegal and why some things *should* be illegal. Walt, who has begun cooking meth at this point, seems to enjoy not quite telling Hank the truth.
- Throughout season 2, the pool (and especially the scorched teddy bear) is a focal point of the black-and-white cold opens that slowly reveal the horrible truth of the Wayfarer crash to the audience.
- In "Over" (2.10), the pool is the scene of Junior's tequila experience, with Hank including Junior on the sly and Walt basically demanding his son drink until he pukes in the pool. Here, Hank's far more the father figure to Junior than Walt is.
- In "Phoenix" (2.12), a poolside party is thrown to celebrate the arrival of baby Holly. Incidentally, the food comes from Los Pollos Hermanos.
- In "Caballo Sin Nombre" (3.02), Walt takes the time to use a pool strainer to fish a floating Band-Aid out of the pool, showing how far

he's come from the pilot episode where he was flipping matches into the water. Now he needs to constantly control his environment.

- In "End Times" (4.12), Walt sits by the pool, idly spinning his .38 on the table, looking for a way out of his increasingly desperate situation. This is when his gaze lands on the lily of the valley plant and he decides to take a further step down the path to amorality.
- In "Fifty-One" (5.04), a family cookout turns bizarre as Skyler walks into the pool to force the gathered family to acknowledge that things are not at all right.
- In "Rabid Dog" (5.12), Walt's habit of thinking things over by the pool continues even when the family has left the house to stay at a hotel.

The hotel pool is not the only other swimming pool where significant events take place. Most notably, Gus's 20-year vendetta against the cartel and the Salamanca family begins at Don Eladio's pool where Gus watches in horror as Max is executed, his blood mixing with the water. This is precisely the place where Gus attains the bloody zenith of his carefully planned revenge.

Madrigal

Original air date: July 22, 2012
Written by: Vince Gilligan **Directed by:** Michelle MacLaren

"There is gold in the streets, just waiting for someone to come and scoop it up." — Walter White

The extent of Gus's network begins to be revealed. Meanwhile, Walt is anxious to get cooking again, but Jesse and Mike aren't so sure it's a good idea.

Humor and tragedy often seem to walk hand in hand, and that's one of the reasons the cold open to this episode is so effective. As Peter Schuler (Norbert Weisser who has had major roles in *The Thing*, *Schindler's List*, *Angels & Demons*, and *Gemini Division*) sits through a presentation by a group of very professional food scientists on their latest gastro-chemical masterpieces of chicken-nugget dipping sauces, he's not really there at all. Mechanically he reaches for a nugget, dips, chews. Reaches, dips, and chews again and again as the head scientist enthuses about "Franch." Schuler's world has come crashing down about his ears, and it's all because of his connection with Gus, as revealed by the German policeman's interest in the picture of Schuler and Gus on a golf course on his office wall. As the Los Pollos Hermanos sign is removed from Madrigal Electromotive's hall of fast food, so too does Schuler remove himself, complete with a final auto-flush in the executive washroom.

Across the Atlantic, Walt wants to start cooking again, but he's got a couple of final loose ends to tie up first, beginning with Jesse, who is almost in tears worrying about the missing ricin. Walt helps him search the house for it, and

Jesse conveniently finds the stuff at last, though it's actually yet another lie of Walt's. In one of the more heartbreaking moments of *Breaking Bad*, Jesse, close to bawling, pours out his heart to Walt, apologizing abjectly for being so willing to kill him, for thinking that Walt might have poisoned Brock. "I don't know what's wrong with me," he says. Walt plays the role of the comforting friend and father figure, reminding Jesse that everything turned out okay, and choosing this most vulnerable moment to tell him that he wants them to start cooking again. Of course, there is nothing at all wrong with Jesse besides not trusting his instincts in "End Times" and blowing Walt

(IZUMI HASEGAWA/PR PHOTOS)

away when he had the chance, and Walt's moral depravity is fully on display here as he accepts the apology and plays upon Jesse's pain and confusion.

Mike, however, sees things clearly, and at first wants nothing to do with Walt's new scheme. Mike has repeatedly proven to be immune to Walt's various attempts at manipulation, and continues to be perhaps the one person who sees Walt for what he is: a brilliant man made extraordinarily dangerous by overweening pride and hubris. Unfortunately for Mike, he soon has no choice about going into business with Walt, because wrecking the police evidence vault in "Live Free or Die" has turned up all of the offshore account numbers for Mike and his men, and thus allowed the DEA, now working hard to close the Fring case as Hank's star begins to rise, to seize all of the cash that was keeping Mike's "guys" quiet while they did their jail time. There's also a new player in the game, Lydia Rodarte-Quayle (Laura Fraser, recognizable from *Lip Service*, *Devil's Gate*, and *Vanilla Sky*) who's a little too nervous about the way things have fallen out and is far too willing to kill whoever she needs to in order to stay safe.

Most disturbing, however, is Walt's relationship with Skyler. Bryan Cranston and Anna Gunn once again do a truly remarkable job of portraying the sheer menace in Walt's new attitude, and the terror it inspires in Skyler. The final scene of the episode recalls the ending to "Pilot/Breaking Bad" when Walt turns a willing, very pregnant, Skyler on her side and makes love to her from behind, only this time Walt's kisses and his hand sliding to cup her breast are something twisted and evil, with no love behind any of it, only power, and a willing joy on Walt's part in how he now so completely dominates his wife. It is a truly chilling rape scene, and Anna Gunn somehow projects Skyler's skin actually crawling at Walt's touch, expressing perfectly the trapped horror she feels. Walt has brought the darkness all the way home at last.

LAB NOTES

HIGHLIGHT

LYDIA: "My God, Duane! How did I not see you sitting back there? So weird!"

DID YOU NOTICE

- The film Mike is watching when Walt and Jesse come to make their business proposition is *The Caine Mutiny* (1954), where Humphrey Bogart's brilliant portrayal of a veteran captain who freezes up under pressure contrasts with Mike's own cool unconcern as the DEA searches his house.
- The CEO of Madrigal is stereotypically German, with a shock of blond-white hair, black turtleneck, and black sport coat, an unusual choice for a show that is usually far more subtle.
- As Walt and Jesse tear up Jesse's apartment looking for the ricin cigarette, they go through a collection of crayons, coloring books, and other evidence that Brock and Andrea have been spending a lot of time there.
- Jesse gives the RV a name for the first time: "The Crystal Ship."
- With his granddaughter Kaylee's (Kaija Bales) mechanical pig, Mike once again uses a children's toy to carry out a hit, just as he did with the balloons in "Full Measure."

- Lydia is not as afraid of dying and being found by her little girl as she is of disappearing without a trace and leaving her daughter to feel she abandoned her. This suggests that Lydia's past is anything but pretty.

SHOOTING UP
- Both the cold open and the opening scenes begin with an extreme close-up of food: honey mustard and a chicken nugget in the cold open, and salt in the first act. Both foods are indirectly connected with death, and the close-ups give each an added significance.
- Herr Schuler's suicide takes place surrounded by bright primary colors: the red executive washroom, the blue defibrillator, red tie, etc., making the scene more uncomfortable for the viewer as a violent death takes place amidst bright, cheery colors.
- There is a nice inside-looking-out POV through the peephole in Chow's door at the tumbling toy pig. The POV from the wall directly behind Chow's head is subtly done, with the blood staining the couch and the exit wound barely visible.

TITLE "Madrigal" alludes to the German multinational corporation, but the term also refers to a song made of multiple parts and multiple voices, symbolizing the various perspectives presented throughout the episode by different characters.

SPECIAL INGREDIENTS

SUICIDE BY PORTABLE DEFIBRILLATOR
Herr Schuler commits suicide with a portable automated external defibrillator (AED), a device that is becoming common in places where large numbers of people gather. You can find them in shopping malls, offices, schools, and casinos. AEDs, which have become quite simple to use, are used on people who are having sudden cardiac arrest. The most common cause of sudden cardiac arrest is a condition known as ventricular fibrillation, in which the heart's lower chambers (the ventricles) quiver rapidly and irregularly instead of beating steadily. If delivered within the first few minutes of the onset of the arrhythmia, an electric shock from an AED can restore the heart's normal rhythm. (Contrary to popular belief, "shocking" the heart

cannot restart a heart that has stopped beating. Restore a normal rhythm, yes. Let you know how Frankenstein's monster felt, no.)

Modern AEDs are often described as "idiot proof" — they have recordings that will talk users through the steps of both defibrillation and CPR. In one study, sixth graders were shown to be able to follow the directions and only took 27 seconds longer than trained paramedics to use the AED. It's an amazing medical breakthrough, made even more so by the fact that the machine is designed to detect arrhythmias and analyze the type before determining if a shock is necessary, at which point the AED will charge itself. If the AED does not detect arrhythmia, no shock will be delivered — such a shock could be dangerous or even fatal to a healthy heart. An AED shock would also be damaging to a heart suffering from a myocardial infarction (a "heart attack"), which is caused by a blockage in the coronary arteries choking off the heart's blood supply, rather than a wonky heart rhythm.

Because modern AEDs analyze the heart rhythms before charging, it is likely that Herr Schuler could not have successfully used this method to commit suicide as the device would not have detected arrhythmia. Still — it looked cool.

FEDERAL AUTHORITY TO SEIZE OFFSHORE
FUNDS IN A DRUG TRAFFICKING CASE (RICO)

Follow the money. It's good, solid advice for anyone trying to get to the bottom of just about any questionable behavior, whether it's a politician's sudden change of heart or a tweaker's shiny new car. The Racketeer Influenced and Corrupt Organizations Act (RICO) gave federal law enforcement some powerful tools to fight crime by providing for severe criminal penalties (read "go to prison for a long time") and also providing for a civil cause of action (read "lose all your assets") for acts performed as part of an ongoing criminal organization. RICO permits the leaders of a criminal enterprise to be tried for crimes that they ordered others to do. This change closed a loophole that had previously allowed bosses to escape punishment by claiming that "Sure, Johnny Loose Lips may be sleeping with the fishes, but I didn't do it!"

First enacted in 1970, RICO was originally used to prosecute the Mafia, although the reach of RICO has grown substantially since then. Drug trafficking is a specific RICO crime, so the DEA certainly could have used it to go after Gus's organization. One part of RICO that has made it so effective is the provision that permits a federal U.S. attorney to seek a pre-trial injunction to seize a defendant's assets, *wherever located*, and prevent the transfer of property from the defendant to another company or person. This is how the funds to pay Gus's jailed henchmen to stay quiet suddenly go away, pushing Mike back into business with Walt.

By the way, it has been speculated that the name and subsequent acronym ("RICO") were selected as a nod to the 1931 Edward G. Robinson movie *Little Caesar*, which features a notorious gangster named Rico who, as he lies dying, says, "Mother of mercy, is this the end of Rico?"

5.03

Hazard Pay

Original air date: July 29, 2012
Written by: Peter Gould **Directed by:** Adam Bernstein

"Listen, Walter: just because you *shot* Jesse James, don't *make* you Jesse James." — Mike Ehrmantraut

Walt, Jesse, and Mike get the business going again. Meanwhile, Skyler has an unexpected breakdown.

Things are looking up for Walter White in "Hazard Pay." Mike has found himself forced to go into business with Walt and Jesse in order to make his imprisoned men "whole," and keep them silent about Gus Fring's business and especially Walt, Jesse, and Mike's part in it. Jesse, devastated by what he thinks was a false accusation against Walt for poisoning Brock, is more than willing to help in order to make up for his actions. Skyler is thoroughly cowed by Walt, as is Saul, while Junior is thrilled to have his dad home, and Marie is supremely grateful to him for using his "gambling winnings" to pay for Hank's medical care. Mostly passive during season 4, Walt is now making up for lost time, and is acting decisively. He is finally, and definitely, in charge.

Yet with this newfound confidence and control also come Walt's greatest failings: pride and arrogance. His scheme to cook under the cover of Vamanos Pest's house tents is brilliant, but also risky, placing the operation right in the middle of upper middle class suburbia. Even more, it is contemptuously callous, cooking and venting poison gas into family neighborhoods where children live and play. Walt's new operation invades the most intimate of human social places — the home — turning it from a space of respite and rest into a crime scene. Of course, Walt is merely taking a cue for Gus, who basically told him in "I.C.U." that the best place to hide is in plain sight. At home, Walt's arrogance is most fully on display. His bedroom is quickly becoming a repository of damning evidence as he places his copy of Walt Whitman's *Leaves of Grass* in plain view atop his bedside table, while the deadly vial of ricin still hides in the outlet cover-plate behind the bed. His attitude towards Skyler is one of complete dominance backed by a hubris that makes him sure that he has the upper hand with her once and for all.

Skyler herself seems to be falling apart. With Marie back to her usual cheerfully carping self and nattering on while Skyler tries to deal with the fact that she will go home to a drug-dealing murderer at the end of the day, Sky crumbles at last in a heart-rending scene that leaves Marie scared and utterly confused. Walt uses Marie's vulnerable state to his full advantage, expertly manipulating her with the truth, though far from the whole of it. Revealing Skyler's affair with Ted shifts Marie's sympathies towards him, and places Skyler, breakdown or no, firmly in the wrong. Marie even gives him a tight, supportive hug as she leaves, and in so doing Betsy Brandt and Bryan Cranston give a very subtle, but enormously telling performance. Marie's love, sympathy, and heartbreak for Walt is evident in her expression, while Walt is stunned at this emotional outpouring. His eyes are shocked, and then his entire face softens. Marie truly cares about him, as the members of Walt's family have always done. The only person who ever felt like Walt wasn't good enough somehow was Walt. He has almost always blinded himself to what he has by looking towards what he thinks he needs.

As the episode ends, however, the bloom is knocked off Walt's rose. Again, despite his brilliance, Walt has failed to recognize the realities of the meth business. Perhaps Walt believed that he could simply step into Gus's shoes, but as Mike points out, that's not how the world works. As Walt's share from the sale of the first cook gets smaller and smaller, Walt gets angrier and more frustrated. Despite the fact that it is in his own self-interest to keep Mike's guys paid up, he can't stand the idea of spending *his* money to do so. Finally, Walt reveals to Jesse that he has either missed the point of Gus's brutal slaying of Victor in "Box Cutter" completely, or has managed to rationalize it into meaning what he wants it to mean. Instead of a demonstration of Gus's true viciousness and willingness to pay any price to protect himself and his business, Walt now views Victor's murder as a just punishment for a man who *dared* to cook Walt's recipe. Walt's continuing attempts to rewrite history and deny the vicious realities of running a highly illegal business will continue to reverberate throughout the lives of those around him.

LAB NOTES

HIGHLIGHT
WALT: "Saul, Mike threatened me, he threatened Jesse, he probably threatened someone before breakfast this morning. It's what he does."

DID YOU NOTICE
* Mike, usually so calm and controlled, really doesn't like visiting prisons where someone else controls when he can and can't leave.
* Mike's "division of labor" speech echoes almost word for word the talk Walt gave to Jesse in "Crazy Handful of Nothin'."
* This is the first time Walt has actually met Brock, yet confronted with the little boy he poisoned, Walt shows not a hint of regret.
* As Jesse re-labels the barrel of methylamine, the new label prominently warns, "Keep out of reach of children," though they'll soon be taking it into a house and neighborhood where kids live.
* During a break in the cook, Walt and Jesse are watching *The Three Stooges*, just as Jesse did in "The Cat's in the Bag" when nerving himself up to dissolve Emilio's body. Walt and Jesse have come a long way, and are far from the bumbling stooges they were in season 1.
* Marie mentions that Walt's birthday is coming up, which places the action of season 5 as taking place roughly one year before the cold open of "Live Free or Die," and one year after the first episode.

SHOOTING UP
* "Hazard Pay" is a subtle episode when it comes to camera work. There is a simple security camera POV shot of Mike as he demands to be let out of the prison in the cold open, but this is really the only "trademark" shot in the episode.

- When Walt and Brock are sitting on opposite ends of Jesse's couch, the stripes on the couch-cover create bars between them that are echoed in the transition to the next scene in the vertical green and yellow stripes of the Vamanos Pest tent.

- The tent also allows for some interesting lighting inside the house as Walt and Jesse cook. The sunlight filtered through the yellow and green turns the interior dim and cave-like, making it a much more claustrophobic space. This allows the bright, white lights used within the cook-tent to provide an almost surgical contrast.

- As the cooking montage (set to the strains of "On a Clear Day You Can See Forever" by the Peddlers) ends, there is an unusual computer-generated shot where the camera moves into the boiling chemicals and the focus shifts to the microscopic to show molecules rapidly forming. This effect is reminiscent of similar sequences often seen on the *CSI* franchise, and it is the only time this kind of effect has been used in *Breaking Bad*.

- There is a nice transition between the poisonous clouds emanating from the cook to the clouds outside the window at the White house.

- The scene in which Skyler finds Walt, Junior, and Holly watching the last few minutes of *Scarface* is beautifully done. The sound of automatic gunfire echoes through the house, and while Walt and the kids are in a pool of light Skyler stands in the shadows, outside the family circle. The camera cuts back and forth from the violence on-screen to Skyler's face lit by the flickering TV, as Skyler seems to envision Junior and Holly caught in a holocaust of gunfire brought down on them all by Walt.

TITLE "Hazard Pay" refers directly to the money supplied to Mike's guys to support them and their families while they are in jail, and to keep them quiet in the face of DEA questioning. The title may also refer to Walt's new attitude and control, which he sees as a reward for paying his own dangerous dues.

INTERESTING FACTS "Hazard Pay" marks the first appearance of Todd, played by Jesse Plemons, who is best known for playing the ultimate good-guy Landry Clarke on the TV series *Friday Night Lights*.

SPECIAL INGREDIENTS

WHY ARE THEY CALLED "SECOND STORY MEN"?

Saul explains that the Vamanos Pest crew are legitimate fumigators, but "they're also top-drawer second story men." The term seems to have first been used back in 1886 to mean a burglar who enters a house through an upstairs window. One source lists the term as meaning a cat burglar, which has more of a romantic flair than the Vamanos gang possesses, but you can't have everything in this life.

Gilligan & Co.'s real-life inspiration for Walt's new operation may have been the story of the K&A Gang, one of the most famous and longest-lasting second story gangs in the United States. Operating out of Philadelphia, the K&A (the name comes from the intersection of two streets — Kensington and Allegheny — where the group is said to have first formed) began as a burglary ring after World War Two, although the enterprise eventually expanded into loansharking and drug trafficking. According to Allen M. Hornblum's book about the gang's decades-long existence, *Confessions of a Second Story Man: Junior Kripplebauer and the K&A Gang*, the gang was highly skilled, but certainly were not debonair, sophisticated cat burglars, à la Cary Grant in *To Catch a Thief*. Hornblum describes a gang of hard-fighting, hard-drinking, not-afraid-to-bite-an-ear-or-nose group of thugs who formed crews to successfully rob wealthy neighborhoods all along the East Coast for roughly 20 years. They seldom carried weapons (more for the added jail time a weapon meant rather than for any "gentleman thief" code) and often dressed in business attire, which meant fewer questions were asked as they cased potential targets in upscale neighborhoods.

With the rise of reliable home alarm systems, the K&A Gang needed to branch out. At the same time houses were increasingly being equipped with motion-sensor cameras and silent alarms, the drug culture was on the rise. Never ones to miss an opportunity, the K&A shifted much of their activity into meth production. In the late 1980s, members and affiliates of the K&A were said to be using the P2P method to manufacture a hundred pounds of meth in a cook, causing a federal U.S. attorney to proclaim the K&A "one of the largest methamphetamine organizations in the nation." By cooking with second story men, it looks like Walt and Jesse are just following in the footsteps of the K&A.

F 5.04 | ifty-One

Original air date: August 5, 2012
Written by: Sam Catlin **Directed by:** Rian Johnson

> "I won't — I will *not* have my children living in a house where dealing drugs, and hurting people, and killing people is shrugged off as 'shit happens.'" — Skyler White

Lydia discovers a problem with the methylamine supply. Meanwhile, Walt is excited about his upcoming birthday, but Skyler gives him a different kind of surprise than he hoped for.

"Fifty-One" begins with Walt on top of the world and feeling like he can do anything he wants, up to and including getting rid of his Aztek and trading up to a Chrysler 300 for him, and another new Challenger for Junior, both with all the extras. The cold open ends with a grinning Walt repeatedly revving the engine of his new ride, riding a testosterone high and acting like a teenager. And why not? Mike's "legacy costs" aside, business is good and Walt is finally in charge. From his perspective things are both hunky and dory. Unfortunately, not everything is under Walt's control, especially Hank and the DEA, who have continued to pick at the remnants of Gus Fring's organization and its connection to Madrigal Electromotive, which has led them to Madrigal's Texas branch . . . and Lydia.

Despite this bump in the road, Walt remains confident, and is very much looking forward to his 51st birthday, expecting Skyler to throw him another shindig like she did a year ago in "Pilot/Breaking Bad." After all of his lies,

all of his threats, posturing, and murderous acts, all of the events of seasons 1 through 4, Walt still believes that his family life can — somehow — return to normal. With his newfound self-assurance, Walt looks forward to a house full of friends and neighbors gathered to celebrate him, because he thinks that he finally deserves celebrating. A year ago, Walt felt like the ultimate sad sack, stuck in a go-nowhere life where he barely broke even and where even punk high-school students looked down on him. At 51, however, Walt is finally proud of himself (to say the least), and thinks that his life is in his control at long last. His pride is so overweening, it blinds him to reality, particularly when it comes to Skyler.

Unable to avoid it, Sky has done the minimum possible to celebrate Walt's birthday: cake and a family dinner with Hank and Marie. She knows that there is nothing to celebrate in what Walt has done, and she knows that his swagger includes a terrifyingly offhand physical and emotional dominance of her own life. As conversation staggers to a halt in the face of Skyler's monosyllabic answers after dinner, and Walt begins to fill the void with an extended pontification about what he has been through the past year and how much his family means to him, Skyler takes drastic and wholly unexpected action at last. In a brilliantly filmed sequence, Skyler floats, open-eyed, deep in the pool, her dress billowing out around her like something out of *Peter Pan*, the bright colors contrasting with her Ophelia-like walk into the pool. Anna Gunn plays the scene beautifully as she enters the water and cuts herself off from the noise of her life, from the meaning of their words as they are totally muffled by the water. While it may be unlikely that Skyler was actually seriously attempting suicide, Gunn's wide-eyed thoughtfulness seems to suggest that it might not be that bad after all to just let go and stay in this cold silence forever.

Despite Walt's cruel countering of every idea she has to keep the kids out of the house and thereby out of harm's way, Skyler wins this particular contest, because, in the end, she is absolutely willing to do whatever it takes for as long as it takes, until Walt's cancer returns and solves her problems, once and for all. Season 5 has presented the viewer with a new Walt, and now we see a new Skyler. She may be terrified and terrorized, but she is far from helpless, and seems to finally be prepared to live up to her words in "Cornered": "Someone has to protect this family from the man who protects this family."

LAB NOTES

HIGHLIGHT

BENNY: "Swapped out your air filter, replaced your fluids — didn't have to replace the windshield this time."

DID YOU NOTICE

- Benny the mechanic (John Ashton) tells Walt that "Nothin' beats free," recalling the words of the Denny's waitress in the cold open to "Live Free or Die." In a season that is filled with reflections of what has come before, this line is interesting since, in terms of the story's timeline, it harks back to something that hasn't been said yet, which, from Walt's perspective, recalls Benny's words here.
- Lydia has to fumble with her "second cell phone," a problem Walt had in seasons 1 and 2.
- After Hank and his men have arrested the warehouse guy, Lydia exaggerates the entire experience beyond all proportion in her frantic phone call with Mike, a not-too-subtle reminder that Lydia, when under pressure, is unreliable.
- Excited about their new wheels, Walt and Junior have not left a place in the driveway for Skyler to park her car, a further indication of Skyler's position outside the circle of family warmth.
- This episode firmly places the cold open to "Live Free or Die" a year in the future. In addition, Holly's age is given as eight months, which

also situates "Fifty-One" in relation to the season 2 episode "Phoenix," when Holly was born and Jane was murdered.

- The only genuine gift Walt is seen to receive for his birthday is a very expensive watch from Jesse, the person he has arguably wronged most of all.
- The morning after his birthday, Walt is eating breakfast alone. His family, for which he has supposedly been doing everything, is gone.

SHOOTING UP

- The shot of Lydia taking a conference call in German opens with the camera looking through and panning out from behind a clear-glass business award that is shaped like the state of Texas, giving the viewer Lydia's geographical location.
- At the dinner table after Walt has bought the new cars, Skyler is largely shadowed, while Walt and Junior's animated conversation takes place in the light, again placing Skyler outside of the family space.
- There is a wonderful crime-board POV shot from behind and through the bulletin board that Hank and Gomez have set up to track the Fring case, and the shot even leaves the strings and backs of the photographs visible.
- The outside shot of the striped Vamanos Pest tent includes a view of a brightly decorated fire hydrant that lends the picture a bit of a circus feel, a nice contrast of something apparently joyous hiding both poison, in the case of the tent, and the means to deal with destructive fire, in the case of the hydrant.
- The pool scene is gorgeously done. When focused on Walt, he is brightly lit from the table lamp as he speaks, while behind him Skyler is slightly out of focus and almost completely silhouetted against the brightness of the pool. As the camera shifts to a close-up of Skyler's face, Walt, Hank, and Marie are blurred in a pool of white light, while Skyler herself is lit by the sickly blue-green glow from the pool that seems to flicker as the water moves. Again divorced from family warmth, Skyler is drained of color and shadows play across her features, while the rest of the family are bright, an effect enhanced by the bright wrapping paper.
- The submerged POV of Marie at the side of the pool looking down

at Skyler recalls a similar shot in "ABQ" when Walt is shown from the perspective of the half-burned teddy bear in his pool. Both the bear and Skyler have been driven into the pool by Walt's actions.

TITLE "Fifty-One" refers to Walt's birthday, placing the episode squarely between his 50th birthday, when the series opens, and his 52nd birthday, where, we are led to believe, the series will end.

SPECIAL INGREDIENTS

HOUSE TENTING

Vamanos Pest provides the perfect cover for Walt's new forays into meth manufacturing. A tented house is avoided by everyone, since the gases being pumped into it to eradicate pests such as roaches and destructive beetles are lethal. But what's involved with tenting, and why do it in the first place? To begin with, if there's another way of dealing with the pest problem, *do that*. Tenting is an elaborate, inconvenient process that involves a great deal of trouble on the part of the homeowner. However, if the house is infested, conventional spraying won't take care of the problem, while the tenting process ensures that the killing chemicals get into absolutely every nook and cranny of the structure.

Because the chemicals are inescapable, the homeowner cannot reside in the house during the process and all furnishings, food, etc. must be prepared for the onslaught. For example, any food items (for people or animals) that have been opened and are going to remain in the house during the fumigation process need to be double-bagged in special bags. Unopened cans, jars, or bottles, as well as cosmetics, toothpaste, and ice (!) don't have to be double-bagged, but you still have to go through everything to determine what has to be bagged up and what is okay "as is." All drawers and doors have to be opened and all waterproof mattresses and pillow coverings must be opened or removed. You need to take all living things with you while the house is being fumigated, including pets and houseplants. Further, all plants and shrubs that are close to the house (18 inches) have to be cut back so the fumigator has room to secure the tenting to the ground with heavy water or sand-filled weights called "snakes." This means that fencing, trellises, and anything else close to the house may need to be removed.

After you've done all of this and given your trusted fumigator your keys, you go away for three days and let the fumigator do the job. The first step is to open all windows and doors, and place fans and hoses throughout the house to guarantee that the fumigating gas gets to every remote location within the house. The house is then tented and sealed.

Now the gassy fun starts. First, a "warning agent" called chloropicrin is released into the house — this gas is similar to tear gas and is designed to double check that no people or pets are still inside, either through an owner's forgetfulness or a neighborhood kid's "double dog dare." Once certain that the house is clear, the fumigating gas is released and spread throughout the house; the gas is sealed inside the house for about 24 hours, depending on the size and layout of the house. The next step, taken on the second day, is to break the seal on the house, remove the tenting, and let the house "actively aerate" for an hour with all windows and doors open. Then the house is closed back up for a day of "passive aeration." On the third day, the fumigator will enter the home and check to be sure that the house is fully aerated and is fit for habitation. Once the house is cleared, humans and pets re-enter a bug-free home. Of course, if the house has been used in the meantime to cook meth, there's a whole new set of problems worse than roaches to deal with.

Dead Freight

Original air date: August 12, 2012
Written and directed by: George Mastras

"Bottom line: I have done this long enough to know that there are two kinds of heists: those where the guys get away with it, and those that leave witnesses." — Mike Ehrmantraut

With Lydia's help, Walt, Jesse, and Mike undertake a daring heist. Meanwhile, Skyler offers Walt a business proposition.

Season 5 has seen *Breaking Bad* return to a focus on family, and a widening of the lens to include several different kinds of family. Walt still insists that everything he has done over the past four seasons has all been for his own family, while Hank and Marie are discovering that they enjoy being parents, and are working hard to help Skyler and Walt sort things out. Skyler has no intention of working things out with Walt, but is willing to do anything to protect her children. However, Gilligan & Co. have quietly developed several other families, which now, at least in part, guide the actions of the central characters. Mike only agrees to go into business with Walt in order to keep his men in prison quiet by getting the money they need to take care of their families. Mike himself is putting all of his "hazard pay" into a massive trust fund for his much-loved granddaughter Kaylee. Jesse continues to support Andrea and Brock even though he and Andrea have split up, because they've become his "instant family." Finally, and perhaps most unexpectedly, Lydia continues to reveal a truly fierce loyalty and love for her daughter,

becoming most distraught when contemplating her little girl being left alone in the world. The ties binding these people together are intricate, dangerous, and go to show that, in *Breaking Bad*, there are no free agents; no one who can go down without hurting "innocents." In fact, everything the central characters do winds up hurting someone, somewhere.

Despite a daring train robbery presented with all of the skill and suspenseful drama of *The Italian Job* or *The Thomas Crown Affair*, at the heart of "Dead Freight" is the truth that, no matter how good they are, no matter how pure their intentions, no matter how much control they are able to exercise, what Walt, Jesse, and Mike do kills people, and there is no avoiding that harsh truth. The boy on the dirt bike is a classic example, and his brief arc is carefully crafted down to the smallest detail.

Sound is vital in this episode. The roar of the kid's bike blocks out everything else, particularly through his protective helmet. It is only because he saw a tarantula and stopped to capture it that he dismounts, takes off his helmet, and lets his bike idle at a much quieter rate. This in turn stops him just long enough, and makes things just quiet enough, for him to hear the train-whistle in the distance. The careful attention to sound effects in the cold open is mirrored in the final scene of the episode where, the theft of 1,000 gallons of methylamine successfully completed, Walt, Jesse, and Todd hoot, holler, and celebrate before turning off the motor to the water pump only to hear a softer but similar sound in the idling of the kid's bike.

What follows is a brilliant use of what TV scholars call intertextuality, when an actor well known for a particular role carries the audience's memory of that role over into a new one. Here, Jesse Plemons, best known for his role on *Friday Night Lights* as Landry Clarke, a lovable, loyal young man, guns down the young kid (Sam Webb). Though the viewer is well aware that Plemons is playing a different character in Todd, seeing an actor associated so strongly with a good guy do something so unforgivably heinous makes the murder of the boy even more shocking (though at the same time the moment could be read as a wink at a particularly ham-fisted *FNL* season 2 plotline).

The look on Aaron Paul's face in this scene speaks volumes, and beautifully conveys his character's horror. Within the narrative of *Breaking Bad*, the kid's cold-blooded murder is Jesse's worst nightmare come true, for Jesse was the one who told Todd that absolutely no one could ever know about the robbery, which Todd understandably interpreted as instructions to ensure that no one would ever know. Like Gus Fring telling his street-dealers "No more children" in "Half Measures," Jesse's unthinking words have led directly to the death of a child. Jesse is suddenly much further on the road to becoming that which he hates, and thus to breaking bad completely.

LAB NOTES

HIGHLIGHT

SKYLER: "Out burying bodies?"
WALT: "Robbing trains."

DID YOU NOTICE

- Walt does not bug Hank's computer. What he connects to the Ethernet cable running into the back of Hank's computer tower is a receiver for the bug in the picture frame, allowing them to pick up and record the bug via the internet.
- Laura Fraser does an excellent job silently broadcasting Lydia's desperation. The viewer can see her trying frantically to figure out something to save her skin.
- Lydia is terrified about the possibility of her daughter ending up in a group home, another glimpse into her own past.
- Hank and Marie are becoming *very* attached to Holly.
- This episode is the third time Jesse has come up with an alternate plan this season: the magnets in "Live Free or Die," the collar and

detachable motor for the portable lab in "Hazard Pay," and now the drain and replace scheme for the train robbery.

+ Jesse James is mentioned for the second time this season, the first being in Mike's warning to Walt in "Hazard Pay."

MISCALCULATIONS For perhaps the first time in *Breaking Bad*'s run, it appears that plot convenience overruled continuity in "Dead Freight." The basic idea behind the heist is that Lydia will find out which car the methylamine is in between midnight and 2 a.m., giving the gang about six to eight hours to get out to the site and get ready. Yet Walt, Jesse, and Mike measure the distance from the crossroads to the small trestle and prepare the site at least a day, if not more, before the heist. The viewer sees Lydia calling Mike after all of the preparations have been made. Although it is possible that they needed to operate from the gully no matter where the methylamine tanker car was located, they simply could not know whether it would be near the front, middle, or rear of the train. Jesse measures 814 feet from the crossing to the gully, which is almost the length of three American football fields. To be able to reach any point on the train quickly and efficiently from the gully, they would have to lug along at least 200 or more yards of hose. This is a miscalculation, and a big one.

SHOOTING UP
+ Several POV shots are used in the cold open, showing the world from the perspective of the foot peg of the dirt bike once, twice from the end of the handlebar, and once from the pillion position behind the kid's right shoulder.

+ As the scene opens with Lydia being questioned in the abandoned warehouse, her face is half in shadow and half illuminated by harsh and sickly fluorescent lights.

+ There is a tabletop, up-and-through POV as Lydia spreads out the map which is seen as transparent, but retains the details of roads and borders.

+ POV shots are used again on the train, echoing those on the kid's dirt bike: from the pilot (or "cowcatcher") at the front of the train, from just behind the air horn, and alongside the wheel.

+ There is an excellent crane shot of the oncoming train, where the camera moves up, to the side, and then down to reveal Walt, Jesse, and Todd crouched under the trestle.

TITLE "Dead Freight" is the term used to denote the money paid by a shipper to a shipping line (or in this case, the company who paid for something to be shipped) for failing to load the amount of cargo spelled out in the contract. In terms of the episode it refers to the money the Chinese manufacturer will eventually have to pay Madrigal for the gang's theft of methylamine, which will appear to have been an error on the manufacturer's part. A second, more lethal meaning for the phrase refers to the dead child at the end of the episode, as well as the tarantula the kid has captured and carried away with him in the cold open.

SPECIAL INGREDIENTS

NORTH AMERICAN TARANTULAS

The kid on the dirt bike was completely prepared to collect a tarantula — he's got a clean, empty jar with air holes punched in the top tucked into his inner jacket pocket. But . . . spiders! Big, hairy spiders! What's the kid thinking? Aren't they dangerous? Actually, the kid's perfectly safe, at least from the spider. Tarantulas are fairly common in the American Southwest, where over 50 native species of the spiders can be found. Although tarantulas can seem frightening due to their size, all species are harmless to humans. Their venom is often compared to a bee sting. Despite what bad horror movies may have you believe, no one has ever died from a tarantula bite. There are deadly spiders, of course — the black widow spider and the brown recluse spider have both been known to kill full-grown adults. And Australia has any number of spiders who want to kill you. In contrast, the tarantula is a useful animal since scorpions and cockroaches are part of its diet.

Most species of tarantulas are nocturnal, but you can find them during the day, just as the kid does. Often, what you find during the day is a male tarantula: the males have a nearly ridiculous drive to find females, which is a quality that makes male tarantulas lousy pets. In the wild, male tarantulas live 10 to 12 years, but in captivity, their lifespan is often measured in months as they will work themselves into an early grave trying to escape and find a lady tarantula. The females live about twice as long and make far better pets, if that's what you're interested in.

POST 9/11 RAIL TRANSPORT SECURITY MEASURES

Following the terrorist attacks on September 11, 2001, the immediate focus was on aviation security, not railway security. This makes sense — resources had to be allocated and jetliners were the focus since they had been used as weapons (you can't hurl a train through the air at a skyscraper). Prior to 9/11, security at rail yards, even ones that were used to store 90-ton tanker cars filled with deadly chemicals, was incredibly lax. Often gates were unlocked and unguarded, which allowed free access to the tracks. Further, many switching devices were unlocked, so anyone could pull a lever and redirect (and possibly derail) a train.

After 9/11, measures to tighten security were implemented, especially at chemical plants, which often have railroad spurs running to main tracks, but it was a slow process and flaws still remain. Part of what makes railway security so difficult is that it involves so many entities. The federal government, state governments, counties, and cities all have a role in rail transport, and a freight train may travel on tracks owned and maintained by different corporations through any number of jurisdictions before reaching its final destination. While new security measures at rail yards may not be as highly visible as security measures in place at airports, it's undeniable that changes were necessary. Consider this: well over 1.7 million shipments of hazardous materials per year are transported by rail and a U.S. Navy study has shown that a terrorist attack involving one single tanker car of chlorine near a densely populated area could kill as many as 100,000 people. Considering that every graffiti-covered tanker car represents a breach in security would make anyone feel queasy.

Buyout

Original air date: August 19, 2012
Written by: Gennifer Hutchison **Directed by:** Colin Bucksey

"I'm in the empire business." — Walter White

Mike and Jesse want to make a career change, but Walt refuses to help. Meanwhile, Jesse has dinner with the Whites.

The cold open to "Buyout" is one of the most chilling of the entire series, not for what it shows but for what it doesn't. There is no natural sound as the Vamanos Pest truck is backed up to the garage and Todd digs out the kid's dirt bike. Even as the bike is carefully disassembled piece by piece, including the frame, which requires an electric cutting tool, the only sound is a moody tone-piece as the bike is broken up, dumped into a barrel, and covered with hydrofluoric acid. Mike, Walt, and Todd go about the task methodically and carefully, and when it is finished, Todd goes up onto the back of the truck and digs a little deeper, uncovering a small hand, while Walt fetches another barrel. The viewer does not see the men dispose of the boy's body, but the bike is enough. They will disassemble the boy as easily as they did steel and plastic, until he too is sealed into a barrel to be dissolved away. Only the tarantula in the jar remains, which Todd has kept in an act of monumental stupidity.

Only Jesse does not participate in the disposal process, and it is only Jesse who wants Todd gone once and for all, though he is unwilling to kill him to make sure he stays quiet. Walt doesn't hesitate to keep Todd alive and on the payroll, because in truth Todd has solved a potential problem rather efficiently, and at this point, all Walt really cares about is his business — a fact reinforced later during a cook as he blithely whistles while he works. This becomes crystal clear as both Mike and Jesse decide that they want out, and Mike makes a deal to sell the stolen methylamine to earn them each a cool $5 million. The problem is the buyer will only agree to buy all of the methylamine and Walt doesn't want to sell his share. In season 5, things have generally been running in Walt's favor, and Skyler's new war against him has been somewhat counterbalanced by the way the meth business has been running so smoothly: a process that can continue indefinitely now that they have 1000 gallons of precursor. If, that is, Walt can keep the methylamine, which Mike most definitely doesn't want to happen. To seal the deal with Declan (Louis Ferreira whose credits include *Shooter*, *SGU Stargate Universe*, and *Motive*), Mike takes the precaution of zip-tying Walt to the office radiator and Walt's not one to forget what he sees as a kind of humiliation at Mike's hands.

With Mike and Jesse both determined to get out of the business, and to force Walt to sell his share of the methylamine if necessary, things look like they're beginning to slip out of Walt's control again. On the home front, things are about to get worse after Skyler's visit with Holly where Marie reveals to her that Walt has blamed everything on Skyler's affair with Ted. This conversation changes a weeping Skyler on the verge of coming clean with her sister to a furious woman. Interestingly, the viewer gets another look into both Walt's past and his motivations as he tells Jesse the story of Gray Matter, revealing that he sold out his share of the company for $5,000, while the company is now worth $2.16 billion, a fact Walt knows because, in an act of weekly self-torture, he checks the company's worth *every Friday*. While Walt doesn't mention his reasons for selling out (viewers have Gretchen's perspective on this from "Peekaboo"), he nonetheless reveals that the buyout has resulted in a 20-year grudge not unlike the one Gus held against Don Eladio and the Salamancas. This one error has been eating away at his pride and self-image for decades, and Walt's not about to let go of the one thing that has managed to heal that wound — *ever*.

In the midst of these murderous familial and psychological shadows, Gilligan & Co. unexpectedly give the viewer what may well be the most laugh-out-loud funny scene in the entire series when Walt invites Jesse to have dinner with Skyler and him. What follows is pure comic relief. Jesse sits between Walt and Skyler, in the chair opposite Junior's usual seat, placing him in the position of both child and guest. Certainly Jesse handles the ensuing frigid company with all of the desperate, awkward attempts at tension-breaking of a kid who's caught between warring parents. He tries several approaches: complimenting Sky on the delicious dinner only to learn that it's all deli carryout; talking about the scabbiness of frozen dinners; and finally telling her that Walt has said nice things about the way she's running the car wash. In between these attempts he takes long drinks of his ice water while his eyes dart from Walt to Skyler and back again. Interestingly, Jesse, the sober addict, is the only one at the table not pounding back the booze as Walt steadily drinks bourbon and Skyler keeps refilling the world's largest wineglass. In a final conversational apocalypse, Skyler asks Jesse if Walt also told him about her affair and then leaves the table, wine in hand. Jesse is left looking away from Walt as if he has suddenly found the curtains to be enormously interesting, until Walt tells him that the kids are gone. "Thank God," Jesse sighs, and the audience can't help but agree.

LAB NOTES

HIGHLIGHT

MIKE: "I would never come to the headquarters of our illegal meth operation draggin' a bunch of cops, Walter. It would be unwise."

DID YOU NOTICE

* Todd's remark that "shit happens," recalls Skyler's furious comment about killing people being dismissed with the same phrase in "Fifty-One."
* Most of the information gleaned from the bug in Hank's office is useless to the gang, including a wonderful tirade on the evils of a certain popular sandwich spread.
* Mike is perhaps the most honest character of the show. Even when he doesn't like the truth he is able to acknowledge it, as when he wearily nods at Hank's assertion that, sooner or later, Mike will make a mistake and get caught.
* As Jesse and Walt watch TV during a break from cooking, an ad for "Kelp Caviar" comes on, showing caviar dripping down from the top

of the screen in the exact same fashion as the final liquid meth drips down onto the catch-tray at the end of a cook.

SHOOTING UP

- The cold open begins with a God's-eye-view down into the dirt-filled dump truck pulling into the Vamanos Pest garage.
- The first natural sound heard in the cold open is the strike of Jesse's lighter wheel as he lights a cigarette.
- As the report about the missing 14-year-old Drew Sharp airs, there is a great close-up of Jesse's face, with tears in his eyes, eerily lit by the sun through a yellow stripe of the Vamanos Pest tent, mixed with the electric blue of the TV itself.
- A ground-level, wide-lens shot of the Vamanos Pest office from the wall opposite where Walt is zip-tied to the radiator creates the illusion that the space is much larger than it actually is, reinforcing Walt's seeming helplessness.

TITLE "Buyout" has three meanings. The term refers to: Mike and Jesse's attempt to buy out of the business; Declan's desire to purchase all of the methylamine, thus buying out all three of the ABQ crew; and also Walt's past sale of his share in Gray Matter, thus being bought out of that now highly successful company. It may also refer to Walt's efforts to get into "the empire business" that have resulted in his becoming respected and successful, even in an illegal enterprise, as well as his sacrifice of his relationship with his wife and his kids.

SPECIAL INGREDIENTS

HOW CAN ELECTRICAL WIRING BURN THROUGH PLASTIC?

Electrical power is a fact of modern life. We rely on it to light our lamps, to heat our water, and to operate our coffeemakers. Walt uses it to escape the humiliation of being zip-tied to the radiator in the Vamanos Pest office. He strips the wires bare, places one under the zip tie, then (after bracing himself — electrical burns hurt!), he turns on the coffeemaker and uses the wild current to burn through the zip-tie. How's that work?

Electricity has the potential to be a killing force, so raw wires are covered in plastic as a type of insulation, which stops the flow of the current. The coating is essential, since the service coming in to the average house (or pest control office) is rated at 200 amperes and it only takes 0.05 amperes of electric current to cause skin damage. Electric devices that are intended to put out heat, like space heaters, hair dryers, and coffeemakers, tend to use more power than other devices, so making sure the wires are properly covered becomes even more important. Appliances with worn or frayed insulation should not be used. Replace the cord (just wrapping it in electrical tape will not prevent a fire) or discard the device. Raw wires can easily short circuit, which means the intended path of the current is altered. Accidental short circuits, often caused by faulty wiring, can create electrical arcs and are responsible for thousands of electrical fires per year. The number of people stripping wires in order to deliberately cause such electrical arcs to burn through zip-ties is presumably much, much lower.

TROS AND EX PARTE ORDERS

Saul works to get a temporary restraining order (TRO) to end the DEA's tailing of Mike. The action succeeds, but Saul makes it clear to his client that this is strictly a stopgap measure; it'll get thrown out. TROs such as this one are granted (although most commonly in situations involving alleged domestic violence), and Saul's right. They don't last for long — with good reason.

The idea behind a TRO is that the situation is so dire that urgent measures must be taken or irreparable harm will result, which justifies a court issuing an ex parte order. *Ex parte* is a Latin term that means "on one side only" and at first glance, it seems to shred the part of the Fifth Amendment to the United States Constitution that says "No person shall . . . be deprived of life, liberty, or property, without due process of law." One of the cornerstones of the American justice system is that those who might be affected by legal proceedings have to have fair notice of those proceedings — ex parte proceedings occur when only *one* side gets to present their version of events to a judge.

This would seem to be inherently unfair, as a TRO can result in restricting someone's movement and, in the case of a domestic violence TRO, can cause the temporary confiscation of firearms, but it is actually an excellent example of the elasticity of the due process concept. TROs are extremely short-term solutions and a full hearing between the parties involved in the dispute must be held swiftly. The notion is to balance the competing interests — on one side, a person's interest in knowing that legal proceedings have been begun against them and on the other, the imminent harm that is likely to occur if relief is delayed in order to provide notice to the other person.

Say My Name

Original air date: August 26, 2012
Written and directed by: Thomas Schnauz

"Shut the fuck up and let me die in peace." — Mike Ehrmantraut

Walt makes a deal that keeps him in business and keeps Mike happy. Meanwhile, Hank gets a new lead, and Jesse makes a fateful choice.

Despite the difficulties with Skyler and Mike, Walt is large and in charge again in the cold open to "Say My Name." Outnumbered and almost certainly outgunned, Walt is calm, confident, and coldly dangerous as he negotiates with Declan to take over Mike's end of the business. Without doing anything more than telling the truth (for once) about his skill as a cook, the benefits of his product compared to Declan's, and his responsibility for Gus Fring's death, Walt completely dominates Declan and his crew, terminating the negotiations by making Declan say his name in a demand that is almost sexual in both its phrasing and its effect when Declan whispers "Heisenberg." Walter White is gone and only Heisenberg remains. This is also another example of Walt's hubris — up until now, no one has really been able to put a face to the name "Heisenberg." He's been a shadowy presence that couldn't be definitively identified and therefore, Walt was safe from being exposed. Now, that safety is gone: Heisenberg is blue meth, and Declan and his crew can describe Heisenberg down to his porkpie hat.

Walt's solution, though effective and elegant, doesn't quite fulfill the promise he made at the end of "Buyout" to create a situation where

(IZUMI HASEGAWA/PR PHOTOS)

everyone is happy. Mike is paid and out, and taking care of his guys out of his share, Walt gets to keep the methylamine and keep cooking, but Jesse still wants out, and here Walt has miscalculated. For most of four seasons, Walt has been able to manipulate Jesse by one means or another, and so he is sure that he can do the same thing again, and convince Jesse to stay in the business. First he tries praise, promising to give Jesse his own lab and his own cook, as if rewarding him for his services. Walt repeatedly tells Jesse that his cook is every bit as good as Walt's own and he even praises him in front of Declan. Walt tells Jesse that he is the best, and that there is far more than $5 million to be made. When Jesse refuses to take the bait, Walt shifts gears, berating him, reminding him that he has no other skills, no opportunities, that he's nothing but a junkie. When that still doesn't get Walt his desired outcome, he finally refuses to buy Jesse out, sure that the money will finally win the argument in his favor.

What happens next may be the most important moment in Jesse's life, because he walks away. Without the money, without any relationship with the man who has become a twisted father figure to him, and without regret, Jesse says "no" once and for all. It is a truly central moment, because Jesse has done what Walt no longer can — he has turned back before he is utterly consumed by the darkness. He has refused to participate further in a business that by its very nature kills men, women, and children; rots the souls of those who practice it; and corrodes the conscience of those who are caught up in its web. Jesse has done some terrible things, but at this moment, he walks away a free man. That's no mean feat.

Walt, on the other hand, remains trapped, and simply cannot understand *how* Jesse could walk away from the source of all of Walt's pride and self-respect. Further, with Jesse gone, Walt can no longer so easily hide from his own addiction to pride and power. As long as Jesse stayed with him, Walt could tell himself that what he was doing, who he was *becoming* couldn't be all that bad. Without Jesse, though, Walt has lost the last remnants of his conscience and moral center. Nor is Jesse the only person confronting Walt with the truth about himself in this episode. In a wonderful, disgusted rage, Mike finally calls him out, pointing out that everything that has happened — the deaths, the encroaching DEA, the progressively wilder schemes — can be laid at Walt's feet as the result of his selfish pride. Mike hammers home his true disdain for Walt, and Walt can't take it. In a fit of pique and wounded pride, Walt kills Mike, all because he can't stand to hear the truth, or for someone to dare to cast aspersions on his abilities. The most dangerous thing about Walter White is that he is a brilliant, spoiled brat who has come to see violence as the solution to all of his problems.

LAB NOTES

HIGHLIGHT

> JESSE: "Vamanos."
> SKYLER: "I wish."

DID YOU NOTICE

- ◆ Hank has to make fundraising calls for the DEA "Fun Run," since Gus Fring is no longer a sponsor.
- ◆ When Walt and Todd take a break from the cook, Walt eats a peanut butter and jelly sandwich with the crusts cut off, recalling the sandwiches he made for Krazy-8 in ". . . And the Bag's in the River."
- ◆ Hank is poring over photos of Mike's house as he sits in the video conference call.

SHOOTING UP

- ◆ There are several POV shots used when Lawyer Dan is first seen filling the safe-deposit boxes, including from inside the drawers and the view from Dan's moving wrist.
- ◆ The slight ringing sound that muffles Hank's boss on the video call

recalls the similar effects used throughout the series to indicate when a character's mind is far removed from his or her present situation.

- ◆ The montage of Walt and Todd's first cook is set to "Goin' Down" by the Monkees, and includes some intricate dolly shots as the camera moves behind and out from the other side of objects in the foreground to transition from scene to scene and through time.
- ◆ The shots of the sunset on the muddy river as Mike dies are nicely done, showing nature unaffected by the sudden violence, and Walt and Mike as just two small creatures in a vast world.

TITLE "Say My Name" not only refers to Walt's demand to Declan, but to Mike's habitual use of Walt's full name whenever he speaks to him, suggesting that, regardless of whoever else may think of him as the Great Heisenberg, Mike knows that he's still just Walter.

INTERESTING FACTS The film Mike watches while Hank and the DEA search his house is *The Big Heat* (1953), directed by Fritz Lang. The film is a noir classic about a cop who takes on the crime syndicate controlling his city after his wife is murdered.

SPECIAL INGREDIENTS

ANTOINE LAVOISIER

Walt tells Todd, now his assistant, that he doesn't need to be Antoine Lavoisier. Good thing too. Antoine Lavoisier (1743–1794) is known today as "the father of modern chemistry" for his numerous contributions to the field, although he met a bloody end. Lavoisier was born to wealthy, upper-class French parents and he completed a degree in law at the behest of his family, although he never practiced that profession. He was interested in mathematics and science; at the age of 25 his thoughts on the best way to light the streets of Paris won him membership in the prestigious Royal Academy of Sciences. That same year he joined Ferme générale ("Farmer's General"), a private tax-farming company that collected taxes and tariffs for the French Crown. His close association with the unpopular and notoriously corrupt company, including his marriage to one of the owner's daughters, would have fateful consequences. On May 8, 1794, all of the owners of Ferme générale were arrested, tried for treason, convicted, and executed. The body of the father of modern chemistry was thrown unceremoniously into a common grave.

Despite the high regard in which he is held by chemists, Lavoisier discovered no new substances and he made few improvements to laboratory methods. Instead, his genius was in taking the work of others, refining it, and explaining it. Because of Lavoisier, however, science gained some truly fundamental knowledge upon which much of modern chemistry rests, including the concept of the chemical element, the naming of oxygen and hydrogen, the role of oxygen in forming rust, the chemical composition of water, the metric system, and the invention of plaster of Paris. Not bad for a lawyer.

5.08 G liding Over All

Original air date: September 2, 2012
Written by: Moira Walley-Beckett **Directed by:** Michelle MacLaren

"I'm out . . . I'm out." — Walter White

Things finally come together for Walt, but Hank makes a game-changing discovery.

The first half of season 5 has spent a lot of time in self-reflection through references to past episodes, but "Gliding Over All" takes this to the extreme (see below for a list). The first and perhaps most important of these is the cold open close-up of a common housefly. In the season 3 episode "Fly," Walt's obsession with killing a fly both masked and mirrored Walt's fierce inner struggle, and marked what was perhaps the last chance Walt really had to turn away from the path he had been walking, and maybe even save his soul. Ultimately, he chose to ignore the buzzing of his conscience and go deeper into his own heart of darkness and moral decay. In the cold open to "Gliding Over All," however, the fly evokes no such pangs of conscience in Walt, only a deep thoughtfulness eventually broken by Todd and the necessity of disposing Mike's body.

In Todd, Walt has at last found the ultimate lackey. Todd never even thinks about questioning Walt's orders or actions, and he is perfectly willing to do whatever Walt tells him to. Todd has even taken over Jesse's form of address, calling Walt "Mr. White." As for Jesse himself, he is shut out completely by a contemptuous Walt, and the meth keeps cooking. In fact, Walt's empire grows larger than ever before with the help of Lydia. The last few people who could rat Walt out are dealt within one of the most violent two-minute-long sequences on television. Walt's precisely orchestrated prison hit on Mike's guys and Lawyer Dan does more than merely protect the business by eliminating witnesses, it sends a message to both the criminal community and law enforcement: Heisenberg is alive and well, and you simply don't want to fuck with him. With this, everything falls into place, and for three months straight Walt's story is one of uninterrupted, highly successful operations: he cooks, Declan and Lydia distribute, and Todd assists. Walt is king of Blue Magic Hill, and his word is law.

(ALBERT L. ORTEGA/PR PHOTOS)

When Skyler confronts him with the knee-high pallet full of stacked bills from his 90 days of labor, however, something shifts. Sky tells him that she wants her family back and for the first time in his life Walt is looking at more money than he could ever possibly spend. More money than Junior or Holly could probably spend, and perhaps even *their* own kids. So much money that paying Jesse $5 million is just a drop in the bucket. It is, finally, enough. In a scene reminiscent of when he agrees to accept treatment for his cancer in "Cancer Man," Walt tells Skyler that he's out, and as the episode moves towards its conclusion, it seems that he actually is. Yet there are some troubling issues that haven't been addressed. Unless Todd has learned to duplicate the cook, without Walt, there is no Blue Magic, and the profit margin for everyone slumps. Exactly how do Declan and Lydia feel about Walt retiring? Walt's kingship may be analogous to having a tiger by the tail: letting go just isn't a good option.

However, all of that may be moot as Hank makes the discovery of a lifetime whilst sitting upon the toilet at the White house. Walt's pride has made him careless and his copy of *Leaves of Grass* rests atop the toilet tank as reading material. The book itself is bad enough, but the inscription is worse. In a single moment, everything comes together for the wide-eyed Hank, the brilliant and dogged detective who has spent the past 15 months of his life trying to track down the mysterious Heisenberg; who was almost killed because of his obsession with the case; and who now is the man in charge of the District Office of the DEA. His prey has been right under his nose all along, even more so than Gus Fring was to ASAC Merkert. And Walt has been toying with him all the while. The reflective nature of season 5 thus far is explained in this single moment. It is a last look back before everything changes: for Walt, Skyler, the kids, Hank, Marie, Jesse, Saul — everyone. What comes next will see this dark tale told.

LAB NOTES

HIGHLIGHT

LYDIA: "Maybe you should order something. Do you want a coffee or something? . . . I think this would play better if you ordered something."

DID YOU NOTICE

* All the references to previous episodes:
    * The shot of Walt in the shower references both "Kafkaesque" in season 3 and "Cornered" in season 4.
    * Lydia's nervousness at meeting Walt in public echoes her meeting with Mike in "Madrigal."
    * Walt tells Lydia to "learn to take 'yes' for an answer," almost word for word what Mike told him in "Thirty-Eight Snub."
    * Lydia in turn tells Walt that "We're going to make a lot of money together," which is exactly what Tuco Salamanca told him in "A No-Rough-Stuff-Type Deal."
    * The print in the crappy motel room where Walt meets with Todd's white supremacist uncle is the same print that was hanging on the wall of Walt's hospital room in "Bit By a Dead Bee."
    * As Walt times the mass murders he's ordered, he is dressed in a light yellow check shirt and khakis for the first time since season 2.

- Walt sees the still dented paper-towel dispenser in the cancer clinic men's room from his fit of rage at the end of "4 Days Out."
- As the White-Schrader clan sits around the table by the Whites' pool, Hank is talking about brewing up a fresh batch of "Schraderbräu," his homebrewed beer recipe last seen in "Breakage."
- The montage of the prison murders Walt ordered is set to "Pick Yourself Up" by Nat King Cole and George Shearing. The question remains as to who is actually starting all over again though: Walt, or Hank?
- When Walt visits Jesse, there is a bong and two bottles of beer on Jesse's coffee table. Jesse is apparently beginning to use again, which unfortunately bears out some of the harsher things Walt said to him in "Say My Name."

MISCALCULATIONS

- As Todd's uncle Jack (Michael Bowen, half brother to Robert, Keith, and David Carradine, and best known for his roles in *Django Unchained* and both *Kill Bill* movies) discusses the difficulties with Walt's hits, he says that "Whackin' bin Laden wasn't this complicated." Although "Gliding Over All" was filmed in 2012, it has only been a little over a year in terms of the story since the show began, making the year the conversation takes place 2010, while SEAL Team Six didn't kill Osama bin Laden until May 2, 2011. Creator and executive Vince Gilligan has since admitted that this was a continuity error.
- On a smaller scale, the time shown on Walt's wristwatch when he begins the countdown for the hits is different from the time shown in the close-up that immediately follows. In the wider shot, the time is 12:01:15, while in the close-up it is 12:00:45.

SHOOTING UP

- The cold open moves from an extreme close-up of the fly to a low angle shot of Todd's cab pulling up to Vamanos Pest to a high crane shot of Todd getting out, a play with perspective that is used regularly in *Breaking Bad*.
- The shot of Walt in the mirror on the closet in the master bedroom

recalls a similar shot from "Live Free or Die," and both appear in scenes where Walt is hiding the small vial of ricin.

- ◆ The seemingly upside-down shot of Walt undergoing a PET/CT scan mirrors the same shot used in "Pilot/Breaking Bad" when his cancer was first diagnosed.
- ◆ The long cooking montage includes every type of "trademark" shot associated with *Breaking Bad*: POVs, up-and-through, exterior time-lapse, accelerated motion, transitioning by moving behind and out from objects in the foreground, forced perspectives, jump cuts, low angles, high angles, close-ups, shot-to-shot transitions, etc. The entire sequence is a love song to the tremendous cinematography used from the very beginning of the series, and is beautifully done.

TITLE "Gliding Over All" is a short poem from Walt Whitman's *Leaves of Grass*:
Gliding o'er all, through all,
Through Nature, Time, and Space,
As a ship on the waters advancing,
The voyage of the soul — not life alone,
Death, many deaths I'll sing.

Walt, of course, has caused a great many deaths in his run, and in this episode he directly causes more all at once than at any time before. (The Wayfarer crash wasn't directly caused by Walt, although those deaths can be laid at his feet.) The poem also reinforces the reflective nature of the episode, and emphasizes what *Breaking Bad* is all about: the voyages of the characters' souls.

SPECIAL INGREDIENTS

METH IN THE CZECH REPUBLIC

Thanks to Gus Fring and his use of Los Pollos Hermanos as a cover for his distribution network, the restaurant division of Madrigal is under investigation, but as Lydia points out, Madrigal is a huge multinational corporation with 14 divisions. She had pitched her plan to expand Gus's empire into Europe but a slight case of death ended that idea. Never one to let an opportunity slide, she extends the same offer to Walt, who's not so sure. The Czech Republic?

Isn't that the country that overthrew the Communists in the so-called Velvet Revolution and then elected a playwright? Well, yes. And Lydia may have a brilliant idea here.

Meth is not a widely used drug in most of Europe. The exception is the Czech Republic, where both production and consumption of the drug has increased dramatically in the last decade. The reason is one of the odder legacies of Communist rule. When the Communists were in power, it was exceedingly difficult to get all sorts of things from the West — Coca-Cola, blue jeans, and drugs were all stopped at the border. During this time, users began manufacturing drugs "in house," which is easier with a totally artificial drug such as meth than it is if you have to get hold of a shipment of opium poppies to turn into heroin, for instance. Add to this the fact that Soviet economic policy favored having different key industries associated with different satellite states, and that one of the largest factories producing ephedrine (a popular precursor in meth production) was located near Prague. When the Iron Curtain fell, both borders and markets opened, and suddenly there was money to be made. Meth labs began popping up in the Czech Republic.

According to the European Monitoring Centre for Drugs and Drug Addiction (EMCDDA), while the number of large-scale meth labs seems to be decreasing, the number of "kitchen cooks" in Europe increased by 22 percent between 2008 and 2009. That being said, Lydia overstates the demand. EMCDDA's figures show that only 0.3 percent of Czech adults have tried meth, rather than Lydia's estimate of 5 percent.

5.09

B lood Money

Original air date: August 11, 2013
Written by: Peter Gould **Directed by:** Bryan Cranston

"Have an A1 day!" — Walter White

Reeling from his discovery, Hank begins to try to build a case against Walt. Meanwhile, Jesse discovers that living with the past is more easily said than done.

Eight episodes after "Live Free or Die," the cold open to "Blood Money" returns to the older, bearded Walt as he visits the house at 308 Negra Arroyo Lane. The former White house has become an abandoned place surrounded by a chain-link fence, and local teenagers have modified Walt's pool into a skate park. This is no longer Walt's — or anyone else's — home. Instead, it is an empty shell collecting litter inside and out, with "Heisenberg" spray-painted in huge letters across what was once the White family living room wall. It seems that Walt has fallen, and so has everything around him. His current chore? Retrieving the small vial of ricin from behind the faceplate of the electrical outlet in what used to be his and Skyler's bedroom. Fittingly, Walt is collecting death from this dead place, a place where he and Skyler had once created life together.

This scene still lies in the future as far as the primary series timeline is concerned, however, and the opening act of the episode shifts the viewer to the White bedroom in better days: clean, furnished, brightly lit, and lived in, as Hank steps slowly out of the master bathroom clutching Whitman's *Leaves of Grass*. It is impossible to overstate the magnificence of Dean Norris's

(JOHN HALE)

performance in this episode. His subtle style perfectly evokes the constantly changing, turbulent array of emotions boiling inside of Hank, from the quiet moment he spends staring out at Walt through the sliding door of the White house, to the final scene's incredible confrontation. The revelation that Walt is Heisenberg is almost too much for Hank, but only almost, and the next morning he is doing what he does best — building a case.

Hank's not the only one who wrestles with powerful emotions in "Blood Money," though. Jesse, who is using again, looks awful. His reddened eyes, darkly circled with heavy bags beneath, speak to sleepless nights and an inner pain that the chemicals cannot erase. With $5 million, Jesse is miserable, because the blood that covers the money, and his own hands, is the blood of children. For Jesse, the money is irrevocably tainted, and has become a horrifying reminder of all the lives dissolved by his and Walt's adventures. In Jesse's mind the only way he might be able to get close to a clean conscience is if he doesn't keep the money. Moreover, he has to give it away in a fashion that will help some of his victims. When his first attempt to get rid of the money through Saul fails, Jesse finally, desperately, hits on the idea of throwing it out of his car, like some demented newspaper boy, in the poorest neighborhood he can find, one that bears a striking resemblance to the area featured in "Peekaboo." It's a nice touch by Gilligan & Co., because when it comes to crystal meth in the U.S., it is the working poor who suffer the most, both directly and indirectly, since every drug house in the country is surrounded by other houses filled with people just trying to get by and raise their kids. Jesse is literally throwing money at the problems he has helped to create.

Of all the memorable moments in the episode, it is the final scene that far and away stands out: Walt's confrontation with Hank. With powerhouse performances by Norris and Cranston (who also directed this episode), Walt and Hank lay all of their cards on the table. Hank's hurt, confusion, and outright fury are more than a match for Walt's attempts at rationalization and manipulation. When Walt tries to talk about protecting their family, Hank shuts him down immediately with some undeniable truth: "Like you give a shit about family!" It is only with the last line of the episode, when all attempts at logical and emotional manipulation have failed, that Walt is able to make Hank pause. In an almost melancholy shift of expression, Walter White fades and only Heisenberg is left, with a chilling warning to Hank to "tread lightly." It's worth noting however, that Heisenberg's eyes are not the coldest ones in the garage. With that final threat, Hank goes hard and frozen, and a terrifying, righteous predator meets Heisenberg's gaze.

LAB NOTES

HIGHLIGHT

SKINNY PETE: "Dude, yo, why do you think McCoy never liked to beam nowhere? 'Cause he's a *doctor*, bitch! Look it up, it's science."

DID YOU NOTICE

- As Walt leaves his former home, he meets his ex-neighbor, Carol, who drops her groceries in shock, causing several oranges to roll out onto the sidewalk, possibly a *Godfather*-like reference to violence and death in the future.
- In the cold open, Walt pauses at the sliding doors to look out at the kids skating in the dry pool, then proceeds down the hallway to the bedroom. In the first act, Hank makes the same journey in reverse,

moving from the back bedroom to come and stand at the sliding doors, looking out at Walt on the poolside patio.

◆ When Hank opens the sliding door, the first intelligible words heard are Marie jokingly telling Walt, "You are the Devil."

◆ When Hank loses control of his SUV, he crashes into a white picket fence, perhaps the ultimate American symbol for home, family, and security, all of which Walt's actions have broken or at least endangered.

◆ At the car wash, Walt and Skyler are both dressed in whites and light beiges, a change from their generally darker clothing in previous episodes, and also the kind of clothes worn by people who do not expect to perform any arduous physical labor during their workday.

◆ "Blood Money" is doing some interesting things with characters' eyes. Walt's eyes disappear in his reflection in the cracked mirror in the cold open, and Lydia's eyes are hidden behind her Jackie-O-style sunglasses except when she is speaking earnestly to Walt.

◆ Walt has come full circle, back to running the cash register at the car wash and asking permission to rearrange the air fresheners. Instead of Bogdan, however, Skyler is now the boss, and appears to be the person who will make all the decisions about the business.

◆ As Hank goes through the Heisenberg files in his garage, elements and characters from throughout the series are seen again, including Krazy-8, Mike, Gus, Gale, Don Eladio, Tyrus, the breathing mask from Walt's high school chemistry lab, and the now easily identifiable sketch of Heisenberg made by the cousins for their shrine to Santa Muerte in "Sunset."

◆ It has been at least a month and likely longer since Walt gave Jesse the $5 million, but it seems that Jesse hasn't spent a dime of it in all that time.

◆ Jesse almost never looks at Walt during their scene together, recalling Hector Salamanca's refusal to look at Gus Fring.

◆ When trying to convince Jesse that Mike is alive, Walt inadvertently says the opposite of what he means: "Jesse. I need you to believe this. It's not true. It's just not."

◆ The towel Walt places under his knees echoes Gus doing the same thing in Don Eladio's bathroom in "Salud."

◆ As Walt searches through the magazines on the back of the toilet, the top one is revealed to be *Family Circle,* while the back of the one on the bottom reveals an ad for Walt's expensive medical center, with the tagline "Dedicated to Treating Cancer."

- Hank's neighbor's kid is playing with a remote-controlled car again, perhaps the one he bought with the money Hank gave him to replace the car destroyed when Marie spitefully ran over it with her VW Bug in "Seven Thirty-Seven."

SHOOTING UP

- The close-up shot of the skateboard wheels recalls the POV shots of the wheels of both Tomas's bicycle in "Mandala," and Drew Sharp's dirt bike wheel in "Dead Freight."
- Again Gilligan & Co. use sound and sight to indicate that a character is under tremendous stress. As Hank drives away from Walt's, Marie's voice becomes indistinct and echoes, while the shots from Hank's POV become blurry, unfocused, and canted. The scene recalls Walt's reaction to the news that he has cancer in the pilot episode. Both pieces of news are traumatic, life-changing events.
- As Hank works through the files in his garage, there is a nice contrast shot of the Schraderbräu logo in the foreground that features a silly, grinning Hank in a bright Hawaiian shirt and lei, while in the background, a blurred Hank, dressed in gray, works intently, with deadly seriousness, and no trace of a smile.
- *Breaking Bad's* iconic bottom-up POV shot is turned on its head in this episode as Jesse is seen from above, looking up through his clear coffee table. Not only has up-and-through become down-and-through, but Jesse himself is occupying the POV that viewers have become so used to seeing, looking up and through his table, as if, like a camera, Jesse can only stare at the world around him without any desire to participate in it.
- The shot of Jesse and Walt sitting on opposite ends of the couch is carefully composed. Verticals in the form of the stacked money bags between them, an upright beer-bottle on the table in the foreground, and the gap between the window curtains in the background divide the two men sharply, while the image is framed by a row of empty beer bottles lying on their sides at the bottom of the shot.

362

TITLE "Blood Money" not only references the ways in which Jesse and Walt have earned their money since season 1, but is also a historical term for the compensation paid by a murderer to the family or clan of the victim. Payment of blood money indemnified the killer and his family from vengeance by the victim's family, and legally settled the matter permanently. By trying to give his money to the family of Drew Sharp and other victims, Jesse is literally attempting to pay for his crimes. Blood money was historically part of legal systems in cultures all around the world, including Northern Europe, the Middle East, Somalia, Japan, and Korea.

MUSIC As the first act opens and Hank comes out of the Whites' bathroom, the song "If I Didn't Love You," by Squeeze is playing outside by the pool. In the song the singer reveals that if he didn't love the woman he's singing about, he'd hate her, a nice parallel for Hank and Walt's relationship as Hank must now deal with such hatred for the man he once loved as a brother. This is a nice bit of continuity with the previous episode, where "Up the Junction," by the same band, was playing as the Whites and Schraders hung out by the pool. In that tune, the singer is a man whose lover becomes ill, so he goes to work, starts a family, and gets everything going well, only to be left high and dry by his wife, at which point his life goes to hell. Someone's playing *Squeeze Greatest Hits* with Walter White in mind.

INTERESTING FACTS This episode was dedicated to "Our Friend, Kevin Cordasco." Kevin was a 16-year-old boy in Los Angeles who was a huge fan of *Breaking Bad* and who also suffered from neuroblastoma, a rare form of cancer. A friend of Kevin's family arranged for Kevin to meet Bryan Cranston, who visited Kevin in the hospital, and later brought Bob Odenkirk and Anna Gunn to visit Kevin at his home in L.A. Kevin was also able to meet *Breaking Bad*'s writing staff in November 2012. The cast and crew were deeply moved by Kevin's story and his continuous positive attitude in the face of his illness. Vince Gilligan planned to write Kevin a role in the show, but the teen was too ill to travel to the set for filming when the time came. As his illness worsened, Kevin was offered the opportunity to read the script for the finale of *Breaking Bad*, but apparently turned it down because he wasn't sure he would be able to keep it to himself. Kevin died in March 2013, and Gilligan decided to dedicate "Blood Money" to him as a gesture of respect and tribute.

SPECIAL INGREDIENTS

FORENSIC HANDWRITING COMPARISON

It's not enough for Hank to *think* he's right when he sees Gale's inscription to "W.W." in Walt's copy of *Leaves of Grass* — he has to be absolutely sure, so we see him using Gale's lab workbook from the evidence collected at the scene of his murder to compare with the *Leaves of Grass* inscription. Hank's not looking for personality traits as revealed in handwriting (a field known as "graphology"); instead, he's looking for proof that the same person produced both writings. Handwriting analysis is a subjective field but, done properly, it generally holds up in court. Hank's looking for the individual characteristics that make one person's handwriting distinct from everybody else's. Even identical twins have individual handwriting styles. While the handwriting of very young children often looks very similar, as we get older, our style changes — usually quite drastically — from the models we learned in elementary school. While it is possible for adults to share a few characteristics, the odds of anyone sharing dozens of individual characteristics are astronomical.

In handwriting analysis, two documents must be compared. The first, known as an "exemplar," is by a known author (Gale's lab workbooks, for instance) and the second is by an unknown author. Clearly, a quality exemplar is the key to the final analysis. The analysis begins by looking for differences in the two samples, rather than similarities, which almost anyone could find with some accuracy. It's the lack of these differences that indicate the two documents were written by the same person. It helps considerably that both samples Hank is looking at are written in uppercase — comparisons between upper- and lower-case letters are nearly worthless. It's also helpful that both samples were provided without coercion, as nervous people tend to do all sorts of wacky things when writing (as do drunk or extremely tired people). In the case of the two documents Hank is looking at, there are no differences, bringing a piece of the puzzle into place.

ALL-SEEING EYE

In Saul's office, a potential client is wearing a T-shirt with the symbol of the all-seeing eye, which is sometimes known as the "Eye of Providence." Eyes and the act of looking (or not looking, in Héctor's case with Gus) are recurring motifs in *Breaking Bad*. Remember Don Eladio's amulet and the teddy-bear eyeball? It seems appropriate that such an image appears in this episode, which is so wrapped up in whether or not characters can — or want to — see things. While there are variations on the symbol, it is most usually depicted as an eye enclosed in a triangle, in turn surrounded by rays emanating out. Often interpreted to represent the eye of a divine God watching over the world, the symbol can be traced back to the Eye of Horus in Egyptian mythology. In medieval and Renaissance Europe, the Eye of Providence was used as a representation of the Christian Trinity. In 1776, the eye was suggested as a design element of the Great Seal of the United States and it was adopted for the reverse of the Great Seal in 1782. The eye also appears on the United States one-dollar bill, the notion being that the Eye of God Himself watches favorably over the success of the United States.

B uried

5.10

Original air date: August 18, 2013
Written by: Thomas Schnauz **Directed by:** Michelle MacLaren

"It was me. I screwed up." — Walter White

Hank moves quickly to get hard evidence against Walt, but finds more obstacles to his investigation than he expected. Meanwhile, Walt is moving fast to cover his tracks, and Marie confronts Skyler.

It looks like things are beginning to fall apart for Walt, and he begins "Buried" one crucial step behind Hank as the latter manages to contact Skyler first. Skyler has been the linchpin to Walt's schemes since discovering his criminal activities back in season 2, because if she flips, Walt doesn't stand much of a chance. So Skyler's choice in this episode is crucial, and the same goes for Anna Gunn's skill at bringing to life the range of emotions Skyler experiences in "Buried." Meeting with Hank, Skyler is cautious, not quite ready to commit to one side or another, but also unwilling to be pushed into making that decision. The scene she creates at the restaurant is part artifice and part emotional breakdown, similar to her walk into the pool in "Fifty-One," but it does what she needs it to, which is buy her some time to think, and to get in touch with Walt — who, on Saul's wise advice, isn't taking her calls.

Walt himself is in full panic mode, and as usual, that means he's moving fast. Importantly, despite the rush and sense of power Walt gets as Heisenberg, he seems to genuinely want to be out of the business for good. His reaction to Saul's suggestion that Hank be killed is uncompromising, claiming Hank as family, and therefore untouchable, a remarkable change in attitude from his view in "One Minute." Walt is apparently truly trying to put Heisenberg firmly in his past. The thing about the past, though, is that it never really goes anywhere, and it crops up at the most unexpected and inconvenient times.

For Skyler, her past choice to keep Walt's secret in order to protect her kids and force him to pay for Hank's medical bills comes back hard as she finally, *finally*, tells Marie the truth. Sort of. Skyler is being exquisitely careful here, and never actually says anything that could be taken as a direct and explicit confession in a court of law. In the first of two extraordi-

(IZUMI HASEGAWA/PR PHOTOS)

narily intimate scenes, Marie confronts Skyler about Walt, and obviously wants Hank to be wrong. Throughout the series, Skyler and Marie's relationship, though far from perfect, has been presented as very, very close. At no time are any other members of their family even mentioned, and the closeness to the Whites and Schraders is built around the core of the sisters' love for one another. Subtly but surely, *Breaking Bad* has emphasized that, when it comes to blood relatives, the sisters have only each other. Skyler's betrayal is therefore horrifically enormous, particularly when she reveals (through her silence when Marie guesses the truth) that she knew about Walt before Hank was shot and almost killed. Like Skyler in "I.C.U.," Marie is not slow in deducing that Walt's activities likely had something to do with the attack on her husband, and if there is one thing Marie is devoted to above anything else, it's Hank and her marriage. Marie's head-snapping slap marks the severing of one of only two relationships that Marie had absolute faith in. Skyler's shocked devastation shows that she is well aware of the true cost of her duplicity.

Perhaps it is this loss that propels Skyler into her final choice of the episode. With Marie seemingly permanently estranged, all Skyler has left are Walt and the kids. She takes tremendously tender care of the exhausted, unconscious Walt as he lies on the bathroom floor. Or, it may be the revelation of his returned cancer that tips the scales, as Walt will likely die and solve all problems. Yet, in what is one of the most beautifully acted scenes in the entire series, it is impossible to deny that, despite everything, there is a deep and abiding affection between Skyler and Walt. Whether or not it is love at this point is another question, but there is a bond there that nothing seems to be quite able to break. Of all the characters in the show, Skyler is the most emotionally complex, and from the get-go Gunn has brought that complexity to her performance. Probably all of the reasons listed above go into making her decision, but as in "Four Corners," Skyler casts her lot with Walt. It's an oddly moving choice.

LAB NOTES

HIGHLIGHT

HUELL: "Mexico. Alls I'm sayin'."

KUBY: "Guy hit 10 guys in jail within a two-minute window. Alls *I'm* sayin'."

DID YOU NOTICE

- After his Robin Hood spree, Jesse is found in a playground, a reminder that his guilt comes from the consequences that his actions have had on children.
- As Walt leaves Hank's garage in the opening act, he turns to look back and the two men face off with their feet apart, arms loose by their side. Walt even twiddles his fingers as if loosening his hand. It's composed like a classic Western showdown scene between two gunfighters, and is undoubtedly deliberate as Vince Gilligan has repeatedly called *Breaking Bad* "a modern-day Western."
- When Hank hugs Skyler in the restaurant, she is stiff and unresponsive in his arms, already maintaining her distance. This display of affection echoes the similarly awkward and uncomfortable embrace between Hank and Skyler in "Seven Thirty-Seven."

- Whether it's dissolving bodies or storing cash, plastic 55-gallon barrels can do it all.
- Walt's collapse on the bathroom floor recalls season 1's "The Cat's in the Bag" where he also spent the night passed out on the bathroom floor.
- Walt asks Skyler if the news of his cancer makes her happy, referring back to her confrontation with him in "Fifty-One."
- Vision, or the lack thereof, continues to be important in this episode, with Lydia arriving at Declan's cook site blindfolded, and leaving with her eyes tightly shut against the results of her actions. She is alternately unwillingly and then willingly blinded. Not seeing things makes them less real, and unable to be recalled or found later. This goes for Walt too, who is almost constitutionally incapable of seeing the truth about himself and his actions.
- The usually loquacious Jesse doesn't have a single spoken line in the entire episode, underlining his precarious emotional state.

SHOOTING UP

- The cold open features another top-down, God's-eye-view of Jesse as he lies on the old merry-go-round in the playground. The scene is beautifully lit as well, with a strong light source to one side casting sharp shadows that slide across Jesse as he slowly rotates.
- The camera work for Walt and Hank's showdown outside the garage is also classically Western. The alternating angles are low, looking up from Hank's leg to Walt and vice versa, or are close-ups of the men's faces. The editing cuts from one view to another, one man to another, in a manner instantly recognizable from any number of middle-of-the-dusty-street Western shoot-outs.
- There are two classic *Breaking Bad* POV shots as Walt buries his cash. The first is a dizzying barrel's-eye-view as Walt rolls it into the pit, and the second an up-and-through POV from the GPS just before Walt smashes it.
- The composition of Lydia's walk through the bodies of Declan and his men is nicely done, with the red soles of her Louboutins matching the fresh blood of the slain men.

TITLE Like most titles in *Breaking Bad*, "Buried" has multiple meanings and references. Walt buries his money, of course, and Declan's meth lab is a buried school bus. In another sense, Declan and his men are buried, and the relationships between the Whites and the Schraders is also dead and buried by the episode's end.

INTERESTING FACTS

- This episode was dedicated to "Our Friend, Thomas Schnauz, Sr." the father of the episode's writer, Thomas Schnauz (Jr.).
- Marie compares Hank to Lone Wolf McQuade, the hero of an eponymous film starring Chuck Norris (presumably no relation to Dean Norris) as Texas Ranger Jim "J.J." McQuade. The movie includes just about every rogue cop-film trope, including a heroic "lone wolf" who doesn't work well with others and has a taste for danger, a ruthless drug kingpin, a retired buddy, a higher-ranking officer who tries to rein in the hero, and a new partner the hero does not want. Chuck Norris has said this movie was a direct inspiration for *Walker, Texas Ranger*.
- The coordinates supposedly associated with Walt's buried money, Latitude 34.59.21 Longitude -106.36.52, are actually the coordinates for Albuquerque Studios, where *Breaking Bad* was filmed.

SPECIAL INGREDIENTS

CHRISTIAN LOUBOUTIN

Vince Gilligan once remarked that "Lydia really is Darth Vader in Louboutins," and she shows it in "Buried." When Lydia walks gingerly through the blood-stained sands, viewers see the scarlet soles of her high-heeled dress shoes — footwear not at all suited for a vicious slaughter, yet somehow perfectly suited to Lydia. The distinctive red soles and towering heels are indicative of French designer Christian Louboutin, and show Lydia's apparent wealth and sense of fashion as these shoes are considered very chic. Louboutin shoes begin at about $500 and can easily reach $5,000 for a crystal-encrusted pair, so it says something about Lydia that she thinks nothing of wearing such impractical shoes to a clandestine meeting in the dusty desert with her meth supplier.

While Louboutin does make some low-heeled shoes, it's the four-inch-plus stilettoes that most people associate with the brand. Louboutin added the distinctive red sole to his shoes in his third year as an independent designer — the color is actually registered as Pantone 18-1663 TPX — and this element has often been copied by others. In fact, Yves Saint Laurent was involved in a lengthy lawsuit with Louboutin over the color of the sole and in September 2012, YSL won the limited right to keep red soles on their shoes, provided that the rest of the shoe was also red. The outer portion of Lydia's shoes was not red and she's not a woman to buy knockoffs, so it seems certain that Lydia's blood-red soles indicated authentic Louboutin. Very nice shoes, and apparently to Lydia, having the funds to buy them is something well worth killing over.

Confessions

Original air date: August 25, 2013
Written by: Gennifer Hutchison **Directed by:** Michael Slovis

"Why don't you kill yourself, Walt?" — Marie Schrader

Walt and Skyler take drastic measures to try to stop Hank's investigation. Meanwhile, Jesse comes to a fateful realization.

"Confessions" is aptly titled, as the revelations come thick and fast for the main characters, though they do not always recognize the significance of what they discover. Nor are the confessions always true in whole or in part. Certainly this is the case with the first two confessions given by Todd. His description of the massacre of Declan and his men as a "change in management" is something of a massive understatement, so much so that Walt is unlikely to pay much attention to the message when he gets it. Shortly thereafter, Todd gives his uncle Jack and Kenny (Kevin Rankin) an edited version of the great train robbery in "Dead Freight," but omits any mention of the murder of Drew Sharp.

The third confession of the episode is more intimate as, in a futile attempt to make Jesse talk, Hank reveals his anger at being manipulated and used by Walt. This is more than just an interrogation tactic. Hank is too intense, too honest in his hurt and anger. Dean Norris brings his usual power and subtlety to the scene, as does Aaron Paul, who speaks little — yet when Hank suggests that Jesse might like to talk about Walt, Jesse whispers, "Not to you." Jesse's eyes reveal a storm of emotion belied by his soft tone, because for the

first time, he really does want to talk. Indeed, Jesse is Walt's biggest problem, and a loose end that he has never quite been able to fully control, and Jesse's soft sentence marks the episode's fourth confession.

Confession number five is one of the more despicable non-murderous things Walt has done, as he tells Junior about his cancer's return in order to use Junior's deep love in order to control him. Of course Junior won't leave for Hank and Marie's once he finds out that his dad has cancer again. The way Walt self-servingly manipulates what is best in his son betrays everything a father should be and do, and Walt's smug expression as he hugs his son, his *pride* in having so effectively overpowered him, is truly abominable. When compared with Hank's confession to Marie that he changed his mind about telling the DEA about Walt, an admission he makes out of the solid core of honesty and respect upon which their marriage is based, the self-seeking nature of Walt's machinations are further underlined.

The seventh confession is both honest and inadvertent. At the remarkably uncomfortable dinner meeting with Hank and Marie, Skyler lets slip that whatever they think Walt has done, it is in the past, a tacit admission of Walt's guilt and her own abetting of his crimes. It is the eighth confession that marks the breaking point for the Whites and Schraders, however. With his falsified DVD recording, Walt tells just enough truth to make his false witness against Hank resonate, and, if further proof was necessary, demonstrates the true disregard Walt actually has for family, no matter what he might say. Betsy Brandt and Dean Norris's performances in this scene are profound. As the DVD plays, Marie and Hank are silent, and so the actors must communicate to the audience and each other wordlessly, and both actors masterfully portray a range of emotions, both singly and in complex combination, without a word. This is much, much harder than Brandt and Norris make it look. Afterwards, Walt's lies are again emphasized by a confession driven by love, as Marie reveals that she accepted money from Walt to pay for Hank's medical care. Returning again to *Breaking Bad*'s original theme of the downfalls of the American health insurance system, Marie tells him that if she hadn't paid for the extra care, Hank likely wouldn't have been able to walk again, because his government-issued insurance wouldn't have provided the care he needed. Hank is devastated by the news, but at the same time, it is so obvious that Marie did what she did in complete innocence and out of true love, that neither Hank nor the viewer can be too angry with her.

Ultimately, however, the most devastating confession in the long run is Saul's. Delivered under threat of death, he admits to having Huell steal the ricin cigarette at Walt's orders. Confirming Jesse's deduction that, one way or another, Walt was behind Brock's poisoning, this confession creates the single enemy that Walt cannot afford to have. With Jesse out for fiery retribution, Walt's world may well be about to come crashing down around him once and for all.

LAB NOTES

HIGHLIGHT

SAUL: "Christ. Some people are immune to good advice."

DID YOU NOTICE

* The scene in the cold open where Jack, Kenny, and Todd's conversation in the diner is interrupted by the waitress foreshadows the much more obvious and uncomfortable scene with the cheery waiter and Walt, Skyler, Marie, and Hank later in the episode.

- As they carefully groom themselves in the diner's bathroom, Kenny mentions to Jack how he hates to see kids being forced to wear bike helmets. Drew Sharp was wearing a helmet as he tooled about on his dirt bike, but that didn't help him when he met Todd.
- As he waits with Jesse in the desert, Saul remarks, "It's always the desert," an open acknowledgment of the space as both private and dangerous.
- Walt's attempt to get Hank and Marie to see the logic of just leaving things alone again recalls the season 3 episode "Fly," where he revealed his belief that the right combination of words should be able to make anyone see things his way.

SHOOTING UP

- The cold open begins with an extreme close-up of Todd lighting his cigarette, evoking earlier shots of Jesse doing the same thing, and the smoke of the show's credits as well.
- Jesse's experience in the interrogation room is distorted, the police officers shown in fast motion and time lapse, their voices made unintelligible by a constant droning. Everything is slightly out of focus as well, altogether revealing Jesse's headspace as he tunes everything out.
- The interrogation room is seen through the vent-grille POV.
- As Walt begins recording his "confession," the camera is focused on the camcorder screen, where the image of Walt is sharp and clear, while in the background, Walt himself is blurred and indistinct, a nice visual commentary on reality and fiction, and how we so often can confuse the two.
- As Walt asks Skyler to take over at the register so he can go to chemo, Sky is sitting in her office with the light off, gazing into space. As Walt recalls her to the present and tells her that the false confession was necessary and worked, Skyler is clearly lit by "natural" light coming in through the window, while Walt is only a silhouette, revealed as a creature of darkness and deception.

TITLE There are 10 different confessions in this episode — some true, some false, and some a bit of both. This is an episode where there's really no need to dig for a deeper meaning in the title than that.

INTERESTING FACTS

- In connection with Todd and Jesse's antics on and under a moving train in "Dead Freight," Jack references Burt Reynolds's *Hooper* — a 1978 action-comedy about an aging stuntman and the increasingly dangerous stunts Reynolds's character tries to pull off to stay ahead of his younger competition.

- The restaurant in this scene, Garduño's, has since become a popular destination for Albuquerque's *Breaking Bad* fans and a must-eat stop for *Breaking Bad* tourists. The wait for the table where the Whites and Schraders have their tense discussion can last up to several hours, though, so make your reservations early. Also, their tableside guacamole really is amazing.

SPECIAL INGREDIENTS

BEAR CANYON ARROYO SPILLWAY DAM

When Jesse is waiting for Saul's mysterious Vacuum Cleaner Guy, viewers were baffled by the structure behind him. Why was Jesse standing in front of a collection of huge, stylized tombstones? Well, he wasn't — although we respect the symbolism of those blank slabs rising up to both block Jesse's further retreat away from his problems and to represent all the lives ruined by Walt's decisions. The scene was filmed at the Bear Canyon Arroyo Spillway Dam in Albuquerque. This spillway was built for an event that hopefully never happens: the sudden flooding of the Bear Canyon Arroyo River. A flood of such proportions is unlikely to happen (such events are often termed "hundred-year floods"), but when such floods do occur, the effects can be devastating.

Spillways provide a controlled release of water from a dam to a downstream area, which is most commonly the original river that was dammed. By releasing the water, the dam is protected from being damaged by the weight and speed of the rising floodwaters. The distinctive design of the Bear Canyon Arroyo Spillway is an example of a stepped chute baffled spillway. The baffles (the "tombstones" behind Jesse) serve to break up the energy of the flowing water, which makes it easier to control. As water passes through the chute and around the baffles, the potential energy of the water is converted to forceful kinetic energy. If this energy is not dissipated, tremendous erosion damage can occur. We're talking about a *lot* of energy here — the engineers who do the math estimate that the spillways at a hydroelectric plant, working at full capacity, could easily produce 10 times the megawattage of the actual power plant served by the spillways.

5.12 | Rabid Dog

Original air date: September 01, 2013
Written and directed by: Sam Catlin

"We've come this far. For *us*. What's one more?"
— Skyler White

Walt moves quickly to minimize the aftereffects of Jesse's gasoline-attack on his house. Meanwhile, Hank gets his biggest chance to crack the case against Walt.

"Rabid Dog" begins with a nice bit of misdirection. The cold open apparently picks up right where "Confessions" left off, with Walt arriving back at his house while Jesse is still inside throwing gasoline all over the living room. Except that Jesse's not there. After the credits, Walt is moving at top speed to eliminate the evidence of Jesse's "visit." This is vital, because, as Skyler made clear during their meeting with Hank and Marie in "Confessions," her cooperation with Walt hinges on all of his criminal activities being behind him. If Walt's sins begin to crop up again, particularly in the form of threats to their home and children, Skyler's attitude is likely to change.

This season, Walt has — mostly — had great success with his lies and manipulations, but with the story he spins to Junior and Skyler he returns to the days of seasons 2 and 3, when he created overelaborate, hyper-detailed lies to cover his cooking and odd absences. Predictably, Skyler and Junior aren't buying what he's selling, but Junior unwittingly provides Walt with a better lie, one that satisfies, but worries, Junior. Skyler, on the other hand, remains to be convinced. Meanwhile, Jesse seems to have disappeared, and Saul's "A-Team" of Huell and Kuby has not even been able to track him down.

"Rabid Dog" showcases three very interesting changes in character; Walt's reactions to Saul's suggestion that he have Jesse killed marks the first. Walt genuinely wants to avoid killing — or even hurting — Jesse, and this is a fundamental shift for a guy who only a few episodes earlier thought nothing of killing Mike, or of arranging an almost operatic mass murder of the imprisoned remnants of Gus and Mike's men. Walt is *out*, and to give him credit, appears to be totally serious about staying that way. The same cannot be said for Skyler, however. In the second, truly tragic, shift of character in the episode, Skyler's determination to protect her family and secure the ill-gotten gains from Walt's cooking days has made murder not merely a possibility for her, but the best option. At this point, Skyler has lost much of her old life and, perhaps most important, her relationship with Marie. She has knowingly aided and abetted in the manufacture of illegal drugs, the murder of several people, and the covering up of all Walt's crimes. The final line for Skyler was helping Walt make the DVD of his false confession; an act that destroyed the strongest family tie she has ever possessed. This was a move into the darkness by which Skyler betrayed everything she has ever thought was true and good about herself. From that psychologically damaged position, murder has truly become something to be shrugged off as "shit happens."

Ironically, Jesse and Hank wind up being the ones who push Walt back into the realm where deadly violence is a viable solution. In a lovely twist, the third act of the episode returns to Jesse rampaging through the White house, and reveals that the first person to arrive at the house was *Hank*, not Walt. Aaron Paul brings the pain in this scene, raging, weeping, so utterly betrayed that his primal scream of "He can't keep getting away with it!" is one of the most heartbreaking moments in the entire series. His insomnia and meth-fueled emotional state gives Hank the perfect opening to forge an alliance to take Walt down, and Jesse has finally been hurt enough by Walt to be willing to betray him. With Jesse in hand, Hank has also finally confided in Gomez, who is present for Jesse's own recorded confession, which is far more detailed and entirely more honest than Walt's.

With no hard evidence, however, Hank has to send Jesse to meet with Walt while wearing a wire, and it is here that arguably the most shocking change in character takes place. Jesse is understandably concerned that Walt wants to meet with him in order to kill him. After Jesse has stormed out, and Gomez raises the very real possibility that he's right about the danger, Hank shrugs it off. To him, even if Jesse is killed, all is well — so long as they get the killing on tape. ASAC Merkert once referred to Hank as a great white shark, and that relentless ruthlessness is now on full display. Walt is swimming in dangerous waters, and he doesn't even know it.

LAB NOTES

HIGHLIGHT

> WALT: "Jesus. Jesse did that?"
> SAUL: "Yeah, but you gotta understand: deep down, he loves me."

DID YOU NOTICE

- When he arrives in his neighborhood, Walt parks in front of a fire hydrant, a sign of both Walt's belief that the law doesn't apply to him, and his fundamental carelessness.
- At the very end of the cold open, a group of neighborhood skate-boarders flashes by. Walt's house will be theirs soon enough.
- When Walt returns to his hotel room, Skyler is emptying her third mini-bottle of vodka.
- Marie and Hank's relationship is such that Marie can get the truth from him with a look and tone of voice. Very different from the games Walt and Skyler play.
- Hank and Marie still have family pictures of Walt and Skyler in their guest room, both looking very happy, seemingly a long time ago, but in reality less than two years in the past.
- Jesse refers to Walt as "the Devil," echoing Marie's first audible line in the cold open to "Blood Money."

SHOOTING UP

- As Walt searches for Jesse in the cold open, the hallway leading back to the master-bedroom door is shot to make the hallway seem especially long and deep. This is the fourth time this composition is used in a row as similar shots appear in "Blood Money," "Buried," and "Confessions."

- As Walt approaches and hesitates before the master-bedroom door, the camera angle is very low, distorting the appearance of the door-knob and making it appear much larger than it actually is.
- The first act of the episode opens with an inside POV shot of a blue wet/dry vacuum cleaner hose. This is another nice misdirection, as the blue tint recalls various meth-making POVs throughout the series.
- As Jesse begins his confession, the same focal composition is used as with Walt's false confession in "Confessions": Jesse's image in the camcorder screen is sharp and clear, while the view of him on the couch in the background is blurred.

TITLE "Rabid Dog" references Saul's comparison of Jesse to Old Yeller. In the 1957 film *Old Yeller*, preteen Travis Coates takes in a yellow-colored, mongrel dog only after initially being repelled by the creature and trying to drive it away. The mutt saves Travis and his family several times, and Travis soon falls in love with the critter, naming him Old Yeller. At the end of the film, however, Old Yeller contracts rabies while defending the family from an infected wolf, and Travis ends up having to put his friend down in order to prevent him from becoming sick and attacking the family. It's a heartbreaking moment. With the character shifts in both Skyler and Hank, either one of them could also be considered as having gone "rabid," and they are now a danger to the people around them.

INTERESTING FACTS
- Kuby's line about Badger going on about *Babylon 5* has a deeper connection to *Breaking Bad* than just fleshing out Badger and Skinny Pete's science fiction TV cred. Way back in 1997, a young Bryan Cranston had a one-time speaking role in the *Babylon 5* fourth season episode "The Long Night." He played Ericsson, the commander of a starship squadron who goes on a death ride as part of a strategy to provide false information to the series' big bad, the Shadows.
- During "Rabid Dog," Jesse and Hank make several references to "DC" and "MDC." Both are referring to Albuquerque's Metropolitan Detention Center, or county jail. The MDC is the 39th largest jail in the U.S. and is classified as a "mega-jail," processing an average of 40,000 inmates every year.

SPECIAL INGREDIENTS

BABYLON 5

When Kuby (played by Bill Burr whose credits include *Date Night* and *New Girl*) reports that he bugged Badger's house and is pretty sure that Jesse isn't hiding out there because, "For three hours straight, all he talked about was something called *Babylon 5*," fans in the know get a giggle in the midst of a grim episode. *Babylon 5* was a space opera created by J. Michael Straczynski that ran for five years (1994–1998, with a pilot movie airing in 1993). *Babylon 5* is remarkable for several reasons, so it's no surprise that Badger could talk about the show for hours on end.

Like Gilligan with *Breaking Bad*, Straczynski conceived *Babylon 5* as a "novel for television," with a discrete story to tell in an intentionally limited number of seasons. Straczynski, however, had the major action and character arcs plotted out before the show went into initial production. In fact, *Babylon 5* is often cited as the origin of the "long arc" on television. Also, there was no "writer's room" for *Babylon 5* — Straczynski wrote 92 of the 110 episodes. (For comparison's sake, Joss Whedon is credited with writing 23 episodes of the 144-episode *Buffy the Vampire Slayer*; Ron Moore wrote 13 episodes of the 73 episodes of *Battlestar Galatica*; Vince Gilligan wrote 13 of the 62 episodes of *Breaking Bad*). *Babylon 5* also ushered in the CGI-era of television and the show received multiple awards for its use of visual effects, including two consecutive Hugo Awards. While advances in technology make some of the effects seem less-than-stellar today, the strong character arcs in *Babylon 5* and consistency in the overall story make these flaws more charming than jarring.

The final aspect of *Babylon 5* that should be mentioned here is Straczynski's use of the internet to promote the show and connect with fans. While today social media outreach is considered an integral part of the marketing campaign for any show (and certainly is a part of *Breaking Bad*), in the early '90s, the World Wide Web didn't exist as it does today — Straczynski was connecting with fans through online communities on Usenet newsgroups, as well as through the GEnie and CompuServe systems. His interaction with the fans no doubt contributed to the passionate fan base that continues to discuss, dissect, and comment on the show. <*>

SAXITOXIN

Marie reveals to Dave-the-therapist that she's been looking up "untraceable poisons," including one called "saxitoxin." When Marie gets in these dark moods, it's probably best to avoid her until she's feeling a little more chipper, as saxitoxin is a particularly nasty poison. Derived primarily from shellfish, such as clams, scallops, and oysters, saxitoxin has also been traced to fish and reef crabs.

Once ingested, saxitoxin acts quickly, resulting in symptoms within 30 minutes. Symptoms include a sensation of floating, vertigo, numbness of the mouth and extremities, along with paralysis. If the victim survives the first 12 hours, the prognosis is good, although muscle weakness may persist for weeks. Death results in about 25 percent of the cases (keep in mind this statistic refers to accidental ingestion while Marie is contemplating the deliberate use of the poison) and is usually the result of respiratory failure. Your lungs essentially paralyze due to "flaccid paralysis." This is the opposite of "spastic paralysis," in which the muscles become stiff and rigid, which is what most of us think of as paralysis. With flaccid paralysis, your muscles become so limp and relaxed that they lose the ability to contract. If this condition affects your respiratory muscles, suffocation can result — and all the while, you're fully conscious and aware of what's happening around you.

5.13 T o'hajiilee

Original air date: September 8, 2013
Written by: George Mastras **Directed by:** Michelle MacLaren

"Walter White, you have the right to remain silent."
— Hank Schrader

Jesse helps Hank and Gomez close in on Walt. Meanwhile, Lydia has concerns about the salability of Todd's product.

Todd has a crush on Lydia, and she knows it. One of the constant themes of *Breaking Bad* is people manipulating others for their own gain, and Lydia is not afraid to use Todd's feelings for her as leverage to get him to improve the quality of his cook. There's something creepy in Todd's timid advances, though. He's part shy schoolboy, trying awkwardly to get close to the girl of his dreams, and part sexual predator, invading her personal space in a really disturbing way. This is Todd all over, however: sweet, clean-cut good looks, and an almost sociopathic disregard for human life, all in one twisted package. Walt's phone call at the end of the scene places the cold open as occurring just slightly before the end of "Rabid Dog," and makes explicit his decision to have Jesse killed.

"To'hajiilee" then becomes something of a merry-go-round of attempted manipulations as Hank and Gomez con Huell into telling them about burying Walt's money; Jack gets Walt to cook for Todd; Walt convinces Andrea to call Jesse; and finally Jesse, Hank, and Gomez trick Walt into revealing where he buried his money. Even Skyler is keeping Junior at the car wash on the slimmest of pretexts. Almost everyone is playing someone in this episode, but none of the maneuvering works out quite like anyone had planned. Ironically, Saul, the lawyer who is so incredibly adept in finessing the legal system, is the one straight-talking character in the episode. His remark that his battered face is an occupational hazard is completely true, and he clearly warns Walt that things are looking grim and to not underestimate Jesse. Like the Greek Cassandra, however, no one believes Saul, and so Walt is quickly, easily, and deliciously suckered by Jesse's text and phone call. For all of his brains, it never even occurs to Walt that he might be getting scammed, and so he leads Hank into the desert. The call also ultimately reveals the real Walt behind all of his prevarication and rationalization as he rages at Jesse: *"Don't you touch my money!"* In the final analysis this is what Walt really cares about. Whatever his reasons may have been in the beginning, the money is not now a route to treating his cancer or insuring his family's security. Now the money *itself* has become the goal, the be-all and end-all of Walt's work, the tangible proof of what he has done.

It turns out that Walt buried his money in the very first place he and Jesse cooked, only a little over a year earlier, and despite all that has happened since, the desert shows no sign of any of it. The desert is again a place untouched by memory and unmarked by man, the perfect place for this particular endgame. Hank has played fast and loose with procedure in his hunt for Walt, but it has paid off big-time, and he finally slaps the cuffs on Heisenberg, and reads him his rights. It is a moment of supreme victory of good over evil, of justice over criminality . . . and it doesn't last. Gilligan & Co. telegraph the punch somewhat with the loving phone call between Hank and Marie, a call that echoes another exchange of "I love yous" in the episode "One Minute," just before the Salamanca cousins showed up. Then too, Hank had been true to himself and things had worked out such that he was happy, and okay with the world. In *Breaking Bad* such peace tends to be shattered violently. Jack and the neo-Nazis arrive loaded for bear, and in the midst of a fusillade of automatic gunfire, things fade to black.

LAB NOTES

HIGHLIGHT

SAUL: "Don't drink and drive, but if you do — call me!"

DID YOU NOTICE

- Lydia and Skyler are both concerned with their respective brands.
- Todd's ringtone for Walt is Thomas Dolby's "She Blinded Me with Science."
- Walt doesn't like to shake Jack's hand, and drops it as soon as he is able to.
- Brock gets very quiet around Walt, and does his best not to interact with him. This was also true when he first met Walt in "Hazard Pay." Brock instinctively knows that something is off about Walt. In comparison, he looks up and lights up when he hears Andrea say Jesse's name.
- As Walt and Saul talk at the car wash, one of Saul's billboards can be seen in the background between them.
- In his taunting phone call, Jesse specifically and scornfully calls Walt by his first name, rather than his usual "Mr. White."
- Back in season 4's "Bullet Points," Hank tells Walt that he wanted to be the one to "slap the cuffs on" Heisenberg and here, he gets his wish.
- Hank notes that he'll call the Tribal Police on his way out, indicating that they are on Native land, and that neither he nor Gomez have told anyone where they are.

SHOOTING UP

- The cold open begins with a familiar up-and-through POV of meth pouring into the pan, only instead of the translucent blue the viewer has become used to, the liquid crystal is an almost opaque, dirty, brownish-gray color.
- There is another ground-level looking-up POV of a slice of blue sky between two overpasses, with Hank looming large as he waits for Gomez to join Jesse and him.
- As Walt is discussing the hit on Jesse with Jack and the neo-Nazis, a low train-whistle is heard in the background, recalling "Dead Freight" and the death of Drew Sharp, the point at which Walt's empire reached its peak and began its fall.
- There is an upwards POV shot from inside the trash can as Marie looks down upon the calf's brains Hank has thrown away after faking the photo of Jesse's death.

TITLE "To'hajiilee" is the name of a Navajo Nation Reservation. Formerly known as the Canoncito Indian Reservation, To'hajiilee is split up into sections of land in Bernalillo, Cibola, and Sandoval counties in New Mexico, west of Albuquerque. The title thus refers to the area where Walt buried his money and where the episode ends, fitting in with Hank needing to call the Tribal Police. To'hajiilee translates as "Bringing Up Water From a Natural Well," and may be a deliberate reference to Walt finally dropping all of his pretenses in his phone conversation with Jesse as he races out into the desert. All of Walt's rage, arrogance, and greed have always been there, but in "To'hajiilee" they come rushing to the surface.

MUSIC The song playing as Todd brings Lydia her tea is "Oh Sherrie" by Steve Perry.

INTERESTING FACTS Kenny suggests that the meth could be dyed "Heisenberg blue," much the same way farm-raised salmon are colored to satisfy market demand. It's true. The flesh of wild salmon has a distinctive pinkish color due to the fishes' diet. In the wild, salmon primarily eat krill and plankton, which contain astaxanthin, a natural antioxidant in the same family as the beta-carotene found in carrots. Salmon and trout retain carotenes in their flesh, which explains why salmon steaks are, well, salmon-colored while catfish are not. Consumers expect salmon to be pink, so farm-raised salmon are fed a diet that includes color additives in the feed.

SPECIAL INGREDIENTS

THE *MIRANDA* CASE

"You have the right to remain silent . . ." If you've ever watched a single cop show, you can probably recite the so-called *Miranda* warning. Most people, however, are unfamiliar with the facts of this important case, which began in the American Southwest, one state over from where Hank reads his brother-in-law his *Miranda* rights. In 1963, Ernesto Miranda was arrested in Phoenix, Arizona, in connection with a kidnapping and sexual assault. He was not told of his right to counsel before being interrogated and two hours into his questioning, police had a written, signed confession. The confession included a typed disclaimer stating that Miranda knew his rights and had knowingly waived them. He did have counsel at his trial and his attorney objected to the use of the signed confession, but the objection was overruled. Miranda was convicted of kidnapping and rape, and received a 20-year sentence.

The question on appeal was, should the confession, which was obtained without warnings against self-incrimination (a right set out in the Fifth Amendment of the U.S. Constitution) and without legal counsel present (a right guaranteed by the Sixth Amendment), be admissible in court? Miranda's attorneys took the position that the police violated his constitutionally guaranteed rights and the confession was obtained illegally; therefore, it should be thrown out and Miranda should get a new trial. The State of Arizona took the position that Miranda (who had a lengthy criminal history) was no stranger to police procedures and that he signed the confession willingly, therefore the prosecution was proper and the conviction should be upheld.

The case made it all the way to the United States Supreme Court, who voted five to four to overturn Miranda's conviction. The court ruled that it is the state's responsibility to ensure that the guarantees embodied in the Constitution are upheld, and Chief Justice Earl Warren made it clear that the police have an unwaivable responsibility to warn a suspect "prior to any questioning that he has the right to remain silent, that anything he says can be used against him in a court of law, that he has the right to the presence of an attorney, and that if he cannot afford an attorney one will be appointed for him prior to any questioning if he so desires." Following the decision, Miranda was tried again in 1967 by the State of Arizona and found guilty of the crime. He was paroled in 1972 and returned to his old neighborhood, where he made a little money autographing police officers' *Miranda* cards that carried the text of the required warning.

5.14

Ozymandias

Original air date: September 15, 2013
Written by: Moira Walley-Beckett **Directed by:** Rian Johnson

"What is *wrong* with you? We're a family!" — Walter White

Walt loses control of his supposed allies, and Jesse finds himself in a dangerous new situation. Meanwhile, Marie reaches out to Skyler, and things take a disastrous turn.

"Ozymandias" is, without a doubt, one of the most intense episodes in the entirety of *Breaking Bad*. The cold open begins with a close-up of a flask of water coming to a fast boil, close to a perfect visual metaphor for what is to come. Yet things don't boil over immediately, and while "To'hajiilee" ended with the shattering sound of automatic weapons firing, "Ozymandias" opens quietly, taking the viewer all the way back to "Pilot/Breaking Bad," when Walt had hair and a mustache, and Jesse was still just a punk kid. The heartbreak lies in the fact that, in terms of time passing within the story, this scene took place less than two years ago. Walt turned 50 in the pilot, 51 in season 5's "Fifty-one," and 52 in the future seen in the cold open to "Live Free or Die." So everything that's happened — all of it — takes place in the space of two years of narrative time, total. Two years in which Walt has gone from wishy-washy high school chemistry teacher to drug kingpin and multiple murderer. Two years in which Jesse has transformed from a shallow kid trying to act cool to a desperately wounded young man with more experience of heartbreak and loss than anyone should have to endure. Almost two years from the phone call between Walt and Skyler in the cold open

(IZUMI HASEGAWA/PR PHOTOS)

of this episode to the one in the last act. Every human life changes over time, but for the characters in *Breaking Bad* the past two years have brought radical and revolutionary change.

Some don't survive. Hank has finally triumphed over Walt, and put the cuffs on Heisenberg, but the moment of his greatest triumph is also the moment of his doom, for he and Gomez are outnumbered, and incredibly outgunned. Walt, who genuinely doesn't want Hank to die, is *still* trying to find the right sequence of words, still trying to make people see "reason" as he sees it, but now, at long last, he is forced to face the fact that he is not in control — of anything. Walt begs and pleads for Hank's life, but both Hank and Jack know what has to happen, and neither flinches from it. *Breaking Bad*'s good guy is dead, buried in an unmarked grave in a desert that neither cares nor remembers what passes through it.

For Walt, things have well and truly spun out of control, but he refuses to see that he is the catalyst for all of this. As usual, Walt is convinced that everything must be someone else's fault — and in this case Jesse's. Nor is it enough for Walt to deliver him up to the neo-Nazis for torture and (so he thinks) death, but he has to crush Jesse under his heel by telling him the truth about Jane. Only in his version, he isn't the tormented, weeping Walter of "Phoenix" and "Fly," but a cold and ruthless killer. Walt's denial of responsibility carries through to Skyler and Junior as well. To Walt, it is not his choices that have caused his son to distrust him, and have finally driven Skyler to stand up to him and demand that he leave them alone, but their own sheer unreasonableness in failing to see that Walt knows best.

His final confrontation with Skyler is violent and bloody, and when he has won, holding Skyler down with one hand while brandishing the knife with the other, it is Flynn (who will never again be "Junior") who leaps on top of him and rips him away. Finally, as he rages against his wife and son for acting the way they have, Walt realizes that the Whites have become a family in name only, and that the responsibility for destroying that bond is his alone. The phone conversation that opens the episode is prosaic, but full of love, respect, and familial devotion — a committed husband and wife quietly rejoicing over a new baby and their life. The one that ends the episode is quite different, and while Walt is indeed trying to shift the entirety of the blame to his own shoulders and away from Skyler, there is also a great deal of truth in his anger, particularly when it comes to recounting how Skyler never believed in him. This is the true tragic flaw of Walter White. Skyler always believed in him, as did Flynn, and Hank, and Marie. Walt had a truly good family who loved him deeply, and supported him in every way that mattered. It was always *Walt* who felt that he wasn't good enough, that he didn't provide well enough, wasn't respected enough. It was not what those around him thought of him that sent Walt down this road, but his own twisted, self-centered self-image. Walter White had an incredible family, and Walter White smashed it to bits.

LAB NOTES

HIGHLIGHT
JACK: "Jesus, what's with all the greed around here? It's unattractive."

DID YOU NOTICE
- One of Walt's first lines in the episode is to tell Jesse that "The reaction has begun," a reference not only to the cook itself, but also to the endless chain reaction that follows their very first cook.
- During the call in the cold open, the phone is lying next to the knife block, just as it is later when Skyler grabs a knife to use against Walt, her choice of instrument in each case reinforcing the framing of the episode and the degree to which things have changed.
- The cold open call is also very similar to the final call between Hank and Marie in "To'hajiilee," complete with exchanged "I love yous."
- When Walt falls to the ground after Hank is killed, his expression,

position, and the camera angle mirror that of Gus in "Hermanos" when Max was killed.

- Jack makes Walt shake his hand again, and Walt still can barely stand it. But he does it.
- When Walt's rolling the barrel, he rolls it past a pair of pants lying on the ground, a nod to the fact that Walt lost his pants when he was out in the same spot in the RV in "Pilot/Breaking Bad."
- Marie does not wear purple in this episode. Instead, she is already in black, the color of mourning.

SHOOTING UP

- The cold open uses a fixed camera and some fancy editing to fade objects and people in and out. The unchanging landscape underlines the uncaring and unnoticing nature of the desert. Much has happened here in the past, and more will happen in the future, but in terms of the land, nothing has lasting consequences and nothing leaves marks for long.
- When Walt, Jesse, and the RV fade away, the only sound is the ambient noises of the desert: wind through the scrub, and the occasional call of a bird, somehow more desolate than even total silence would be. This ambient noise returns in the "silence" after the shootout, and again when Walt zones out after Hank is killed.
- Time lapse is used for the hours spent digging up the money barrels, as well as to emphasize just how long Walt spends lying on his side in the desert.
- As Jesse is dragged out from under the car, he looks up, and the camera pans away to show two carrion birds circling high over the desert. This pair of buzzards — just waiting for the killing to be done so their work can begin — is a very traditional image in the Western genre.
- Walt hands the elderly Navajo man a bundle of cash through a barbed-wire fence and beside a sun-bleached cow's skull. The composition not only reinforces the pain and death associated with Walt's money, but also recalls Jane's death by reminding us of her love of Georgia O'Keeffe, who was famous for a series of paintings featuring such skulls.
- There is yet another long shot of the hallway in the White house as Walt rushes from room to room, packing.

TITLE "Ozymandias" is the title of a sonnet published in 1818 by Percy Bysshe Shelley:

I met a traveller from an antique land
Who said: "Two vast and trunkless legs of stone
Stand in the desert. Near them, on the sand,
Half sunk, a shattered visage lies, whose frown,
And wrinkled lip, and sneer of cold command,
Tell that its sculptor well those passions read
Which yet survive, stamped on these lifeless things,
The hand that mocked them and the heart that fed.
And on the pedestal these words appear —
'My name is Ozymandias, king of kings:
Look on my works, ye Mighty, and despair!'
Nothing beside remains. Round the decay
Of that colossal wreck, boundless and bare
The lone and level sands stretch far away."

Shelley is thought to have been writing about the ruins of a gigantic statue of the Pharaoh Ramses II, but in terms of *Breaking Bad*, "Ozymandias" speaks directly to the dreams and delusions of Walter White, who once upon a time was in "the empire business." The poem, read by Bryan Cranston over images of the empty New Mexico desert, also featured as a promo ad for the second half of season 5 in 2013.

MUSIC The song playing as Walt laboriously rolls his barrel of money through the desert is "Take My True Love by the Hand" by the Limeliters.

INTERESTING FACTS In the scene with Walt in the restroom as he changes her, Holly (played in this episode by Elanor Anne Wenrich) begins saying "mommy" again and again. This was totally unscripted, and Bryan Cranston just went with it and improvised around Elanor, creating one of the episode's many powerful scenes.

SPECIAL INGREDIENTS

AMBER ALERTS

After Walt leaves the house with Holly, viewers see the place swarming with police officers. One is holding a large snapshot of the missing toddler and talking on the phone to set up an "AMBER Alert." Originating in the United States in 1996, this is a child abduction alert system, and similar systems are used in many other countries. AMBER Alerts are distributed widely, using multiple media methods, including television stations, cable TV, internet radio, commercial radio, satellite radio, email, text messages, and electronic billboards such as traffic condition signs. The notion is that when a child abduction occurs, the first few hours are absolutely crucial, so messages are sent thick and fast to blanket the area and put the public on notice regarding the appearance of the child, the abductor, and/or the vehicle.

The term "AMBER Alert" is a "backronym" (meaning a phrase constructed so an acronym fits an existing word) for "America's Missing: Broadcast Emergency Response." The backronym arose out of a 1996 case in which a nine-year-old girl named Amber Hagerman was abducted in Arlington, Texas, while riding her bicycle in her grandparents' neighborhood. A neighbor witnessed the abduction and called the police and Amber's younger brother also rode his bike to his grandparents' house to tell his family what happened. The police and media were alerted within minutes of the abduction, but four days after her abduction, the body of Amber Hagerman was found dumped in a storm drainage ditch. Her killer has never been identified.

Following Amber's tragic murder, her family began calling for tougher laws to protect children, which jumpstarted the movement to create sex offender registries and ultimately established the AMBER Alert system. In 1998, the Child Alert Foundation created the first completely automated notification system, and by 2005, all 50 states had AMBER Alert systems in place to operate seamlessly across state and jurisdictional lines.

To avoid false alarms, there are four general guidelines put forth by the U.S. Department of Justice for issuing an AMBER Alert, although each state sets its own specific criteria:

- the child must be under 18 years of age;
- law enforcement must confirm that an abduction has taken place;
- there must be sufficient descriptions of the child, the abductor, or the vehicle; and
- the child must be at risk of death or serious injury.

The second criterion is somewhat "soft," with many law enforcement agencies ignoring that guideline in order to issue an alert in the event of parental abductions, such as Walt's taking of Holly.

HANK & MARIE & KIDS

Hank and Marie Schrader don't have kids of their own, but they are shown to be deeply involved in the family life of the Whites. Family get-togethers are a common occurrence and, while Hank and Marie have different relationships with Junior, both are shown to be comfortable interacting with him, with Hank often acting as a father figure to the teen.

But when baby Holly enters the picture, the Schraders go into overdrive. As Walt and Skyler's marital problems become more pronounced in season 5, it becomes obvious that Hank and Marie are ready, willing, and able to step in to ensure that the kids have a safe place to live, shielded from the tsunami of bad that is the White marriage. For example:

* In "Dead Freight" (5.05), Hank calls baby Holly "*my* little girl."
* In "Buyout" (5.06), Marie is referring to Holly when she tells Sky, "This little munchkin — I could just keep her *forever*."

The Schraders may want to reunite Walt and Sky with their kids, but make no mistake — they're ready to take on the roles of full-time parents, and with Holly being shown dressed in purple, it seems that Marie has marked her niece very clearly as being her own "little munchkin."

5.15

G ranite State

Original air date: September 22, 2013
Written and directed by: Peter Gould

"It's over." — Saul Goodman

Walt and Jesse struggle to escape their fates and regain some measure of control over their lives. Meanwhile, Skyler, Marie, and Flynn have to deal with the fallout from Walt's exploded empire.

Things have fallen apart for Walter White and most of the people he was closest to, both "professionally" and personally. In a nice bit of misdirection and subversion of viewer expectations, the cold open of "Granite State" reveals the already instantly recognizable red minivan to be carrying Saul, rather than Walt. Albuquerque's best-advertised lawyer is disappearing, his own *criminal* law practice rendered unsustainable by his representation of Walt. "Granite State" collapses time repeatedly, and the revelation that Walt is still hiding out in Ed the Vacuum Cleaner Guy's basement reveals that at least several days have passed since the end of "Ozymandias."

Walt's temporary prison is a basement room, and Jesse's is a much more literal cage, while Todd, Jack, and the neo-Nazis are moving from success to success. They have some $80 million in cash, have stolen what is apparently the only copy of Jesse's confession from Marie and Hank's house, and have the second greatest meth cook in history as their slave. This latter fact is of grave importance to Todd, who uses Jesse's abilities to continue to strengthen his ties to Lydia. Todd's crush continues, and the scene where he meets with

Lydia in the same coffeehouse where she used to meet with Walt — right down to the same table — is a wonderfully written exchange where Todd speaks the language of a romantic relationship, and Lydia unconsciously follows the same path, including telling him, "We're gonna have to take a break."

Of course, while Lydia likes the new purity levels, she's still incredibly risk-averse, and so Todd and Kenny and one of their neo-Nazi compatriots confront Skyler over Holly's crib to make sure that she'll never say a word about Lydia. It's a chilling scene, and underlines just how dangerous Lydia can be. This is the same woman who, in "Madrigal," begged Mike both to spare her daughter, and to leave Lydia's body somewhere it would be found, so that her daughter would not grow up with the pain of having her mother just disappear. Yet Lydia seems entirely comfortable in sending Todd to threaten both Skyler and Holly — or worse. In the end, Lydia is every bit as vicious as Gus Fring, and just as willing to eliminate any and all possible threats to her business.

Walt meanwhile has traded one self-imposed prison for another, this one in the rural mountains of New Hampshire: a one-room cabin with no access to the outside world, not even broadcast television. The difference between

Walt and Jesse's prisons is that Walt can leave his whenever he wants. In fact, Walt considers doing so the first day, only to be overwhelmed by his fear, whispering a promise of "Tomorrow. Tomorrow," like the usurper in the final scene of the final act of *Macbeth*:

> *Tomorrow, and tomorrow, and tomorrow,*
> *Creeps in this petty pace from day to day,*
> *To the last syllable of recorded time;*
> *And all our yesterdays have lighted fools*
> *The way to dusty death. Out, out, brief candle!*
> *Life's but a walking shadow, a poor player*
> *That struts and frets his hour upon the stage*
> *And then is heard no more. It is a tale*
> *Told by an idiot, full of sound and fury*
> *Signifying nothing.*

It is hard not to see Walt's promise to himself as a direct reference to the Bard by Gilligan & Co., for many tomorrows will pass before Walt actually leaves his gates. Again the episode collapses time. Walt apparently went in for chemo treatment once a month back home, and the last time was in "Confessions," when things began to spin out of Walt's control for the last time. Judging by the fact that the Vacuum Cleaner Guy has so much news to bring Walt, and that he has flubbed the needle stick for Walt's chemo once before, several months have passed since "Mr. Lambert" arrived in New Hampshire.

Walt finally realizes that he has lost almost everything when he manages to call Junior, now going officially by the name of "Flynn White," and is rejected by his son, whom once loved him above all others. Walt makes the error of thinking that money will fix everything, and that he still has the ability or the right to provide for Flynn and Skyler (who is now going by her maiden name). Not to mention that Walt proposes to do so by endangering Flynn's best friend Lewis. In a beautiful scene, Flynn tells Walt off once and for all, leaving no room for Walt to doubt or rationalize away the fact that he has destroyed his relationship with his son forever. In fact this is the moment of total despair for Walter White as he begs his son, and perhaps whatever higher powers exist in the *Breaking Bad* universe, to not let everything he has done, everything he has been through, "be for nothing."

Meanwhile, Jesse has his relationship with Andrea brutally torn away before his eyes as Todd guns her down on her own porch as an object lesson of the cost of defying Jack. The choices of both Walt and Jesse have come back to hurt the people they love the most, while also destroying their own lives.

Yet it turns out that Walt has a couple of things left after all: pride and revenge. Walt doesn't act from any noble reason. He is motivated by the Schwartzes' appearance on *The Charlie Rose Show*, where they dismiss Walt's involvement in the early days of Gray Matter as inconsequential. Walt's pride cannot bear that. Nor can he stand the fact that blue meth is apparently still being cooked and sold. For Walter White's reputation to be destroyed is bad enough, but to add insult to injury by eliminating the memory of Walt as the one and only Heisenberg is unacceptable, and enraging. And so Walt evades the police, and disappears again, bent on revenge, and in all likelihood, death.

LAB NOTES

HIGHLIGHT

SAUL: "A month from now — *best case scenario* — I'm managing a Cinnabon in Omaha."

DID YOU NOTICE

- Gilligan & Co. avoid showing us Ed the Vacuum Cleaner Guy's face for as long as possible in the cold open.
- As the neo-Nazis watch Jesse's confession and Jesse details Todd's murder of Drew Sharp, Todd smirks, both proud of having gunned down a kid in cold blood and hurt by hearing Jesse insult him.
- Saul's predictions of what will happen to Skyler if Walt leaves turn out to be 100 percent correct.
- Todd is a touchy-feely guy, but his touches, while always a little creepy, carry different messages. With Skyler, his hand on her shoulder is an implicit threat. With Lydia, his hesitant brushing of lint off of her shoulder is a sign of true, albeit twisted, affection.
- Lydia is happy to finally be working with someone who will allow her to use her "tradecraft" of sitting and talking back-to-back, something Mike and Walt never put up with.
- After his first abortive trip to the gates of his property, Walt never dons

the Heisenberg porkpie hat again, leaving it hanging on the antler of the stuffed buck's head in his cabin.

- When Vacuum Cleaner Guy is updating Walt on news from home, he tells Walt that Skyler is going by her maiden name. Skyler's maiden name is "Lambert," the same name Walt has adopted while on the lam.

- Flynn's final words to Walt are very similar to the ones he used in "Cancer Man," when Walt was trying to justify his refusal to seek treatment: "Then why don't you just fucking die already? Just give up and die."

SHOOTING UP

- Michael Slovis and his crew use a lot of dark tones in this episode, from the shadowy interiors of Walt's cabin and Jesse's pit to the neo-Nazis' clubhouse and the bar in the final act of the episode. The darkness creates a kind of claustrophobic feel and somber mood, subtly but powerfully reinforcing Walt and Jesse's imprisonments.

- The broken camcorder at Hank and Marie's is shot from a floor-level, close-up POV.

- When the lawyers are talking to Skyler, we hear the same high-pitched tinnitus sound that — since its first use in "Pilot/Breaking Bad" when Walt got his cancer diagnosis — has become indicative of characters being out of reality and in their own little worlds, usually as a result of some traumatic experience.

- As Walt arrives in New Hampshire he is seen from an inside-the-tanker POV.

- There is a POV shot from the interior of the woodstove as Walt lights a fire.

TITLE "Granite State" is the official nickname for New Hampshire. The title may also be a reference to the three months or so that Jesse and Walt spend in their respective prisons, where each day is the same, unrelieved by any pleasant difference, just an endlessly repetitive routine of worry, fear, and pain that must come to feel like a permanent state of affairs, as if their lives have been turned into a granite state of mind-numbing sameness.

INTERESTING FACTS

- Saul's Vacuum Cleaner Guy is played by Robert Forster, who rose to fame as the lead character in *Banyon* in the early 1970s. Quentin Tarantino rescued him from bit roles by giving him a part in 1997's *Jackie Brown*, which earned Forster an Academy Award nomination. Most recently he played Arthur Petrelli in *Heroes* and George Clooney's father in *The Descendants*.
- The drink Walt orders in the final scene is The Dimple Pinch, a blended Scotch whiskey, which, if not extreme upper-shelf stock, is right up there with Chivas Regal. Nor is this the first time Walt's seen drinking it. Ironically, he and Hank toasted Holly's birth with The Dimple Pinch in "Phoenix," and Walt pours himself some to celebrate killing Gus in "Live Free or Die."
- In the Charlie Rose interview with Gretchen and Elliott, Rose mentions an article about Walter White in *The New York Times* written by Andrew Sorkin. After the episode aired, Sorkin added a layer of verisimilitude to the scene by actually writing a fake column that was published in the *Times'* "Deal B%k" section on September 23, 2013.

SPECIAL INGREDIENTS

MR. MAGORIUM'S WONDER EMPORIUM

It may be true, as Sartre said, that hell is other people, but being stuck in an isolated New Hampshire hunting cabin with two copies of *Mr. Magorium's Wonder Emporium* might at least count as purgatory. The 2007 family comedy-fantasy has a solid cast, with lead roles played by Dustin Hoffman as a 243-year-old toy store owner and Natalie Portman as the young woman who is set to inherit the unusual business. However, *Wonder Emporium* failed to connect with moviegoers.

Zach Helm wrote *Wonder Emporium* and also made his directorial debut with it. Helm had a strong writing track record at that point, having won awards for the play *Good Canary*, and for his screenplay, *Stranger than Fiction*. His choice to direct *Wonder Emporium* in addition to writing it turned out to be an unfortunate decision. The film with the fun-to-say title was a commercial flop, costing $65 million and barely making half that at the American box office. Worldwide, the movie scraped the break-even point, but it's still considered a failure.

Helm maintains a sense of humor about the film and has even joined in the criticism of his own movie. When asked by the entertainment show *TMZ* for his thoughts on having *Wonder Emporium* appear in "Granite State," his reply was that having two copies of his directorial debut in the cabin was unrealistic since "that is exactly two more copies than are allowed in my house."

5.16

F elina

Original air date: September 29, 2013
Written and directed by: Vince Gilligan

"I did it for me. I liked it. I was *good* at it and . . . I was *alive.*"
— Walter White

Walt returns to New Mexico to put his affairs in order once and for all.

Running throughout "Felina" is the classic Marty Robbins tune "El Paso," which tells the story of a cowboy whose love for a beautiful woman leads him to commit the "foul, evil deed" of murdering a competitor, an act that forces him to flee from Texas to New Mexico before his love eventually drives him back to El Paso, where he is certain to be killed. Rather than a woman, however, Walt's Felina is the Blue, and the pride and power that come with his extraordinary skill as a meth cook. This is what has made Walt a multiple murderer and cost him everything.

Gilligan & Co. leave no major loose ends in this series finale, but one of the most interesting elements they tie off is the suggestion of a Greater Force running throughout *Breaking Bad*. Walt himself has commented on it in the season 3 episode "Fly" when he pondered the chances of meeting Don Margolis in a bar so very shortly before Jane's murder. When Walt first attempts to hot-wire the Volvo, he's trying too hard, taking a complicated approach to a problem before exhausting all of the alternatives. Yet, when the attempt fails, for the first time in the series, Walter White prays, promising that if some force will just let him get home he will "take care of the rest," presumably including his own death. This is a tremendous change for a man who, in the season 1 episode ". . . And the Bag's in the River," insisted that there was nothing to life but chemistry. It is after this brief, honest prayer that everything starts going Walt's way at long last.

Walt is on a death ride, and it is that which makes him so successful in this final episode. He is a man with almost nothing left to lose, so all of the fear, anger, and frenetic action that has always been present as he tries to accomplish his immediate goals and come out *alive* is absent. For Walt, there is no possibility of surviving, and no point. Bryan Cranston gives one of his most powerful, most subtle, performances of the series in "Felina," as Walt goes through the episode calmly, calculatedly, and oddly relaxed. He also finally lets go of the biggest lie of the series: that he did all of this for his family. His admission that he did it for himself, because he liked it, is an incredible moment in television history. After he tells this truth, Walt's eyes close, and the viewer can literally see a weight lift from him, because it's not just Skyler to whom he is admitting this for the first time, but himself. Anna Gunn's bravura performance is central as well, as Skyler too takes a moment to *hear* this truth. For this is not just a final moment of honesty from and by Walt, it is also the very last gift and tribute he can pay to the memory of their marriage and their love. It is a kind of reconciliation and good-bye all at once.

Indeed, Walt is saying his good-byes throughout the episode. As he leaves his former house, he flashes back two years to the pilot episode, when he celebrated his 50th birthday surrounded by a house full of friends and a loving family, and Hank invited him on the ride-along that would change everything. The transition from the Walt of "Pilot/Breaking Bad" to the Walt of "Felina" is astonishing. From healthy-looking, brightly lit, and innocent, to gaunt, shadowed, and a face weathered with pain and knowledge — the change in the man is visible and profound. Jesse too has his moment of reflection, of a warm past shattered by the dark present. In a lovely, heartbreaking scene, a teenage Jesse is seen creating the box he told the NA group about in season 3's "Kafkaesque" — painstakingly, lovingly. He uses all hand tools, and joins the pieces together without nails or screws, but only careful woodworking, and stains the box with a handmade mixture until it is absolutely perfect, wonderfully beautiful. He told the story in "Kafkaesque" as if it were a dream, then brought it crashing back to a bitter reality with the admission that he sold the box for an ounce of weed. The potential that the box held — a gift for his mom, a future of

being the good son she'd be proud of — is cut short by what he did with it instead. And now, the memory of innocence and incredible possibilities is literally brought up short by the jerk of the cable attached to his chains in the neo-Nazis' meth lab. Here Jesse is ragged, scarred, bearded, and filthy, the ultimate end-point of a seemingly innocuous decision he made so long ago. Beaten down and enslaved, with seemingly no possibilities left at all.

While Walt was largely responsible for taking those possibilities away, it is also Walt who gives them back to Jesse in the end, not only by freeing Jesse from his captors, but literally taking a bullet for him. The two do not part friends, and certainly not as the surrogate-father and son they came so close to being, but things between them are at least settled, and both men know it is for the last time. Jesse told Walt that he was done taking orders from him, and here he stands by that declaration, refusing to kill Walt when Walt asks him to. What happens to Jesse? Anything, and that's the point. He is free, and all the possibilities that were his when he made the box are his once again.

As for Walt, his last act is to say good-bye to the lab that grew out of the Vamanos Pest lab that he and Jesse built, the place where he was able to be his true self. His tour is loving, and upon finding a breathing mask of a similar make to the ones he first stole from the high school chemistry lab, he smiles, and the final musical frame is put in place by Badfinger's "Baby Blue." Again, Walt's special love, his "Baby Blue," isn't a woman, but the meth, the cook, the danger, the ride. Here at the end of it all, Walter White has finally come home, and there his story ends.

It was a hell of a ride.

LAB NOTES

HIGHLIGHT

WALT: "Elliott, if we're gonna go that way, you'll need a bigger knife."

DID YOU NOTICE

- In the cold open, there is yet another view of Walt in a mirror. The last eight episodes of season 5 regularly feature such mirror images, reflecting that Walt is increasingly unable to avoid seeing himself for who and what he really is.
- The car Walt steals in New Hampshire and drives to New Mexico is an older model Volvo, the same make of car that Gus drove. When he switches it out for a different car in the Denny's parking lot, he's driving an old, four-door, Ford LTD–style car, like Mike's.
- Walt makes Elliott and Gretchen shake his hand to seal their deal. His insistence and their reluctance and distaste echo Walt's own reaction every time he was made to shake Jack's hand.
- Walt makes every effort to appear down on his luck, dirty, sick, and desperate when he meets Lydia and Todd at the coffee shop. Judging by his ability to get cleaned up and change clothes before meeting with Skyler, this — including the coughing fit — is likely almost completely an act on Walt's part.
- When Walt is in the desert building the remote controlled armature for the M60, he is singing "El Paso" under his breath.
- When a cleaned-up Walt visits Skyler, he is wearing the same outfit he wore in "Pilot/Breaking Bad": khakis, green shirt, and light khaki windbreaker, as if reminding her of the man he used to be.
- Walt caresses Holly with his left hand. When he is trying to jimmy the car in the cold open, he hurts his right hand, the same hand Skyler cut in "Ozymandias," and the same hand, bloodied, that he uses in the last

scene to caress one of the tanks in the lab. This a lovely reversal from the traditional view of the left, or "sinister," hand as the bad one, and a play on the biblical phrase that "the left hand doesn't know what the right is doing."

* As the neo-Nazis search Walt, a low train-whistle can be heard in the background, a reminder of Drew Sharp's murder.
* The seemingly endless, overwhelming sound of the M60 machine gun as it mows down the neo-Nazis is almost exactly the same as the sound effect Skyler woke up to in "Hazard Pay" when Walt, Flynn, and Holly were watching the climactic scene of Scarface. This is Walt's very own "Say hello to my little friend" moment.
* Walt dies with his eyes wide open, finally willing and able to see things as they are, rather than as he wants them to be.

MISCALCULATIONS When Walt arrives at the neo-Nazis' compound, Kenny carefully checks out the interior of his car, and then has Walt thoroughly searched, during which process they even confiscate his keys and wallet, yet they *never think to check the trunk*. This is a little bit *too* convenient given the enormous size of the trunk on that style of car, and the neo-Nazis' otherwise meticulous security measures.

SHOOTING UP

* There are some truly tremendous shots in this episode, beginning with the close-up of the snow-covered car window. At first, no borders are seen, just the snow, and when the camera moves it is somewhat disorienting, because the snow, which turns the incoming light slightly blue, at first reads like another up-and-through POV, when it is actually a simple, horizontal shot.
* The first upward-looking POV is actually an under dashboard view as Walt tries to jimmy the car.
* The play of red-and-blue police lights filtered by the snow-covered windows is just tremendous, and amps up the tension beautifully.
* The color palette used for Gretchen and Elliott and their house is an interesting play on their name, Schwartz, which is German for "black," on Walt's last name, and on the combination of the two in Gray Matter. While the Schwartzes have been associated with black and gray, their

clothing and home are clean, uncluttered, and *white*, while Walt emerges from black shadows outside, and is dirty, dark, and gray in appearance.

♦ In the flashback of Jesse making his box, the light is a deep, warm, buttery-gold, which interacts with the generally pale wood to create an idyllic, softly welcoming atmosphere, literally the golden age of Jesse's past.

♦ There is a rolling-bag level POV of Lydia's Louboutins as she enters the coffee shop.

♦ As Lydia stirs the stevia into her mug, the camera focuses on her tea and slowly moves in as the sweetener dissolves, underlining the importance of the action, and foreshadowing the consequences of it.

TITLE "Felina" is a reference to the woman in Marty Robbins's song, and thereby to the Blue that Walt is obsessed with, but it is also an anagram for "finale." When the title of the series finale was announced in late 2013, fans noticed that "Felina" could be broken down into the abbreviations for three elements: Fe (iron), Li (lithium), and Na (sodium). Much was made of the three elements being shorthand for "blood, meth, and tears," but this stretches things a bit too far, as lithium has absolutely nothing to do with the manufacture of crystal meth.

MUSIC "El Paso" and "Baby Blue" are discussed above, but there is one more significant piece of music in this episode: as Gretchen and Elliott enter their house, followed by Walt, the classical music playing is "Ballet Music" from Charles Gounod's opera *Faust*, about a man who makes a deal with the devil in order to gain ultimate power and knowledge. It's a fitting piece as it echoes Walt's own journey. The music also harkens back to the characterization of Walt as the Devil by Marie in "Blood Money," and by Jesse in "Rabid Dog." In "Felina," of course, the Schwartzes are forced to make a deal with the Devil — a nice touch.

INTERESTING FACTS After completing his call to the Schwartzes' assistant, Walt takes off his watch and leaves it on top of the pay phone. Vince Gilligan later admitted that, as "Felina" was being filmed, they remembered that Walt was not wearing a watch when he was seen in the cold opens of "Live Free or Die" and "Blood Money," so they had to have him leave it somewhere along the way to avoid a continuity error.

SPECIAL INGREDIENTS

IRREVOCABLE TRUSTS

Walt's plan is to get the remnants of his meth fortune to his children through an irrevocable trust supposedly set up by Gretchen and Elliott Schwartz of Gray Matter Technologies. Walt's very clear about the structure of the trust and how it is to be funded, and, honestly, it's one of his better ideas. Legally speaking, a "trust" is a contractual relationship in which one party holds property for the benefit of another. In this case, Walt is the "settlor" (or "grantor"), the person who transfers his property to the "trustees," who are the Schwartzes. The trustees are charged with holding the property (in this case, over $9 million) for the benefit of Flynn, who is to receive the full sum of money on his 18th birthday. Trustees have legal title to the property, but are obligated to act for the good of the beneficiaries. While they may be compensated for their work (and certainly can have their expenses, such as legal fees and taxes, reimbursed), trustees are obligated to remit all profits, such as interest and dividends, from the trust "corpus" (the money, in this case) to the beneficiaries. Of course, Gretchen and Elliott think the "two best hitmen west of the Mississippi" have them in their crosshairs, so this is one trust that's going to be set up rapidly and run prudently.

There are all sorts of reasons to set up a trust and there are many different forms of trusts. Walt is insistent upon an "irrevocable trust," which is one whose terms cannot be revised. That brings up another point — since Walt's using the Schwartzes as his cats-paws in this matter, the trust will be set up to make it appear that they are the settlors and they will probably use a financial institution as the trustee. The Schwartzes are still alive, so this is technically an "irrevocable living trust," since it is being established during the lifetimes of the settlors.

Walt's not putting conditions on how Flynn uses the money, although restrictions are very common with trusts. Many are established to be used only for the "health, education, and welfare" of the beneficiary, although "welfare" can be a very broad category. Walt's intent is for Flynn to turn 18 and be given a great big whopping windfall of money that Flynn is not expecting and knows nothing about. This is how lottery winners wind up broke in two years. Let's hope Flynn has better sense.

SPEED KILLS (SEASON 5)

BODY COUNT

Walt: 19 (Mike; Mike's guys and their lawyer; Jack, Kenny, and the neo-Nazis; Lydia)

Jesse: 1 (Todd)

Lydia: 10 (Declan and his men)

Todd: 2 (Drew Sharp, Andrea)

Jack & the Neo-Nazis: 2 (Hank and Gomez)

BEATDOWNS

Walt: 2 (by Hank, also Skyler with knife)

Jesse: 1+ (by Todd)

Saul: 1 (by Jesse)

THE ONES WHO KNOCK

VIOLENTIZATION IN *BREAKING BAD*

How does a mild-mannered, middle-class, high school chemistry teacher go from being a milquetoast who is incapable of standing up to his boss at the crappy second job he has to work as a car-wash attendant to being a man able to bomb a nursing home; calculatedly poison a child; order the assassination of 10 men; rationalize the murder of a young teenager as regrettable, but necessary; and cold-bloodedly plan to mow down 10 more men with a machine-gun? This is the journey that Walter White takes across five seasons of *Breaking Bad*, but the change from nonviolent person to dangerously violent criminal is one that happens all too often in real life as well. While the events depicted in *Breaking Bad* are entirely fictional, Vince Gilligan & Co. portray Walt and other characters' experience of violent behavior in a very realistic way, adding to the believability of the show as a whole.

The high level of "emotional realism" in *Breaking Bad* was discussed in the first essay in this book, and to examine that feeling of reality in Walt's transformation to a dangerous criminal the work of sociologist Lonnie Athens again becomes central. After years spent developing case studies of violent criminals, sometimes at serious risk to himself, Athens has termed the social experience of violence "violentization" (as in "socialization"), defining it in his 1992 book *The Creation of Dangerous Violent Criminals* as a four-stage process arising from particular social experiences. According to Athens, the violentization of a person occurs through a process of brutalization, belligerency, violent performances, and virulency. These stages are experienced in order, can occur over a variable amount of time, and the entire process is subject to both temporary and permanent interruption. In other words, someone like Jesse Pinkman can experience most of these phases without being doomed to progress to the point of virulency. On the other hand, someone like Tuco Salamanca has progressed through the entire process and, when we first meet him, already resorts to deadly violence as a response to even the slightest perceived provocation.

Athens breaks down the first stage, brutalization, into three parts: violent subjugation, personal horrification, and violent coaching. Though each experience differs from the others in certain details, each part involves a person being traumatized by others through cruel treatment, usually a mix of physical and psychological abuse. Violent subjugation happens when someone is forced to submit to another's authority, which is achieved through the threat or actual use of violence to force obedience, or through the use of violence in retaliation for disobedience. Violent subjugation is also often used as a tool to condition the subject to show proper respect to a putative authority figure. In *Breaking Bad*, we see this process most clearly in the case of Jesse Pinkman, who is repeatedly the victim of violent subjugation. In the pilot he is pistol whipped and kicked by his ex-partner Emilio. He is beaten to the point of hospitalization by Tuco in "Crazy Handful of Nothin'," is threatened and smacked into obedience by Mike in "ABQ," is again hospitalized after being beaten by Hank in "One Minute," and is brutally beaten and tortured by Todd and the neo-Nazis in "Ozymandias." In each case, Jesse is helpless before the violence of his attackers and through fear and pain is forced to submit to their will. Violent subjugation in one form or another occurs to characters frequently throughout *Breaking Bad*, but Jesse is the most obvious case.

The second aspect of brutalization, personal horrification, is basically the reverse of violent subjugation. Instead of undergoing the subjugation him or herself, the person sees it happen to someone else. Walt and Jesse both witness Tuco brutally beating one of his lieutenants to death in "A No-Rough-Stuff-Type Deal," Jesse witnesses another deadly example in "Peekaboo," and Jesse deals with Combo being gunned down in "Mandala." He and Walt are both forced to watch Gus's execution of Victor in "Box Cutter," Gus sees Max murdered in "Hermanos," Skyler spends most of the first half of season 5 terrified by what Walt has done to Gus, Walt watches Jack murder Hank, and Walt and Jesse each see the other subjugated through the threat of violence multiple times throughout the series.

The final aspect of brutalization is violent coaching. Simply put, the subject is coached to perform violent acts by another, often older, person. In *Breaking Bad* there are many violent coaches. Walt eggs Jesse on to recover the meth stolen from one of their dealers in "Peekaboo," and again urges him to violence in the final dramatic scenes of "Full Measure." Jesse in turn coaches Walt to kill Krazy-8 in "The Cat's in the Bag," and ". . . And the Bag's in the River," and in "Seven Thirty-Seven" urges him to murder Tuco. Walt receives further coaching from both Saul and Mike at various points, including a story told by the latter in "Half Measures" that will influence Walt towards drastic action later. In addition, we see other characters involved in elements of violent coaching, particularly and very importantly, in the cold open to season 3's "One Minute," where we see a young Héctor Salamanca engage in all three aspects of brutalization at once to the two young brothers who will become the murderous cousins in their adulthood.

The end result of the process of brutalization is an individual who has undergone a deeply traumatic and chaotic process, leaving him fundamentally disturbed and distraught as he attempts to integrate these experiences into his life. Thus the beginning of Athens's second phase, belligerency, can be seen as a kind of existential crisis. The person is faced with a divergence between how people are *supposed* to interact with one another, and how his own experience of brutalization demonstrates how they *actually* interact. Soon enough, however, the individual brings his thinking back from the realm of society as a whole to his specific case. It is important to remember that the person has been deeply and often repeatedly brutalized, and such trauma defeats any attempt to disregard or discard it. It must be dealt with, for better or worse. The question in the person's mind has changed from "Why did this happen to me?" to "What can I do to stop it from happening again?"

The obvious answer is to take violent action against those who threaten to hurt or who unduly provoke the subject or the subject's loved ones. The person has now resolved to use potentially deadly violence, up to and including killing another human being, but only under certain conditions. This is not necessarily where people begin to break bad, however. Indeed, this is the level of violentization possessed by many trained soldiers, police officers, and even untrained people faced with a threat to themselves or their loved ones. The program of controlled brutalization found in military boot camps and law enforcement training is specifically designed to take recruits from a nonviolent civilian status to this level of belligerency, where they are willing and able to use deadly violence "to protect and serve." This is the level of violentization reached by Hank and Gomez as DEA agents, and eventually by Jesse.

When people move from willingness to commit violence under certain circumstances to actually committing such acts, they have progressed to the third stage, violent performances. The effects of violent performances on the perpetrator depend largely on their outcome, Athens stresses. If the violent performance is clearly effective, the possibility of moving onto the next level of violentization becomes that much greater. A draw, or contest with no clear-cut winner, will result in the subject remaining in the violent performances stage until a clear-cut victory (or defeat) occurs at a later time. A clear defeat or series of defeats can break the chain of violentization completely as the subject rethinks his resolution to employ violence, or it can actually continue the subject's violent progression as his resolution to be violent remains unchanged despite proof that he is not very good at it.

In Walter White we see a series of successful violent acts lead to an increasing willingness to resort to violence as a means of solving problems. His gassing of Krazy-8 and Emilio in a situation of immediate danger in the pilot episode is followed by the deliberate killing of Krazy-8 in ". . . And the Bag's in the River" in a situation that can still be rationalized as self-defense, but which lacks the element of imminent danger. This is followed by Walt's use of fulminated mercury to force Tuco to pay for the meth he took from Jesse in "Crazy Handful of Nothin'," and though Walt rejects Jesse's plans to shoot Tuco, he is soon ready with a plan to use ricin to poison the gang lord. Again this can be rationalized as pre-emptive self-defense, but he is turning ever more quickly to potentially deadly violence to achieve his ends. In "Full Measure," Walt runs down two street-dealers, then picks up one fallen thug's gun and uses it to finish the second, coolly and efficiently. Later, Walt convinces Jesse to murder Gale. Walt then poisons a child and uses a bomb to kill both Héctor and Gus, and by season 5, Walt views killing Mike's imprisoned men as the most efficient way to ensure their silence, and doesn't hesitate to slaughter Todd, the neo-Nazis, and Lydia.

After killing the two thugs, who were street-level members of Gus's drug organization, Gus, Mike, and Victor all treat Walt differently. While not afraid of him, they are wary, and now view him as a potentially dangerous liability to the organization. Indeed, it is after this incident that Gus makes the decision to have Walter killed. Walt has proven that he is capable of committing deadly violence, and has done so in an unpredictable manner. Walt's action has brought him notoriety and even a kind of increased respect and standing among these violent men. This status is increased in season 5 after word gets out that Walt killed Gus, and his reputation grows even larger when he arranges for the death of Mike's men in "Gliding Over All." Psychologically, this kind of recognition can prove to be intoxicating, and can lead to a drastic change in the subject's thinking — as Walt comes to believe that he *is* the danger.

Walt's use of violence clearly escalates as the series progresses, and is usually successful. In terms of Athens's theory of violentization, Walt has traveled the road to the fourth and final stage of virulency. In this phase, a person makes what Athens calls "an unmitigated violent resolution" to severely harm other human beings without serious or repeated provocation. Tuco is perhaps the series' main example of someone who has reached the point of virulency to become what Athens defines as a dangerous violent criminal. Yet while Tuco is the most obvious, the same level has been reached by Gus, Héctor, Don Eladio, Tyrus, Victor, Todd, Jack, and even Walt himself. Walt's ultimate solution is a violent one, and it must always been borne in mind that it was not his only choice. Turning himself in would have accomplished the goal of protecting Skyler, and he would still have conned the Schwartzes into giving Flynn money. Walt didn't *have* to kill Todd and the Nazis — he *wanted* to.

Thus the characters of *Breaking Bad* follow a very realistic progression of violence, and unfortunately it is one that viewers recognize from the real world. This attention to the realities of violence, of how and why real people break bad, is one of the truly brilliant themes of the series. Gilligan & Co. never shy away from showing us the brutal truths of their characters' choices, and by giving us a largely accurate portrayal of the effects of violence on human souls, *Breaking Bad* comes more chillingly alive than ever. Because if the mild-mannered Mr. White can become the mass murderer Heisenberg, then so could anyone. Even us.

SPEED KILLS (SERIES TOTALS)

BODY COUNT
Walt: 24
Walt/Don Margolis: 167 (with Wayfarer 515)
Walt/Héctor: 3
Gus: 13+
Salamanca cousins: 11
Mike: 6
Gaff: 4
Jesse: 3
Hank: 2
Tuco: 1+
Jack & Neo-Nazis: 2+
Lydia: 10
Todd: 2

BEATDOWNS
Walt: 4
Jesse: 5+
Saul: 1
Gonzo: 1

SOURCES

"2 Cleared in 'Macho' Camacho's Death." ESPN.com. ESPN.go.com. 6 Feb 2013.

"2012 Chrysler 300." BreakingBad.wikia.com.

"Abiquiú." BreakingBad.wikia.com.

"About Georgia O'Keeffe." OKeeffeMuseum.org.

"About LoJack." LoJack.com.

"About PET/CT." PetScanInfo.com.

Adams, Cecil. "Did the Civil War Create 500,000 Morphine Addicts?" TheStraightDope.com. 9 Jul 1999.

Alcindor, Yamiche. "Cops: Woman shoplifted and cooked meth inside Walmart." *USA Today*. UsaToday.com. 9 Jun 2012.

"All Seeing Eye." MasonicDictionary.com.

"AMBER Alert Timeline." Office of Justice Programs. OJP.USDOJ.gov.

"Ambulance Chaser." TVTropes.org.

Ang, Ien. *Watching Dallas: Soap Opera and the Melodramatic Imagination.* Trans. Della Couling. New York: Methuen & Co., 1985.

"Animal Fact Sheet — Tarantula." Arizona-Sonora Desert Museum. DesertMuseum.org.

"Animal Feed." SustainableTable.org.

Ankrom, Sheryl. "Anxiety Attacks Versus Panic Attacks: What's the Difference?" PanicDisorder.about.com. 29 Jun 2009.

"Anti-Hero." TVTropes.org.

"Anti-heroes: Aaron Paul on *Breaking Bad*." AMCTV.com.

"Antoine Laurent Lavoisier." University of Virginia. Cti.Itc.virginia.edu.

Armstrong, W.P. "The Castor Bean." Wayne's Word. WaynesWord
    .palomar.edu. March 1999.

Associated Press. "Police: Mom killed two children, two others and herself
    after taping herself smoking meth." FoxNews.com. 17 Jan 2012.

Athens, Lonnie. *The Creation of Dangerous Violent Criminals*. Chicago:
    University of Illinois Press, 1992.

—. "Dramatic Self Change." *The Sociological Quarterly 36*, No. 3 (Summer),
    1995.

—. "Self as Soliloquy." *The Sociological Quarterly 35*, No. 3 (August), 1994.

"Augusto Pinochet." Brittanica.com.

Bachelard, Gaston. *The Poetics of Space*. Trans. Maria Jones. New York:
    The Orion Press, 1964.

Baker, Debbi. "Mylar Balloons Cause Power Lines to Fall in El Cajon."
    UTSanDiego.com. 12 June 2012.

"Bear Canyon Arroyo Spillway Dam." Wikimapia.org.

Bedard, Megan. "'Food Inc.' Chicken Farmer Goes Rogue — Says Goodbye
    to Factory Farms." TakePart.com. 7 May 2012.

Bennett, Drake. "Abducted!" Boston.com. 20 Jul 2008.

"Blue Sky." BreakingBad.wikia.com.

Blum, Mitch. "Stop Breaking Down: What the Cars on *Breaking Bad* Tell Us
    about the True Nature of the Characters." MitchBlum.com. 14 Jul 2011.

Boden, Robert F. "Five Years After *Bates*: Lawyer Advertising in Legal and
    Ethical Perspective." Marquette Law Scholarly Commons. Scholarship.
    law.marquette.edu.

Bodine, Alicia. "Homemade Ice Packs." eHow.com.

Bonander, Ross. "Pablo Escobar: 5 Things You Didn't Know." AskMen.com.

"Bonnie and Clyde." FBI.gov.

"Bonnie and Clyde's Death Car." RoadsideAmerica.com.

"Both Sides Claim Victory in *YSL v. Louboutin* Shoe Case." Forbes.com.
    5 Sep 2012.

"BP Announces Class-Action Settlement in 2010 Gulf Oil Disaster."
    CNN.com. 19 Apr 2012.

Breaking Bad. TV Series. Executive Producers Vince Gilligan, Mark Johnson, Michelle MacLaren. AMC. 2008–2013.

Brentplummerwest. "Czech Meth: Is *Breaking Bad* Accurate?" Across the Pond. Iuwest.wordpress.com. 7 Sep 2012.

"A Brief History of Methamphetamine." Vermont Department of Health. HealthVermont.gov. 2013.

Britt, Ryan. "All Alone in the Night: When *Babylon 5* Invented 21st Century Fandom." Tor.com. 8 Oct 2012.

"*Brown v. Board of Education* (1954)." PBS.org. 2007.

Buttimer, Anne. "Home, Reach, and the Sense of Place." *The Human Experience of Space and Place*. Eds. Anne Buttimer and David Seamon. New York: St. Martin's Press, 1980.

Calabro, Tina. "'Breaking Bad' actor RJ Mitte finds 'perfect role' prepared him to become an activist." *Pittsburgh Post-Gazette*. Post-Gazette.com. 17 Mar 2010.

"*California v. Carney*." Legal Information Institute. Law.cornell.edu.

"Can a Desert Eagle Be Suppressed?" Answers.yahoo.com.

Caverly, N. Brian and Jordan S. Simon. "Revocable versus Irrevocable Trusts." Dummies.com. 2013.

Celebi, Sarah. "Why Are Electrical Wires Covered in Plastic?" eHow.com.

"Cerebral Palsy." MayoClinic.com.

"Chemotherapy." Cancer.org.

"Chemotherapy." MayoClinic.com.

"The Clarence Darrow Award." Oklahoma Criminal Defense Lawyers Association. OCDLAOklahoma.com. 2013.

Clark, Josh. "How Many Things Can You Plug into an Electrical Outlet Before It Catches Fire?" HowStuffWorks. Home.howstuffworks.com.

Cohen, Brad. "Inside Pablo Escobar's Medellín Cartel." BBC.com. 18 Oct 2011.

Collins & Collins, P.C. "New Mexico Retreat Law Reviewed in Light of the Trayvon Martin Case." NewMexicoInjuryAttorneyBlog.com. 11 May 2012.

"Contingency Fees: Read This Before You Hire a Lawyer." ThompsonHall.com.

Costandi, Mo. "The Dissociative Fugue State: Forgetting One's Own Identity." NeuroPhilosophy.wordpress.com. 18 Apr 2007.

Cresswell, Tim. *In Place/Out of Place: Geography, Ideology, and Transgression.* Minneapolis: University of Minnesota Press, 1996.

—. *Place: A Short Introduction.* Oxford: Blackwell Publishing, 2004.

Curley, Bob. "DSM-V — Major Changes to Addictive Disease Classifications." RecoveryToday.net. March 2010.

"Czech Capital Becomes EU Crystal Meth Capital." RT News. RT.com. 14 Jul 2010.

D'Addario, Daniel. "The Music of the *Breaking Bad* Finale." Salon.com. 29 September 2013.

"Defending Skyler White: Sexism in *Breaking Bad.*" Feminist, Unplugged. AwkwardSong.wordpress.com. 31 Jul 2012.

"Difference between Rock and Mineral." DifferenceBetween.com. 13 Jan 2011.

"Do You Think Gus Fring of *Breaking Bad* Walking Away from a Blast Might Have Been a Bit 'Overblown'?" Answers.yahoo.com.

Dryden-Edwards, Roxanne. "Gambling Addiction (Compulsive or Pathological Gambling)." OnHealth.com. 2013.

"The Evil Eye." LuckyMojo.com.

"Evil Eye Protection Beads." EvilEyeProtection.com.

"Ex Parte." Legal-Dictionary.thefreedictionary.com.

"Facts about Ricin." Centers for Disease Control & Prevention. Bt.cdc.gov. 9 May 2013.

"Facts and Case Summary — *Miranda.*" United States Courts. UScourts.gov.

"The Famous B5 Jumpgate Pin." JumpgatePins.com.

Farrell, John A. "Clarence Darrow: Jury Tamperer?" *Smithsonian Magazine.* SmithsonianMag.com. Dec 2011.

"Flaccid Paralysis." Medical-Dictionary.thefreedictionary.com.

Flintoff, Cory. "A Look at Mexico's Drug Cartels." NPR.org. 16 Apr 2009.

Folsom, Ed and Kenneth M. Price, Eds. The Walt Whitman Archive. WhitmanArchive.org.

Ford, D'Lyn. "O Fair (Dry, Windy, Stormy) New Mexico." New Mexico State University. ACES.nmsu.edu. Reprint Summer 1997.

Forte, Stephen M. "What the Attorney-Client Privilege Really Means." Smith, Gambrell & Russell, LLP. SGRLaw.com. Fall 2003.

"Four Corners Monument." ArizonaGuide.com.

"Four Corners Monument." Navajo Nation Parks & Recreation. NavajoNationParks.org.

"Four Corners Monument Still the Legally Recognized Landmark despite Reports." Navajo Nation Parks & Recreation. NavajoNationParks.org. 22 Apr 2009.

"Fourth Amendment — Search and Seizure." Constitution.findlaw.com.

Freeman, Shanna. "How Forensic Dentistry Works." HowStuffWorks. Science.howstuffworks.com.

Freese, Kevin. "The Death Cult of the Drug Lords Mexico's Patron Saint of Crime, Criminals, and the Dispossessed." Foreign Military Service Office. FMSO.leavenworth.army.mil.

Gambling Disorders 360°. Blog.ncrg.org. 2013.

"General Guide to Criminal Jurisdiction in Indian Country." Tribal Court Clearinghouse. Tribal-Institute.org.

George, Patrick. "Why *Breaking Bad* Has the Best Cars on TV Right Now." Jalopnik.com. 2 Feb 2013.

"Georgia O'Keeffe." MetMusuem.org.

Glenn, Brandon. "Chemotherapy 19% cheaper in doctors' offices than hospitals, study says." MedCityNews.com. 4 Apr 2012.

Godkin, Michael A. "Identity and Place: Clinical Applications Based on Notions of Rootedness and Uprootedness." *The Human Experience of Space and Place*. Eds. Anne Buttimer and David Seamon, New York: St. Martin's Press, 1980.

"GPS Tracker — SkyTRX GPS Tracking System." Spy Chest. SpyTechs.com.

Grady, Denise. "Defibrillators Let Lay People Save Heart Attack Victims, Studies Say." HeartSaveSolutions.com. 2004.

Gray, Steven. "Santa Muerte: The New God in Town." *Time*. Time.com. 16 Oct 2007.

"The Great Seal of the United States." U.S. Department of State. State.gov.

Greco, Michael R. "Ex Parte TRO's: Courts Don't Like Them." Fisher & Phillips LLP. NonCompeteNews.com. 8 Feb 2012.

Grell, Jeffrey E. "Ricoact.com LLC." RicoAct.com.

"GS Pay Scale FAQs." Govcentral.monster.com.

Gupta, Prachi. "5 facts about Walter White's not-so-favorite Movie, 'Mr. Magorium's Wonder Emporium.'" Salon.com. 23 Sep 2013.

Harris, Malcolm. "Upping the Antihero." TheNewInquiry.com. 24 Aug 2011.

"Hazards of Meth Ingredients." KCI.org.

Helmenstine, Anne Marie. "Mercury Fulminate — *Breaking Bad*." About .com. 5 Mar 2008.

Hendrixson, Brent. "'So You Found a Tarantula!'" The American Tarantula Society. ATSHQ.org. 2008.

Henry, Alan. "How to Plant a Dead Drop (Without Everyone Finding It)." Lifehacker.com. 14 Nov 2012.

Herman, Marc. "Would *Breaking Bad*'s Czech Scheme Work?" Salon.com. 5 Sep 2012.

Hibberd, James. *"Breaking Bad* Series Finale Ratings Smash All Records." EW.com. InsideTV.ew.com. 30 Sep 2013.

"History of Anti-Money Laundering Laws." Financial Crimes Enforcement Network — Department of the Treasury. www.FinCEN.gov.

Hornblum, Allen M. "Road Companies, Brutes and Safecrackers." *Philadelphia CityPaper*. Archives.citypaper.net. 26 May–1 Jun 2005.

"Horrific Murder No Surprise in U.S. Meth Capital." USAToday.com. 21 Jan 2012.

"The Housefly." Newton: Ask A Scientist! Newton.dep.anl.gov. June 2012.

"The Housefly — A Common Pest." KidzWorld.com.

"How Does Tent Fumigation Work?" Key Fumigation, Inc. KeyFumigation .com.

"How Do I Handle My Professional Car Wash Wastewater?" Illinois EPA. EPA.state.il.us. 2011.

"How Meth Destroys the Body." *Frontline*. PBS.org. 2011.

"How to Define Anode and Cathode." Av8n.com.

"How to Make a Battery." MonkeySee.com.

"How to Make Thermite." How2DoStuff.com. 30 Jan 2006.

"How Zombie Computers Work." HowStuffWorks. Computer.howstuff works.com.

"Huntington's Disease." Alzheimer's Association. Alz.org. 2013.

"Huntington's Disease." MayoClinic.com. 2013.

"Huntington Disease." National Library of Medicine (US). Genetics Home Reference. GHR.nlm.nih.gov. 21 Oct 2013.

"I Hate Marie Schrader." Facebook.com.

IMDb.com.

"Income, Poverty, and Health Insurance Coverage in the United States: 2010." United States Census Bureau. Census.gov. 13 Sept 2011.

"Ingredients Used to Cut Meth and Side Effects." KCI.org.

"Irrevocable Living Trusts." Nolo.com.

Jones, Tom. "Police: Mom on meth doesn't feed baby." WSBTV.com.
    30 Mar 2012.

Joseph, Richard. "History of Meth." AlbuquerqueBreakingBad.com. 2009.

Kapsin, Kirsten. "Underground Heated Flooring." FindAnyFloor.com.
    24 Sep 2008.

"The Kelly Criterion." WizardOfOdds.com. 11 Nov 2009.

"The Kelly Criterion and Blackjack." BlackJackTactics.com.

"Kill Off Skyler White." Facebook.com.

Kilroy, Chris. "Special Report: Tenerife." AirDisaster.com.

"Kinetic and Potential Energy." Library.thinkquest.org.

Kocieniewski, David. "Despite 9/11 Effect, Railyards Are Still Vulnerable."
    NYTimes.com. 27 Mar 2006.

Largo, Michael. *God's Lunatics: Lost Souls, False Prophets, Martyred Saints,
    Murderous Cults, Demonic Nuns, and Other Victims of Man's Eternal Search
    for the Divine.* New York: HarperCollins, 2010.

"Law Enforcement: IRS Criminal Investigation Special Agent." United
    States Internal Revenue Service. Jobs.irs.gov. 2013.

"Lawyer Retainer Fees." LawyerRetainerFees.com.

Layton, Julia. "How Handwriting Analysis Works." HowStuffWorks.
    Science.howstuffworks.com. 2013.

—. "How Money Laundering Works." HowStuffWorks. Money.howstuff
    works.com. 2013.

—. "What Is Ricin?" HowStuffWorks. Science.howstuffworks.com. 2013.

Lee, David. "*Killing Pablo* by Mark Bowden." MedellinLiving.com. 3 Jan 2011.

Levey, Noam. "Global push to guarantee health coverage leaves U.S.
    behind." *Los Angeles Times.* LATimes.com. 12 May 2012.

Lewit, Meghan. "Bad Husband, Bad Wife, Good TV: The Fascinating Rise
    of Antihero Marriages." TheAtlantic.com. 30 Apr 2013.

Limbert, Travis. "The Heroic Narrative Breaking: Bad Heroes or Good
    Villains." Academia.edu. 26 Apr 2012.

Linder, Douglas. "Who Is Clarence Darrow?" University of Missouri-Kansas
    City. law2.umkc.edu.

Lindsey, John. "Mylar Balloons Are Hazardous to Power Lines." *The Tribune*
    (San Luis Obispo). SanLuisObispo.com. 10 Mar 2012.

"Lobectomy as a Treatment for Lung Cancer." LungCancer.about.com.

"LoJack Corporation History." FundingUniverse.com.

"Lung Cancer." MedicineNet.com.

"Lung Lobectomy." Lung Cancer Channel. Lung-Cancer.emedtv.com.

"The Lurker's Guide to Babylon 5." MidWinter.com.

Mahany, Brian. "IRS Criminal Investigations — Will I Get Charged?"
    Mahany & Ertl. MahanyErtl.com. 2009.

Marcotte, Amanda. *Breaking Bad* TV Expectations." The American
    Prospect. Prospect.org. 17 Aug 2012.

"Marital Privilege." LexisNexis.com.

Marshall, Kelli. "I Don't Like Skyler White, But Probably Not for the
    Reasons You Think." MediAcademia. KelliMarshall.net. 7 Aug 2012.

Mattson, Bruce. "Antoine Lavoisier." Creighton University. Mattson.
    creighton.edu.

Maugh, Thomas H. "General Electric chemist invented process for making
    diamonds in lab." LATimes.com. 31 July 2008.

"May 23, 1934 — Bonnie and Clyde Are Killed in Police Ambush." *The New
    York Times*. Learning.blogs.nytimes.com. 23 May 2012.

McElroy, Griffin. *Breaking Bad* Easter Egg Discovered in *Rage*." Joystiq.com.
    8 Oct 2011.

McKinney, Devin. "Violence: The Strong and the Weak." *Film Quarterly* 40,
    No. 9, 1993.

"Meaning of Names." BehindTheName.com.

Meeks, Brock N. "U.S. Announces Steps to Bolster Rail Security."
    NBCNews.com. 22 Mar 2004.

"Methamphetamine Laboratories Put Responders at Risk." RKI
    Instruments. www.RKIInstruments.com. 2013.

"Mexican Cartels Go Back to Basics." BorderlandBeat.com. 16 Dec 2009.

"Mexico: Crimes at the Border." *Frontline*. PBS.org. 27 May 2008.

"Mexico's Zetas Cartel Rewrites Drug War in Blood." NBCNews.com. 2013.

Michelson, Miles. "What Is the Kelly Criterion?" Horseracing.about.com.

Mikkelson, Barbara and David P. "RICO Suave." Snopes.com. 21 Dec 2004.

Mine, Alice Neece. "Walking the Ethical Line with Lawyer Advertising."
    North Carolina State Bar. www.NCBar.gov.

"The Mineral Quartz." The Mineral and Gemstone Kingdom. Minerals.net.

"Minerals vs Rocks." Diffen.com.

"*Miranda v. Arizona* (1966)." InfoPlease.com.

Mitchell, Chase. "Real Stories: Eddie Plein, Owner of Eddie's Gold Teeth." Creative Loafing Atlanta. CLAtl.com. 17 Sept 2006.

"Model Rules for Professional Conduct." ABA. AmericanBar.org.

"Monkey Trial." PBS.org. 2001.

Morrow, Sean. "The Cars of *Breaking Bad*." Portable.tv. 2013.

"Mr. Magorium's Wonder Emporium." RottenTomatoes.com.

Mrotek, Bob. "Eye for an Eye." MexicoBob.blogspot.com. 26 Nov 2011.

"Music from *Breaking Bad* Season 1." AMCTV.com. 2008.

National Transportation Safety Board. NTSB.gov.

Neuman, Clayton. "Music from *Breaking Bad* Season 2." AMCTV.com. 2009.

—. "Music from *Breaking Bad* Season 3." AMCTV.com. 2010.

—."Music from *Breaking Bad* Season 4." AMCTV.com. 2011.

Nichols, Scott E. "Why Are Salmon Pink?" Verlasso.com. 30 Apr 2012.

"Occupational Outlook Handbook — Air Traffic Controllers." U.S. Bureau of Labor Statistics. BLS.gov.

Outlaw, Kofi. "*Breaking Bad* & Meth in America." ScreenRant.com. 10 Feb 2012.

"Pablo Escobar." Biography.com.

"Passive GPS Tracking." LandAirSea.com.

"Pay & Leave — Salaries & Wages." U.S. Office of Personnel Management. OPM.gov.

"The Phoenix Legend." Shades-of-Night.com.

"Pinochet Tried Defying Defeat, Papers Show." NYTimes.com. 23 Feb 2013.

Poniewozik, James. "Dead Tree Alert: Walter White, the Greatest American Antihero." *Time*. Entertainment.time.com. 9 Jul 2012.

Preece, John. Weak Interactions: Screen Science Explained. WeakInteractions.wordpress.com.

"Preparing Your Home for Termite Fumigation." Dow AgroSciences. DowAgro.com.

"Product Placement — Top Five Ads You Couldn't Skip Over." The M/C/C Minute. MCCom.com. 15 Aug 2012.

"Q&A — Los Cuates de Sinaloa (Narcocorrido Band)." AMC Blogs. Blogs.amctv.com.

"Quantum Physics: Werner Heisenberg." On Truth & Reality. SpaceAndMotion.com. 2012.

"Questions and Answers about Chemotherapy." WebMD.com.

"Really Cool Portable GPS Tracker." Coolest-Gadgets.com.

Rees, Clair. "Multiple Threat Magnum." Remtek.com. 1998.

"Regarding Immigration, What Is a Coyote?" wiseGEEK.com.

Relph, Edward. *Place and Placelessness*. London: Pion Ltd., 1976.

Rivers, Dacia. "Climate in Albuquerque, New Mexico." *USA Today*.
    TravelTips.usatoday.com.

"Rocks and Their Properties." Teaching Assistance Program. eTap.org.

Rojas, Peter. "Cellphone Bomb Detonator." Engadget.com. 4 Mar 2005.

"Roman Houses." History Learning Site. HistoryLearningSite.co.uk.

Rose, Ananda. "Death in the Desert." NYTimes.com. 21 Jun 2012.

Rosenberg, Alyssa. "From *The Shield* to *Breaking Bad*: How Anti-Hero Shows
    Make Women Do the Hard Work." ThinkProgress.org. 17 Jul 2012.

—. "Stop Hating the Wives: In Praise of *Breaking Bad*'s Skyler White."
    Slate.com. 16 Jul 2012.

Rosenberg, Eli. "Q&A — Aaron Paul (Jesse Pinkman)." AMCTV.com. 2011.

Rowles, Dustin. "*Breaking Bad* Creator Vince Gilligan Calls Skyler White
    Haters Misogynists, 'Plain and Simple.'" Warming Glow. Uproxx.com.
    14 May 2013.

Rowney, Jess, Teresa Hermida and Donald Malone. "Anxiety Disorders."
    The Cleveland Clinic Foundation. ClevelandClinicMedEd.com, 2011.

Russell, Mallory. "Here Are Some of TV's Most Successful Product
    Placements." BusinessInsider.com. 14 Mar 2012.

"Salary Table 2011-GS." U.S. Office of Personnel Management. OPM.gov.

Schorr, Melissa. "Defibrillators Easy to Use, Save Lives." ABC News.
    ABCNews.go.com. 2013.

"Self Defense." LexisNexis.com.

"Self Defense Overview." FindLaw. Criminal.findlaw.com.

"Series: *Babylon 5*." TVTropes.org.

"Seriously Funny Lawyer Ads?" LoweringTheBar.net.

Silver, Stephen. "Essay: 'Skyler Is Such a Bitch!,' and Other Unfair *Breaking
    Bad* Observations." EntertainmentTell. TechnologyTell.com. 13 Jul 2012.

Slovis, Michael. "Inside *Breaking Bad*: Jesse's House." AMCTV.com. 2012.

—. Telephone Interview with Author. 10 Aug 2013.

Soniak, Matt. "How Does an Etch A Sketch Work?" MentalFloss.com.
    28 Dec 2010.

—. "How Poisonous Is Lily of the Valley?" MentalFloss.com. 11 Oct 2011.

"Spastic Paralysis." InfoPlease.com.

Steen, Margaret. "Safeguarding the Rails: Four Avenues for Increasing Security." Emergency Management. EmergencyMGMT.com. 29 Nov 2010.

Stevenson, Mark and Arturo Perez. "Mexico Meth Bust: Army Finds 15 Tons of Pure Methamphetamine." HuffingtonPost.com. 9 Feb 2012.

Stritof, Sheri and Bob. "The Language and Meaning of Flowers for Married Couples." Marriage.about.com.

"Supreme Court Confirms Attorney-Client Privilege, Even After Death." National Association of Criminal Defense Lawyers. NACDL.org. 25 June 1998.

Szymanski, Mike. "Mylar Balloons Can Be Dangerous, and Short-Circuit Power Lines." Patch. StudioCity.patch.com. 6 Jun 2012.

Tannenbaum, Rob. "Bob Odenkirk on Saul Goodman: 'I'm Amazed that People Like Him.'" RollingStone.com. 24 Sep 2013.

Tanz, Jason. "How *Breaking Bad* Resurrects Its Antihero Again and Again." Wired.com. 3 Jul 2012.

"The Tenerife Crash — March 27, 1977." 1001Crash.com.

Thomas, Dana. *Deluxe: How Luxury Lost Its Luster.* New York: Penguin, 2007.

"Top Ten Solar States." CleanEnergyAuthority.com. 16 May 2012.

Tuan, Yi-Fu. "A View of Geography." *Geographical Review* 81, No. 1 (January), 1991.

—. *Space and Place: The Perspective of Experience.* Minneapolis: University of Minnesota, 1977.

"Underfloor Heating — The Roman Legacy." Robbens Systems Underfloor Heating. UnderfloorHeating.co.uk.

"Universal Pain Assessment Tool." White Plains Hospital. WPHospital.org.

"U.S. Contract Tower Association Annual Report, 2011." U.S. Contract Tower Association. ContractTower.org. 2012.

Valdes-Dapena, Peter. "Most-Stolen Cars: Old Hondas." CNN. Money.cnn.com. 2 Aug 2011.

Valencia, Nick and Michael Martinez, "Champion Boxer Hector 'Macho' Camacho Dies After Shooting." CNN.com. 11 Dec 2012.

VanDerWerff, Todd. "Vince Gilligan walks us through *Breaking Bad*'s 4th Season. (Part 2 of 4)." AVClub.com. 11 Oct 2011.

Vantuono, William. "Railroading in a Post 9/11 World." RailwayAge.com. 18 Jan 2012.

"Walt Whitman." Poets.org.

Ware, Michael. "Los Zetas called Mexico's most dangerous drug cartel." CNN.com. 6 Aug 2009.

Weisstein, Eric W. "Lavoisier, Antoine (1743–1794)." Wolfram Research. Scienceworld.wolfram.com. 2007.

"Welcome to Class Action Lawsuits." Class Action Lawsuits. Web-Access.net.

"Werner Heisenberg." American Institute of Physics. AIP.org. 2013.

Westervelt, Celina. "High Bail in Mom's Meth, Stabbing Case." KRQE.com. 24 Feb 2012.

"What Are Billable Hours?" wiseGEEK.com.

"What Are Marine Shellfish Toxins?" Food Safety Network. FoodSafety.ksu.edu. 14 Jun 2004.

"What is a loan out corporation?" ABSPayroll.net.

"What Is Marital Privilege?" wiseGEEK.com.

"What is Meth, Effects of Meth & Facts About Methamphetamine." MethProject.org.

"What Is the Color Code of Christian Louboutin Red Soles?" Cars & Life. Uygarr.blogspot.com. 9 Dec 2012.

"When Should an Automated External Defibrillator Be Used?" National Institutes of Health. NHLBI.nih.gov. 2 Dec 2011.

Wickell, Janet. "Step-by-Step Look at Tent Fumigation." HomeBuying. about.com.

Wiley, Arlo J. "TV Viewer's (and TV's) Wife Problem." GobbledyGeekPodcast.com. 20 Nov 2012.

Wilkinson, Tracy. "Mexico has arrested a leader of Santa Muerte 'church.'" *Los Angeles Times*. Articles.LATimes.com. 5 Jan 2011.

Wilkinson, Tracy and Ken Ellingwood. "Mexico's army no match for drug cartels." *Los Angeles Times*. Cleveland.com. 2 Jan 2011.

Wilson, Michael. "A Season of Open Windows, and the Second-Story Man." NYTimes.com. 8 Jun 2012.

"Winchester Black Talons." TheGunZone.com.

"Winchester Ranger Talon (Ranger SXT/Black Talon) Wound Ballistics." FirearmsTactical.com.

Zapani. "Desert Eagle list." Listal.com. 31 Oct 2010.

Zimmerman, Amy. "'Breaking Bad' Meets 'Mr. Magorium's Wonder Emporium' . . . And It Is Glorious." TheDailyBeast.com. 25 Sep 2013.

Zyada. "Universal Pain Scale." Boards.straightdope.com. 12 Jun 2008.

INDEX OF
SPECIAL INGREDIENTS